# California 1990 PUBLISHING MARKET PLACE

# California 1990 PUBLISHING MARKET PLACE

*A comprehensive directory of markets, resources, and opportunities for writers.*

*Edited by: Marjorie Gersh and Meera Lester*

Writers Connection
*Cupertino, California*

**California Publishing Marketplace**
**1990 Edition**



**Publisher:** Steve Lester

**Editors:** Marjorie Gersh, Meera Lester

**Marketing Director:** Cliff Feldman

**Cover Design:** Detta Penna

To order additional copies, see page 249.

Writers Connection
1601 Saratoga-Sunnyvale Road, Suite 180
Cupertino, CA 95014
(408) 973-0227, FAX (408) 973-1219

Printed and bound in the United States of America
Second Printing, 1989

ISBN 0-9622592-0-9

# Table of Contents

# Acknowledgements

Our warmest thanks go to Michael Crisp, John Fremont, Pamela Jekel, Michael Larsen, Nancy Mulvaney, Bill Oliver, Phyllis Pianka, and Bob Reed, who so freely gave their suggestions, support, and advice on this project.

For their conscientious and diligent work verifying information, typesetting, and proofreading the manuscript, we'd like to thank Writers Connection staff members Peggy Gilbertson, Kate Hendon, Pat Kasper, Lee Kucera, Mardeene Mitchell, Jan Stiles, Dean Stark, Burton Sukhov, and Moira Uplinger.

A special thanks goes to Holly Pedersen and Phyllis Schuette for their contributions.

For sharing our belief that "writers helping writers strengthens our West Coast writing and publishing community," and for supporting our work over the years, we extend a heartfelt thanks to all our Writers Connection members.

*This book is dedicated to writers everywhere,
but especially to those in California who have long needed
and frequently requested a definitive guide
to publishing markets, information, and resources
in "the Golden State."*

# Introduction

We know what writers need. Writers Connection has been in the business of providing information and services to writers, organizations, small presses, and self-publishers for nearly a decade. Now, as a small press, we've produced our first book—*California Publishing Marketplace*.

## Markets

We're confident that whatever you're writing, there's a market for it in California, and you'll find it in the following pages. California, the birthplace of the small press movement in the 1960s, is expected to continue to be a hotbed of publishing activity in the 1990s. That means oportunities for writers. Because we designed and developed this book specifically for writers, we've included the names of book and magazine submissions editors along with editorial guidelines and submission information, payment rates, preferred method of query, rights purchased, and much more. For newspapers, we've listed submissions and book review editors.

## Professional Organizations

For those interested in expanding their professional network, we've included wherever possible the address, phone number, and contact for the national headquarters of each organization and then listed information on the California chapters. You're sure to find one in your area.

## Writers' Conferences

Writers' conferences are great sources of valuable information, professional contacts, and motivation renewal. We contacted over 40 in the state and included comprehensive information on those that responded. If you're serious about writing, plan to attend at least one this year.

## Literary Agents

One question we are frequently asked is, "Where can I find a literary agent to represent my work?" While our list does not include every agent in the state, we did send out hundreds of surveys and spent weeks verifying information on the phone. The result is a list of agents that includes not only names, addresses, and phone numbers, but substantial information on the kinds of literary properties the agencies are seeking, agency commission fees, and rights handled by the agency.

## Books and Resources

For many years, Writers Connection teachers, members, and seminar participants have offered insights and suggestions about the kinds of books they need for honing their skills. Writers Connection has responded by creating a bookstore filled with how-to-write books, style guides, reference books, market books, and business writing books. Since these books have proved so helpful to our writers, we thought you'd like to know about them, too. An annotated list of books is included in this directory as well as other resources you, the writer, might need.

## Updates

We realized from its inception that this book would require regular updating of information. Some of that information will appear in the monthly 16-page *Writers Connection* newsletter. In addition, we plan to issue a new edition of this book every two years.

In the process of compiling and verifying information for the book, we mailed thousands of questionnaires. If any publishers, agents, organizations, or conferences are not listed, it is likely that their surveys were not returned, they requested deletion, or their information could not be verified.

We realize much of the information in this book will change with time—organizations elect new officers each year; book publishers, magazines, and newspapers hire new editors; and conference directors find new locations, change formats, and offer new speakers.

When using this book, if you come across information that is incomplete or has changed, please let us know. If you know of a book, magazine, or newspaper publisher that should be included, tell us—we'll send the appropriate survey forms. Let us know if you would like your organization or conference listed. Listings are free.

If you wish to be notified of future editions of *California Publishing Marketplace*, please send us your name and address. Finally, we appreciate feedback. Let us know if the book works well for you, or if it doesn't, and why.

Meera Lester, Editor
Co-founder Writers Connection

# About Writers Connection

Writers Connection was founded in 1983 by Steve and Meera Lester to serve writers and publishing professionals in California. Writers Connection has 2,000 members and provides a wide range of services, including two unique seminar programs, a bookstore offering more than 200 titles on writing- and publishing-related topics, a resource library, a job shop specializing in contract or full-time placement of technical and other writers, special events, two West Coast writers' conferences (including the popular "Selling to Hollywood"), and a 16-page monthly newsletter.

In addition to single memberships for individuals, Writers Connection also offers a group membership rate for six or more individuals joining through a single company or organization. Benefits to members include: discounts on seminars, conferences, and books, and access to wide range of resource material.

The monthly *Writers Connection* newsletter features updated information on markets, events, contests, industry news, and articles on various aspects of writing and publishing. Members receive the newsletter free and subscriptions are available to nonmembers.

The company's general seminar program targets professional writers as well as hobbyists with over 250 seminars each year in the areas of fiction, nonfiction, and career enhancement. Classes average three to six hours in length and cover a multitude of subjects such as "Constructing the Novel," "Writing Mystery and Suspense," "Travel Writing," and "Tapping the Creative Power of Dreams."

The business and technical classes are directed toward the professional writer working in a business or technical environment. Typical classes include "Researching and Writing Procedures Manuals," "Indexing Computer Documentation," "Basic Grammar for Writers," and "High-Tech Public Relations Writing."

If you would like to join Writers Connection or subscribe to the monthly newsletter, an order form appears on page 249. The form may also be used to request course catalogs, a free sample newsletter, or additional information about Writers Connection and the next edition of *California Publishing Marketplace*.

# Book Publishers

We assume that you have a manuscript (or an idea for one) which you wish to have published. We have obtained and organized the following information to help you decide where to send your submission, what to include in and on the envelope, when to anticipate an initial response, and in general, what to expect in terms and payment if you are offered a publishing contract.

## How to Use the Information in This Section

The first paragraph of each entry identifies the publishing company, lists its location, and describes its publishing history. Your initial contact should be directed to the submissions editor named in the entry.

## Subjects of Interest

We divided this into three main fields: nonfiction, fiction, and other. We listed the publishers' areas of interest within each field and included titles of recent publications. What publishers don't want is as important as what they do want; don't waste your time trying to force through an exception.

## Initial Contact

Follow the instructions. Send editors what they want. There are many resources in the Books for Writers section which will help you prepare an effective query letter or persuasive book proposal. Include any additional material requested. When sending a requested resumé, biography (bio), or curriculum vitae, include only those details of your life which are relevant to your authority and ability to write the book.

## Acceptance Policies

**Unagented manuscripts:** Many medium to large publishers will look only at manuscripts submitted by an agent. To find an agent, turn to the Literary Agents section, send a query about your project to several of the agents listed, then choose the agent you feel will best represent you and your project.

**Simultaneous submissions:** If the publisher's information says "yes" to simultaneous submissions, you may submit your manuscript to several different publishers at the same time, but you should inform each publisher that the manuscript is being simultaneously submitted.

**Disk submissions:** Many publishers are willing to accept your *final* manuscript on a disk compatible with the publisher's computer system, but almost all of them prefer the initial contact be in the form of hard copy (a print-out on paper).

**Response time to initial inquiry:** Response time varies greatly. Be patient and avoid phoning the publisher unless you've been instructed to do so by the publisher in question. A week or two *after* the specified response time (listed in the publisher's entry), you are entitled to send a written request for information concerning the status of your submission. As with any correspondence to a publisher or agent, remember to include your SASE.

**Average time until publication:** This information (always dependent upon a number of factors) provides an approximate idea of how long the process takes after the publisher has received the completed manuscript.

**Advance royalty:** When dealing with small or midsize presses, the advances (if given at all) tend to be small. The money goes primarily into production and promotion. An advantage of working with small presses is that your book is not "just another on their big list." The lists tend to be smaller and thus your book gets more attention.

**Royalty:** Some royalties are computed on the retail cover price, but most are computed on the publisher's gross sales income, which combines sales to distributors with sales to retail stores. If your personal negotiations with a publisher have reached the contract stage, pay an agent or a publishing attorney to review and evaluate the contract before you sign.

**First run:** The number of copies to be printed is usually based on the publisher's best estimate of the number of copies that can be sold in the initial one- to two-year period.

**Subsidy basis:** In general, this means that the author pays some portion of the production and promotion costs and potentially stands to earn more than a basic royalty if the book sells well. Many legitimate small publishing houses simply do not have the money to finance all costs, and for that reason they encourage author investment. Subsidy deals take many forms, so obtain all the facts, get the terms in writing, and seek legal advice before signing.

## Marketing Channels

Most publishers market books through direct mail sales to individuals, rep sales to book stores, and distributor sales (distributors stock, sell, and distribute books to bookstores and libraries). In addition, some publishers promote special sales through book clubs, social organizations, and special interest groups. If your book has such special sales potential, be sure to mention that fact in your initial contact with the publisher.

**Subsidiary Rights:** Most of the rights listed are self-explanatory. Serialization and reprint rights often involve technical and monetary implications which can best be evaluated by an experienced agent or attorney.

## Additional Information

This is the publisher's opportunity to supply any supplemental information not covered in the preceding sections. Tips are specific recommendations from the publisher to the author and should be seriously considered.

**Catalog:** We suggest that your first step toward any publisher be to send for the catalog of books already published. This will give you the "flavor" of that press and enable you to draft a more focused query or submission.

### Abbreviations

n/i means no information was given to us by the publisher.
n/a means that this particular question did not apply to the publisher.

---

**AAMES-ALLEN PUBLISHING COMPANY.** 1106 Main St. Huntington Beach, CA 92648-2719. (714) 536-4926. Submissions Editor: Peggy Glenn. Not accepting manuscripts.

**ACCENT ON MUSIC.** PO Box 417. Palo Alto, CA 94302. (415) 328-1889. Submissions Editor: Mark Hanson. Founded: 1987. Number of titles published: cumulative—2, 1989—1. Softback 100%.

**Subjects of Interest. Nonfiction**—how-to, music instructions. Recent publications: *Art of Contemporary Travis Picking; Solo Style Contemporary Travis Picking* (both instructional book plus audio cassette). Do not want: nonmusic subjects.

**Initial Contact.** Query letter; outline of book. Include author bio.

**Acceptance Policies.** Unagented manuscripts: yes. Simultaneous submissions: yes, query letter first. Disk submissions: no. Response time to initial inquiry: 4 weeks. Average time until publication: n/i. **Advance**: none. **Royalty**: negotiable. First run: 2000.

**Marketing Channels.** Distribution houses; independent reps. Subsidiary rights: English language publication outside United States and Canada.

**Additional Information.** We are looking for other high-quality books to distribute in our catalog. Catalog: upon request.

**ACROBAT BOOKS.** PO Box 480820. Los Angeles, CA 90048. (213) 578-1055. Submissions Editor: Anthony Cohan. Founded: 1975. Number of titles published: cumulative—19, 1989—4. Hardback 25%, softback 75%.

**Subjects of Interest. Nonfiction**—instruction and interviews in the creative arts (film, music, video, etc.). Recent publications: *Directing the Film* (interviews with 75 famous film directors); *Stolen Moments* (conversations with contemporary musicians). Do not want: poetry; children's books.

**Initial Contact.** Query letter.

**Acceptance Policies.** Unagented manuscripts: yes. Multiple submissions: yes. Disk submissions: no. Response time to initial inquiry: 4 weeks. Average time until publication: 6 months. **Advance**: none. **Royalty**: 15-20%. First run: 3000-4000.

**Marketing Channels.** Distribution houses; direct mail; independent reps; in-house staff. Subsidiary rights: all.

**Additional Information.** Catalog: upon request.

**ACS PUBLICATIONS.** PO Box 16430. San Diego, CA 92116-0430. (619) 297-9203. Submissions Editor: Maritha Pottenger. Founded: 1976. Number of titles published: cumulative—70, 1989—8. Hardback 5%, softback 95%.

**Subjects of Interest. Nonfiction**—astrology; metaphysical; holistic health. Recent publications: *Houses of the Horoscope*; *Spirit Guides.* Do not want: fiction or thinly disguised autobiographies.

**Initial Contact.** Query letter; outline of book.

**Acceptance Policies.** Unagented manuscripts: yes. Simultaneous submissions: query letter first. Disk submissions: no. Response time to initial inquiry: 1 month. Average time until publication: 2 years. **Advance:** none. **Royalty**: 15% of monies received. First run: 3000.

**Marketing Channels.** Distribution houses; direct mail; in-house staff; special sales. Subsidiary rights: all.

**Additional Information.** We do not accept deterministic (the planets are doing it to you) astrology; personal power and responsibility vital. Tips: Request "Guidelines for Potential Authors." Catalog: 8 1/2 x 11 manila envelope, 3 first class stamps.

**AFCOM PUBLISHING.** PO Box H. Harbor City, CA 90710-0330. (213) 326-7589. Submissions Editor: Juanita Ferrey. Founded: 1986. Number of titles published: cumulative—5, 1987—4. Softback 100%.

**Subjects of Interest. Nonfiction**—health related topics; how-to activity books for children. Recent publications: *The Complete Guide to Home Remedies*; *Why Do I Eat More Than I Want Diet Book?*; *Why Do I Drink More Than I Want?; Over 101 Inexpensive Ways to Entertain Children.*

**Initial Contact.** Query letter; sample chapters.

**Acceptance Policies.** Unagented manuscripts: no. Disk submissions: no. Response time to initial inquiry: 1 month. Average time until publication: n/i. **Advance:** n/i. **Royalty**: n/i. First run: n/i.

**Marketing Channels.** Cooperative distribution; direct mail; independent sales reps; in-house staff; special sales. Subsidiary rights: none.

**Additional Information.** We usually use "in-house" material for our books. Catalog: write to publisher.

**ALLEN PUBLISHING COMPANY.** PO Box 1889. Reseda, CA 91335. (818) 344-6788. Submissions Editor: Michael Wiener. Founded: 1979. Number of titles published: cumulative—18, 1987—2. Softback 100%.

**Subjects of Interest. Nonfiction**—self-help book aimed at the "opportunity seeker" market. Recent publications: *How-to Start A Money-Making Business for $15; How-to Start Your Own Mail Order Business.* Do not want: any other subject than our specialty.

**Initial Contact.** Query letter; SASE is mandatory.

**Acceptance Policies.** Unagented manuscripts: yes. Simultaneous submissions: no. Disk submissions: no. Response time to initial inquiry: 2 weeks. Average time until publication: 6 months. **Advance:** negotiable. **Royalty**: negotiable. First run: varies.

**Marketing Channels.** Mail order only. Subsidiary rights: none.

**Additional Information.** Our audience consists of people, usually with limited financial assets, who want to start a business or find some other way to make money. Catalog: SASE.

**ALTA NAPA PRESS.** (Imprints: Gondwana Books). 1969 Mora Ave. Calistoga, CA 94515. (707) 942-4444. Submissions Editor: Carl T. Endemann. Founded: 1976. Number of titles published: cumulative—16, 1989—4. Hardback 10%, softback 90%.

**Subjects of Interest. Nonfiction**—philosophy. Recent publications: *Wherever I Went* (travel sketches). **Other**—poetry (Gondwana Books). Recent publications: *Crossroads at the Antipodes* (experimental poetry in 7 languages, all originals). Do not want: manuscripts with emphasis on sentimental and personal feelings.

**Initial Contact.** Query letter; 2 chapters; outlines. Poetry: 3 poems. Include biographical background and philosophy; poetic goals and principles; and hour, date, and place of your birth.

**Acceptance Policies.** Unagented manuscripts: yes. Simultaneous submissions: no. Disk submissions: no. First novels: yes. Response time to initial inquiry: 6 weeks. Average time until publication: 6 months. **Advance:** none. **Royalty:** n/i. First run: 500. Subsidy basis: yes.

**Marketing Channels.** Direct mail. Subsidiary rights: translation and foreign.

**Additional Information.** We want material on any subject of universal appeal which is clear and concise. Tips: Read our catalog. Catalog: $1.30 plus $1.30 postage.

American Astronautical Society *see* **UNIVELT, INC.**

**AMERICAN BUSINESS CONSULTANTS.** 1540 Nuthatch Lane. Sunnyvale, CA 94087. (408) 738-3011. Submissions Editor: Wilfred F. Tetreault. Founded: n/i. Number of titles published: cumulative—100, 1987—5. Hardback 1%, softback 99%.

**Subjects of Interest.** **Nonfiction**—appraising, buying, selling and financing all types of businesses; start-up companies; fraud in business. Recent publications: *Buying and Selling Business Opportunities; Starting Right in Your New Business.* Do not want: anything other than the above.

**Initial Contact.** Entire manuscript.

**Acceptance Policies.** Unagented manuscripts: yes. Simultaneous submissions: yes. Disk submissions: no. Response time to initial inquiry: 15 days. Average time until publication: 3 months. **Advance:** open. **Royalty:** open. First run: open.

**Marketing Channels.** Direct mail; special sales. Subsidiary rights: none.

**Additional Information.** I conduct seminars every week throughout the country. Tips: It would be a good idea to attend a seminar. Catalog: write and ask.

**AMERICAN INDIAN STUDIES.** Campbell Hall, UCLA. Los Angeles, CA 90024. (213) 825-4777. Submissions Editor: Dr. Duane Champagne. Founded: 1970. Number of titles published: cumulative—37, 1987—not numbered yet. Softback 100%.

**Subjects of Interest.** **Nonfiction**—scholarly approach to American Indian culture. Recent publications: *American Indian Policy and Cultural Values: Conflict and Accommodation; Preserving Traditional Arts; Migration Tears.* Do not want: poetry.

**Initial Contact.** Query letter; book proposal with sample chapters or entire manuscript; precis. Include author bio.

**Acceptance Policies.** Unagented manuscripts: yes. Simultaneous submissions: no. Disk submissions: IBM; Macintosh. Response time to initial inquiry: 1 month. Average time until publication: 3-6 months. **Advance:** none. **Royalty:** none. First run: 1000-2500.

**Marketing Channels.** Cooperative distribution; direct mail; in-house staff. Subsidiary rights: none.

**Additional Information.** We seek primarily to publish scholarly research on American Indian topics. Tips: Submit 4 double-spaced copies; follow *Chicago Manual of Style* for end notes. Catalog: upon request.

**AMERICAN POETRY ASSOCIATION.** 250 A Potrero St. PO Box 1803. Santa Cruz, CA 95061. (408) 429-1122. Submissions Editor: Richard Elliot. Founded: 1981. Number of titles published: cumulative—25, 1987—8. Hardback 100%.

**Subjects of Interest.** **Other**—poetry. Recent publications: *American Poetry Anthology; Poetry of Life; Love's Greatest Treasures.* Do not want: prose.

**Initial Contact.** 5 poems, each no more than 20 lines. Include name and address on each.

**Acceptance Policies.** Unagented manuscripts: yes. Simultaneous submissions: yes; prefer previously unpublished. Disk submissions: no. Response time to initial inquiry: 3 weeks. Average time until publication: 6-9 months. **Advance**: none. **Royalty**: none. 152 contest winners receive $11,000 in prizes including $1000 grand prize. Two contests per year. First run: 2000.

**Marketing Channels.** Direct mail. Subsidiary rights: none; all rights remain with poet.

**Additional Information.** Every poet who sends poems automatically enters the poetry contest. Every poet receives a copy of the *Poet's Guide to Getting Published.*

**APACHE CORRAL.** 3048 Champion #2. Oakland, CA 94602. (415) 261-5592. Submissions Editor: Apache Corral. Founded: 1983. Number of titles published: cumulative—1. Softback 100%.

**Subjects of Interest.** ethnic material; nontraditional poetic works.

**Initial Contact.** Query letter; entire manuscript; phone.

**Acceptance Policies.** Unagented manuscripts: yes. Simultaneous submissions: yes. Disk submissions: no. First novels: yes. Response time to initial inquiry: 2 weeks. Average time until publication: varies. **Advance**: none. **Royalty**: n/i. First run: up to writer. Subsidy basis: yes; negotiable terms.

**Marketing Channels.** Distribution houses; cooperative distribution; independent sales reps. Subsidiary rights: all.

**APPLETON AND LANGE.** (Subsidiary of Simon and Schuster). 2755 Campus Dr. San Mateo, CA 94403. (415) 377-0977. Submissions Editor: Alexander Kugushev (basic science); Nancy Evans (clinical science). Founded: 1938. Number of titles published: 1988—12, 1989—14. Softback 100%.

**Subjects of Interest.** **Nonfiction**—medical. Do not want: anything outside of medicine.

**Initial Contact.** Book proposal with 2 sample chapters. Include table of contents; affiliations.

**Acceptance Policies.** Unagented manuscripts: yes. Simultaneous submissions: no. Disk submissions: yes. Response time to initial inquiry: 3 months. Average time until publication: depends on subject. **Advance**: none. **Royalty**: yes. First run: n/i.

**Marketing Channels.** Distribution houses; direct mail; independent reps; in-house staff; special sales. Subsidiary rights: direct mail or direct sales; book club; translation and foreign Enlish language publication outside the United States and Canada.

**Additional Information.** The authors and editors of our books are practicing physicians or Ph.D.'s on the faculty of medical schools and hospitals. Catalog: upon request.

**APPLEZABA PRESS.** PO Box 4134. Long Beach, CA 90804. (213) 591-0015. Submissions Editor: D. H. Lloyd. Founded: 1977. Number of titles published: cumulative—31, 1989—4. Hardback 10%, softback 90%.

**Subjects of Interest.** **Nonfiction**—cookbooks. Recent publications: *College Quickies Cookbook.* **Fiction**—modern novels; short story collections. Recent publications: *Case of the Missing Blue V.W.; Flight to Freedom.* **Other**—poetry; children's (soon). Recent publications: *Bible Bob Responds to a Jesus Honker; Blood and Bones; Elegy to a Gay Giraffe*. Do not want: genre fiction (romance, detective, etc.).

**Initial Contact.** Query for fiction and nonfiction; entire manuscript for poetry.

**Acceptance Policies.** Unagented manuscripts: yes. Simultaneous submissions: yes; inform us. Disk submissions: no. First novels: yes. Response time to initial inquiry: 5-8 weeks. Average time until publication: 3 years. **Advance**: up to $100. **Royalty**: 8%-12%. First run: 1000-3000.

**Marketing Channels.** Distribution houses; cooperative distribution; direct mail. Subsidiary rights: all.

**Additional Information.** Catalog: #10 SASE.

**ARCHIVES, THE.** 4546 El Camino Real, B-10-318. Los Altos, CA 94022. (415) 326-6997. Submissions Editor: G.H. Harrison (general); T. M. Watson (computers, equestrian). Founded: 1969. Hardback 50%, softback 50%.

**Subjects of Interest. Nonfiction**—computer science; metaphysical; archaeology; equestrian; hang gliding; sociology; Irish history. Recent publications: *Apple 16—A Comprehensive Guide to Apple IIgs Computing; The Dead Books. Vol. I & II—Social History of the Haight-Ashbury; The Holy Grail—An Ethno-Archaeological Study*; *The Hole in the Wind—Hang Gliding and the Quest for Flight*. **Fiction**—mystery/adventure. Recent publications: *Computer Smut* (zany, computer-inspired adventure mystery). Do not want: romantic fiction.

**Initial Contact.** Query letter; sample chapters. Include brief history of author's works; reason for proposed manuscript; future manuscript ideas. (If hard copy, double spaced, spiral bound.)

**Acceptance Policies.** Unagented manuscripts: yes. Simultaneous submissions: yes. Disk submissions: Macintosh or IBM (Microsoft Word or MacWrite). First novels: yes. Response time to initial inquiry: 4-6 weeks. Average time until publication: 3-6 months. **Advance:** none. **Royalty**: by arrangement. First run: by arrangement.

**Marketing Channels.** Distribution houses; direct mail; independent sales reps. Subsidiary rights: all.

**Additional Information.** Short-run specialist. Catalog: SASE.

**ARIEL VAMP PRESS.** PO Box 33496. Berkeley, CA 94703. (415) 654-4849. Submissions Editor: Jolene Babyak. Founded: 1987. Number of titles published: 1988—1. Softback 100%.

**Subjects of Interest. Nonfiction**—prison; prisoners; serious jazz musicians. Recent publications: *Eyewitness on Alcatraz; True Stories of Families Who Lived on The Rock.*

**Initial Contact.** Query letter.

**Acceptance Policies.** Unagented manuscripts: no. Simultaneous submissions: yes. Disk submissions: no. Response time to initial inquiry: 4-6 weeks. Average time until publication: 18 months. **Advance:** n/i. **Royalty**: n/i. First run: n/i.

**Marketing Channels.** Distribution houses; direct mail. Subsidiary rights: n/i.

Asian Humanities Press *see* **JAIN PUBLISHING COMPANY**

**ASTRONOMICAL SOCIETY OF THE PACIFIC.** 390 Ashton Ave. San Francisco, CA 94112. (415) 337-1100. Submissions Editor: Andrew Fraknoi. Founded: 1889. Number of titles published: cumulative—25.

**Subjects of Interest. Nonfiction**—space science; astronomy. Recent publications: *The Mars Kit; Astronomy As a Hobby; Worlds In Comparison.* Do not want: astrology.

**Initial Contact.** Very little work by outsiders accepted; authors must have track record in science or science writing.

**Acceptance Policies.** Unagented manuscripts: yes. Simultaneous submissions: no. Disk submissions: WordPerfect. Response time to initial inquiry: depends on project. Average time until publication: depends. **Advance:** n/i. **Royalty:** n/i. First run: n/i.

**Marketing Channels.** n/i. Subsidiary rights: n/i.

**Additional Information.** We are a nonprofit scientific educational organization publishing educational materials. We publish *Mercury* magazine, as well as a newsletter for teachers, and a catalog of educational materials.

**ATHLETIC PRESS.** (Subsidiary of Golden West Books). PO Box 80250. San Marino, CA 91118. (818) 283-3446. Submissions Editor: Donald Duke. Founded: 1971. Number of titles published: cumulative—4, 1987—2. Softback 100%.

**Subjects of Interest. Nonfiction**—conditioning for sports. Recent publications: *Stretching for All Sports.*

**Initial Contact.** Query letter; general description.

**Acceptance Policies.** Unagented manuscripts: yes. Simultaneous submissions: no. Disk submissions: no. Response time to initial inquiry: 4-6 months. Average time until publication: 1 year. **Advance:** none. **Royalty:** 10%. First run: 3000.

**Marketing Channels.** Distribution houses; direct mail; independent sales reps. Subsidiary rights: none.

**AUTHORS UNLIMITED.** 3330 Barham Blvd., Ste. 201. Los Angeles, CA 90068. (213) 874-0902. Submissions Editor: Renais Hill, Jon Rappaport, S. E. Bernstein. Founded: 1981. Number of titles published: cumulative—150, 1989—75. Hardback 10%, softback 90%.

**Subjects of Interest. Nonfiction**—Recent Publications: *The Evil Empire; How-to Balance the Budget.* **Fiction**—Recent Publications: *Kill Kadaffi; Grief Merchants.* **Other**—poetry. Do not want: anything pornographic.

**Initial Contact.** Query letter; sample chapters.

**Acceptance Policies.** Unagented manuscripts: yes. Simultaneous submissions: yes, if informed who else submitted to. First novels: yes. Disk submissions: no. Response time to initial inquiry: 2 weeks. Average time until publication: 9 months. **Advance:** none. **Royalty:** scale. First run: 2000.

**Marketing Channels.** Distribution houses; cooperative distribution; direct mail; in-house staff; special sales. Subsidiary rights: all.

**Additional Information.** Send clean manuscript in good form. Catalog: SASE plus $.90.

**AUTO BOOK PRESS.** PO Bin 711. San Marcos, CA 92069. (619) 744-3582. Submissions Editor: William Carroll. Founded: 1955. Number of titles published—1987: 4. Hardback yes, softback yes.

**Subjects of Interest. Nonfiction**—automotive material; technical or definitive how-to.

**Initial Contact.** Query letter; synopsis; 3 sample chapters.

**Acceptance Policies.** Unagented manuscripts: yes. Simultaneous submissions: yes. Response time to initial inquiry: 2 weeks. Average time until publication: 1 year. **Advance:** varies. **Royalty:** 15%.

**Additional Information.** Tips: Take time to research the market.

**AVIATION BOOK COMPANY.** 1640 Victory Blvd. Glendale, CA 91201. (818) 240-1771. Submissions Editor: W. P. Winner. Founded: 1964. Number of titles published: cumulative—13, 1989—4. Hardback yes, softback yes.

**Subjects of Interest.** **Nonfiction**—technical aviation; pilot training; aeronautical history. Recent publications: *Instrument Flight Training Manual; 1989 Federal Aviation Regulations for Pilots; 1989 Airman's Information Manual.*

**Initial Contact.** Query letter; outline.

**Acceptance Policies.** Unagented manuscripts: yes. Response time to initial inquiry: 2 months. Average time until publication: 9 months. **Advance**: none. **Royalty**: paid on retail price.

**Additional Information.** Tips: Let us know you are aware of how your book is better than what else is out there and what is unique about your book. We are willing to look at artwork and photos. Catalog: 9x12 SASE, $1 postage.

**BANYAN TREE BOOKS.** 1963 El Dorado Ave. Berkeley, CA 94707.

Not accepting new manuscripts.

**BARN OWL BOOKS.** (Imprints: Amazon Press) PO Box 7727. Berkeley, CA 94707. (415) 644-9488. Submissions Editor: Gina Covina. Founded: 1983. Number of titles published: cumulative—3, 1989—1. Hardback 10%, softback 90%.

**Subjects of Interest.** **Nonfiction**—Recent Publications: *Windbreak: A Woman Rancher on the Northern Plains* (a year on a South Dakota cattle ranch). **Fiction**—Recent Publications: *The City of Hermits* (an odd assortment of northern California characters cope with the next BIG earthquake). Do not want: poetry.

**Initial Contact.** Query letter with book proposal and sample chapters.

**Acceptance Policies.** Unagented manuscripts: yes. Simultaneous submissions: yes, query first. First novels: yes. Disk submissions: 3.5" disk for Macintosh. Response time to initial inquiry: 1 month. Average time until publication: 1 year. **Advance**: negotiable. **Royalty**: 7.5%—15% depending on situation. First run: 2000—5000.

**Marketing Channels.** Distribution houses; cooperative distribution; direct mail; special sales. Subsidiary rights: all.

**Additional Information.** We are so small and eccentric that we are difficult to categorize. The publisher must fall in love with the manuscript—and believe that it is marketable—and falling in love is an unpredictable phenomenon. Catalog: upon request.

**BARR-RANDOL PUBLISHING COMPANY.** 136A N. Grand Ave. West Covina, CA 91791. (818) 339-0270. Submissions Editor: G. F. Coats. Founded: 1985. Number of titles published: cumulative—1. Softback 100%.

**Subjects of Interest.** **Nonfiction**—real estate and mortgage investment. Recent publications: *Smart Trust Deed Investment in California, 2nd Edition.* Do not want: manuscripts which require more than minor editing.

**Initial Contact.** Book proposal with sample chapters.

**Acceptance Policies.** Unagented manuscripts: yes. Simultaneous submissions: yes. Disk submissions: no. Response time to initial inquiry: 3 weeks. Average time until publication: n/i. **Advance**: n/i. **Royalty**: n/i. First run: n/i.

**Marketing Channels.** Distribution houses; cooperative distribution; direct mail; in-house staff. Subsidiary rights: all.

**Additional Information.** We have a very narrow focus and know exactly what we want.

## BC STUDIO PUBLICATIONS.

PO Box 5908. Huntington Beach, CA 92615. Submissions Editor: S. Kaye. Founded: 1976; reformatted 1987 for folio publishing. Number of titles published: cumulative—44, 1987—16. Softback 100%.

**Subjects of Interest. Nonfiction**—how-to folios: hobbies; moneymaking; crafts; small business investment; home remedies; directories; plans. Do not want: fiction; poetry; pornography.

**Initial Contact.** Send for guidelines, list of titles plus sample, $2.00.

**Acceptance Policies.** Unagented manuscripts: almost all. Simultaneous submissions: yes, we should be informed and advised if they would allow retitling. Disk submissions: no. Response time to initial inquiry: 2-3 weeks. Average time until publication: 3-5 months. **Advance**: $250-$1000. **Royalty**: 20% of our own sales; 10% of our dealer's sales. First run: varies.

**Marketing Channels.** Cooperative distribution; direct mail. Subsidiary rights: all.

**Additional Information.** We don't publish "books" rather, paperbound folios ranging from 2 to 38 pages of very specialized information. All facts—no frills. Tips: Magazine writing is wrong for us, as are the kind of reports you learned to write in school. Check our sample first. Catalog: send $2 for catalog, guidelines and sample.

## BEDFORD ARTS, PUBLISHER.

250 Sutter St. San Francisco, CA 94108. (415) 362-3730. Submissions Editor: Stephen Vincent. Founded: 1986. Number of titles published: cumulative—5, 1987—3. Hardback 65%, softback 35%.

**Subjects of Interest. Nonfiction**—art books; books on typography; illustrated biographies; reprints of art and criticism.

**Initial Contact.** Book proposal with sample chapters; art work, if possible.

**Acceptance Policies.** Unagented manuscripts: yes. Simultaneous submissions: yes. Disk submissions: WordPerfect; MultiMate; IBM DW3; Wang; WordStar; Volksriter; Microsoft Word; Smana; ASCII. Response time to initial inquiry: 1 month. Average time until publication: varies. **Advance**: varies. **Royalty**: 4% of gross sales. First run: 5000+/-.

**Marketing Channels.** Distribution houses; cooperative distribution; direct mail; special sales. Subsidiary rights: first serialization; second serialization; reprint rights; direct mail or sales rights; book club rights; translation and foreign rights; English language publication outside the United States and Canada.

**Additional Information.** Catalog: upon request.

## BENMIR BOOKS.

2512 9th St., Ste. 8. Berkeley, CA 94710. (415) 849-9117. Submissions Editor: Boris Bresler. Founded: 1983. Number of titles published: cumulative—5 , 1989—2. Hardback 30%, softback 70%.

**Subjects of Interest. Nonfiction**—Jewish themes. Recent publications: *One and One Make Three* (dual autobiography). **Fiction**—Jewish themes. Recent publications: *Imaginary Number* (short stories). Do not want: poetry.

**Initial Contact.** sample chapters; entire manuscript; biographical information.

**Acceptance Policies.** Unagented manuscripts: yes. Simultaneous submissions: yes. Disk submissions: no. First novels: yes. Response time to initial inquiry: 2 months. Average time until publication: 12 months. **Advance**: varies. **Royalty**: 15% on net. First run: 3000.

**Marketing Channels.** distribution houses; cooperative distribution; direct mail; in-house staff. Subsidiary rights: none; for now, no policy.

**Additional Information.** We only want books on Jewish themes. Tips: No poetry. Catalog: upon request.

Benziger *see* **GLENCOE PUBLISHING COMPANY.**

**BICYCLE BOOKS, INC.** 32 Glen Dr., PO Box 2038. Mill Valley, CA 94941. (415) 381-0172. Fax: (415) 381-6912. Submissions Editor: Christina Nau. Founded: 1985. Number of titles published: cumulative—11, 1989—4. Hardback 33%, softback 66%.

**Subjects of Interest. Nonfiction**—how-to, sports, recreational and travel books related to bicycling. Recent publications: *The Mountain Bike Book; Bicycling Fuel/Nutrition for the Bicycle Riders; Biography of Bicycle Racer "Major Taylor."*

**Initial Contact.** Entire manuscript; photographs and art work.

**Acceptance Policies.** Unagented manuscripts: yes. Simultaneous submissions: yes. Disk submissions: IBM PC formatted discs in 360KB; Wordstar or similar program that processes ASCII files. Response time to initial inquiry: 6 weeks. Average time until publication: 1 year. **Advance**: none. **Royalty**: 7 1/2%. First run: 5000-8000.

**Marketing Channels.** Distribution houses; cooperative distribution; direct mail; in-house sales. Subsidiary rights: all.

**Additional Information.** Catalog: SASE.

**BIOFEEDBACK PRESS.** (Subsidiary of Biofeedback Institute of San Francisco). 3428 Sacramento St. San Francisco, CA 94118. (415) 921-6500. Submissions Editor: Dr. George von Bozzay, president. Founded: 1973. Number of titles published: cumulative—n/i; 1987:4. Hardback 25%, softback 75%.

**Subjects of Interest. Nonfiction**—stress management; behavioral medicine; biofeedback. Recent publications: *Biofeedback Methods and Procedures* (introductory manual); *Behavioral Medicine, Stress Management and Biofeedback* (clinician's desk reference); *Projects in Biofeedback* (text/workbook); *What is Biofeedback?* (information paperback for students and patients).

**Initial Contact.** Query letter.

**Acceptance Policies.** Unagented manuscripts: yes. Simultaneous submissions: no. Disk submissions: no. Response time to initial inquiry: 30 days. Average time until publication: 1 year. **Advance**: negotiable. **Royalty**: negotiable. First run: varies.

**Marketing Channels.** Direct mail; independent reps. Subsidiary rights: none.

**Additional Information.** Most titles are specifically targeted to health professionals specializing in behavioral health. Catalog: upon request.

Black Lizard Books *see* **CREATIVE ARTS BOOK COMPANY.**

**BLAKE PUBLISHING.** (Subsidiary of The Graphic Center). 2222 Beebee St. San Luis Obispo, CA 93401. (805) 543-6843. Submissions Editor: Vicki Leon. Founded: 1983. Number of titles published: cumulative—14, 1989—4-6. Softback 100%.

**Subjects of Interest. Nonfiction**—nature; regional travel; food and cooking. Do not want: poetry; fiction.

**Initial Contact.** Query letter. Include credits.

**Acceptance Policies.** Unagented manuscripts: no. Simultaneous submissions: no. Disk submissions: no. Response time to initial inquiry: 4-6 weeks. Average time until publication: 6 12 months. **Advance**: varies. **Royalty**: varies. First run: varies.

**Marketing Channels.** Distribution houses; independent reps; in-house staff. Subsidiary rights: none.

**Additional Information.** Catalog: upon request.

**BLUE DOLPHIN PUBLISHING, INC.** 12380 Nevada City Hwy. Grass Valley, CA 95945. (916) 265-6925. Submissions Editor: Paul M. Clemens. Founded: 1985. Number of titles published: cumulative—15, 1989—5. Hardback 1, softback 14.

**Subjects of Interest. Nonfiction**—psychology (lay and professional); comparative spiritual traditions (Zen, Tibetan, Sufi); health; death and dying; children's; audio and video cassettes. Recent publications: *A Practical Guide to Creative Senility; Sad but OK...My Daddy Died Today*.

**Initial Contact.** Query letter; book proposal with sample chapters; or, entire manuscript. Include author biography and references.

**Acceptance Policies.** Unagented manuscripts: yes. Simultaneous submissions: yes; inform us. Disk submissions: IBM; ASCII. Response time to initial inquiry: 6 weeks to a year. Average time until publication: 6 months. **Advance**: none. **Royalty**: 10% on invoice total. First run: 2000-5000. Subsidy basis: yes; split net sales 50-50 with investor.

**Marketing Channels.** Distribution houses; direct mail. Subsidiary rights: all.

**Additional Information.** We also own and run Blue Dolphin Press, Inc., and produce all work in-house. Tips: We generally require a financial investment from author or outside agent. Catalog: upon request.

Body Press *see* **PRICE STERN SLOAN.**

**BORGO PRESS.** Box 2845. San Bernardino, CA 92406. (714) 884-5813. Submissions Editor: Robert Reginald. Founded: 1975. Number of titles published: cumulative—800, 1989—100. Hardback, softback, we do everything in both versions.

**Subjects of Interest. Nonfiction**—scholarly books for the library and academic markets; scholarly monographs. Do not want: fiction; poetry; children's books; trade books; popular nonfiction; etc.

**Initial Contact.** Query letter. Include some evidence the author has looked at our books, not our catalog.

**Acceptance Policies.** Unagented manuscripts: yes. Simultaneous submissions: no. Disk submissions: no. Response time to initial inquiry: 2 months plus. Average time until publication: 2 years plus. **Advance**: none. **Royalty**: 10%. First run: 100-1000.

**Marketing Channels.** Direct mail. Subsidiary rights: all.

**Additional Information.** We throw away submissions without SASEs. All of our books are published in open-ended, numbered, monographic series. Tips: Do not submit manuscripts unless you have seen our books. Catalog: SASE with $.65 postage.

**BOXWOOD PRESS.** 183 Ocean View Blvd. Pacific Grove, CA 93950. (408) 375-9110. Submissions Editor: Dr. Buchsbaum. Founded: 1952. Number of titles published—5 a year average. Hardback 50%, softback 50%.

**Subjects of Interest. Nonfiction**—biology; natural history; area studies; psychology; psychiatry; mathematics; economics; biography. Recent publications: *Ano Nuevo; Natural History of Monterey Bay Area; Monarch Butterfly; What is a California Sea Otter?; Living Invertebrates; Basic Ecology.*

**Initial Contact.** Entire manuscript (no proposals). Include curriculum vitae (indicate your expertise).

**Acceptance Policies.** Unagented manuscripts: yes. Simultaneous submissions: yes. Disk submissions: yes. Response time to initial inquiry: 3 weeks approximately. Average time until publication: 5 months from clean manuscript. **Advance**: none. **Royalty**: 10%. First run: 1000 (up to 5000). Subsidy basis: Project must be sound and have an identifiable market.

**Marketing Channels.** Distribution houses; direct mail; independent reps; in-house staff; special sales. Subsidiary rights: all.

**Additional Information.** Tips: Have it neat, double-spaced, and clean. Catalog: upon request.

**BRENNER INFORMATION GROUP.** (Subsidiary of Brenner Microcomputing, Inc.). 13223 Black Mountain Rd., Ste. 430. San Diego, CA 92129. (619) 693-0355. Submissions Editor: Robert C. Brenner. Founded: 1982/1988. Number of titles published: cumulative—2, 1989—5. Softback 100%.

**Subjects of Interest.** **Nonfiction**—how-to; self-help; reference. Recent publications: *Silent Speech of Politicians—Body Language in Government*. In process: *How to Read Your Customer/Client Like a Book; Index to Desktop Publishing* (articles and books)*; Patient's Guide to Medical Tests*. Do not want: novels.

**Initial Contact.** Query letter; book proposal with sample chapters. Include biography.

**Acceptance Policies.** Unagented manuscripts: yes. Simultaneous submissions: yes; inform us. Disk submissions: MS-DOS; Macintosh. Response time to initial inquiry: 2-4 weeks. Average time until publication: 2-6 months. **Advance**: variable. **Royalty**: 9-17%. First run: 2000-5000. Subsidy basis: Will produce finished product from initial manuscript; will consult on marketing and sales; also do share-cost publishing.

**Marketing Channels.** Distribution houses; direct mail; in-house staff; special sales. Subsidiary rights: all.

**Additional Information.** Our purpose is to collect, process, format, package, and distribute information of value to people. Tips: Request guidelines. Catalog: upon request.

Broadway Books *see* **HUNTER HOUSE PUBLISHERS.**

**BULL PUBLISHING COMPANY.** 110 Gilbert. Menlo Park, CA 94025. (415) 322-2855. Submissions Editor: David C. Bull. Founded: 1974. Number of titles published: cumulative—75. 19089—4. Hardback 5%, softback 95%.

**Subjects of Interest.** **Nonfiction**—health; nutrition; fitness; cancer care and prevention. Recent publications: *The Nutrition Debate: Sorting Out Some Answers; Keeping Abreast: Breast Changes That Are Not Cancer; Child of Mine: Feeding with Love and Good Sense*. Do not want: books with only trade potential; must have some cross-over to professional markets (medical and allied health).

**Initial Contact.** n/i. Book proposal with sample chapters. Include listing of potential markets.

**Acceptance Policies.** Unagented manuscripts: yes. Simultaneous submissions: no. Disk submissions: no. Response time to initial inquiry: 2 weeks. Average time until publication: 9 months. **Advance**: varies. **Royalty**: 10-15% of net. First run: 5000+ (depending on the book).

**Marketing Channels.** Distribution houses; direct mail; special sales. Subsidiary rights: all.

**Additional Information.** Catalog: upon request.

• **CADMUS EDITIONS.** Box 687. Tiburon, CA 94920. (707) 431-8527. Submissions Editor: Jeffrey Miller. Founded: 1979. Number of titles published: cumulative—40, 1987—2. Hardback 20%, softback 80%.

**Subjects of Interest. Fiction**—Recent Publications: *She Woke Me Up So I Killed Her* (selected short translation of Paul Bowles); *The Pigeon Factory; Early Routines.* **Other**—poetry. Recent publications: *How a City Sings* (Federico Garcia Lorca); *Yellow Lola; The Great Naropa Poetry Wars.*

**Initial Contact.** Query letter. Include curriculum vitae with list of publications to date.

**Acceptance Policies.** Unagented manuscripts: yes. Simultaneous submissions: no. Disk submissions: no. First novels: yes. Response time to initial inquiry: 30-45 days. Average time until publication: 12 to 18 months. **Advance**: usually none. **Royalty**: negotiable. First run: 2000-3000.

**Marketing Channels.** Distribution houses; independent reps. Subsidiary rights: all.

**Additional Information.** Catalog: request from Subterranean Co., PO Box 10233, Eugene, OR 97440.

## C & T PUBLISHING.

PO Box 1456. Lafayette, CA 94549. (415) 937-0605. Submissions Editor: Carolie Hensley. Founded: 1983. Number of titles published: cumulative—28, 1989—6. Softback 100%.

**Subjects of Interest. Nonfiction**—how-to quilting books. Recent publications: *Three Dimensional Design; A Celebration of Hearts, Light and Shadows: Optical Illusion in Quilts.* Do not want: any material outside quilting and quilt making field.

**Initial Contact.** Query letter; perhaps photos of quilts to be included.

**Acceptance Policies.** Unagented manuscripts: yes. Simultaneous submissions: no. Disk submissions: ASCII file. Response time to initial inquiry: 1 week. Average time until publication: 9-12 months. **Advance**: negotiable; subsidizes author's photographic expenses. **Royalty**: 8% retail or 10% wholesale. First run: 5000-15,000.

**Marketing Channels.** Direct mail; independent reps; craft product distributors. Subsidiary rights: all.

**Additional Information.** We only publish quilt making and quilting books. Tips: Send for author's packet.

product distributors. Subsidiary rights: all.

## CANTERBURY PRESS.

Box 2151C. Berkeley, CA 94702. (415) 843-1860. Submissions Editor: Ian Faircloth and Norine Brogans. Number of titles published: 1988—4.

**Subjects of Interest. Nonfiction**—philosophy; social justice; sociology; studies on the "third world"; minorities; underprivileged. Recent publications: *Living Outside Inside* (problems of the disabled). **Fiction**—adventure; experimental; fantasy; humor; needs to have a social or political or cultural insight. Recent publications: *Perigrina* (children's bilingual). Do not want: books which do not exhibit our philosophy.

**Initial Contact.** Query letter; outline.

**Acceptance Policies.** Unsolicited manuscripts: query first; all unsolicited manuscripts are returned unopened. Unagented manuscripts: yes. Disk submissions: query. Response time to initial inquiry: 1 month, queries; 2 months, manuscripts. Average time until publication: 4 months. **Advance**: $500. **Royalty**: 5-8%. Subsidy basis: yes; 50%.

**Additional Information.** We are appealing to a mature audience that appreciates innovative writing, new ideas, and insights. Tips: Send for manuscript guidelines; #10 SASE. Catalog: #10 SASE.

## CAREER PUBLISHING, INC.

910 N. Main St. PO Box 5486. Orange, CA 92613-5486. (714) 771-5155. Submissions Editor: Sherry Robson. Founded: 1972. Number of titles published: cumulative—60, 1989—10. Softback 100%.

**Subjects of Interest.** **Nonfiction**—vocational courses; medical; computer, word processing; truck driving textbooks. Recent publications: handbook/workbook for Wordstar, Wordperfect, Wordstar 2000 plus Rel 3; *Occupational Outlook Handbook; Trucking*. Do not want: fiction or poetry.

**Initial Contact.** Query letter.

**Acceptance Policies.** Unagented manuscripts: yes. Simultaneous submissions: no. Disk submissions: yes; Apple and IBM compatibles. Response time to initial inquiry: 30 days. Average time until publication: 1 year. **Advance**: none. **Royalty**: 10%. First run: 3000-5000.

**Marketing Channels.** Cooperative distribution; in-house staff. Subsidiary rights: all.

**Additional Information.** Write for guidelines. Catalog: upon request.

**CAROUSEL PRESS.** PO Box 6061. Albany, CA 94706. (415) 527-5849. Submissions Editor: Carole T. Meyers. Founded: 1976. Number of titles published: cumulative—10, 1988—1, 1989—1. Hardback 5%, softback 95%.

**Subjects of Interest.** **Nonfiction**—family travel; California travel. Recent publications: *Weekend Adventures for City-Weary People: Overnight Trips in Northern California.*

**Initial Contact.** Book proposal with sample chapters. Include SASE.

**Acceptance Policies.** Unagented manuscripts: yes. Simultaneous submissions: no. Disk submissions: no. Response time to initial inquiry: 2 weeks. Average time until publication: 1 year. **Advance**: n/i. **Royalty**: n/i. First run: 5000.

**Marketing Channels.** Distribution houses; direct mail; in-house staff; special sales. Subsidiary rights: all.

**Additional Information.** Catalog: SASE with $.45 postage.

**CASSANDRA PRESS.** PO Box 868. San Rafael, CA 94915. (415) 382-8507. Submissions Editor: Gurudas. Founded: 1985. Number of titles published: cumulative—11, 1988—6. Softback 100%.

**Subjects of Interest.** **Nonfiction**—new age; metaphysical; holistic health; astrology; psychology.

**Initial Contact.** Query letter; or book proposal with sample chapters.

**Acceptance Policies.** Unagented manuscripts: yes. Simultaneous submissions: yes. Disk submissions: no. Response time to initial inquiry: 1 -2 months. Average time until publication: 9-12 months. **Advance**: none. **Royalty**: 6% on retail; higher as sales increase. First run: 8000-14,000.

**Marketing Channels.** Distribution houses; direct mail. Subsidiary rights: all.

**Additional Information.** Catalog: upon request.

**CASTLEROCK PRESS.** 4090 Ben Lomond. Palo Alto, CA 94306. (415) 856-1062. Submissions Editor: Bill Oliver. Founded: 1988. Number of titles published: cumulative—1, 1989—1. Softback 100%.

**Subjects of Interest.** **Nonfiction**—travel with historical flavor. Recent publications: *San Mateo! A Sketchbook Tour of the San Francisco Peninsula's Past.* Do not want: fiction; poetry.

**Initial Contact.** Query letter; brief description. Include author's background; potential market.

**Acceptance Policies.** Unagented manuscripts: yes. Simultaneous submissions: yes. Disk submissions: no. Response time to initial inquiry: 2 weeks. Average time until publication: 6-9months. **Advance**: none. **Royalty**: 10%. First run: 5000+/-. Subsidy basis: yes.

**Marketing Channels.** Distribution houses; direct mail; in-house staff; special sales. Subsidiary rights: all.

**Additional Information.** We are looking for education through travel orientation. Tips: We want authors who can help promote their books. Catalog: upon request.

## CATALYSTS PUBLICATIONS.

143 Dolores St. San Francisco, CA 94103. (415) 552-5045. Submissions Editor: Bonnie Weiss. Founded: 1985. Number of titles published: cumulative—3. Softback 100%.

**Subjects of Interest.** **Nonfiction**—how-to's—publicity, promotion, writing. Recent publications: *How-to Publicize Your Way to Success: A Step by Step Guide; The Power of Publicity* (cassette album); *"Spotlight"* (a newsletter on musical theater/film).

**Initial Contact.** Query letter.

**Acceptance Policies.** Unagented manuscripts: yes. Simultaneous submissions: no. Disk submissions: no. Response time to initial inquiry: 3 weeks. Average time until publication: n/i. **Advance**: n/i. **Royalty**: n/i. First run: n/i.

**Additional Information.** Catalog: upon request.

## CCC PUBLICATIONS.

20306 Tau Place. Chatsworth, CA 91311. (818) 407-1661. Submissions Editor: Cliff Carle. Number of titles published—5-10 per year. Softback 100%.

**Subjects of Interest.** **Nonfiction**—humorous how-to/self-help. Recent publications: *No Hang-Ups.*

**Initial Contact.** Query letter; complete manuscript; SASE.

**Acceptance Policies.** Unagented manuscripts: yes. Simultaneous submissions: yes. Response time to initial inquiry: 1 month, queries; 3 months, manuscripts. Average time until publication: 1 year. **Advance**: n/i. **Royalty**: 5-10% on wholesale.

**Additional Information.** We have a reputation for humor titles with a long shelf life which will appeal to the impulse buyer. Catalog: 8 1/2 x 11 SASE, 2 first class stamps.

## CELESTIAL ARTS.

(Division of Ten Speed Press). Box 7327. Berkeley, CA 94707. (415) 524-1801. Submissions Editor: Mariah Bear. Founded: 1983. Number of titles published: cumulative—200, 1989—20. Softback 100%.

**Subjects of Interest.** **Nonfiction**—biography; cookbooks/cooking; holistic health; psychology; social sciences; new age; philosophy; self-help. Recent publications: *Garlic Lover's Cookbook* (several volumes). **Fiction**—very limited; some children's. Recent publications: *Longing; The UnAmericans in Paris.* **Other**—Gordo comics; audio cassettes; posters. Do not want: poetry; channeling.

**Initial Contact.** Query letter; book proposal with sample chapters. Include SASE.

**Acceptance Policies.** Unagented manuscripts: yes. Simultaneous submissions: yes. Disk submissions: IBM; Word Perfect. Response time to initial inquiry: 4-6 weeks. Average time until publication: 1 year. **Advance**: varies. **Royalty**: standard. First run: 5000.

**Marketing Channels.** Distribution houses; direct mail; independent reps; in-house staff; special sales. Subsidiary rights: all.

**Additional Information.** Tips: Do not submit manuscripts to both Ten Speed Press and Celestial Arts. Do not phone us. Catalog: 9x12 SASE, $1.92 postage.

## CHANDLER & SHARP PUBLISHERS, INC.

11 A Commercial Blvd. Novato, CA 94945. (415) 883-2353. Submissions Editor: Jonathan Sharp. Founded: 1972. Number of titles published: cumulative—38, 1989—3. Hardback 5%, softback 95%.

**Subjects of Interest.** **Nonfiction**—an occasional trade book with subject matter related to our textbook interests. **Other**—college-level texts in anthropology and political science. Recent publications: *The Sophists; The Study of Culture; Anthropology in the High Valleys: Essays on the New Guinea Highlands*. Do not want: fiction; poetry; drama.

**Initial Contact.** Query letter; book proposal with sample chapters. Include author's resumé or vitae.

**Acceptance Policies.** Unagented manuscripts: yes. Simultaneous submissions: yes; we request that author listen to our best offer before making a final decision. Disk submissions: no (we hope to in the future). Response time to initial inquiry: 10 days to 2 weeks. Average time until publication: 9 months to 2 years. **Advance**: small, but negotiable. **Royalty**: 15% of net (cash received). First run: 3000-6000 copies. Subsidy basis: yes; negotiable, but author is expected to pay at least one-half of costs.

**Marketing Channels.** Direct mail; independent reps; in-house staff. Subsidiary rights: all.

## CHILDREN'S BOOK PRESS.

1461 Ninth Ave. San Francisco, CA 94122. Submissions Editor: Harriet Rohmer. Founded: 1975.

**Subjects of Interest.** **Fiction**—multicultural literature for children; picture books only. Recent publications: *The Invisible Hunters* (Nicaragua); *The Legend of Food Mountain* (Mexico); *Aekyung's Dream* (Korea).

**Initial Contact.** Entire manuscript; explain why you feel it is important to publish the story at this time.

**Acceptance Policies.** Unagented manuscripts: yes. Simultaneous submissions: yes. Disk submissions: no. Response time to initial inquiry: 4-6 weeks. Average time until publication: 1 year. **Advance**: varies. **Royalty**: 5% author; 5% artist. First run: 7500.

**Marketing Channels.** Distribution houses; direct mail; independent reps; special sales. Subsidiary rights: all.

**Additional Information.** We publish bilingual and multicultural folk tales and contemporary stories reflecting the traditions and culture of Third World communities both in the United States and in the Third World. **Tips:** Send for editorial guidelines. Catalog: SASE; $.45 postage.

## CHINA BOOKS AND PERIODICALS, INC.

2929 24th St. San Francisco, CA 94110. (415) 282-2994. Submissions Editor: Bob Schildgen. Founded: 1965. Number of titles published: cumulative—38, 1989—12. Hardback 20%, softback 80%.

**Subjects of Interest.** **Nonfiction**—books about China; Chinese topics; Chinese Americans. Recent publications: *Buddhist Art of the Tibetan Plateaus; 5000 Years of Chinese Costumes*; *Easy Tao* (on Chinese exercise). **Fiction**—mostly translations from Chinese literature; we have a new fiction series. Do not want: books that are not related to China.

**Initial Contact.** Query letter.

**Acceptance Policies.** Unagented manuscripts: yes. Simultaneous submissions: no. Disk submissions: MS-DOS (preferably Wordperfect or Microsoft Word). Response time to initial inquiry: 1 month. Average time until publication: 8 months. **Advance**: $500. **Royalty**: 8% of retail. First run: 5000 average. Subsidy basis: yes; occasionally.

**Marketing Channels.** Distribution houses; direct mail; independent reps. Subsidiary rights: all.

**Additional Information.** Catalog: upon request.

**CHRONICLE BOOKS.** 245 - 5th St. San Francisco, CA 94103. (415) 777-7240. Submissions Editors: Nion McEvoy, Executive Editor (nonfiction); Victoria Rock (children's); David Barich (cook books); Jay Schaefer (fiction and topical nonfiction). Founded: 1966. Number of titles published: 1989—85. Hardback yes, softback yes.

**Subjects of Interest. Nonfiction**—high quality, full color coffee-table books; cookbooks; craftbooks (new to our list); regional California—art, cooking, foods, design, nature, photography, recreation, travel. Recent publications: *Chinese American Portraits; Restaurants of San Francisco; The Great Family Getaway Guide*. Fiction—children's (we are just entering this field).

**Initial Contact.** Query letter; book proposal with sample chapters. Include sample art work.

**Acceptance Policies.** Unagented manuscripts: yes. Simultaneous submissions: yes. Response time to initial inquiry: 1 month. Average time until publication: 18 months. **Advance:** $3000, average. **Royalty:** 6-10% of retail.

**Marketing Channels.** Independent reps; in-house staff. Subsidiary rights: first serialization; second serialization; newspaper syndication; reprint; book club; translation and foreign.

**Additional Information.** We are in the process of expanding our nonfiction and children's line and welcome submissions. Catalog: 9x12 SASE, 4 first class stamps.

**CITY LIGHTS BOOKS.** 261 Columbus Avenue. San Francisco, CA 94133. (415) 362-1090. Submissions Editor: Robert Sharrard. Founded: 1953. Number of titles published: cumulative—200, 1987—20. Hardback 10%, softback 90%.

**Subjects of Interest. Nonfiction**—philosophy, art and history studies. Recent publications: *Spinoza: Practical Philosophy; The Tears of Eros; Duras by Duras*. **Fiction**—alternative, unconventional novels; fiction in translation. Recent publications: *Story of the Eye; Simbi and the Satyr of the Dark Jungle; Without Falling*. **Other**—poetry. Recent publications: *Passionate Journey; Twenty Prose Poems* (Baudelaire)*; The Stiffest of the Corpse: Exquisite Corpse Reader; City Lights Review No. 2* (Ferlinghetti).

**Initial Contact.** Query letter; book proposal with sample chapters; SASE.

**Acceptance Policies.** Unagented manuscripts: 50%. Simultaneous submissions: yes. Disk submissions: no. First novels: yes; very few. Response time to initial inquiry: 6 weeks. Average time until publication: 18 months. **Advance:** $500-2000. **Royalty:** 7% annual payment. First run: 2500. Subsidy basis: yes.

**Marketing Channels.** Cooperative distribution. Subsidiary rights: all.

**CLEIS PRESS.** PO Box 14684. San Francisco, CA 94114. Submissions Editor: Frederique Delacoste. Founded: 1980. Number of titles published: cumulative—16, 1989—6. Softback 100%.

**Subjects of Interest. Nonfiction**—human rights; feminist; gay/lesbian; women's issues; by and about Latin American women; government/politics. Recent publications: *Sex Work: Writings by Women in the Sex Industry* (anthology of essays). Do not want: religious or spiritual works; topics that have been overworked. **Fiction**—feminist; gay/lesbian; literary. Recent publications: *Unholy Alliances: New Fiction by Women* (anthology). Do not want: romance.

**Initial Contact.** Query letter; or outline and sample chapters; or complete manuscript. fiction: complete manuscript.

**Acceptance Policies.** Unagented manuscripts: yes. Simultaneous submissions: yes; inform us as to who and when. Disk submissions: query. Response time to initial inquiry: 1 month. Average time until publication: 6 months. **Advance**: n/i. **Royalty**: varies.

**Additional Information.** We are interested in books which will sell in feminist and progressive bookstores and will sell in Europe for translation rights. Tips: Author should spend time in bookstore whose clientele resembles her audience. Know your market. Catalog: #10 SASE and 2 first class stamps.

**CLIFFHANGER PRESS.** Box 29527. Oakland, CA 94604-9527. (415) 763-3510. Submissions Editor: Nancy Chirich. Founded: 1985. Number of titles published: cumulative—15, 1988—4. Softback 100%.

**Subjects of Interest.** **Fiction**—mystery; suspense. Recent publications: *Death in a Small Southern Town.* Do not want: spy stories; hardboiled detective type characters.

**Initial Contact.** Outline; 2-3 chapters; SASE.

**Acceptance Policies.** Unagented manuscripts: yes. Simultaneous submissions: yes. Response time to initial inquiry: 2 months. Average time until publication: 9-12 months. **Advance**: none. **Royalty**: 8%. First run: n/i.

**Marketing Channels.** Distribution houses. Subsidiary rights: n/i.

**Additional Information.** Our focus is mystery/suspense with a strong regional or foreign feel, a strong plot and believable characters. Catalog: #10 SASE.

**CLOTHESPIN FEVER PRESS.** 5529 N. Figueroa. Los Angeles, CA 90042. (213) 254-1373. Submissions Editor: Jenny Wren. Founded: 1985. Number of titles published: cumulative—5, 1989—4. Softback 100%.

**Subjects of Interest.** **Nonfiction**—autobiography; how-to. **Fiction**—anthologies. Recent publications: *Leaving Texas. Self-Portraits Anthology: From a Different Light; Shitkickers and other Texas Stories.* **Other**—poetry. Recent publications: *Dark Passages.* Do not want: works on AIDS; gay male works.

**Initial Contact.** Query letter; book proposal with sample chapters.

**Acceptance Policies.** Unagented manuscripts: yes. Simultaneous submissions: yes; inform us. Disk submissions: Macintosh Word 3.0. First novels: yes. Response time to initial inquiry: 1 month. Average time until publication: 1 year. **Advance**: none. **Royalty**: none. First run: 250-500. Subsidy basis: yes; if manuscript is accepted, we will negotiate printing costs and imprint name.

**Marketing Channels.** Direct mail; in-house staff; special sales at conventions. Subsidiary rights: none.

**Additional Information.** We are a lesbian publisher and our audience is primarily lesbian. Heterosexual material is not of interest to us. Tips: Read one of our books. Catalog: upon request.

**COMMUNICATION UNLIMITED.** (Imprint: Write to Sell). PO Box 6405. Santa Maria, CA 93456. Submissions Editor: Gordon Burgett. Founded: 1980. Number of titles published: cumulative—6, 1989—1. Hardback 40%, softback 60% (all but first book comes out in both forms).

**Subjects of Interest.** **Nonfiction**—information dissemination by writing and speaking. Recent publications: *Empire Building by Writing and Speaking; Query Letters/Cover Letters: How They Sell Your Writing; How-to Sell 75% of Your Freelance Writing; Speaking for Money.* Do not want: anything but information dissemination by writing and speaking.

**Initial Contact.** Query letter. Include explanation of who would buy the book, why, and what else like it exists.

**Acceptance Policies.** Unagented manuscripts: yes. Simultaneous submissions: no. Disk submissions: yes; if book accepted, we want copy on disk; will discuss format. Response time to initial inquiry: to query, quickly; no response to any other form. Average time until publication: varies. **Advance**: varies. **Royalty**: varies. First run: depends on perceived market.

**Marketing Channels.** Distribution houses; direct mail. Subsidiary rights: none.

**Additional Information.** We are very small by intention and are closely linked with seminars, plus audio cassette production. Tips: Try someone else unless it serves the speaking and writing market directly. Catalog: upon request.

**COMSOURCE PUBLISHING.** PO Box 26216. San Francisco, CA 94126. (415) 775-5879. Submissions Editor: J.R. Pierce. Founded: 1972. Number of titles published: cumulative—9. Hardback 20%, softback 80%.

**Subjects of Interest. Nonfiction**—food and wine; travel guides; horse racing; computers and software; parapsychology, paranormal. Recent publications: *Little Restaurants of San Francisco; Computers in Business; Out of This World* (parapsychological phenomenon). Do not want: fiction.

**Initial Contact.** Query letter; author biography; outline or table of contents. Include writing sample.

**Acceptance Policies.** Unagented manuscripts: yes. Simultaneous submissions: no. Disk submissions: no. Response time to initial inquiry: 2 months. Average time until publication: varies to 1 year. **Advance**: negotiable. **Royalty**: n/i. First run: 10,000.

**Marketing Channels.** Distribution houses; direct mail; independent reps. Subsidiary rights: all.

**Additional Information.** Catalog: upon request.

**COMSTOCK EDITIONS, INC.** 3030 Bridgeway Blvd. Sausalito, CA 94965. (415) 332-3216. Submissions Editor: George Young. Founded: 1971. Number of titles published: cumulative—28, 1987—4. Softback 100%.

**Subjects of Interest.** All of the following publications are reprints: **Nonfiction**—biography; history; nature. Recent publications: *Bagdhad-By-the-Bay; Sea Routes to the Gold Fields.* **Fiction**—western; historical; out-of-print classics. Recent publications: *Medicine Calf; The Distant Music; Paul Bunyan.* **Other**—folklore; popular local history. Do not want: poetry; new age; health; sports.

**Initial Contact.** Query letter; book proposal; brief synopsis.

**Acceptance Policies.** Unagented manuscripts: no. Simultaneous submissions: no. Disk submissions: no. Response time to initial inquiry: 1-2 months. Average time until publication: up to 1 year. **Advance**: $250-500. **Royalty**: 6%-8%. First run: 5000.

**Marketing Channels.** Distribution houses; direct mail. Subsidiary rights: all.

**Additional Information.** There is a very slight chance that I would do an original book in the next two years. Tips: If you previously published a book in the mass market, I might be more useful. Catalog: upon request.

**CONARI PRESS.** 713 Euclid Avenue. Berkeley, CA 94708. (415) 527-9915. Submissions Editor: Mary Jane Ryan. Founded: 1987. Number of titles published: cumulative—5 (through 1989). Softback 100%.

**Subjects of Interest. Nonfiction**—psychology; self-help. Recent publications: *Coming Apart: Why Relationships End and How-to Live Through the Ending of Yours; Just in Case: A Handbook of All of the Information and Legal Forms Californians Need to Control Their Lives.* Do not want: fiction.

**Initial Contact.** Entire manuscript.

**Acceptance Policies.** Unagented manuscripts: yes. Simultaneous submissions: yes; just tell us. Disk submissions: IBM Wordperfect. Response time to initial inquiry: 1-2 months. Average time until publication: 1 year. **Advance**: varies. **Royalty**: varies. First run: 3000-10,000.

**Marketing Channels.** Distribution houses; direct mail. Subsidiary rights: all.

**Additional Information.** Catalog: SASE.

## CONTEMPORARY ARTS PRESS.

PO Box 3123, Rincon Station. San Francisco, CA 94119. (415) 431-7672. Submissions Editor: Carl Loeffler. Founded: 1975. Number of titles published: cumulative—2.

**Subjects of Interest. Nonfiction**—experimental arts and new communication technology; contemporary art; new forms of art; performance art; art and video; telecom and art. Recent publications: *Performance Anthology: Sourcebook for a Decade of California Performance Art; Correspondence Art: Art Sent through the Mail.* Also publishes a quarterly magazine via electronic publishing.

**Initial Contact.** Query letter; mansucript.

**Acceptance Policies.** Unagented manuscripts: yes. Simultaneous submissions: no. Disk submissions: yes. Response time to initial inquiry: 2 months. Average time until publication: 1-2 months. **Advance**: n/i. **Royalty**: n/i.

**Marketing Channels.** 70 country electronic network.

## CRAFTSMAN BOOK COMPANY.

6058 Corte Del Cedro. Carlsbad, CA 92009. (619) 438-7828. Submissions Editor: Laurence D. Jacobs. Founded: 1953. Number of titles published: cumulative—65, 1989—10. Softback 100%.

**Subjects of Interest. Nonfiction**—"how-to" construction manuals for professional builders. Recent publications: *National Construction Estimator; Residential Electricians Handbook; Painter's Handbook; Drywall Contracting; Running Your Remodeling Business; Masonry Estimating*. Do not want: anything not for professional builders.

**Initial Contact.** Query letter; book proposal. Include author's qualifications.

**Acceptance Policies.** Unagented manuscripts: yes. Simultaneous submissions: yes. Disk submissions:; MS-DOS (IBM compatible). Response time to initial inquiry: 3 weeks. Average time until publication: 1 year. **Advance**: 0-$500. **Royalty**: 12 1/2% of gross. First run: 5000.

**Marketing Channels.** Direct mail. Subsidiary rights: reprint; video distribution; sound reproduction and recording; direct mail or direct sales; book clubs; translation and foreign; computer and other magnetic and electronic media; commercial; English language publication outside the United States and Canada.

**Additional Information.** Must be straight "how-to" material. Catalog: upon request.

## CREATIVE ARTS BOOK COMPANY.

(Imprint: Black Lizard Books). 833 Bancroft Way. Berkeley, CA 94710. (415) 848-4777. Submissions Editor: Peg O'Donnell (Creative Arts); Barry Gifford (Black Lizard Books; crime fiction line). Founded: 1976. Number of titles published: cumulative—150, 1988—40 (1/2 reprints; 1/2 original). Hardback 50%, softback 50%.

**Subjects of Interest. Nonfiction**—essays; biographies; memoirs; "armchair travel"; California history (literary); music (biographies, memoirs, some technique and form but not how-to). Recent publications: *Things Ain't What They used To Be; Improvisation; Music From the Inside Out; Lethal Injection; Silk Stalkings: When Women Write of Murder*. **Fiction**—serious literature; short stories; mainstream/contemporary (not "pop"). Recent publications: *California Childhood: Recollections and Stories of the Golden State; Jesus and Fat Tuesday and Other Stories*. Do not want: poetry; romance; science fiction; children's;

young adult; war/adventure; new age; travel guides; health/fitness; technical; arts and crafts; photography; how-to; military history; self-help.

**Initial Contact.** Outline; table of contents; sample chapters. Include author bio and SASE in order to return materials.

**Acceptance Policies.** Unagented manuscripts: yes. Simultaneous submissions: yes. Disk submissions: no. First novels: yes. Response time to initial inquiry: 6-8 weeks. Average time until publication: 1 year. **Advance**: $500-$1500. **Royalty**: 6%-7 1/2%. First run: 5000-10,000.

**Marketing Channels.** Distribution houses; independent reps; special sales. Subsidiary rights: first serialization; second serialization; newspaper syndication; reprint rights; dramatization; motion picture and broadcast; book club; translation and foreign; English language publication outside United States and Canada.

**Additional Information.** Tips: Do not phone for follow-up information. If we are not interested in a writer's work we do not give lengthy explanations. Catalog: upon request.

**CREATIVE MEDIA SERVICES.** 2936 Domingo Ave., Ste. 5. Berkeley, CA 94705. (415) 843-3408. Submissions Editor: Linda Harris. Number of titles published: cumulative—35. Softback 100%.

**Subjects of Interest. Other**—clip art; camera-ready art. Recent publications: *CMS Custom Clip Art.*

**Initial Contact.** Query letter; samples of artwork.

**Acceptance Policies.** Unagented manuscripts: yes. Simultaneous submissions: n/i. Disk submissions: n/i. Response time to initial inquiry: immediate. Average time until publication: 6 months. **Advance**: n/i. **Royalty**: n/i. First run: n/i.

**Marketing Channels.** Direct mail. Subsidiary rights: none.

**Additional Information.** Catalog: upon request.

**CREATIVE WITH WORDS PUBLICATIONS.** PO Box 223226. Carmel, CA 93922. (408) 649-1682. Submissions Editor: Brigitta Geltrich. Founded: 1975. Number of titles published: cumulative—79, 1988—2. Softback 100%.

**Subjects of Interest. Fiction**—folklore genres (e.g Christmas tales, Easter tales; lore around the world); creative writing and language arts work of children. Recent publications: *Children in Folklore/Children and Their Folklore; We Are Poets and Authors, Too!* (anthology of children's writings). Do not want: pornography; controversial issues.

**Initial Contact.** Query letter; book proposal with sample chapters; always include cover letter stating to which project author is submitting (see writer's guidelines).

**Acceptance Policies.** Unagented manuscripts: yes. Simultaneous submissions: no. Disk submissions: TRS 80 or Xerox 6085/8010. Response time to initial inquiry: 1 month; then according to deadline. Average time until publication: deadline is observed. **Advance**: none. **Royalty**: none. First run: n/i.

**Marketing Channels.** In-house staff. Subsidiary rights: none.

**Additional Information.** We offer authors a 20% price reduction on copies 1-9 ordered and 30% reduction on orders 10 and above. Tips: Be creative, be proficient, be brief. Catalog: SASE.

**CREATIVITY UNLIMITED.** 30819 Casilina. Rancho Palos Verdes, CA 90274. (213) 541-4844. Submissions Editor: Shelley Stockwell. Founded: 1983. Number of titles published: cumulative—11. Softback 100%.

**Subjects of Interest. Nonfiction**—new age; love yourself; hypnosis. Recent publications: *Insides Out; Sex and Other Touchy Subjects.* Other—poetry; self-hypnosis tapes. Recent publications: *Enlightenment Poetry.*

**Initial Contact.** Query.

**Acceptance Policies.** Unagented manuscripts: yes. Simultaneous submissions: n/i. Disk submissions: no. Response time to initial inquiry: 2 weeks. Average time until publication: 6 months. **Advance**: n/i. **Royalty**: n/i. First run: n/i.

**CRISP PUBLICATIONS.** 95 First St. Los Altos, CA 94022. (415) 949-4888. Michael G. Crisp. Founded: 1984. Number of titles published: cumulative—1987: 25+ per year. Softback 100%.

**Subjects of Interest. Nonfiction**—management training; communications; office management; self-management; sales training/customer service; entrepreneurship; career guidance; study skills; retirement and life planning. Recent publications: *Fifty-Minute Series: Team Building: An Exercise in Leadership; Effective Meeting Skills. How-to Succeed in College; The Unfinished Business of Living: Helping Aging Parents Help Themselves.*

**Initial Contact.** Query letter. Include table of contents; preface.

**Acceptance Policies.** Unagented manuscripts: yes. Simultaneous submissions: no. Disk submissions: no. Response time to initial inquiry: 3 weeks. Average time until publication: 6 months. **Advance**: none. **Royalty**: 10%. First run: 5000 +/-.

**Marketing Channels.** Distribution houses; cooperative distribution; direct mail; independent reps; special sales.

**Additional Information.** Most books are from experienced trainers/authors. Tips: If subject is unique and author has developed a widely attended workshop, chances for placement are improved. Catalog: upon request.

**CROSSING PRESS, THE.** 22-D Roache Rd. PO Box 1048. Freedom, CA 95019. (408) 722-0711. Submissions Editor: John and Elaine G. Gill. Founded: 1971. Number of titles published: cumulative—120, 1989—40. Hardback, softback, we do both cloth and paperback editions of all titles.

**Subjects of Interest. Nonfiction**—cookbook series; women's health series; parenting series; men's series; gay men's series; women's spirituality series. Recent publications: *Red Flower: Rethinking Menstruation; Street Food; Treasure of Nature: Seashells.* **Fiction**—literary; feminist; general, mysteries; sci-fi feminist. Recent publications: *Mundane's World; Through Other Eyes* (animal stories by women); *Clio Browne: Private Investigator* (A WomanSleuth Mystery). **Other**—some calendars and b/w postcards of famous people. Do not want: romance novels; historical fiction; children's stories.

**Initial Contact.** Query letter. Include outline or table of contents.

**Acceptance Policies.** Unagented manuscripts: yes. Simultaneous submissions: yes. Disk submissions: no. First novels: yes. Response time to initial inquiry: 3-4 weeks. Average time until publication: 6-12 months. Advance: negotiable. Royalty: 7-71/2% list or 10% net. First run: 5000-10,000.

**Marketing Channels.** Independent reps. Subsidiary rights: all; except video distribution; sound reproduction and recording rights.

**CYNTHIA PUBLISHING COMPANY.** 4455 Los Feliz Blvd. Suite 1106. Los Angeles, CA 90027. (213) 664-3165. Submissions Editor: Dick Mitchell. Not accepting submissions until January, 1991.

**JOHN DANIEL AND COMPANY.** PO Box 21922. Santa Barbara, CA 93121. (805) 962-1780. Submissions Editor: John Daniel. Founded: 1985. Number of titles published: cumulative—38, 1989—10. Harback 10%, softback 90%.

**Subjects of Interest.** **Nonfiction**—memoirs; essays. Recent publications: *In My Father's House* (memoir of a southern politician). **Fiction**—short stories; novels. Recent publications: *Big Chocolate Cookies* (novel about jazz and the stock market). **Other**—poetry (very little). Recent publications: *A Soldier's Time, Vietnam War Poems.*

**Initial Contact.** Query letter.

**Acceptance Policies.** Unagented manuscripts: yes. Simultaneous submissions: yes. Disk submissions: Macintosh or IBM compatible. First novels: yes. Response time to initial inquiry: 6-8 weeks. Average time until publication: 6-12 months. **Advance**: none. **Royalty**: 10% of net receipts. First run: 1000-2000.

**Marketing Channels.** Cooperative distribution. Subsidiary rights: all.

**Additional Information.** We are very small, specializing in belles lettres. Tips: Query first. Catalog: SASE.

**MAY DAVENPORT, PUBLISHERS.** 26313 Purissima Rd. Los Altos Hills, CA 94022. (415) 948-6499. Submissions Editor: May Davenport. Founded: 1975. Number of titles published: cumulative—32, 1989—2-3. Hardback and softback.

**Subjects of Interest.** **Nonfiction**—children's: animals, art, music, nature. **Fiction**—children's (elementary, secondary): fantasy, adventure. Recent publications: *Comic Tales Anthology #2* (fantasy, fun-to-read short stories, plays and poems for teens); *Willy Zilly and the Little Bantams.* **Other**—We are looking for 30-minute, one-act plays for TV-oriented junior and senior high school students; be humorous. Do not want: picture books, easy readers.

**Initial Contact.** Query letter. Include SASE.

**Acceptance Policies.** Unagented manuscripts: yes. Simultaneous submissions: yes. Disk submissions: no. Response time to initial inquiry: 3 weeks. Average time until publication: 1-3 years. **Advance**: none. **Royalty**: 15% on retail. First run: 2000. Subsidy basis: will consider for special junior or senior high textbooks, i.e. economics, international markets, finance, and money and banking. 50% cash down for editing/illustration/layout/dummy for approval; 25% down for printing/binding; 25% before delivery of books.

**Marketing Channels.** Distribution houses; direct mail; independent reps. Subsidiary rights: 50/50 negotiable.

**Additional Information.** We will contract for small business or club newsletter: collect news, edit, illustrate, layout, and see to the printing, binding and mailing. Tips: Be yourself! Your talent with words will speak for itself. And, if you can make people laugh, or smile, that's precious. Catalog: SASE.

**DELLEN PUBLISHING COMPANY.** (Subsidiary of Macmillan Inc.). 400 Pacific Ave., 3rd Fl. East. San Francisco, CA 94133. (415) 433-9900. Submissions Editor: Donald E. Dellen. Founded: 1976. Number of titles published: cumulative—40, 1988—10. Hardback 90%, softback 10%.

**Subjects of Interest.** **Other**—college textbooks; mathematics; statistics; computer science.

**Initial Contact.** Query letter; book proposal.

**Acceptance Policies.** Unagented manuscripts: n/a. Simultaneous submissions: n/i. Disk submissions: yes. Response time to initial inquiry: n/i. Average time until publication: n/i. **Advance**: n/i. **Royalty**: n/i. First run: n/i.

**Marketing Channels.** In-house staff. Subsidiary rights: all.

**DEMORTMAIN PUBLISHING.** PO Box 1280 . Pine Grove, CA 95665. (209) 295-4644. Submissions Editor: E. S. Matz. Founded:1983. Number of titles published: cumulative—2. Softback 100%.

**Subjects of Interest. Nonfiction**—dogs. We are looking for mansucripts on the crafts business (homebased). Recent publications: *Pit Bull Fact and Fable; The American Pit Bull Terrier.*

**Initial Contact.** Query letter.

**Acceptance Policies.** Unagented manuscripts: yes. Simultaneous submissions: yes. Disk submissions: yes. Response time to initial inquiry: n/i. Average time until publication: n/i. **Advance**: n/i. **Royalty**: 10-15% of gross. First run: 1000.

**Marketing Channels.** Distribution houses; Direct mail. Subsidiary rights: n/i.

**Additional Information.** We're a small independent and want to publish books on homebased craft business. We already publish a trade newspaper for homebased craft professionals, *The CA Craft Connection Newspaper* (a regional publication for California and Nevada). We are always in the market for articles on marketing crafts and how-to books on operating a home-based crafts business.

Don't Call it Frisco Press *see* **LEXIKOS PRESS.**

Doodle Art *see* **PRICE STERN SLOAN.**

**DOUBLE M PRESS.** 16455 Tuba St. Sepulveda, CA 91343. (818) 360-3166. Submissions Editor: Charlotte M. Stein. Founded: 1975. Number of titles published: cumulative—12, 1989—3. Hardback, softback, simultaneous production.

**Subjects of Interest. Nonfiction**—history and biography, geared to the school market, libraries, and parents. **Fiction**—children's (pre-school through young adult): history; contemporary problems; humor; fantasy. Do not want: gratuitous violence or sex.

**Initial Contact.** Query letter first.

**Acceptance Policies.** Unagented manuscripts: yes. Simultaneous submissions: yes. Disk submissions: no. First novels: yes. Response time to initial inquiry: 2 weeks. Average time until publication: 1 year. **Advance**: none. **Royalty**: 8% minimum of gross. First run: 1000.

**Marketing Channels.** Direct mail; special sales. Subsidiary rights: First serialization; newspaper syndication; book club; translation and foreign; English language publication outside the United States and Canada.

**Additional Information.** Catalog: not until fall.

**DOWN THERE PRESS/YES PRESS.** (Subsidiary of Open Enterprises, Inc.). PO Box 2086. Burlingame, CA 94011-2086. (415) 550-0912, 342-2536. Submissions Editor: Joani Blank. Founded: 1970. Number of titles published: cumulative—10, 1989—2. Softback 100%.

**Subjects of Interest. Nonfiction**—sexual self-help, education and awareness. Recent publications: *Men Loving Themselves; Kids First Book About Sex; Let's Talk About Sex and Loving* (for kids). **Fiction**—erotica. Recent publications: *Herotica: A Collection of Women's Erotic Fiction.*

**Initial Contact.** Query letter; book proposal with 1-3 sample chapters; chapter outline.

**Acceptance Policies.** Unagented manuscripts: yes. Simultaneous submissions: yes; please advise. **First novel:** maybe. Disk submissions: prefer hard copy for initial contact. Response time to initial inquiry: 2 months. Average time until publication: 1 year. **Advance**: minimal. **Royalty**: 8%-10% cover. First run: 2000-5000.

**Marketing Channels.** Distribution houses; cooperative distribution; direct mail; special sales. Subsidiary rights: all.

**Additional Information.** We are a very small press with very specific views of the kind of sex information to be made available. Catalog: #10 SASE.

**DRAGON'S TEETH PRESS.** El Dorado National Forest. Georgetown, CA 95634. Submissions Editor: Cornel Lengyel. Founded: 1970. Number of titles published: cumulative—40, 1987—5. Softback 100%.

**Subjects of Interest. Nonfiction**—music; philosophy. **Other**—poetry.

**Initial Contact.** Query letter; or outline and sample chapters. Include artwork or photos. Poetry: 10 samples or complete manuscript.

**Acceptance Policies.** Unagented manuscripts: yes. Simultaneous submissions: yes. Disk submissions: no. Response time to initial inquiry: 1 month. Average time until publication: 1 year. **Advance**: none. **Royalty**:10% on retail; or in copies. First run: n/i. Subsidy basis: if book has literary merit, uncertain market.

**Marketing Channels.** Distribution houses; direct mail. Subsidiary rights: all.

**Additional Information.** Tips: Looking for brilliant, highly original work. Catalog: SASE; 3 first class stamps.

**DROPZONE PRESS.** PO Box 882222. San Francisco, CA 94188. (415) 776-7164. Submissions Editor: Roy T. Maloney. Founded: 1978. Number of titles published: cumulative—2, 1989— 2 video. Softback 100%.

**Subjects of Interest. Nonfiction**—real estate; business; science. Recent publications: *Real Estate Quick and Easy; Roy's Rot* (business quotations). **Other**—video. Do not want: novels.

**Initial Contact.** Query letter.

**Acceptance Policies.** Unagented manuscripts: call first. Simultaneous submissions: yes; call first. Disk submissions: no. Response time to initial inquiry: 2 weeks. Average time until publication: 3 months. **Advance**: negotiable. **Royalty**: negotiable. First run: negotiable.

**Marketing Channels.** Distribution houses; direct mail; special sales. Subsidiary rights: none.

**Additional Information.** My books are in their 10th edition. Catalog: phone.

**DUSTBOOKS.** Box 100. Paradise, CA 95967. (916) 877-6110. Submissions Editor: Len Fulton. Founded: 1963. Number of titles published: cumulative—100+, 1988—5. Hardback and softback.

**Subjects of Interest. Nonfiction**—microcomputers; writing and publishing. Recent publications: *Small Press Record of Books in Print; Black and Blue Guide to Literary Magazines; International Directory of Little Magazines and Small Presses.* **Other**—poetry.

**Initial Contact.** Outline; sample chapters.

**Acceptance Policies.** Unagented manuscripts: yes. Simultaneous submissions: yes; inform us. Disk submissions: no. Response time to initial inquiry: 2 months. Average time until publication: 1 year. **Advance**: $500+\-. **Royalty**: 15%. First run: n/i.

**Marketing Channels.** Mail order. Subsidiary rights: all.

**Additional Information.** We have a small general trade list. Our energy is directed toward directories dealing with small press book/magazine directories. Tips: Writer's guidelines available; #10 SASE. Catalog: upon request.

**EDUCATIONAL INSIGHTS.** (Imprints: Laurel Park Publishing). 19560 S. Rancho Way. Dominguez Hills, CA 90220. (213) 637-2131. Submissions Editor: Dennis Graham. Founded: 1962. Number of titles published: cumulative—600, 1987—50. Softback 100%.

**Subjects of Interest. Nonfiction**—educational only—preschool through junior high.

**Initial Contact.** Book proposal with sample chapters or entire manuscript.

**Acceptance Policies.** Unagented manuscripts: yes. Simultaneous submissions: yes. Disk submissions: no. Response time to initial inquiry: 30 days. Average time until publication: 9 months. **Advance**: varies. **Royalty**: varies. First run: varies. Subsidy basis: yes; terms vary.

**Marketing Channels.** Distribution houses; direct mail; in-house staff. Subsidiary rights: all.

**Additional Information.** Catalog: upon request.

**ELECTRONIC TREND PUBLICATIONS.** 12930 Saratoga Ave., Ste. D-1. Saratoga, CA 95070. (408) 996-7416. Submissions Editor: Gene Selven. Founded: 1978. Number of titles published—7-10 per year. Softback perfect bound.

**Subjects of Interest. Nonfiction**—all technology subjects; technology market reports. Recent publications: *Start Up: Founding a High Tech Company and Securing Multi-Round Financing; Critical Trends in Contract Assembly* (impact of parallel processing on high performance computing); *Mimic Program; SMT Surface Mail Technology.*

**Initial Contact.** Call first.

**Acceptance Policies.** Unagented manuscripts: yes. Simultaneous submissions: yes. Disk submissions: Wordstar; WordPerfect. Response time to initial inquiry: immediately (on phone). Average time until publication: 6 months. **Advance**: negotiable. **Royalty**: might be **Royalty** or payment in full. First run: 75-150.

**Marketing Channels.** Direct mail; promote through magazine and newspaper reviews. Subsidiary rights: none.

**Additional Information.** This is a market research company and its needs are exclusively in that field. Catalog: upon request.

**ELYSIUM GROWTH PRESS.** (Imprints: Golden Eagle; Sun West). 700 Robinson Rd. Topanga, CA 90290. (213) 455-1000. Submissions Editor: Ed Lange. Founded: 1961. Number of titles published: cumulative—25, 1989—4. Hardback 40%, softback 60%.

**Subjects of Interest. Nonfiction**—source for books about the human body with and without clothes. Recent publications: *Body Self Acceptance; Body Self Image; Nudism in Australia; Nudity as Therapy.* **Other**—nudist travel guides, United States and international.

**Initial Contact.** Query letter; book proposal.

**Acceptance Policies.** Unagented manuscripts: yes. Simultaneous submissions: yes. Disk submissions: yes; Macintosh. Response time to initial inquiry: 10 days. Average time until publication: 12 months. **Advance**: 2000+. **Royalty**: 10%. First run: 5000.

**Marketing Channels.** Distribution houses; cooperative distribution; direct mail; special sales. Subsidiary rights: all.

**Additional Information.** Tips: Review our Catalog for type of material sought. Catalog: SASE.

**EMPIRE PUBLISHING SERVICE.** 7645 Le Berthon St. Tujunga, CA 91042. (818) 784-8918. Submissions Editor: Wendy Landes. Founded: 1970. Number of titles published: cumulative—190, 1988—3. Hardback 20%, softback 80%.

**Subjects of Interest. Nonfiction**—how to; texts; technical, entertainment industry. Recent publications: *Producing Your First Film; Television Production Techniques; Young Directors and Their Films*. **Other**—dramas; musicals; poetry. Do not want: novels.

**Initial Contact.** Query letter. Include #10 SASE.

**Acceptance Policies.** Unagented manuscripts: yes. Simultaneous submissions: yes. Disk submissions: no. Response time to initial inquiry: 60-90 days. Average time until publication: 90-180 days. **Advance**: varies. **Royalty**: varies. First run: 2000-20,000. Subsidy basis: yes; terms vary.

**Marketing Channels.** Distribution houses; cooperative distribution; direct mail; independent reps; in-house staff; special sales. Subsidiary rights: yes.

**Additional Information.** Catalog: $1.00 plus SASE with $.65 postage.

Enrich *see* **PRICE STERN SLOAN.**

**EPISTEMICS INSTITUTE PRESS.** PO Box 77508. Los Angeles, CA 90007. (213) 389-0307. Submissions Editor: Dr. Larry Gower. Founded: 1983. Number of titles published: cumulative—1. Hardback 40%, softback 60%.

**Subjects of Interest. Nonfiction**—philosophy; epistemology; epistemological historical philosphies. Recent publications: *Prisoners of Aristotle; The Miracle of Abduction.*

**Initial Contact.** Query letter; entire manuscript.

**Acceptance Policies.** Unagented manuscripts: yes. Simultaneous submissions: yes. Disk submissions: no. Response time to initial inquiry: 1 week. Average time until publication: 2 months. **Advance**: none. **Royalty**: 40%. First run: varies. Subsidy basis: yes; 50/50 author/publisher.

**Marketing Channels.** Direct mail. Subsidiary rights: none.

**Additional Information.** Small press confined to nonfiction. Interdisciplinary with epistemological method of inquiry dealing with language as a vehicle. Tips: Make sure your manuscript has originality and has been researched. Catalog: upon request.

**ROBERT ERDMANN PUBLISHING.** 28441 Highridge Road, Ste. 101. Rolling Hills Estates, CA 90274. (213) 544-5071. Submissions Editor: Dr. Glenn Austin. Founded: 1978. Number of titles published: cumulative—18, 1989—10. Hardback 20%, softback 80%.

**Subjects of Interest. Nonfiction**—self-help; family medical; health; travel. Recent publications: *Love and Power: Parent and Child; New Perspectives in Raising Healthy, Happy Competent Children.* Do not want: fiction.

**Initial Contact.** Book proposal with sample chapters. Include author background.

**Acceptance Policies.** Unagented manuscripts: n/i. Simultaneous submissions: yes. Disk submissions: yes. Response time to initial inquiry: 30 days. Average time until publication: 1 year. **Advance**: varies. **Royalty**: varies. First run: 10,000 (varies). Subsidy basis: yes; negotiable.

**Marketing Channels.** Distribution houses; direct mail; independent reps; special sales. Subsidiary rights: all.

**Additional Information.** We look for timely subjects. Catalog: upon request.

**ESOTERICA PRESS.** PO Box 170. Barstow, CA 92312. Submissions Editor: Yoly Zentella. Founded: 1985. Number of titles published—beginning publication in 1988. Softback 100%.

**Subjects of Interest. Nonfiction**—biographies, history dealing with travel or human situations. **Fiction**—novellas dealing with humanist themes; universal issues; women in and out of United States, especially Latinas. Recent publications: *Blood At the Roots* (novella based on true story by Aisha Eshe). **Other**—poetry on humanist themes. Recent publications: *Proud Ones: Poems by Koryne*. Do not want: frivolities; love stories with emphasis on sex.

**Initial Contact.** Query letter; sample chapters; must include SASE; source for contact with Esoterica Press.

**Acceptance Policies.** Unagented manuscripts: yes. Simultaneous submissions: yes; condition that if we are first to accept, writer withdraws manuscript from other presses, gives us first rights. Disk submissions: no. First novels: yes. Response time to initial inquiry: 6-12 weeks. Average time until publication: 6-12 months. **Advance**: none. **Royalty**: after expenses, 60/40 author/publisher. First run: depends on market.

**Marketing Channels.** Distribution houses; cooperative distribution; direct mail; in-house staff. Subsidiary rights: first serialization; second serialization; reprint; book club; translation and foreign; English language publication outside United States and Canada.

**Additional Information.** Our emphasis is on fiction writing by Latino-Americans, Asian-Americans, Arab-Americans, Black-Americans, and Native-Americans. This of course does not exclude others. Tips: Just send it. Catalog: SASE.

## ETC PUBLICATIONS.

Drawer ETC. Palm Springs, CA 92263. (619) 325-5352. Submissions Editor: LeeOna S. Hostrop. Founded: 1972. Number of titles published: cumulative—120, 1989—6. Hardback and softback.

**Subjects of Interest. Nonfiction**—business management; educational management; gifted education, texts.

**Initial Contact.** complete manuscript.

**Acceptance Policies.** Unagented manuscripts: yes. Simultaneous submissions: yes. Disk submissions: no. Response time to initial inquiry: 3 weeks. Average time until publication: 1 year. **Advance**: none. **Royalty**: standard. First run: 2500. Subsidy basis: will consider.

**Marketing Channels.** n/i. Subsidiary rights: all.

**Additional Information.** Catalog: upon request.

## FALLEN LEAF PRESS.

PO Box 10034. Berkeley 94709. (415) 848-7805. Submissions Editor: Ann Basart. Founded: 1984. Number of titles published: cumulative—7, 1989—3. Softback 100%

**Subjects of Interest. Nonfiction**—music reference books; monographs on contemporary American composers. Recent publications: *Schoenberg Discography*; discography of music on forte-pianos; bibliography of Baroque oboe music; guides to early and 19th-century American choral music; index to journal *Perspectives of New Music*. Do not want: anything not related to music.

**Initial Contact.** Query letter; book proposal with sample chapters; front matter, sample indexes (if ref. book); author's background and expertise, current position, interest in and knowledge of subject, published works.

**Acceptance Policies.** Unagented manuscripts: yes. unagented: 100%. Simultaneous submissions: no. Disk submissions: IBM compatible. Response time to initial inquiry: 1-2 months. Average time until publication: varies. **Advance**: none to $500. **Royalty**: 10%-15%; except for esoteric books with none. First run: 450-750.

**Marketing Channels.** Distribution houses, direct mail. Subsidiary rights: vary; usually not relevant, except in case of foreign translation. English language publication outside United States and Canada. Direct mail or sales.

**Additional Information.** At this time we are requesting camera-ready copy for our reference books. Tips: Look at our catalog and our published books. Catalog: upon request.

## MICHEL FATTAH.

933 Pico Blvd. Santa Monica, CA 90405. (213) 450-9777. Submissions Editor: Darrell Houghton. Founded: 1982. Number of titles published: cumulative—23, 1989—9. Hardback 75%, softback 25%.

**Subjects of Interest. Nonfiction**—celebrity biographies; how-to; self-help. Recent publications: *My Days with Errol Flynn; The Senator Must Die: The Murder of Robert F. Kennedy; Earthquake Ready.* **Fiction**—historical fiction. Recent publications: *Eternal Fire* (historical novel of Persia). **Other**—children's books. Do not want: pornography/erotica.

**Initial Contact.** Query letter.

**Acceptance Policies.** Unagented manuscripts: no. Simultaneous submissions: no. Disk submissions: no. Response time to initial inquiry: 4-6 weeks. Average time until publication: 1 year. **Advance**: varies. **Royalty**: varies. First run: 5000. Subsidy basis: no.

**Marketing Channels.** Distribution houses; independent reps. Subsidiary rights: all.

**Additional Information.** Do not send any fiction at this time. Tips: SASE is very important. Catalog: 81/2 x 11 SASE; $1.00.

## FELS AND FIRN PRESS.

33 Scenic Ave. San Anselmo, CA 94960. (415) 457-4361. Submissions Editor: John M. Montogomery. Founded: 1967. Number of titles published: 1987—1.

**Subjects of Interest. Nonfiction**—Jack Kerouac. Recent publications: *Jack Kerouac at the Wild Boar, and Other Skirmishes.* **Fiction**—would consider if on Jack Kerouac.

**Initial Contact.** Query letter.

**Acceptance Policies.** Unagented manuscripts: yes. Simultaneous submissions: yes. Disk submissions: no. Response time to initial inquiry: 10 days. Average time until publication: 6 months. **Advance**: varies. **Royalty**: 10% of wholesale price of run. First run: 1500. Subsidy basis: yes; I could.

**Marketing Channels.** Distribution houses; direct mail. Subsidiary rights: none.

**Additional Information.** Catalog: upon request.

## FESTIVAL PUBLICATIONS.

PO Box 10180. Glendale, CA 91209. (818) 718-8494. Submissions Editor: Alan Gadney. Founded: 1976. Number of titles published: cumulative—15 books; 7 audio tapes. Hardback 50%, softback 50%.

**Subjects of Interest. Nonfiction**—reference books and audio cassette tapes in the fields of film, video, television, screenwriting, and related subjects. Recent publications: series of books on contests, festivals, grants, scholarships, fellowships in film, video, television broadcasting, writing.

**Initial Contact.** Query letter.

**Acceptance Policies.** Unagented manuscripts: yes. Simultaneous submissions: yes. Disk submissions: IBM PC. Response time to initial inquiry: 3-6 months. Average time until publication: 6-12 months. **Advance**: negotiable. **Royalty**: negotiable. First run: 3000-5000. Subsidy basis: yes.

**Marketing Channels.** Distribution houses; cooperative distribution; direct mail; in-house staff; special sales. Subsidiary rights: all.

**Additional Information.** We are interested in manuscripts, seminars, courses, other materials that can be offered on audio cassette tapes in the fields of film, video, television, and screenwriting. We are also interested in short manuscripts that can be offered as "special reports" on specific areas in the above categories. Catalog: upon request.

**FIESTA CITY PUBLISHERS.** PO Box 5861. Santa Barbara, CA 93150. (805) 733-1984. Submissions Editor: Frank E. Cooke. Founded: 1980. Number of titles published: cumulative—4, 1987—1. Hardback 25%, softback 75%.

**Subjects of Interest. Nonfiction**—music; cooking; how-to. Recent publications: *Anything I Can Play, You Can Play Better* (self-taught guitar method); *Kids Can Write Songs Too!* (for young teens). Do not want: personal accounts of difficult situations.

**Initial Contact.** Query letter; brief description of proposed material.

**Acceptance Policies.** Unagented manuscripts: yes. Simultaneous submissions: yes. Disk submissions: no. Response time to initial inquiry: 2-4 weeks. Average time until publication: 6 months (varies). **Advance**: none. **Royalty**: varies. First run: 1000.

**Marketing Channels.** Distribution houses; direct mail; special sales. Subsidiary rights: none.

**Additional Information.** Catalog: upon request.

Firehole Press *see* **NATURE'S DESIGN.**

**FITHIAN PRESS.** PO Box 21022. Santa Barbara, CA 93121. (805) 962-1780. Submissions Editor: John Daniel. Founded: 1986. Number of titles published: cumulative—21; 1987:10. Softback 100%.

**Subjects of Interest. Nonfiction**—all subjects; including poetry. Recent publications: *Morelling: The Joys of Hunting and Preparing Morel Mushrooms; Bicentennial Blues: 200 Years of the US Presidency* (humorous poetry). **Fiction**—novels, short stories. Recent publications:*SALT Twelve* (political science fiction). Do not want: pornography.

**Initial Contact.** Query letter; book proposal with 2 sample chapters; length of manuscript.

**Acceptance Policies.** Unagented manuscripts: yes. Simultaneous submissions: yes. Disk submissions: IBM, Macintosh. First novels: yes. Response time to initial inquiry: 6 to 8 weeks. Average time until publication: 6 to 8 months. **Advance**: n/a. **Royalty**: 50% of net receipts. First run: 500-1000. Subsidy basis: yes; author pays production costs in return for larger **Royalty**. Books remain property of author.

**Marketing Channels.** Direct mail; special sales. Subsidiary rights: first serialization; reprint; dramatization, motion picture and broadcast; translation and foreign.

**Additional Information.** We call ourselves "co-publishers." Catalog: upon request.

**FLUME PRESS.** 644 Citrus Ave. Chico, CA 95926. (916) 342-1583. Submissions Editor: Casey Huff. Founded: 1984. Number of titles published: cumulative—5, 1987—1. Softback 100%.

**Subjects of Interest. Nonfiction**—poetry chapbooks. Recent publications: *The Centralia Mine Fire; Common Waters, Running Patterns.*

**Initial Contact.** Through our annual chapbook contest; send for information.

**Acceptance Policies.** Unsolicited manuscripts: just through contest. Unagented manuscripts: n/a. Simultaneous submissions: yes; if chosen by Flume Press, author must withdraw from other publisher. Disk submissions: no. Response time to initial inquiry: 6 weeks after contest deadline. Average time until publication: 3 to 4 months. **Advance, Royalty**: contest prize—$50. + 50 copies. First run: 250.

**Marketing Channels.** Distribution houses; direct mail.

**Additional Information.** Flume is a not-for-profit press. Catalog: upon request.

**FOGHORN PRESS.** 212 Prentiss St. San Francisco, CA 94110. PO Box 77845, San Francisco, CA 94107. (415) 641-5777. Submissions Editor: Vicki I. Morgan. Founded: 1985. Number of titles published: cumulative—9, 1989—4. Softback 100%.

**Subjects of Interest. Nonfiction**—sports and recreation. Recent publications: *California Camping* (guidebook describing more than 1500 campgrounds); *California Golf* (guidebook to 600 courses). Do not want: fiction; children's books.

**Initial Contact.** Query with cover letter; book proposal with a few sample chapters.

**Acceptance Policies.** Unagented manuscripts: yes. Simultaneous submissions: yes. Disk submissions: no. Response time to initial inquiry: 4-6 weeks. Average time until publication: 9 months. **Advance**: none. **Royalty**: 10-15% of net. First run: n/i.

**Marketing Channels.** Distribution houses; in-house staff; special sales. Subsidiary rights: all.

**Additional Information.** We believe in promoting every title we take on as fully as possible. The marketability of a book is a major consideration. Tips: At this time, we are oriented toward the western states. We are looking for recreational titles that are not overly narrow in scope and are marketable. Catalog: call or write.

**FORMAN PUBLISHING.** 11611 San Vicente Blvd., Ste. 206. Los Angeles, CA 90049. (213) 820-8672. Submissions Editor: Ashley Summers. Founded: 1982. Number of titles published: cumulative—4, 1987—2. Hardback 50%, softback 50%.

**Subjects of Interest. Nonfiction**—self-help. Recent publications: *PMS; Stepmothering; After 50.* Do not want: fiction.

**Initial Contact.** Synopsis.

**Acceptance Policies.** Unagented manuscripts: yes. Simultaneous submissions: yes. Disk submissions: no. Response time to initial inquiry: 4 weeks. Average time until publication: 1 year. **Advance**: n/i. **Royalty**: standard. First run: n/i.

**Marketing Channels.** Independent reps. Subsidiary rights: all.

**Additional Information.** We distribute through Publishers Marketing Services. Catalog: upon request.

**FRIENDS OF PHOTOGRAPHY.** 101 The Embarcadero, Ste. 210. San Francisco, CA 94105. (415) 391-7500. Submissions Editor: David Featherstone. Founded: 1967. Number of titles published: cumulative—53, 1989—3. Softback 100%.

**Subjects of Interest. Nonfiction**—photographic monographs containing critical introductions; books of critical essays on fine art photography. Recent publications: *Landscapes from the Middle of the World; EW: Centennial Essays in Honor of Edward Weston.*

**Initial Contact.** Query letter. Include resumé and writing samples.

**Acceptance Policies.** Unagented manuscripts: yes. Simultaneous submissions: no. Disk submissions: no. Response time to initial inquiry: 3-4 weeks. Average time until publication: varies. **Advance**: none. **Royalty**: paid on books sold through retailers, not on those distributed to membership. First run: 12,000-15,000.

**Marketing Channels.** Distribution houses; direct mail.

**Additional Information.** Catalog: upon request.

**FROG IN THE WELL.** PO Box 170052. San Francisco, CA 94117. (415) 431-2113. Submissions Editor: Susan Hester. Founded: 1980. Number of titles published: cumulative—6, 1987—0. Softback 100%.

**Subjects of Interest.** **Nonfiction**—feminist social change. Recent publications: *Crimes Against Women* (testimony from women from 40 countries). **Fiction**—feminist social change. Recent publications: *The Honesty Tree* (12 year old discovers her employers/friends are lesbians). Do not want: pornography.

**Initial Contact.** Query letter; book proposal with sample chapters. Include short list of published works.

**Acceptance Policies.** Unagented manuscripts: yes. Simultaneous submissions: yes; inform us. Disk submissions: yes; Apple compatible. First novels: yes. Response time to initial inquiry: 3-4 months. Average time until publication: up to 1 year. **Advance**: none. **Royalty**: 50% of net after expense have been paid. First run: 2500+. Subsidy basis: open to possibility.

**Marketing Channels.** Distribution houses; cooperative distribution; direct mail; in-house staff; special sales. Subsidiary rights: all.

**Additional Information.** Catalog: upon request.

**FRONT ROW EXPERIENCE.** (Imprints: Kokono). 540 Discovery Bay Blvd. Byron, CA 94514. (415) 634-5710. Submissions Editor: Frank Alexander. Founded: 1974. Number of titles published: cumulative—22, 1989—2. Softback 100%.

**Subjects of Interest.** **Nonfiction**—special education; perceptual-motor development with emphasis in movement education; lesson plans teacher guidebooks for pre-K and elementary school teachers. Recent publications: *Perceptual-Motor Development Guide.* Do not want: authors who are not active in their field and not conducting workshops, seminars, talks, etc. that promote their ideas.

**Initial Contact.** Query letter; convincing case why book will do well.

**Acceptance Policies.** Unagented manuscripts: yes. Simultaneous submissions: yes. Disk submissions: no. Response time to initial inquiry: 2-3 weeks. Average time until publication: 9-12 months. **Advance**: none. **Royalty**: 5% of first 2000; 10% thereafter. First run: 500 minimum; more if author convinces us their promotional efforts will result in larger sales. Subsidy basis: yes; initial investment returned when first printing sells out.

**Marketing Channels.** Direct mail. Subsidiary rights: all.

**Additional Information.** Tips: Authors must be willing to sell and promote their own books. Catalog: upon request.

**GATEWAY BOOKS.** 31 Grand View Ave. San Francisco, CA 94114. (415) 821-1928. Submissions Editor: Donald Merwin. Founded: 1985. Number of titles published: cumulative—5, 1988—8. Softback 100%.

**Subjects of Interest.** **Nonfiction**—self-help in retirement field; United States, foreign or seasonal living sites. Recent publications: *Retirement Choices: Choose Mexico; Choose Latin America;* Do not want: unrelated self-help or travel works.

**Initial Contact.** Query letter; table of contents.

**Acceptance Policies.** Unagented manuscripts: yes. Simultaneous submissions: yes. Disk submissions: check first. Response time to initial inquiry: 1 month. Average time until publication: 1 year. **Advance**: small. **Royalty**: 12% of net; negotiated. First run: 2500-5000.

**Marketing Channels.** Distribution houses.

**Additional Information.** Catalog: upon request.

**GAY SUNSHINE PRESS.** (Imprint: Leyland Publications). Box 40397. San Francisco, CA 94140. (415) 824-3184. Submissions Editor: Winston Leyland. Founded: 1970. Number of titles published: cumulative—50+, 1988—10. Hardback and softback.

**Subjects of Interest. Nonfiction**—how-to and gay lifestyle; creative literary nonfiction. **Fiction**—erotica; ethnic; historical; mystery; science fiction; short stories. Do not want: any topic too limited or academic; long personal narratives.

**Initial Contact.** Query letter first; then outline and sample chapters if we request.

**Acceptance Policies.** Unsolicited manuscripts: we return them unopened. Unagented manuscripts: yes. Disk submissions: n/i. Response time to initial inquiry: 1 month. Average time until publication: n/i. **Advance**: none. **Royalty**: standard or outright purchase. First run: 5000.

**Marketing Channels.** Distribution houses; direct mail; special sales. Subsidiary rights: all.

**Additional Information.** Catalog: $1.

**GEM GUIDE BOOK COMPANY** 3677 San Gabriel Parkway. Pico Rivera, CA 90660. (213) 692-5492. Submissions Editor: Al Mayerski, George Wilson. Founded: 1965. Number of titles published: cumulative—7, 1988—6. Softback 100%.

**Subjects of Interest. Nonfiction**—Gem Trail of (several Southwest states); Ghost Towns of. . . ; Hiking and Backpacking In. . . . Recent publications: *Midwest Gem, Fossil and Mineral Trails; Gem Trails of Oregon; Day Hikes and Trail Rides In and Around Phoenix.*

**Initial Contact.** Query letter.

**Acceptance Policies.** Unagented manuscripts: yes. Simultaneous submissions: yes. Disk submissions: no. Response time to initial inquiry: 2 weeks. Average time until publication: 6-9 months. **Advance**: n/i. **Royalty**: n/i. First run: n/i.

**Marketing Channels.** Distribution houses; direct mail; independent reps; in-house staff. Subsidiary rights: none.

**Additional Information.** We publish books about outdoor adventures—rock collecting, gold and gem hunting.

**GHOST TOWN PUBLICATIONS.** PO Drawer 5998. Carmel, CA 93921. (408) 373-2885. Submissions Editor: Debbie McCabe. Founded: 1971. Number of titles published: cumulative—12, 1988—1. Hardback 25%, softback 75%.

**Subjects of Interest. Nonfiction**—regional history of Monterey Peninsula, Central California; children's series: *History and Happenings of California."* Recent Publications: *Otters, Octopuses and Odd Creatures of the Deep; The Strange Case of the Ghosts of the Robert Lewis Stevenson House* (children's). Do not want: fiction.

**Initial Contact.** Query letter.

**Acceptance Policies.** Unagented manuscripts: no. Simultaneous submissions: no. Disk submissions: no. Response time to initial inquiry: 1 month. Average time until publication: varies. **Advance**: n/i. **Royalty**: 10% negotiable.

**Marketing Channels.** Special sales. Subsidiary rights: none.

**Additional Information.** Catalog: upon request.

**GLENCOE PUBLISHING COMPANY.** (Subsidiary of Macmillan Publ. Co.). (Imprints: Benziger). 15319 Chatsworth St. Mission Hills, CA 91345. (818) 898-1391. Submissions Editor: Murray Giles, Editorial Director. Founded: 1971. Number of titles published: cumulative—425, 1989—80. Hardback 75%, softback 25%.

**Subjects of Interest.** **Nonfiction**—Benziger Imprint: Catholic religious education texts for preschool through adult. Glencoe Imprint: junior high/high school; junior college text in vocational subjects (business, home economics, technical/industrial education, careers); junior high/high school texts in selected general curriculum subjects (English, math, social studies, health, art). Do not want: trade books, fiction or nonfiction.

**Initial Contact.** Query letter; book proposal with 1 sample chapter. Include curriculum vitae.

**Acceptance Policies.** Unagented manuscripts: yes. Simultaneous submissions: yes. Disk submissions: only by prior arrangement. Response time to initial inquiry: 2 weeks. Average time until publication: 1 year. **Advance**: varies. **Royalty**: varies. First run: varies.

**Marketing Channels.** Direct mail; in-house staff. Subsidiary rights: all.

**Additional Information.** We are interested only in textbooks for established courses offered by public schools, parochial schools or private business/trade schools. Tips: We frequently employ writers, copyeditors, indexers, etc. on a freelance or for hire basis. Catalog: upon request.

**GLGLC MUSIC.** (Subsidiary of La Costa Music Business Consultants). PO Box 147. Cardiff, CA 92007. (619) 436-7219. Submissions Editor: Robert Livingston. Founded: 1979. Number of titles published: cumulative—12, 1988—3. Hardback 10%, softback 80%.

**Subjects of Interest.** **Nonfiction**—music business; music trade; tax law; contracts; copyright law. Recent publications: *Livingston's Complete Music Business Reference, Vols 1 & 2*.

**Initial Contact.** Query letter.

**Acceptance Policies.** Unagented manuscripts: yes. Simultaneous submissions: no. Disk submissions: yes; IBM PC. Response time to initial inquiry: 30 days. Average time until publication: n/i. **Advance**: varies. **Royalty**: standard 6%-12%. First run: varies; specialize in short run.

**Marketing Channels.** Direct mail. Subsidiary rights: none.

**Additional Information.** Catalog: upon request.

Golden Eagle *see* **ELYSIUM GROWTH PRESS.**

**GOLDEN WEST BOOKS.** (Subsidiary of Pacific Railroad Publications, Inc.). PO Box 80250. San Marino, CA 91108. (213) 283-3446. Submissions Editor: Donald Duke. Founded: 1961. Number of titles published: cumulative—10, 1987—5. Hardback 100.

**Subjects of Interest.** **Nonfiction**—railroad transportation histories; American transportation. Recent publications: *Time of the Trolley* (100-year history of the trolley car); *Los Angeles and Salt Lake Railway*.

**Initial Contact.** Query letter; general description.

**Acceptance Policies.** Unagented manuscripts: yes. Simultaneous submissions: no. Disk submissions: no. Response time to initial inquiry: 4-6 months. Average time until publication: 1 year. **Advance**: none. **Royalty**: 10%. First run: 3000-4000.

**Marketing Channels.** Distribution houses; direct mail; independent reps. Subsidiary rights: none.

**Additional Information.** Catalog: upon request.

Gondwana Books *see* **ALTA NAPA PRESS.**

**H. M. GOUSHA.** (Subsidiary of Simon and Schuster). PO Box 49006. San Jose, CA 95161. In-house only.

**GREENHOUSE REVIEW PRESS.** 3965 Bonny Doon Rd. Santa Cruz, CA 95060. (408) 426-4355. Submissions Editor: Gary Young. Founded: 1975. Number of titles published: cumulative—20, 1989—2. Hardback 10%, softback 90%.

**Subjects of Interest. Other**—poetry; broadside series, single sheets, illustrated poems.

**Initial Contact.** Entire manuscript. Include SASE.

**Acceptance Policies.** Unagented manuscripts: yes. Simultaneous submissions: no. Disk submissions: no. Response time to initial inquiry: 1 month. Average time until publication: 2 years. **Advance**: none. **Royalty**: pays in copies. First run: 350.

**Marketing Channels.** Direct mail. Subsidiary rights: none.

**Additional Information.** Limited edition, finely printed, letter press, hand-made paper for book collectors, libraries, and museums.

**GREENLEAF CLASSICS, INC.** PO Box 20194. San Diego, CA 92120. (619) 56-5711. Submissions Editor: Paul J. Estok. Number of titles published: 1987—400+. Softback 100%.

**Subjects of Interest. Fiction**—adult erotic novels; sexual theme; contemporary; women's point of view; involve serious everyday problems.

**Initial Contact.** Request guidelines before submitting anything; then complete manuscript (preferred); or at least 3 sample chapters.

**Acceptance Policies.** Unagented manuscripts: yes. Disk submissions: no. Response time to initial inquiry: 1-2 months. Average time until publication: n/i. **Advance**: Pays by outright purchase 6 months after acceptance.

**Marketing Channels.** Distribution houses; direct mail; independent reps. Subsidiary rights: all.

**Additional Information.** Tips: Include return postage if you want your manuscript returned. Catalog: SASE.

**GREEN TIGER PRESS.** 1061 India St. San Diego, CA 92101. (619) 238-1001. Submissions Editor: Editorial Committee. Founded: 1970. Number of titles published: cumulative—50, 1989—12. Hardback and softback.

**Subjects of Interest. Fiction**—illustrated children's books; words must evoke visual sense of wonder. Recent publications: Do not want: science fiction.

**Initial Contact.** Query letter; entire manuscript (never send the original).

**Acceptance Policies.** Unagented manuscripts: yes. Simultaneous submissions: yes. Disk submissions: n/i. Response time to initial inquiry: allow 3 months. Average time until publication: n/i. **Advance**: n/i. **Royalty**: standard on retail. First run: 5000-10,000.

**Marketing Channels.** Distribution houses. Subsidiary rights: vary according to project.

**Additional Information.** We also publish greeting cards; calendars; posters; and stationery. Tips: Words should stimulate the imaginative world of children; evoke a mythical quality. Catalog: upon request.

**GURZE DESIGNS AND BOOKS.** Box 2238. Carlsbad, CA 92008. (619) 434-7533. Submissions Editor: Leigh Cohn. Founded: 1980. Number of titles published: cumulative—10, 1989—7. Softback 100%.

**Subjects of Interest.** **Nonfiction**—health; pop-psych; self-help. Recent publications: *Bulimia: A Guide to Recovery; Dear Kids of Alcoholics.* Do not want: poetry; fiction; heavily academic works.

**Initial Contact.** Query letter.

**Acceptance Policies.** Unagented manuscripts: yes. Multiple submissions: yes. Disk submissions: MAC; Osborne. Response time to initial inquiry: 6-8 weeks. Average time until publication: 6-8 months. **Advance**: $1000. **Royalty**: 10% net. First run: 7500.

**Marketing Channels.** Distribution houses; cooperative distribution; direct mail; special sales. Subsidiary rights: direct mail or direct sales; book club; sound reproduction and recording.

**Additional Information.** Catalog: upon request.

## HARCOURT BRACE JOVANOVICH, CHILDREN'S BOOKS DIVISION.

1250 6th Ave. San Diego, CA 92101. (619) 699-6810. **Submissions:** Manuscript Submissions. Number of titles published: 1989—75+. Hardback and softback.

**Subjects of Interest.** **Nonfiction**—juvenile. Recent publications: *A Voice From Japan.* **Fiction**—picture books; novels for all ages. Recent publications: *Elbert's Bad Word; The First Dog; In the Beginning.*

**Initial Contact.** Nonfiction: query first. Fiction: query; or submit outline and sample chapters. Picture books: complete manuscript.

**Acceptance Policies.** Unagented manuscripts: yes. Simultaneous submissions: no. Disk submissions: no. Response time to initial inquiry: 6-8 weeks. Average time until publication: 1-2 years. **Advance**: varies. **Royalty**: varies; some outright purchases. First run: n/i.

**Marketing Channels.** Distribution houses; independent reps. Subsidiary rights: all.

**Additional Information.** Tips: Send for manuscript guidelines for #10 SASE, 1 first class stamp. Catalog: 9x12 SASE, 4 first class stamps.

## HARPER AND ROW.

151 Union St. Ice House One, Ste. 401. San Francisco, CA 94111. (415) 477-4400. Submissions Editor: Thomas Grady. Founded: 1870. Number of titles published: 1988—12. Hardback 60%, softback 40%.

**Subjects of Interest.** **Nonfiction**—religions (all denominations); self-help; new-age; psychology. Recent publications: *Caring and Commitment: Learning to Live the Love We Promise; The Addictive Organization; Women and the Blues; Harper's Bible Commentary; The Enneagram; The Chalice and the Blade; Codependent No More.* Do not want: fiction.

**Initial Contact.** Query; or outline and sample chapters.

**Acceptance Policies.** Unagented manuscripts: no. Simultaneous submissions: yes; inform us. Disk submissions: no. Response time to initial inquiry: 2-3 months. Average time until publication: 12-18 months. **Advance**: varies. **Royalty**: standard. First run: varies.

**Marketing Channels.** Direct mail; in-house staff; special sales. Subsidiary rights: all.

**Additional Information.** Catalog: upon request.

## HARPER JUNIOR BOOKS GROUP, WEST COAST.

(Division of Harper and Row Publishers). Box 6549. San Pedro, CA 90734. (213) 547-4262. Submissions Editor: Linda Zuckerman. Number of titles published: 1988—15. Hardback 100%.

**Subjects of Interest.** **Nonfiction**—juvenile; all areas. **Fiction**—juvenile; all areas. **Other**—poetry. Do not want: Dr. Suess-type verse.

**Initial Contact.** Nonfiction: query; or complete manuscript. Fiction: complete manuscript only. Poetry: complete manuscript.

**Acceptance Policies.** Unagented manuscripts: yes. Simultaneous submissions: yes; inform us. Disk submissions: no. Response time to initial inquiry: 4 months. Average time until publication: 18 months. **Advance**: negotiable. **Royalty**: standard on wholesale. First run: n/i.

**Marketing Channels.** Distribution houses. Subsidiary rights: all.

**Additional Information.** We are looking for material for ages pre-school through young adult. Tips: Writers should be familiar with children's literature, be professional in their writing and know the field. Catalog: 10x13 SASE; 4 first class stamps. Includes guidelines.

## HAY HOUSE, INC.

501 Santa Monica Blvd. #602 Mailing: PO Box 2212. Santa Monica, CA 90406. (213) 394-7445. Submissions Editor: Lin Laucella. Founded: 1985. Number of titles published: cumulative—12, 1987—4. Softback 100%.

**Subjects of Interest. Nonfiction**—self-help; psychology; biography; metaphysical; new age. Recent publications: *You Can Heal Your Life; Rebirthing Made Easy; Love Your Disease; Heal Your Body; The AIDS Book.* Do not want: negative books; satanism; psychic occurrences.

**Initial Contact.** Book proposal with sample chapters or entire manuscript. Include previous writing experience: articles, books, etc.

**Acceptance Policies.** Unagented manuscripts: yes. Simultaneous submissions: no. Disk submissions: no. Response time to initial inquiry: 4-6 weeks. Average time until publication: 1 year. **Advance**: $2000-$15,000. **Royalty**: 5-10%. First run: 7500.

**Marketing Channels.** Distribution houses; direct mail; in-house staff; special sales. Subsidiary rights: all (except computer, magnetic and electronic media).

**Additional Information.** Tips: Typewritten manuscripts only—no handwriting will be accepted. Catalog: upon request.

## HERE'S LIFE PUBLISHERS, INC.

(Subsidiary of Campus Crusade for Christ). Box 1576. San Bernardino, CA 92404. (714) 886-7981. Submissions Editor: Dan Benson. Number of titles published: 1988—25. Hardback and softback.

**Subjects of Interest. Nonfiction**—self-help; evangelism; Christian campus ministry; family; personal growth. Do not want: new-age; metaphysical; missionary biography.

**Initial Contact.** Query; or outline with sample chapters.

**Acceptance Policies.** Unagented manuscripts: yes. Simultaneous submissions: yes. Disk submissions: yes; query. Response time to initial inquiry: 1-3 months. Average time until publication: 1 year. **Advance**: n/i. **Royalty**: 15% of wholesale. First run: 5000.

**Marketing Channels.** Independent reps; special sales. Subsidiary rights: all.

**Additional Information.** Tips: The writer has the best chance to sell to us if they use a Biblical approach to problem solving. Catalog: guidelines; 8 1/2 x 11 SASE; 2 first class stamps.

## HEYDAY BOOKS.

Box 9145. Berkeley, CA 94709. (415) 549-3564. Submissions Editor: Malcolm Margolin. Founded: 1974. Number of titles published: cumulative—22, 1989—4. Hardback 5%, softback 95%.

**Subjects of Interest. Nonfiction**—California Indians; natural history; history and travel (must have California focus). Recent publications: *East Bay Out: A Guide to East Bay Regional Parks; Cyclists Route Atlas: A Guide to the Gold Country and High Sierra; The Harvest Gypsies: On the Road to the Grapes of Wrath* by John Steinbeck (a series of newspaper articles originally published in 1936 about migrant farm workers). Do not want: fiction; poetry; books outside California.

**Initial Contact.** Query letter (minimal).

**Acceptance Policies.** Unagented manuscripts: yes. Simultaneous submissions: no. Disk submissions: no. Response time to initial inquiry: 10 days. Average time until publication: 6 months. **Advance**: rarely more than $1000. **Royalty**: 8-10% of list. First run: 4000-7000. Subsidy basis: no.

**Marketing Channels.** Distribution houses; independent reps; in-house staff. Subsidiary rights: all.

**Additional Information.** Manuscript should be literate, sensitive and useful. Catalog: manila envelope, $.45 postage.

**HOLDEN DAY, INC.** 4432 Telegraph Avenue. Oakland, CA 94609. (415) 428-9400. Submissions Editor: Martha Murphy. Founded: 1959. Number of titles published: 1988—5+/-; 1989: 10. Hardback 50%, softback 50%.

**Subjects of Interest.** **Nonfiction**—operation research; physics; college level market software. Recent publications: *Storm* (quantitative modeling package); *VP Expert for Business Applications*. Do not want: trade books.

**Initial Contact.** Query letter. Include biography, markets, and table of contents.

**Acceptance Policies.** Unagented manuscripts: yes. Simultaneous submissions: yes. Disk submissions: ASCII code. Response time to initial inquiry: 2-3 weeks. Average time until publication: contract dependent. **Advance**: negotiable. **Royalty**: negotiable. First run: market dependent.

**Marketing Channels.** In-house staff; direct mail; data base of users. Subsidiary rights: none.

**Additional Information.** Tips: Include a representative or unique chapter. Catalog: upon request.

**HOLLOWAY HOUSE PUBLISHING COMPANY.** 8060 Melrose Ave. Los Angeles, CA 90046. (213) 653-8060. Submissions Editor: Raymond F. Locke. Number of titles published: 1988—30. Softback 100%.

**Subjects of Interest.** **Nonfiction**—games (i.e., backgammon, gin rummy); gambling (how to win.). **Fiction**—Black Experience literature; contemporary stories. Recent publications: *Secret Music*.

**Initial Contact.** Outline; 3 sample chapters.

**Acceptance Policies.** Unagented manuscripts: yes. Simultaneous submissions: yes. Disk submissions: query first. Response time to initial inquiry: 8 weeks. Average time until publication: 6 months. **Advance**: n/i. **Royalty**: standard. First run: 15,000-20,000.

**Marketing Channels.** Distribution houses; direct mail; independent reps. Subsidiary rights: n/i.

**Additional Information.** We are the largest publisher of Black Experience literature. Tips: Check guidelines. Catalog: and guidelines; SASE.

**HOOVER INSTITUTION PRESS.** (Subsidiary of Hoover Institution on War, Revolution and Peace). Stanford University, Stanford, CA 94305. (415) 723-3373. Submissions Editor: Pat Baker, Executive Managing Editor. Number of titles published: 1988—20, 1989—8. Hardback 50%, softback 50%.

**Subjects of Interest.** **Nonfiction**—international studies; domestic studies; political science; history; public policy; arms control; Soviet-U.S. relations. Recent publications: *The Kazakhs*

(Martha Brill Olcott); *The Red Orchestra: The Case of Africa* (D. Bark). Do not want: fiction of any type—all manuscripts must be scholarly.

**Initial Contact.** Query letter; book proposal with 3 sample chapters. Or, query letter with abstract and 3 sample chapters with footnotes.

**Acceptance Policies.** Unagented manuscripts: yes. Simultaneous submissions: to be discussed with managing editor. Disk submissions: check with managing editor. Response time to initial inquiry: 4-6 weeks. Average time until publication: to be discussed with managing editor. **Advance**: negotiable. **Royalty**: n/i. First run: n/i.

**Marketing Channels.** Distribution houses; in-house staff; direct mail; special sales. Subsidiary rights: first serialization; newspaper syndication; reprint; book club; translation and foreign; English language publication outside the United States and Canada.

**Additional Information.** Catalog: upon request.

HP Books *see* **PRICE STERN SLOAN.**

## HUNTER HOUSE PUBLISHERS.

(Imprints: Broadway Books; Sufi Publishing; Light Wave Press). Box 847. Claremont, CA 91711. (714) 624-2277. Submissions Editor: Jennifer D. Trzyna. Founded: 1978. Number of titles published: cumulative—70, 1989—8. Hardback 10%, softback 90%.

**Subjects of Interest.** **Nonfiction**—women's health; family health; psychology. Recent publications: *Menopause Without Medicine; The Enabler; Trauma in the Lives of Children; Healthy Aging; Writing From Within; Helping Your Child Succeed After Divorce; Getting High in Natural Ways.* **Fiction**—womanist/mythical, historical. Recent publications: *The Adventures of Huru on the Road to Baghdad.* **Other**—"infobooks" for teens. Do not want: erotica; science fiction; illness biographies.

**Initial Contact.** Query letter; book proposal with 2-3 sample chapters. Include author's background and resumé.

**Acceptance Policies.** Unagented manuscripts: yes. Simultaneous submissions: yes; we request author notify us immediately if he/she decides to sign with another publisher. Disk submissions: no. First novels: yes. Response time to initial inquiry: 1-2 months. Average time until publication: 12-18 months. **Advance**: $100-$500. **Royalty**: 7 1/2-15% on 2500; 10% after. First run: varies. Subsidy basis: yes; common interest.

**Marketing Channels.** Distribution houses; cooperative distribution; direct mail; in-house staff; special sales. Subsidiary rights: all.

**Additional Information.** We offer comprehensive book production services to both self-publishing authors and other publishers. Tips: Do not send full manuscripts unless requested. SASE required. Catalog: SASE 9 x 12, $.65 postage.

## IGNATIUS PRESS.

(Subsidiary of Guadalupe Assoc., Inc.). 2515 McAllister St. San Francisco, CA 94118. (415) 387-2324. Submissions Editor: Rev. Joseph D. Fessio, S.J. Founded: 1978. Number of titles published: cumulative—210, 1989—60. Hardback 10%, softback 90%.

**Subjects of Interest.** **Nonfiction**—Catholic theology and devotional works; biographies of saints; reprints of Chesterton and Newman. Recent publications: *The Cantata of Love: A Verse by Verse Reading of the Song of Songs; Woman to Woman; Fundamentals of the Faith.*

**Initial Contact.** Book proposal with 3 sample chapters and table of contents.

**Acceptance Policies.** Unsolicited manuscripts: we do not return them. Unagented manuscripts: most. Simultaneous submissions: yes. Disk submissions: IBM compatible. Response time to initial inquiry: could be as long as 1 year. Average time until publication: 1 year. **Advance**: varies, minimal. **Royalty**: varies. First run: usually 3000.

**Marketing Channels.** Distribution houses; cooperative distribution; direct mail; independent reps. Subsidiary rights: all.

**Additional Information.** At this time we have commitments to many manuscripts so we are not looking for new ones. It would take an exceptional book to be accepted! Catalog: upon request.

**ILLUMINATIONS PRESS.** 2110-B 9th St. Berkeley, CA 94710. (415) 849-2102. Submissions Editor: Norman Moser (poetry); Randy Fingland (prose). Founded: 1965. Number of titles published: cumulative—6, 1989—2. Softback 100%.

**Subjects of Interest.** **Nonfiction**—personal essays on art, zen, mysticism, etc. Recent publications: *El Grito del Norte* (stories and tales); *The Illuminations Reader: Anthlogy of Writing and Art.* **Other**—poetry; plays. Recent publications: *Cleft Between Heaven and Earth* (poetry); *Between Me and Thee* (poetry); *Forester Whacks* (poetry). Do not want: Christian verse.

**Initial Contact.** Query letter; book proposal with sample chapters; 5-10 pages of poetry. Include subscription to anthology; bio of author; credits. We can be contacted by phone.

**Acceptance Policies.** Unagented manuscripts: yes. Simultaneous submissions: yes. Disk submissions: no. Response time to initial inquiry: 2-3 months. Average time until publication: 12-18 months. **Advance**: none. **Royalty**: percent of profits based on investment. First run: 400-800 (poetry); 800-1500 (prose). Subsidy basis: 50% or less of costs.

**Marketing Channels.** Distribution houses; direct mail; special sales; subscription. Subsidiary rights: all.

**Additional Information.** Most of what we publish is local or regional and with people we know. Tips: Phone afternoons or evenings to discuss possibilites. Catalog: SASE.

**INTEGRATED PRESS.** 526 Comstock Dr. Tiburon, CA 94920. (415) 435-2446. Submissions Editor: Jack Gaines. Founded: 1979. Number of titles published: 1987—3. Hardback 30%, softback 70%.

**Subjects of Interest.** **Nonfiction**—psychology, biography. Recent publications: *Fritz Perls: Here and Now.* Do not want: anything which is not quality.

**Initial Contact.** Query letter.

**Acceptance Policies.** Unagented manuscripts: yes. Simultaneous submissions: no. Disk submissions: no. Response time to initial inquiry: 3 weeks. Average time until publication: n/i. **Advance**: $500. **Royalty**: 6/10/12. First run: 2500.

**Marketing Channels.** n/i. Subsidiary rights: n/i.

**INTELLIGENT CHOICE INFORMATION.** 4771 La Cresta. San Jose, CA 95129. (408) 249-4747. Publishes only *Complete Car Cost Guide.*

International Academy of Astronautics *see* **UNIVELT, INC.**

**INTERURBAN PRESS/TRANS ANGLO BOOKS.** Box 6444. Glendale, CA 91205. (213) 240-9130. Submissions Editor: Mac Sebree. Number of titles published: 1988—10. Hardback and softback.

**Subjects of Interest.** **Nonfiction**—transportation and transportation history (emphasis on railroads); Western Americana (logging, gold rush, mining); preservation movement; business and economics; travel. Recent publications: *Monon—The Hoosier Line.*

**Initial Contact.** Query letter.

**Acceptance Policies.** Unagented manuscripts: yes. Simultaneous submissions: n/i. Disk submissions: no. Response time to initial inquiry: 2 weeks. Average time until publication: n/i. **Advance**: none. **Royalty**: 5-10% on gross. First run: 2000.

**Marketing Channels.** Distribution houses; special sales. Subsidiary rights: n/i.

**Additional Information.** Catalog: upon request.

Irio I O *see* **STRAWBERRY HILL PRESS.**

**IRIS COMMUNICATION GROUP.** 1278 Glenneyre, Ste. 138. Laguna Beach, CA 92651. (714) 497-2101. Submissions Editor: Marlene Miller. Founded: 1987. Number of titles published: cumulative—1.

**Subjects of Interest. Nonfiction**—business communications. Recent Publications: *Business Guide to Print Promotion.*

**Initial Contact.** Book proposal with 3 sample chapters.

**Acceptance Policies.** Unagented manuscripts: yes. Simultaneous submissions: no. Disk submissions: straight ASCII file. Response time to initial inquiry: 2-3 weeks. Average time until publication: n/i. **Advance**: n/i. **Royalty**: n/i. First run: n/i.

**Marketing Channels.** Distribution houses; direct mail; special sales. Subsidiary rights: direct mail or direct sales; book club.

**Additional Information.** We are especially interested in the practical applications of cognitive science and communications theory. Catalog: upon request.

**ISLAND PRESS.** Star Route 1, Box 38. Covelo, CA 95428. (707) 983-6432. Submissions Editor: Barbara Dean. Founded: 1978. Number of titles published: cumulative—55, 1989—16. Hardback and softback. We do simultaneous editions.

**Subjects of Interest. Nonfiction**—practical information and analysis for professionals and concerned citizens on the conservation and management of natural resources. Recent publications: *Reforming the Forest Service; Hazardous Waste Management; Western Water Made Simple.* Do not want: anything outside our carefully defined niche.

**Initial Contact.** Book proposal with 2 sample chapters. Send for author information packet.

**Acceptance Policies.** Unagented manuscripts: yes. Simultaneous submissions: yes; if author informs us. Disk submissions: final manuscript can be on disk; initial submission must be hard copy. Response time to initial inquiry: 1-3 months. Average time until publication: 7 months from finished manuscript. **Advance**: none. **Royalty**: 5-7.5% net. First run: varies considerably.

**Marketing Channels.** Distribution houses; direct mail; special sales. Subsidiary rights: all.

**Additional Information.** Tips: Send for author information packet. Catalog: upon request.

**JAIN PUBLISHING COMPANY.** (Imprints: Asian Humanities Press; AHP Paperbacks). PO Box 4177. Santa Clara, CA 95054-0177. (408) 727-3151. Submissions Editor: Mukesh K. Jain. Founded: 1976. Number of titles published: cumulative—45, 1989—7. Hardback 70%, softback 30%.

**Subjects of Interest. Nonfiction**—new age; Asian studies—religions, cultures and philosophies. Recent publications: *Shamanism: The Spirit World of Korea; Death Was His Koan: The Samurai Zen of Suzuk Shosan.* Do not want: fiction.

**Initial Contact.** Book proposal with 2 sample chapters. Include curriculum vitae.

**Acceptance Policies.** Unagented manuscripts: yes. Simultaneous submissions: no. Disk submissions: IBM/Apple compatible; coding instructions available. Response time to initial inquiry: 4-8 weeks. Average time until publication: 9-12 months. **Advance**: none. **Royalty**: 6%-7.5%; usually offered with second and successive printings. First run: 1000-2000 copies. Subsidy basis: yes; whereas we do not ask for direct subsidy from the author, occasionally we do expect higher cooperation with third party subventions.

**Marketing Channels.** Distribution houses; direct mail. Subsidiary rights: all.

**Additional Information.** Tips: Manuscripts should be no more that 400 pages and preferably with no color art. Catalog: upon request.

## JALMAR PRESS.

(Subsidiary of B.L. Winch and Assoc.). 45 Hitching Post Dr., Bldg. 2. Rolling Hill Estates, CA 90274-4297. (213) 547-1240. Submissions Editor: B.L. Winch. Founded: 1971. Number of titles published: cumulative—44, 1989—4. Hardback 10%, softback 90%.

**Subjects of Interest.** **Nonfiction**—positive self-esteem; personal development; parenting; popular psychology; self-help; right brain/whole brain learning (trade oriented). Recent publications: *Present Yourself! Captivate Your Audience With Great Presentation Skills; Openmind/Wholemind; Learning the Skills of Peacemaking*. Do not want: novels.

**Initial Contact.** Book proposal with sample chapters; survey of why product is needed; evidence author is visible and can sell the book; information on competitive products; who the market is.

**Acceptance Policies.** Unagented manuscripts: yes. Simultaneous submissions: yes. Disk submissions: no. Response time to initial inquiry: 6-8 weeks. Average time until publication: 12-18 months. **Advance**: very small, but negotiable. **Royalty**: 7.5%-15%. First run: 5000-25,000. Subsidy basis: yes; open to discussion.

**Marketing Channels.** Distribution houses; cooperative distribution; direct mail; independent reps; special sales. Subsidiary rights: all.

**Additional Information.** Have 5 best-sellers (over 100,00 copies sold) out of 20 current titles. Very strong back-list. Keep books in stock if sales justify. Tips: Present strong proposal covering market and competition for the book. Catalog: upon request.

## WILLIAM KAUFMANN, INC.

95 1st St. Los Altos, CA 94022.

No longer accepting unsolicited manuscripts.

Kazan Books *see* **VOLCANO PRESS.**

## KEY BOOKS PRESS.

1111 S. Arroyo Parkway, Ste. 410. PO Box 90490. Pasadena, CA 91109-0490. (818) 441-3457. Not accepting submissions.

Kokono Books *see* **FRONT ROW EXPERIENCE.**

## KONOCTI BOOKS.

Rt. l, Box 216. Winters, CA 95694. (916) 662-3364. Not currently accepting submissions.

## KOSTELLO DESIGN AND PUBLISHING COMPANY

PO Box 11606. Oakland, CA 94611. (415) 652-1286. Submissions Editor: Delores C. Booth. Founded: 1978. Number of titles published: cumulative—8. Softback 100%.

**Subjects of Interest.** **Nonfiction**—time management. **Other**—educational workbooks and books, K-10; artwork for children; short stories (2-12 pages). Recent publications: *The Success is Best* (series). Do not want: novels.

**Initial Contact.** Query letter (short is better).

**Acceptance Policies.** Unagented manuscripts: yes. Simultaneous submissions: yes. Disk submissions: no. Response time to initial inquiry: 2 weeks. Average time until publication: depends. **Advance**: varies. **Royalty**: none. First run: 2500-5000.

**Marketing Channels.** Direct mail; independent reps; in-house staff. Subsidiary rights: n/i.

**Additional Information.** We are interested in purchase of artwork and short stories for K-10. Tips: Type on one side of page; address on manuscript. Catalog: upon request.

**LAGOON PUBLICATIONS.** 9 Channel Landing. Tiburon, CA 94920. (415) 381-4601. Submissions Editor: Karen Misuraca. Founded: 1988. Number of titles published: 1989—1. Softback 100%.

**Subjects of Interest. Nonfiction**—book marketing. Recent publications: *Selling Books in the (San Francisco) Bay Area: A Directory and Guide for Small Press and Self Publisher.*

**Initial Contact.** Phone.

**Acceptance Policies.** Unagented manuscripts: yes. Simultaneous submissions: yes. Disk submissions: Macintosh Word; Works. Response time to initial inquiry: 1 week. Average time until publication: n/i. **Advance**: n/i. **Royalty**: n/i. First run: 3000.

**Marketing Channels.** Distribution houses; cooperative distribution; direct mail; special sales. Subsidiary rights: first serialization; second serialization.

**Additional Information.** Display ads available.

**LAHONTAN IMAGES.** PO Box 1093. Susanville, CA 96130. (916) 257-4546. Submissions Editor: Tim I. Purdy. Founded: 1986. Number of titles published: cumulative—2, 1988-3. Softback 100%.

**Subjects of Interest. Nonfiction**—general interest, specializing in the history of Northeastern California and the Great Basin. Recent publications: *Eagle Lake; Flanigan: Anatomy of a Railroad Ghost Town; Frontier Times: The 1874-1875 Journals of Sylvester Daniels.* Do not want: fiction.

**Initial Contact.** Query letter.

**Acceptance Policies.** Unagented manuscripts: yes. Simultaneous submissions: yes. Disk submissions: no. Response time to initial inquiry: 1 month. Average time until publication: 6 months. **Advance**: none. **Royalty**: 10% on retail and wholesale. First run: 1500.

**Marketing Channels.** Cooperative distribution; direct mail; in-house staff. Subsidiary rights: none.

**Additional Information.** We are a small regional publisher, specializing on topics of Northeastern California and Nevada. Catalog: upon request.

Laugh and Learn *see* **PRICE STERN SLOAN.**

Laurel Park Publishing *see* **EDUCATIONAL INSIGHTS.**

**LEXIKOS.** (Imprints: Don't Call It Frisco Press). 4079 19th Ave. San Francisco, CA 94132-3009. (415) 584-1085. Submissions Editor: Michael R. Witter. Founded: 1982. Number of titles published: cumulative—44, 1989—5. Softback 100%.

**Subjects of Interest. Nonfiction**—regional and city histories; walking guides; hiking; outdoors. Recent publications: *Short History of Los Angeles; Short History of Santa Fe; The Bay Area at Your Feet; Living Legacy* (architectural history); *Inside Cannery Row.* Do not want: self-help; politics.

**Initial Contact.** Book proposal with 3 sample chapters.

**Acceptance Policies.** Unagented manuscripts: yes. Simultaneous submissions: yes. Disk submissions: no. Response time to initial inquiry: 1 month. Average time until publication: 8 months. Advance: varies up to $1000. Royalty: 10% of list (average). First run: 4000-5000.

**Marketing Channels.** Distribution houses; cooperative distribution; independent reps. Subsidiary rights: all.

**Additional Information.** Catalog: SASE.

**LIBRA PUBLISHERS, INC.** 3089C Clairmont Dr., Ste. 383. San Diego, CA 92117. (619) 581-9449. Submissions Editor: William Kroll. Founded: 1960. Number of titles published: cumulative—200, 1987—15. Hardback 90%, softback 10%.

**Subjects of Interest. Nonfiction**—all categories. Recent publications: *Hidden Bedroom Partners* (needs and motives that destroy sexual pleasure); *Manual for Retirement Counselors; Sexual Friendship—A New Dynamics in Relationships*. Fiction—all categories. Recent publications: *The Long Wind* (novel of woman's self-realization); *Tarnished Hero.*

**Initial Contact.** Entire manuscript. Include author's background; previously published works.

**Acceptance Policies.** Unagented manuscripts:yes. Simultaneous submissions: yes; inform us. Disk submissions: no. First novels: yes. Response time to initial inquiry: 3 weeks. Average time until publication: 8-12 months. **Advance**: none. **Royalty**: 10-15%. First run: 1000-5000. Subsidy basis: on occasion if we like the book but feel it has limited sales potential, we offer assistance in self-publishing.

**Marketing Channels.** Direct mail; in-house staff; special sales. Subsidiary rights: all.

Light Wave Press *see* **HUNTER HOUSE.**

**LINDEN PUBLISHERS.** 1750 N. Sycamore. Hollywood, CA 90028. Not accepting submissions.

Little Miss *see* **PRICE STERN SLOAN.**

**LONE EAGLE PUBLISHING, INC.** 9903 Santa Monica Blvd. Ste. 204. Beverly Hills, CA 90212. (213) 471-8066. Submissions Editor: Joan Singleton. Founded: 1982. Number of titles published: cumulative—17, 1989—8. Hardback and softback.

**Subjects of Interest. Nonfiction**—motion picture and video: self-help; technical; how-to; specialities. Recent publications: *Film Scheduling; Filmmakers Dictionary; Screen Acting*. Do not want: biographies; anything unrelated.

**Initial Contact.** Outline; synopsis; sample chapters.

**Acceptance Policies.** Unagented manuscripts: yes. Simultaneous submissions: yes. Disk submissions: query. Response time to initial inquiry: 8 weeks. Average time until publication: 1 year. **Advance**: $250. **Royalty**: 5-10%. First run: n/i.

**Marketing Channels.** Distribution houses; in-house sales; Direct mail. Subsidiary rights: all.

**Additional Information.** We are looking for professionals in the movie/video field with a specialty that has not been overworked. Tips: Expect to work hard on promotion. Catalog: #10 SASE, 2 first class stamps.

**LONELY PLANET PUBLICATIONS.** 112 Linden St. Oakland, CA 94607. (415) 893-8555. Submissions Editor: Eric Kettunen, Sales Manager. Founded: 1973. Number of titles published: cumulative—80, 1988—20, 1989—25. Softback 100%.

**Subjects of Interest. Nonfiction**—travel guides (series): Travel Survival Kits; the On a Shoestring series; phrase books; trekking guides. Recent publications: *Eastern Europe on a Shoestring; Tahiti—A Travel Survival Kit.* Do not want: anything outside of travel.

**Initial Contact.** Query letter; book proposal with cover letter.

**Acceptance Policies.** Unagented manuscripts: yes. Simultaneous submissions: n/i. Disk submissions: no. Response time to initial inquiry: varies, if promising it must go to Australian office. Average time until publication: varies. **Advance**: n/i. **Royalty**: n/i. First run: n/i.

**Marketing Channels.** Direct mail; independent sales reps; in-house staff; special sales. Subsidiary rights: all.

**Additional Information.** We're the leading publisher of guides for the independent traveler. We cover the more exotic destinations. Tips: Look at our catalog before making submissions. Catalog: call or write.

**LURAMEDIA.** 7060 Miramar Rd., Ste. 104. San Diego, CA 92121. (619) 578-1948. Submissions Editor: Lura Jane Geiger. Founded: 1962. Number of titles published: cumulative—17, 1989—8. Hardback 5%, softback 95%.

**Subjects of Interest. Nonfiction**—spiritual and religious growth; psychology; health; women; ministry. Recent publications: *Seasons of Friendship* (uses biblical theme of Naomi and Ruth). Do not want: poetry; children's stories.

**Initial Contact.** Query letter; book proposal with sample chapters; biography; annotated chapter outline; uniqueness of book; competition.

**Acceptance Policies.** Unagented manuscripts: yes. Simultaneous submissions: yes. Disk submissions: no. First novels: yes. Response time to initial inquiry: 3-4 weeks. Average time until publication: 9 months. **Advance**: None to $500. **Royalty**: 10% of sales; negotiable. First run: 2000-5000.

**Marketing Channels.** Distribution houses; direct mail; in-house staff; special sales. Subsidiary rights: all.

**Additional Information.** We select books that have a long shelf life and keep reprinting them. Tips: Tell me why you think your book will interest readers. Catalog: upon request.

Mad Libs *see* **PRICE STERN SLOAN.**

**M AND T PUBLISHING, INC.** 501 Galveston Dr. Redwood City, CA 94063. (415) 366-3600. Submissions Editor: Ellen Ablow. Founded: 1982. Number of titles published: cumulative—50, 1987—12. Softback 100%.

**Subjects of Interest. Nonfiction**—programming; computer books and software. Recent publications: *Dr. Dobb's Tool Book of 80286/80386 Programming; Dr. Dobb's Essential Hypertalk Handbook; Graphic Programming Inc.; Public-Domain Software and Shareware.*

**Initial Contact.** Book proposal with sample chapters; or outline.

**Acceptance Policies.** Unagented manuscripts: yes. Simultaneous submissions: yes. Disk submissions: IBM PC (clone); MS-DOS. Response time to initial inquiry: 4 weeks. Average time until publication: 6 months. **Advance**: varies. **Royalty**: varies. First run: varies.

**Marketing Channels.** Distribution houses; direct mail; independent reps. Subsidiary rights: all.

**Additional Information.** Catalog: call or write.

**MANUAL 3, INC.** 1150 S. Bascom Ave., Ste. 17. San Jose, CA 95128. (408) 293-9654. Submissions Editor: Phil Gold. Founded: 1981. Number of titles published: cumulative—300+; 1988: 15. Hardback 15%; Softback 85%.

**Subjects of Interest.** **Nonfiction**—very technical programs directed to the electronics industry; documentation, telecommunications; hardware documentation.

**Initial Contact.** Query letter. Include previous experience.

**Acceptance Policies.** Unagented manuscripts: yes. Simultaneous submissions: yes. Disk submissions: Microsoft Word for Macintosh—3.01 or higher. Response time to initial inquiry: 30 days. Average time until publication: 4-5 months. **Advance**: negotiable. **Royalty**: negotiable. First run: 1000-25000.

**Marketing Channels.** distribution houses. Subsidiary rights: none.

**Additional Information.** We publish for a variety of different companies: Apple, H-P, IBM, etc. Rarely does a book have our own company name on it. Tips: Manuscripts should be complete, accurate and well-written. Catalog: upon request.

**MARKETSCOPE BOOKS.** 119 Richard Ct. Aptos, CA 95003. (408) 688-7535. Submissions Editor: Ken Albert. Founded: 1985. Number of titles published: cumulative—7; 1988: 2. Softback 100%.

**Subjects of Interest.** **Nonfiction**—fishing, outdoors. Recent publications: *Trout Fishing in California; Saltwater Fishing in California.* Do not want: fiction.

**Initial Contact.** Query letter.

**Acceptance Policies.** Unagented manuscripts: yes. Simultaneous submissions: yes. Disk submissions: no. Response time to initial inquiry: 1 week. Average time until publication: 6 months. **Advance**: varies. **Royalty**: varies. First run: 10,000.

**Marketing Channels.** Distribution houses; independent reps. Subsidiary rights: all.

**Additional Information.** Catalog: upon request.

**MARK PUBLISHING, INC.** 15 Camp Evers Lane. Scotts Valley, CA 95066. (408) 438-7668. Submissions Editor: Bill Myers. Founded: 1987. Number of titles published: cumulative—5; 1988: 3. Softback 100%.

**Subjects of Interest.** **Nonfiction**—how-to books. Recent publications: *You Can Make Money from Your Arts and Crafts; You Can Spend Less and Sell More* (advertising for small businesses); *Yellow Page Report* (how to advertise in the yellow pages).

**Initial Contact.** Query letter; book proposal; call Bill Myers and describe project.

**Acceptance Policies.** Unagented manuscripts: yes. Simultaneous submissions: yes. Disk submissions: yes. Response time to initial inquiry: 1 week. Average time until publication: varies. **Advance**: none. **Royalty**: n/i. First run: n/i.

**Marketing Channels.** n/i. Subsidiary rights: n/i.

**Additional Information.** Catalog: upon request.

**MAYFIELD PUBLISHING COMPANY.** 1240 Villa St. Mountain View, CA 94041. (415) 960-3222. Submissions Editor: Thomas Broadbent. Founded: 1946. Number of titles published: cumulative—185 (in print), 1989—30. Hardback 40%, softback 60%.

**Subjects of Interest.** **Nonfiction**—college textbooks in English (composition and literature); education; dance; theater; art; music; health; physical education and recreation; psychology; anthropology; sociology; journalism; communication; speech. Do not want: books not intended for college courses.

**Initial Contact.** Query letter; or book proposal; tentative outline of contents.

**Acceptance Policies.** Unagented manuscripts: yes. Simultaneous submissions: yes; inform us. Disk submissions: yes; Wordstar for IBM compatibles; Wordperfect, Microsoft Word for IBM or Macintosh; Macwrite. Response time to initial inquiry: 2 weeks. Average time until publication: varies. **Advance**: varies. **Royalty**: varies. First run: varies.

**Marketing Channels.** Direct mail; in-house staff. Subsidiary rights: all.

**Additional Information.** Catalog: write to marketing director for materials pertinent to your subject.

**MAZDA PUBLISHERS.** 2991 Grace Lane. PO Box 2603. Costa Mesa, CA 92626. (714) 751-5252. Submissions Editor: Ahmad Jabbari. Founded: 1980. Number of titles published: cumulative—38; 1988: 4. Hardback and softback.

**Subjects of Interest.** **Nonfiction**—Middle East and North Africa in the areas of: art; business; cooking and foods; history; politics; sociology; social sciences; informational books; emphasis on scholarly approach. **Fiction**—related to geographic specifications. **Other**—poetry; translations and works of Middle Eastern poets only.

**Initial Contact.** Outline; summary; sample chapters.

**Acceptance Policies.** Unagented manuscripts: yes. Disk submissions: query. Response time to initial inquiry: 2-6 weeks. Average time until publication: 4 months. **Advance**: none. **Royalty**: standard on wholesale. First run: 2000.

**Marketing Channels.** n/i. Subsidiary rights: n/i.

**Additional Information.** Our audience is the academic and the educated layperson. Tips: Send SASE for guidelines. Catalog: upon request.

**MCCUTCHAN PUBLISHING COMPANY.** 2940 San Pablo Ave. PO Box 774. Berkeley, CA 94701. (415) 841-8616 (outside of CA 800-227-1540). Submissions Editor: John McCutchan. Founded: 1963. Number of titles published: cumulative—300+; 1988: 8. Hardback 100%.

**Subjects of Interest.** **Nonfiction**—college texts: education; administration; hotel and restaurant management; criminal justice. Recent publications: *Purchasing for Food Service Managers; Leaders for America's Schools; Introduction to Criminal Evidence Court Procedure.* Do not want: not many unsolicited manuscripts.

**Initial Contact.** Prospectus on the topic; publishing plan.

**Acceptance Policies.** Unagented manuscripts: yes. Disk submissions: n/i. Response time to initial inquiry: 1 month. Average time until publication: 8-10 months. **Advance**: none. **Royalty**:10-12%. First run: 2500.

**Marketing Channels.** Direct mail. Subsidiary rights: none.

**Additional Information.** We publish for professionals in the field. We don't publish trade books. Catalog: upon request.

**MCKINZIE PUBLISHING COMPANY.** (Subsidiary of Aaims Press). 11000 Wilshire Blvd., #241-777. Los Angeles, CA 90024. (213) 934-7685. Submissions Editor: Elizabeth Campbell. Founded: 1969. Number of titles published: n/i. Softback 100%.

**Subjects of Interest.** **Nonfiction**—family. Recent publications: *Family Reunions: How to Plan Yours; Names from East Africa; Women in Boxing.* **Fiction**—romance. **Other**—poetry.

**Initial Contact.** Book proposal with sample chapters. Include resumé.

**Acceptance Policies.** Unagented manuscripts: yes. Multiple submissions: yes. Disk submissions: no. First novels: yes. Response time to initial inquiry: 90 days. Average time until publication: 2 years. **Advance**: none. **Royalty**: none. First run: 500. Subsidy basis: yes.

**Marketing Channels.** Cooperative distribution; direct mail. Subsidiary rights: first serialization; newspaper syndication; dramatization, motion picture and broadcast; direct mail or direct sales; translation and foreign; computer and other magnetic and electronic media; commercial rights; English language publication outside the US and Canada.

**Additional Information.** Catalog: SASE.

## MCNALLY AND LOFTIN, PUBLISHERS.

5390 Overpass Rd. Santa Barbara, CA 93111. (805) 964-5117. Submissions Editor: W.J. McNally. Founded: 1956. Number of titles published: cumulative—100+, 1989—4. Hardback 10 %, softback 90%.

**Subjects of Interest.** **Nonfiction**—history; travel; regional. Recent publications: *California's Channel Islands; Santa Barbara Mountain Bike Routes; Hikers Guide to the Dick Smith Wilderness; San Rafael Wilderness.*

**Initial Contact.** Book proposal with sample chapters.

**Acceptance Policies.** Unagented manuscripts: yes. Simultaneous submissions: yes. Disk submissions: no. Response time to initial inquiry: 60 days. Average time until publication: 9 months. **Advance:** n/i. **Royalty:** 10% gross. First run: 2500-5000.

**Marketing Channels.** Independent reps; in-house staff. Subsidiary rights: n/i.

**Additional Information.** Catalog: upon request.

## MERCURY HOUSE.

300 Montgomery St., Ste. 700. San Francisco, CA 94104. (415) 433-7042. Submissions Editor: Carol Pitts. Founded: 1985. Number of titles published: cumulative—41, 1987—14. Hardback 90%, Softback 10%.

**Subjects of Interest.** **Nonfiction**—quality in all subjects. Recent publications: *Crunching Gravel; Growing Up in Wisconsin in the Thirties.* **Fiction**—quality in all subjects. Recent publications: *Such Was the Season; The Story of Annie Eliza, the Matriarch of a Black Family in Atlanta.* **Other**—Biography/Lively Arts Series, reprints of classic entertainment books. Recent publications: *Fun In a Chinese Laundry* Do not want: genre fiction.

**Initial Contact.** Book proposal with 3 sample chapters.

**Acceptance Policies.** Unagented manuscripts: yes. Simultaneous submissions: no. Disk submissions: no. First novels: yes. Response time to initial inquiry: 1 month. Average time until publication: 1 year. **Advance:** n/i. **Royalty:** n/i. First run: 3000-15000.

**Marketing Channels.** Distribution houses. Subsidiary rights: all.

**Additional Information.** Catalog: request by mail.

## MHO & MHO WORKS.

Box 33135. San Diego, CA 92103. (619) 488-4991. Submissions Editor: Douglas Cruickshank. Founded: 1969. Number of titles published: cumulative—n/i. Hardback 10%, softback 90%.

**Subjects of Interest.** **Nonfiction**—travel; sexuality; metaphysical; new age; gay; media (broadcast); handicapped literature. **Fiction**—short stories; above nonfiction topics. Do not want: poorly written, self-serving stories.

**Initial Contact.** Book proposal with 2 sample chapters.

**Acceptance Policies.** Unagented manuscripts: yes. Simultaneous submissions: n/a. Disk submissions: MS-DOS; Wordperfect. First novels: yes. Response time to initial inquiry: 1 month. Average time until publication: 6-12 months. First run: 2000. Subsidy basis: yes (only); author pays total cost of book. We handle publicity and distribution.

**Marketing Channels.** Distribution houses. Subsidiary rights: all.

**Additional Information.** Unlike the "vanity presses" we have a very high success rate. Our books have been reviewed in the *NY Times, LA Times, Washington Post, San Francisco Chronicle*, etc. Tips: Remember, we are very good and very expensive.

**Additional Information.** Catalog: 4 first class stamps.

**R AND E MILES PUBLISHERS.** PO Box 1916. San Pedro, CA 90733. (213) 833-8856. Submissions Editor: Robert Miles. Founded: 1980. Number of titles published: cumulative—21; 1988: 4. Hardback 30%, softback 70%.

**Subjects of Interest. Nonfiction**—ecology; quilts; politics; travel. Recent publications: *Ecologist's Guide to France; The Green Alternative.*

**Initial Contact.** Book proposal.

**Acceptance Policies.** Unagented manuscripts: yes. Simultaneous submissions: no. Disk submissions: no. Response time to initial inquiry: 3 weeks. Average time until publication: 6 months. **Advance**: negotiable. **Royalty**: 10%. First run: 1000-7000.

**Marketing Channels.** Distribution houses; direct mail; independent reps. Subsidiary rights: all.

**Additional Information.** Catalog: SASE.

**MILLER BOOKS.** 2908 W. Valley Blvd. Alhambra, CA 91803. (213) 284-7607. Submissions Editor: Joseph Miller. Number of titles published: 1988—4. Hardback and softback.

**Subjects of Interest. Nonfiction**—how-to; self-help; cookbooks; Americana; history; nature; philosophy; politics; emphasis on remedial. **Fiction**—western; historical; humor; mystery; adventure. Do not want: anything erotic.

**Initial Contact.** Complete manuscript.

**Acceptance Policies.** Unagented manuscripts: yes. Simultaneous submissions: yes. Disk submissions: n/i. Response time to initial inquiry: 2 months. Average time until publication: 1 year. **Advance**: n/i. **Royalty**: 10-15% on retail; some manuscripts bought outright. First run: n/i.

**Marketing Channels.** Distribution houses; direct dial; in-house staff. Subsidiary rights: all.

**Additional Information.** Approach subject in a positive vein; negativity doesn't sell. We need remedial texts in all areas. Catalog: upon request.

**MINA PRESS PUBLISHERS.** PO Box 854. Sebastopol, CA 95473. (707) 829-0854. Submissions Editor: Adam David Miller (poetry); Mei Nakano (all others). Founded: 1981. Number of titles published: cumulative—4, 1987—1. Softback 100%.

**Subjects of Interest. Fiction**—range of subject and types of good literature (adult and children). Do not want: any materials that glorify war, portray gratuitous violence or demean a group of human beings.

**Initial Contact.** Query letter.

**Acceptance Policies.** Unagented manuscripts: yes. Simultaneous submissions: yes. Disk submissions: no. First novels: yes. Response time to initial inquiry: 2-3 months. Average time until publication: 12-18 months. **Advance**: none. **Royalty**: 10%. First run: 2000.

**Marketing Channels.** Distribution houses; direct mail; special sales. Subsidiary rights: all.

**Additional Information.** Our motto is "giving life to good books". We are a small press dedicated to the preservation and publication of good literature. We give particular attention to previously unpublished writers and non-mainstream writers, though we consider other works too. Tips: We like children's books of the variety which conveys some meaningful learning experience, which is not all fluff and prettiness. Catalog: none.

## MOON PUBLICATIONS.
722 Wall St. Chico, CA 95928. (916) 345-5473. Submissions Editor: Mark Morris or Deke Castleman. Founded: 1973. Number of titles published: cumulative—27, 1988—4. Softback 100%.

**Subjects of Interest.** **Nonfiction**—comprehensive travel guidebooks for independent travelers of all stripes. Recent publications: *Hawaii Handbook* (a comprehensive resource—covers history, politics, culture, natural features, recreation, and all travel practicalities; *Utah Handbook; Washington Handbook; New Zealand Handbook*; etc. Do not want: fiction; travel narrative; how-to guides.

**Initial Contact.** Query letter; discussion of writer's previous experience and credentials.

**Acceptance Policies.** Unagented manuscripts: yes. Simultaneous submissions: yes; inform us. Disk submissions: DOS; IBM compatible. Response time to initial inquiry: 2 weeks. Average time until publication: 12-15 months. **Advance**: up to $5000. **Royalty**: standard. First run: 5000-20,000.

**Marketing Channels.** Distribution houses; direct mail; special sales. Subsidiary rights: all.

**Additional Information.** Tips: Study any of our guides first to find out what we do and do not publish. Catalog: SASE; legal-sized envelope with 2 first class stamps.

Mr. Men *see* **PRICE STERN SLOAN.**

National Space Society *see* **UNIVELT, INC.**

## NATUREGRAPH PUBLISHERS, INC.
(Imprints: Prism Editions). 3543 Indian Creek Rd. PO Box 1075. Happy Camp, CA 96039. (916) 493-5353. Submissions Editor: Barbara Brown. Founded: 1946. Number of titles published: cumulative—100+, 1989—6. Hardback 5%, softback 95%.

**Subjects of Interest.** **Nonfiction**—natural history; Native American; health; crafts dealing with natural history or Native Americans. Recent publications: *Self-Actuated Healing* (the alternative to doctors and drugs is within you); *Northwoods Wildlife Region* (covers common plants, wildlife). Do not want: anything outside our category.

**Initial Contact.** Query letter; give reasons why book would sell, places to market it; a good sales pitch; how this book differs from other books on the subject.

**Acceptance Policies.** Unagented manuscripts: yes. Simultaneous submissions: yes; alert us; encourages quick publisher response. Disk submissions: no. Response time to initial inquiry: 1 week if not interested; 2 months if interested. Average time until publication: 18 months after contract. **Advance**: none. **Royalty**: 10% of net amount invoiced. First run: 2500. Subsidy basis: rarely; maybe 3%-5% and then we repay the investment at a rate of so much per book sold. Occurs when we want a book and can't afford to produce it without outside help.

**Marketing Channels.** Distribution houses; direct mail; independent reps; special sales. Subsidiary rights: reprint; dramatization, motion picture and broadcast; direct mail or direct sales; book club; translation and foreign; commercial; English language publication outside US and Canada.

**Additional Information.** We are both publishers and printers. Predominantly we print only our own publications, but we also produce books commercially. Tips: We appreciate neatly typed, double spaced, properly margined pages with a black typewriter ribbon. Catalog: upon request.

**NATURE'S DESIGN.** (Imprints: Firehole Press). PO Box 255. Davenport, CA 95017. (408) 426-8205. Submissions Editor: Frank S. Balthis. Founded: 1980. Number of titles published: cumulative—8, 1989—1. Softback 100%.

**Subjects of Interest. Nonfiction**—natural history and travel; wildlife; guides to parks; children's guides to parks. Recent publications: *Mirounga: A Guide to Elephant Seals; Children's Guides to Yellowstone, Ano Nuevo, Pt. Reyes; Winter at Old Faithful.*

**Initial Contact.** Query letter. Include concise list of book, magazine and newspaper credits; concise description of expertise.

**Acceptance Policies.** Unagented manuscripts: yes. Simultaneous submissions: yes. Disk submissions: no. Response time to initial inquiry: 1 week. Average time until publication: 1 year. **Advance**: varies. **Royalty**: varies. First run: 5000-10,000.

**Marketing Channels.** Independent reps; in-house staff; special sales. Subsidiary rights: n/a.

**Additional Information.** As photographers, we wish to "team up" with writers on natural history projects for books and periodicals. Tips: It is very helpful if the writer is familiar with the location and potential market for a book or periodical project. Catalog: SASE.

**NETWORK PUBLICATIONS.** PO Box 1830. Santa Cruz, CA 95061-1830. (408) 438-4060. Submissions Editor: Lance Sprague. Founded: 1981. Number of titles published: cumulative—150, 1989—25. Hardback 1%, softback 99%.

**Subjects of Interest. Nonfiction**—education: adolescent pregnancy; AIDS; sexuality; reproductive health; child sexual abuse. Recent publications: *Does Aids Hurt?* (Contmproary Health Series); *Teaching AIDS: A Resource Guide on Acquired Immune Deficiency Syndrome.* **Fiction**—interactive books for young adults (ages 9-14) on substance abuse prevention. Recent publications: *Serena's Secret* (alcohol); *Christy's Chance* (marijuana). **Other**—photonovela; curricula; resource guides and pamphlets on family life education; sexuality education.

**Initial Contact.** Query letter.

**Acceptance Policies.** Unagented manuscripts: yes. Disk submissions: n/i. Response time to initial inquiry: 1 month. Average time until publication: n/i. **Advance**: n/i. **Royalty**: n/i. First run: n/i.

**Marketing Channels.** Distribution houses; direct mail; in-house staff; special sales. Subsidiary rights: n/i.

**Additional Information.** Our primary audience is secondary-level educators; our emphasis is prevention education within the context of comprehensive health education. Catalog: upon request.

**NEWCASTLE PUBLISHING COMPANY, INC.** 13419 Saticoy. North Hollywood, CA 91605. (213) 873-3191. Submissions Editor: Alfred Saunders. Number of titles published: 1988—10. Softback 100%.

**Subjects of Interest. Nonfiction**—how-to, self-help; metaphysical; new age; fitness; holistic health; psychology; religion. Do not want: biography; travel; children's; poetry; cookbooks; fiction.

**Initial Contact.** Query letter; or summary and sample chapters.

**Acceptance Policies.** Unagented manuscripts: yes. Simultaneous submissions: yes. Disk submissions: no. Response time to initial inquiry: 3-6 weeks. Average time until publication: n/i. **Advance**: none. **Royalty**: 5%-10% on retail. First run: 3000-5000.

**Marketing Channels.** Distribution houses. Subsidiary rights: all.

**Additional Information.** Tips: Include something that will grab the reader. Know your market. Catalog: upon request; guidelines, SASE.

## NEW DAY BOOKS.

(Sister company to Greenhaven Press). PO Box 289011. San Diego, CA 92128-9011. (619) 485-7424. Submissions Editor: Carol O'Sullivan. Founded: 1987. Number of titles published: 1989—16.

**Subjects of Interest.** **Nonfiction**—overview series–controversial topics written in an objective manner. Recent projects included endangered species; garbage; smoking. Also some fun books. Recent publications: *Garbage* (an overview of the environmental problems caused by legal and illegal disposal of trash and garbage); *Special Effects in the Movies* (techniques and equipment used in modern and older movies); subseries entitled *Great Disasters: Eruption of Vesuvius in AD 79* (with historical and cultural context); *Pompeii; The Black Death; and The Dust Bowl.* Do not want: fiction; anthologies; textbookish manuscripts.

**Initial Contact.** Query letter. In the initial contact, the idea will be sufficient. If we like the idea, we'll ask for a proposal, statement of purpose, and chapter outline. We also require a sample chapter. The initial contact should reflect a developed idea, i.e. slant or angle. Author should do some research to see what is already available in order to present a unique approach.

**Acceptance Policies.** Unagented manuscripts: yes. Simultaneous submissions: yes; inform us. Disk submissions: no. Response time to initial inquiry: 2 weeks. Average time until publication: 6 months. **Advance**: none. **Royalty**: flat fee, negotiable. First run: n/i.

**Marketing Channels.** Distribution houses; direct mail. Subsidiary rights: English language publication outside the United States and Canada.

**Additional Information.** We are a new company. We are interested in books for our Overview Series which will focus on issue-oriented books written at a 5-8 grade level. Tips: Request our guidelines and policies. Be familiar with our needs and requirements. Catalog: We don't have one yet. Greenhaven does. Write and request.

## NEW SAGE PRESS.

PO Box 41029. Pasadena, CA 91104-8029. (818) 795-0266. Submissions Editor: Maureen Michelson. Founded: 1984. Number of titles published: cumulative—4. Hardback, softback, often published simultaneously.

**Subjects of Interest.** **Nonfiction**—photo essay books (primarily). Recent publications: *Women and Work; Portrait of American Mother and Daughters; Death Valley, Ground Afire; The New Americans; Common Heroes; Exposures: Women and Their Art.* Do not want: fiction; how-to.

**Initial Contact.** Query letter; book proposal with 1 sample chapter. Include a strong sense of the author's conviction of the worthwhile nature of the project; markets.

**Acceptance Policies.** Unagented manuscripts: yes. Simultaneous submissions: no. Disk submissions: no. Response time to initial inquiry: 3 months. Average time until publication: 1 year. **Advance**: depends on project. **Royalty**: negotiable. First run: 5000-10,000.

**Marketing Channels.** Distribution houses; direct mail; independent reps; special sales. Subsidiary rights: all.

**Additional Information.** We are interested in quality, both production and content. Tips: Clearly delineate the market for your book in your query letter. We're not just interested in "good photos." Catalog: SASE.

## NEW SEED PRESS.

PO Box 9488. Berkeley, CA 94709. (415) 540-7576. Submissions Editor: Helen Chetin. Founded: 1971. Number of titles published: 1988—11, 1989—12. Softback 100%.

**Subjects of Interest.** feminist press looking for nonsexist, nonracist stories for children which actively confront bigotry issues—Recent Publications: *Green March Moons; My Mother and I Are Growing Strong* (Spanish/English).

**Initial Contact.** Query letter; brief summary; SASE.

**Acceptance Policies.** Unagented manuscripts: yes. Simultaneous submissions: yes. Disk submissions: no. First novels: yes. Response time to initial inquiry: 2 weeks. Average time until publication: 1 year. **Advance**: % of Royalty. **Royalty**: 10%. First run: 2000-4000.

**Marketing Channels.** Distribution houses; direct mail. Subsidiary rights: none.

**Additional Information.** Tips: Your manuscript should be the best possible. Make sure who your market is. Catalog: upon request.

**NEW SOCIETY PUBLISHERS.** (Subsidiary of New Society Educational Foundation). PO Box 582. Santa Cruz, CA 95061. (408) 458-1191. Submissions Editor: David H. Albert, West Coast editorial coordinator. Founded: 1981. Number of titles published: cumulative—14, 1988—15. Hardback, softback, all dual editions.

**Subjects of Interest.** **Nonfiction**—books which help create a more peaceful and just world through nonviolent action. Do not want: poetry; plays; fiction; electoral politics; crystals.

**Initial Contact.** Request manuscript guidelines.

**Acceptance Policies.** Unagented manuscripts: yes. Simultaneous submissions: yes. Disk submissions:required; MS-DOS. Response time to initial inquiry: 1 month. Average time until publication: 8-12 months. **Advance**: negotiable. **Royalty**: negotiable. First run: 4000+.

**Marketing Channels.** Distribution houses; direct mail; independent reps; in-house staff; special sales. Subsidiary rights: all.

**Additional Information.** We publish books promoting fundamental social change through nonviolent action only. Tips: Ask yourself whether a world where trees are scarce and book plentiful needs yours to add to the ecological burden. Catalog: SASE.

**NEW WORLD LIBRARY.** 58 Paul Dr. San Rafael, CA 94903. (415) 472-2100. Submissions Editor: Cheryl White. Founded: 1977. Number of titles published: cumulative—55, 1988—7. Softback 100%.

**Subjects of Interest.** **Nonfiction**—self-improvement; new age; uplifting titles on a variety of subjects such as careers, prosperity, writing, psychology. Recent publications: *Reflections in the Light* (Shakti Gawain); *Embracing Our Selves*; *Maps to Ecstasy*. **Other**—audio and video cassettes. Do not want: poetry; military; books about specific gurus; crystals; channeling.

**Initial Contact.** Query letter; book proposal with 1 sample chapter.Include something about the author; SASE.

**Acceptance Policies.** Unagented manuscripts: yes. Simultaneous submissions: yes; inform us. Disk submissions: no. Response time to initial inquiry: 4-8 weeks. Average time until publication: 12 months. **Advance**: varies widely. **Royalty**: reasonable. First run: 3000-10,000.

**Marketing Channels.** Distribution houses; direct mail. Subsidiary rights: all.

**Additional Information.** We're a solid, profitable company with a distribution network in place that can sell as well as anybody. Tips: Be nice. Catalog: upon request.

**NORTH ATLANTIC BOOKS.** (Wholly owned, nonprofit; program of the Society for the Study of Native Arts and Sciences). 2800 Woolsey St. Berkeley, CA 94705. (415) 540-7934. Submissions Editor: Linda Hough. Founded: 1974. Number of titles published: cumulative—200+, 1987—25. Hardback 30%, softback 70%.

**Subjects of Interest.** **Nonfiction**—internal martial arts; homeopathy; Pervuian/Brazilian studies; women's (autobiography, biography); wholistic health; social implications or technology; new science; traditional arts; dance; women artists; visual arts; sports; film; theater. Recent publications: *The Monuments of Mars*. Do not want: manuscripts from people unfamiliar with what we publish.

**Initial Contact.** Query letter. Include SASE; publishing history; academic/writing background.

**Acceptance Policies.** Unagented manuscripts: yes. Simultaneous submissions: no. Disk submissions: no. Response time to initial inquiry: 1 week. Average time until publication: 6 months. **Advance**: none. **Royalty**: 10%. First run: 1000-3000.

**Marketing Channels.** Distribution houses; cooperative distribution; direct mail; independent reps; special sales. Subsidiary rights: all.

**Additional Information.** We are a strong trade press with an eclectic, but focused, catalog. Tips: Be sure to query first. Catalog: SASE; $1.00 postage.

**NORTH POINT PRESS.** Box 6275. Albany, CA 94706. (415) 527-6260. Submissions Editor: Jack Shoemaker. Founded: 1978. Number of titles published: cumulative—250, 1989—30-40. Hardback and softback, depends on project.

**Subjects of Interest.** **Nonfiction**—literary essays. Recent publications: *Horse-Trading and Ecstasy*. **Fiction**—serious and experimental; literary; short stories. Recent publications: *Failure to Zigzag* (novel); *Dusk and Other Stories*. Do not want: Press absolutely does not accept unsolicited fiction or poetry.

**Initial Contact.** Query first to "editorial." Include SASE.

**Acceptance Policies.** Unagented manuscripts: yes. Simultaneous submissions: no. Disk submissions: no. Response time to initial inquiry: 60-90 days. Average time until publication: 1 year. **Advance**: yes. **Royalty**: standard. First run: 5000-10,000.

**Marketing Channels.** Distribution houses (Farrar, Straus and Giroux); in-house staff. Subsidiary rights: all.

**Additional Information.** We have an extensive list of fiction and poetry in translation. Catalog: SASE, $.75

**OAK TREE PUBLICATIONS.** (Subsidiary of Vizcom, Inc.). 3870 Murphy Canyon Rd., Ste. 203. San Diego, CA 92123. (619) 560-5163. Submissions Editor: Linda Alioto. Number of titles published: 1988—10-15. Hardback 100%.

**Subjects of Interest.** **Juvenile Fiction**—picture books with toy tie-in. Recent publications: *I Wish I Had a Computer That Makes Waffles; Value Tales (an ongoing series).*

**Initial Contact.** Book proposal with sample chapters; full-color sample illustrations.

**Acceptance Policies.** Unagented manuscripts: yes. Simultaneous submissions: yes. Disk submissions: no. Response time to initial inquiry: 4-6 weeks. Average time until publication: 8 months. **Advance**: $500. **Royalty**: varies. First run: n/i.

**Marketing Channels.** Distribution houses; in-house staff; direct mail. Subsidiary rights: all.

**Additional Information.** We gear our books to ages 2-8. One of our subsidiaries is Value Tale Communications. Tips: Send request and SASE for manuscript guidelines. Catalog: 8 1/2x11 SASE, 3 first class stamps.

**OAKWOOD PUBLICATIONS.** 616 Knob Hill. Redondo Beach, CA 90277. (213) 378-9245. Submissions Editor: Philip Tamoush. Founded: 1987. Number of titles published: cumulative—4, 1989—2. Hardback 90%, softback 10%.

**Subjects of Interest.** **Nonfiction**—iconography, eastern Christian art; liturgical arts; Orthodox Christian materials. Recent publications: *The Icon; Dynamic Symmetry.*

**Initial Contact.** Query letter.

**Acceptance Policies.** Unagented manuscripts: yes. Disk submissions: n/i. Response time to initial inquiry: 1 month. Average time until publication: n/i. **Advance**: n/i. **Royalty**: n/i. First run: 2000. Subsidy basis: yes; percentage of sales.

**Marketing Channels.** Distribution houses; direct mail. Subsidiary rights: translation and foreign .

**Additional Information.** Catalog: upon request.

**OASIS PRESS.** 720 S. Hillview Dr. Milpitas, CA 95035. (408) 263-9671. Submissions Editor: Emmett Ramey. Founded: 1975. Number of titles published: cumulative—60+, 1988: 30. Hardback 100%.

**Subjects of Interest. Nonfiction**—business related topics; economics. Do not want: anything else.

**Initial Contact.** Query letter.

**Acceptance Policies.** Unagented manuscripts: n/i. Simultaneous submissions: yes. Disk submissions: query. Response time to initial inquiry: 1 week. Average time until publication: 10 months. **Advance**: none. **Royalty**: 8%-15%. First run: n/i.

**Marketing Channels.** Distribution houses; mail order. Subsidiary rights: all.

**Additional Information.** Catalog: upon request.

**OCEAN VIEW BOOKS.** (Imprint: SF West; Ocean View Press). Box 4148. Mountain View, CA 94040. (415) 965-3721. Submissions Editor: Lee Ballentine. Founded: 1981. Number of titles published: cumulative—16, 1989—3. Hardback and softback, we do two versions of each book.

**Subjects of Interest. Nonfiction**—bibliography. Recent publications: *Bibliographic Studies of the Work of Yoko Ono* and *Philip Lamantia.* **Fiction**—science fiction; surrealist fiction. Recent publications: *Poly-New Speculative Writing* (anthology with Ray Bradbury, Tom Disch, William Stafford, et al.) **Other**—speculative and surrealist poetry. Recent publications: *Co-Orbital Moons* (poems of science and science fiction). Do not want: "mainstream" anything; we are a literary publisher.

**Initial Contact.** Query letter. Include clips of published works and evidence that the author has seen our books and understands our requirements.

**Acceptance Policies.** Unagented manuscripts: 90%. Simultaneous submissions: no. Disk submissions: after acceptance only. Response time to initial inquiry: 3 months. Average time until publication: 2 years. **Advance**: negotiable. **Royalty**: negotiable. First run: 500-5000.

**Marketing Channels.** Distribution houses; indpendent reps; in-house staff. Subsidiary rights: first serialization; reprint; book club; translation and foreign; English language publication outside United States and Canada.

**Additional Information.** Tips: Be familiar with our books and refer to our focus in cover letter. Catalog: 9x12 SASE.

**OHARA PUBLICATIONS, INC.** 1813 Victory Place. Box 7728. Burbank, CA 91510-7728. Submissions Editor: Editor. Number of titles published: 1988—12. Softback 100%.

**Subjects of Interest. Nonfiction**—martial arts (systems, how-to, history, philosophy). Recent publications: *Advanced Wing-Chun.*

**Initial Contact.** Query letter first; outline, summary and sample chapter. Include author's credentials.

**Acceptance Policies.** Unagented manuscripts: yes. Simultaneous submissions: yes. Disk submissions: no. Response time to initial inquiry: 3-8 weeks. Average time until publication: n/i. **Advance**: none. **Royalty**: yes. First run: n/i.

**Marketing Channels.** Distribution houses; direct mail. Subsidiary rights: n/i.

**Additional Information.** Tips: Write for guidelines.

**OLD ADOBE PRESS.** Box 115. Penngrove, CA 94951. Submissions Editor: Rafael Cunin. Not accepting manuscripts.

**OLIVE PRESS PUB.** PO Box 99. Los Olivos, CA 93441. Submissions Editor: Addis Lynne Noris. Not accepting manuscripts.

**C. OLSON AND COMPANY.** PO Box 7800. Santa Cruz, CA 95061. (408) 458-3365. Submissions Editor: Clay Olson. Founded: 1977. Number of titles published: cumulative—5, 1989—2. Softback 100%.

**Subjects of Interest.** **Nonfiction**—health—natural hygiene. Recent publications: *For the Vegetarian in You; The New Abolitionists: Animal Rights and Human Liberation.* Do not want: fiction; manuscripts without a query.

**Initial Contact.** Query letter. Include SASE.

**Acceptance Policies.** Unagented manuscripts: yes. Simultaneous submissions: yes. Disk submissions: WordPerfect for Macintosh or IBM; ASCII on 3 1/2" discs. Response time to initial inquiry: 2-3 weeks. Average time until publication: 6-9 months. **Advance**: negotiable. **Royalty**: negotiable. First run: 5000-10,000.

**Marketing Channels.** Distribution houses; direct mail; telemarketing. Subsidiary rights: negotiable; we work from our standard contract.

**Additional Information.** Looking for an author to take a series of newsletters on the subject of fruit trees to convert it to book form. Tips: Query first with SASE. Keep it short. Catalog: SASE; $1.

**ORTHO INFORMATION SERVICES.** (Subsidiary of Chevron Chemical Co.). (Imprint: 101 Productions). 6001 Bollinger Canyon Road. San Ramon, CA 94583. (415) 842-5537. Submissions Editor: Christine L. Robertson. Number of titles published: cumulative—106, 1989—10. Hardback and softback.

**Subjects of Interest.** **Nonfiction**—cookbook; how-to; reference; pictorial; hobbies; nature; gardening; home repair.

**Initial Contact.** Query first; outline and summary to follow on expressed interest of editors.

**Acceptance Policies.** Unsolicited manuscripts: we return them unopened. Unagented manuscripts:yes. Simultaneous submissions: yes. Disk submissions: query. Response time to initial inquiry: 2 months. Average time until publication: 2 years. **Advance**: purchase outright. First run: n/i.

**Marketing Channels.** Distribution houses; in-house staff; special sales. Subsidiary rights: all.

**Additional Information.** Also publishes quarterly *Chevron Travel Club Magazine.* Tips: We decide on total project, assign writers, photographers, etc. after viewing proposal. Check our catalog for topics not already covered. No first-person how-to. Catalog: 9x12 SASE, 2 first class stamps.

**OYEZ.** PO Box 5134. Berkeley, CA 94705. Submissions Editor: Robert Hawley. Not accepting manuscripts.

**PACIFIC BOOKS, PUBLISHER.** PO Box 558. Palo Alto, CA 94302-0558. (415) 965-1980. Submissions Editor: Henry Ponleithner. Founded: 1945. Number of titles published: cumulative—258, 1987—7. Hardback 65%, softback 35%.

**Subjects of Interest.** **Nonfiction**—general and scholarly; professional and technical reference; college level textbooks, including paperbacks. Recent publications: *Heroes of the Golden Gate; Economic and Political Change in the Middle East; Really Now, Why Can't Our Johnnies Read.* Do not want: fiction; poetry.

**Initial Contact.** Query letter; description of manuscript; outline or table of contents. Include potential market(s).

**Acceptance Policies.** Unagented manuscripts: yes. Simultaneous submissions: yes. Disk submissions: yes. Response time to initial inquiry: 3-5 weeks. Average time until publication: 9-15 months. **Advance**: none. **Royalty**: standard. First run: 1500-10,000.

**Marketing Channels.** Direct mail; independent reps; in-house staff; special sales. Subsidiary rights: all.

**Additional Information.** Catalog: upon request.

**PANJANDRUM BOOKS.** 11321 Iowa Ave., Ste. 7. Los Angeles, CA 90025. (213) 477-8771. Submissions Editor: Dennis Koran. Founded: 1971. Number of titles published: cumulative—40+; 1988: 6. Hardback and softback.

**Subjects of Interest.** **Nonfiction**—biography; cooking; health; music; philosophy; theater; vegetarianism; childhood sexuality; juvenile. **Fiction**—avant-garde; experimental. **Other**—poetry. Do not want: religion; humor.

**Initial Contact.** Query letter; or outline and sample chapters. Include SASE.

**Acceptance Policies.** Unagented manuscripts: yes. Simultaneous submissions: yes. Disk submissions: no. Response time to initial inquiry: 2-4 weeks. Average time until publication: n/i. **Advance**: varies. **Royalty**: standard; varies. First run: n/i.

**Marketing Channels.** Distribution houses. Subsidiary rights: all.

**Additional Information.** Catalog: #10 SASE.

**PANORAMA WEST PUBLISHING.** (Imprints: Pioneer Publishing). PO Box 4638. Fresno, CA 93744. (209) 226-1200. Submissions Editor: Polly Powell. Founded: 1983. Number of titles published: cumulative—90, 1989—20. Hardback 60%, softback 40%.

**Subjects of Interest.** **Nonfiction**—California and Western American history; subjects relating to agriculture and rural living in the West; California ethnology. Recent publications: *Bacon and Beans from a Gold Pan; Mineral King Country: Visalia to Mt. Whitney.* **Fiction**—fictionalized biographies of persons reflecting the history of the west.

**Initial Contact.** Book proposal with 3 sample chapters; book outline. Include description of potential market size; dates for completion of manuscript and book (if known).

**Acceptance Policies.** Unagented manuscripts: yes. Simultaneous submissions: yes; inform us. Disk submissions: yes; alos send hard copy. Response time to initial inquiry: 3-4 weeks. Average time until publication: 4 months. **Advance**: none. **Royalty**: 10% of retail price. First run: 3000-5000. Subsidy basis: yes; we will publish for distribution by the author or distribute some of their books.

**Marketing Channels.** Direct mail; independent reps; in-house staff. Subsidiary rights: none.

**Additional Information.** We specialize in high-quality local histories written for general audiences. Catalog: 6x9 SASE.

**PAPERWEIGHT PRESS.** 761 Chestnut Street. Santa Cruz, CA 95060. (408) 427-1177. Submissions Editor: Jenny D'Angelo. Founded: 1969. Number of titles published: cumulative—15; 1988: 2. Hardback 90%, softback 10%.

**Subjects of Interest.** **Nonfiction**—paperweights. Recent publications: *Art of the Paperweight*. Do not want: anything else.

**Initial Contact.** Query letter.

**Acceptance Policies.** Unagented manuscripts: no. Disk submissions: Macintosh. Response time to initial inquiry: n/i. Average time until publication: n/i. **Advance**: n/i. **Royalty**: n/i. First run: n/i.

**PAPIER-MACHÉ PRESS.** 34 Malaga Pl. E. Manhattan Beach, CA 90266. (213) 545-3812. Submissions Editor: Sandra Martz. Founded: 1984. Number of titles published: cumulative—5, 1989—4. Softback 100%.

**Subjects of Interest.** **Nonfiction**—women/feminism. **Fiction**—women's issues; short story collections. Recent publications: *When I Am an Old Woman I Shall Wear Purple* (anthology of poetry, short stories, and photographs about women and aging); *The Tie that Binds: Stories, Poems, Photos* (about opposite sex parent/child relationships). **Other**—poetry. Recent publications: *Poetry Collection* (Sue Saniel Elkind).

**Initial Contact.** Query. Include SASE. (We will provide guidelines and current theme list.)

**Acceptance Policies.** Unagented manuscripts: yes. Simultaneous submissions: yes; inform us. Disk submissions: query first; IBM compatible. First novels: yes. Response time to initial inquiry: 4 weeks. Average time until publication: 6 months. **Advance**: negotiable. **Royalty**: 10-15% (single author). First run: 2500-3000.

**Marketing Channels.** Distribution houses; direct mail. Subsidiary rights: none.

**Additional Information.** We are a small, but hard working press, specializing in anthologies about issues of interest to women; we publish a few single author titles. Tips: Must query first. We are looking for material that is high quality and with a feminist/humanist perspective. Catalog: SASE.

**PARA PUBLISHING.** PO Box 4232-826. Santa Barbara, CA 93140-4232. (805) 968-7277. Submissions Editor: Daniel Poynter. Founded: 1969. Number of titles published: cumulative—48, 1989—7. Hardback 10%, softback 90%.

**Subjects of Interest.** **Nonfiction**—parachutes/skydiving; book publishing and promotion. Recent publications: *The Parachute Manual; Parachuting, the Skydiver's Handbook; The Self-Publishing Manual.* Do not want: anything other than parachutes/skydiving.

**Initial Contact.** Query letter. Include how many parachute jumps you have made.

**Acceptance Policies.** Unagented manuscripts: yes. Simultaneous submissions: yes. Disk submissions: IBM and Microsoft Word preferred; 3.5 or 5.25 disk. Response time to initial inquiry: 48 hours. Average time until publication: 90 days. **Advance**: $100. **Royalty**: 8%. First run: 2000-5000.

**Marketing Channels.** Cooperative distribution; direct mail; special sales. Subsidiary rights: all.

**Additional Information.** Catalog: upon request.

**PARKER & SON PUBLICATIONS, INC.** Box 60001. Los Angeles, CA 90060. (213) 727-1088. Submissions Editor: Managing Editor. Founded: 1898. Number of titles published: cumulative—51, 1989—57. Hardback 80%, softback 20%.

**Subjects of Interest. Nonfiction**—law books, especially on litigation topics, for the practicing attorney. Recent publications: *Land Use Procedure; California Community Property Law; Guide to California Evidence.*

**Initial Contact.** Query letter. Include author's resumé; author's publications; intended market; proposed length; jurisdiction of subject addressed.

**Acceptance Policies.** Unagented manuscripts: yes. Simultaneous submissions: no. Disk submissions: no. Response time to initial inquiry: . Average time until publication: 4 months. **Advance**: n/i. **Royalty**: n/i. First run: n/i.

**Marketing Channels.** In-house staff; direct mail. Subsidiary rights: all.

**Additional Information.** Our editorial department is staffed with legal editors with law degrees. Tips: We are particularly interested in practical law handbooks which can be updated annually, books for legal assistants, litigators, office practitioners. Catalog: upon request.

## PERIVALE PRESS. 13830 Erwin St. Van Nuys, CA 91401-2914.

(818) 785-4671. Submissions Editor: Lawrence P. Spingarn. Founded: 1968 (London, England). Number of titles published: cumulative—22, 1988—1. Hardback 10%, softback 90%.

**Subjects of Interest. Nonfiction**—anthologies of poetry; translations of poetry; literary criticism. Recent publications: *Contemporary French Women Poets; Sympathetic Manifesto.* **Fiction**—novels, short story collections. Do not want: first novels; mysteries; gothics; westerns.

**Initial Contact.** Query letter. Include publishing credits; willingness to promote book through readings.

**Acceptance Policies.** Unagented manuscripts: yes. Simultaneous submissions: yes; author must notify us of acceptance. Disk submissions: no. Response time to initial inquiry: 2 weeks. Average time until publication: 9 months. **Advance**: $150 maximum. **Royalty**: 10%. First run: 500-1000. Subsidy basis: yes; author eventually recovers full investment from sales.

**Marketing Channels.** Distribution houses; direct mail; in-house staff. Subsidiary rights: all.

**Additional Information.** Acquire our catalog. Tips: Clean copy to follow MLA style sheet. Catalog: SASE.

## PERSEVERANCE PRESS. PO Box 384. Menlo Park, CA 94025.

Submissions Editor: Meredith Phillips. Founded: 1979. Number of titles published: cumulative—10; 1988: 2. Trade softback 100%.

**Subjects of Interest. Fiction**—old-fashioned mystery without gratuitous violence, exploitive sex, or excessive gore. Recent publications: *Revolting Development; Murder Once Done.* Do not want: nonfiction; other genres.

**Initial Contact.** Book proposal with 3 sample chapters; cover letter with writing/publishing background.

**Acceptance Policies.** Unagented manuscripts: 85%. Simultaneous submissions: yes; inform us. Disk submissions: no. Response time to initial inquiry: 1 month. Average time until publication: 12 months. **Advance**: none. **Royalty**: 10% of net receipts. First run: 2000.

**Marketing Channels.** Distribution houses; cooperative distribution; direct mail; independent reps. Subsidiary rights: all.

**Additional Information.** Will not consider any material not meeting our guidelines. Tips: Characterization, background, plot, suspense, wit, humanity—all are essential. Catalog: upon request.

Pioneer Publishing *see* **PANORAMA WEST PUBLISHING.**

Plain Jane Books *see* **STRAWBERRY HILL PRESS.**

**PLAYERS PRESS, INC.** Box 1132. Studio City, CA 91604. (818) 789-4980. Submissions Editor: Robert W. Gordon. Founded: 1965. Number of titles published: cumulative—275, 1988—305. Hardback 1%, softback 99%.

**Subjects of Interest.** **Nonfiction**—theater; film; television. Recent publications: *Survival; An Entertainment Industry Guide* (the how-to of finding work for actors, directors and producers); *Stage Make-Up*. **Other**—plays; scenes; monologues; musicals, music, music how-to. Recent publications: *Rhyme Tyme* (musical for children); *Old Loves Die Hard* (play for adults).

**Initial Contact.** Query letter. Include SASE.

**Acceptance Policies.** Unsolicited manuscripts: plays and musicals only. Unagented manuscripts: yes. Simultaneous submissions: no. Disk submissions: no. Response time to initial inquiry: 90-180 days. Average time until publication: 6-24 months. **Advance**: optional. **Royalty**: varies. First run: 5000-20,000.

**Marketing Channels.** Distribution houses; direct mail; independent reps; in-house staff; special sales. Subsidiary rights: all.

**Additional Information.** For plays and musicals—submit only produced work. Catalog: send $1.00.

**PRESIDIO PRESS.** 31 Pamaron Way. Novato, CA 94949. (415) 883-1373. Submissions Editor: Adele Horwitz. Number of titles published: cumulative—120, 1989—25. Hardback and softback.

**Subjects of Interest.** **Nonfiction**—military. Recent publications: *The Last of the Bengal Lancers; Alpha Strike Vietnam; Space Shuttle*. **Fiction**—military setting. Recent publications: *Team Yankee; The Fire Dream*. Do not want: academic works.

**Initial Contact.** Query letter; or outline and 3 sample chapters.

**Acceptance Policies.** Unagented manuscripts: yes. Disk submissions: query. Response time to initial inquiry: 3 months. Average time until publication: 10 months. **Advance**: nominal. **Royalty**: 15% of net. First run: 5000+.

**Marketing Channels.** Distribution houses; special sales. Subsidiary rights: all.

**Additional Information.** Catalog: upon request.

**PRICE STERN SLOAN INC.** (Imprints: HP Books; The Body Press; Price Stern Sloan; Enrich; Troubador Press; Mr. Men; Little Miss; Mad Libs; Wonder Books; Storybook Special; Questron; Treasure Books; Serendipity; Laugh and Learn; Wee Sing; Doodle Art). 360 N. La Cienega Blvd. Los Angeles, CA 90048. (213) 657-6100. Submissions Editor: Lisa Ann Marsoli (juvenile); Spencer Humphrey (humor); Mary Kirby (adult); Doug Morrison (health and fitness). Founded: 1964. Number of titles published: 1989—120. Hardback 20%, softback 80%.

**Subjects of Interest.** **Nonfiction**—adult humor; how-to; health and fitness. Recent publications: *Microwave Cooking; Complete Guide to Prescription and Non-Prescription Drugs*. **Fiction**—juvenile; humor. Recent publications: *Wee Sing Series; How and Why Series; The Gigglesnitcher*. Do not want: religious books.

**Initial Contact.** Query letter; book proposal with 1-3 sample chapters. Do not send original art. Include SASE.

**Acceptance Policies.** Unagented manuscripts: yes. Simultaneous submissions: yes. Disk submissions: no. Response time to initial inquiry: 4-6 weeks. Average time until publication: 6-8 months. **Advance**: varies. **Royalty**: varies. First run: varies. Subsidy basis: yes.

**Marketing Channels.** Direct mail; independent reps; in-house staff; special sales. Subsidiary rights: all.

**Additional Information.** We look for original ideas not themes that have been done over and over again. We want chiren's books that teach as well as entertain. Catalog: SASE, $2.50 postage.

**PRIMA PUBLISHING AND COMMUNICATIONS.** PO Box 1260. Rocklin, CA 95677. (916) 624-5718. Submissions Editor: Ben Dominitz. Founded: 1984. Number of titles published: cumulative—67, 1989—30.

**Subjects of Interest. Nonfiction**—business; cooking; self-help; travel; general nonfiction. Recent publications: *The Complete Franchise Book; Lean and Luscious Cookbook; Raising Self Reliant Children in a Self Indulgent World.* Do not want: poetry; stories of people's vacations.

**Initial Contact.** Query letter. Include author's credentials; market for the book; name, publisher, sales history of previously published works; SASE.

**Acceptance Policies.** Unagented manuscripts: yes. Simultaneous submissions: yes. Disk submissions: no. Response time to initial inquiry: 3-4 weeks. Average time until publication: varies; seasonal. **Advance**: varies. **Royalty**: varies. First run: varies.

**Marketing Channels.** Distribution houses (St. Martin's Press). Subsidiary rights: all.

**Additional Information.** Tips: Be concise in your query. We want books with originality, written by highly qualified individuals. Catalog: 8 1/2x11 SASE, $1.25 postage.

Prism Editions *see* **NATUREGRAPH PUBLISHERS, INC.**

**PROFESSIONAL PUBLICATIONS, INC.** 1250 Fifth Ave. Belmont, CA 94002. (415) 593-9119. Submissions Editor: Lynda Schembri. Founded: 1975. Number of titles published: cumulative—45, 1987—10. Hardback 8%, softback 92%.

**Subjects of Interest. Nonfiction**—engineering and CPA exam review materials; other texts on engineering, business; architecture; professional exams; licensing review materials. Recent publications: 7 titles in the *CPA Examination Review Series,* including auditing and business law. Do not want: romance novels; cookbooks.

**Initial Contact.** Book proposal with sample chapters. Include curriculum vitae; proposed market.

**Acceptance Policies.** Unagented manuscripts: yes. Simultaneous submissions: yes. Disk submissions: IBM 51/4 format; must be accompanied by print-out. Response time to initial inquiry: 2-4 weeks. Average time until publication: varies. **Advance**: varies. **Royalty**: varies. First run: depends on title, market.

**Marketing Channels.** Distribution houses; direct mail; independent reps; special sales. Subsidiary rights: first serialization; sound reproduction and recording; direct mail or direct sales; book club; translation and foreign rights; computer and magnetic and electronic media; English language publication outside United States and Canada.

**Additional Information.** Tips: Provide plenty of information on anticipated sales. Catalog: contact Wendy Nelson.

**PUBLITEC EDITIONS.** 271 Lower Cliff Dr., Ste. A. Laguna Beach, CA 92652. (714) 497-6100. Submissions Editor: Maggie Rowe. Founded: 1984. Number of titles published: cumulative—5, 1989—2. Hardback 10%, softback 90%.

**Subjects of Interest.** **Nonfiction**—sports; health and fitness; how-to. Do not want: fiction; poetry.

**Initial Contact.** Query letter.

**Acceptance Policies.** Unagented manuscripts: yes. Simultaneous submissions: yes. Disk submissions: yes. Response time to initial inquiry: 1 month. Average time until publication: varies. **Advance**: varies. **Royalty**: varies. First run: varies.

**Marketing Channels.** Distribution houses; cooperative distribution; direct mail; special sales. Subsidiary rights: all.

**Additional Information.** "We" are a one-person operation producing one or two titles per year on average. Catalog: upon request.

**PUMA PUBLISHING.** 1670 Coral Dr. Santa Maria, CA 93454. (805) 925-3216. Submissions Editor: John Baptiste. Founded: 1986. Number of titles published: cumulative—3, 1987—1. Softback 100%.

**Subjects of Interest.** **Nonfiction**—small business areas; housekeeping; defensive driving and traffic ticket avoidance. Recent publications: *Speedy Housekeeping; Free Help From Uncle Sam To Start Your Own Business*. Do not want: fiction.

**Initial Contact.** Query letter.

**Acceptance Policies.** Unagented manuscripts: yes. Simultaneous submissions: yes. Disk submissions: not initially; can accept any format once manuscript is accepted. Response time to initial inquiry: 2 weeks. Average time until publication: 9 months. **Advance**: n/i. **Royalty**: 10% of retail. First run: 2000.

**Marketing Channels.** Distribution houses; cooperative distribution; direct mail; special sales. Subsidiary rights: direct mail or sales; book club; commercial; English language publication outside United States and Canada.

**Additional Information.** Need jokes, anecdotes, slogans, success stories of small businesses to be included in book in progress. Tips: No handwritten, no dot matrix.

**QED PRESS.** (Subsidiary of Comp-Type, Inc.). 155 Cypress St. Fort Bragg, CA 95437. (707) 964-9520. Submissions Editor: Cynthia Frank (poetry); John Fremont (prose). Founded: 1985. Number of titles published: cumulative—18, 1987—9. Hardback 25%, softback 75%.

**Subjects of Interest.** **Nonfiction**—social sciences; religion. Recent publications: *African Memories; Comedy Mafia*. **Fiction**—historical; romance; science fiction. Recent publications: *Path of Many Windings; Red Zambesi*. **Other**—poetry. Recent publications: *Expressions of the Heart*. Do not want: pornography; hate literature.

**Initial Contact.** Query letter. Include publishing history.

**Acceptance Policies.** Unagented manuscripts: yes. Simultaneous submissions: yes; inform us. Disk submissions: no. Response time to initial inquiry: 3 months. Average time until publication: 9 months. **Advance**: none. **Royalty**: 10%. First run: 3000. Subsidy basis: yes; 90% of our books are on a subsidy basis with author retaining all rights. Send for brochure.

**Marketing Channels.** Distribution houses; direct mail; in-house staff. Subsidiary rights: all.

**Additional Information.** Catalog: upon request.

Questron *see* **PRICE STERN SLOAN.**

**R & E PUBLISHERS.** PO Box 2008. Saratoga, CA 95070. (408) 866-6303. Submissions Editor: Bob Reed. Founded: 1967. Number of titles published: cumulative—1000+, 1989—26. Hardback 10%, softback 90%.

**Subjects of Interest. Nonfiction**—self-help; psychology; education; abuse; AIDS; health reference; how-to. Recent publications: *Self Esteem; Personality Plus; Free to Fly; Power Study to Up Your Grades; Rewards Offered the US*. Do not want: poetry; fiction; computer; animal; gardening.

**Initial Contact.** Query letter; book proposal with 1 sample chapter. Include market; author's plans (seminars, classes, tours); when project complete.

**Acceptance Policies.** Unagented manuscripts: yes. Simultaneous submissions: yes. Disk submissions: ok, but want hard copy also. Response time to initial inquiry: 60 days. Average time until publication: 6 months. **Advance**: none. **Royalty**: 10%, 12 1/2%, 15%. First run: 2000-10000. Subsidy basis: 10% of our books are with authors who market and sell their books along with our sales.

**Marketing Channels.** Distribution houses; direct mail; independent reps; special sales. Subsidiary rights: all.

**Additional Information.** We have published nearly 1000 titles and have been successful for 20 plus years. Tips: We want to work with authors who will work on efforts to make a book popular—a team effort. Catalog: upon request.

**REBECCA HOUSE.** 1550 California St. San Francisco, CA 94109. (415) 752-4080. Submissions Editor: Joni Roaki. Founded: 1985. Number of titles published: 1989— 1. Hardback.

**Subjects of Interest. Fiction**—children's books.

**Initial Contact.** Entire manuscript.

**Acceptance Policies.** Unagented manuscripts: yes. Simultaneous submissions: no. Disk submissions: no. First novels: yes. Response time to initial inquiry: 30 days. Average time until publication: 1 year. **Advance**: open. **Royalty**: to be negotiated. First run: open.

**Marketing Channels.** Direct mail; in-house staff; special sales. Subsidiary rights: all.

**Additional Information.** We are a new, small press looking for our growth to occur with innovative children's authors and illustrators. Tips: It is best to speak with us directly. Catalog: We are too new to have one yet.

**REBIS PRESS.** PO Box 2233. Berkeley, CA 94702. (415) 527-3845. Submissions Editor: Betsy Davids. Not accepting manuscripts.

**RED ALDER BOOKS.** Box 2992. Santa Cruz, CA 995063. (408) 426-7082. Submissions Editor: David Steinberg. Founded: 1977. Number of titles published: cumulative—6, 1989—1. Hardback 20%, softback 80%.

**Subjects of Interest. Nonfiction**—fathering, changing men's roles. Recent publications: *Fatherjournal* (one man's experience during first 5 years of involved parenting). **Fiction**—quality erotica. Recent publications: *Erotic by Nature* (a fine-quality hardcover collection of imaginative, provocative, non-pornographic photography, writing and drawing). **Other**—poetry. Recent publications: *Beneath This Calm Exterior*. Do not want: pornography.

**Initial Contact.** Query letter; sample material.

**Acceptance Policies.** Unagented manuscripts: yes. Simultaneous submissions: yes. Disk submissions: Macintosh. Response time to initial inquiry: 2-4 weeks. Average time until publication: 1 year. **Advance**: none. **Royalty**: varies. First run: 1000-5000.

**Marketing Channels.** Distribution houses; direct mail. Subsidiary rights: all.

**REFERENCE SERVICE PRESS.** 1100 Industrial Road, Ste. 9. San Carlos, CA 94070. (415) 594-0743. Submissions Editor: Stuart Hauser. Founded: 1976. Number of titles published: cumulative—16, 1987—4. Hardback 100%

**Subjects of Interest.** **Nonfiction**—directories of financial aid for special groups or situations; careers; education. Recent publications: *Directory of Financial Aids for Women, 1989-1990; . . for Minorities, 1989-1990*. Do not want: anything outside our area.

**Initial Contact.** Book proposal.

**Acceptance Policies.** Unagented manuscripts: yes. Simultaneous submissions: no. Disk submissions: no. Response time to initial inquiry: 30 days. Average time until publication: depends on project. **Advance**: n/i. **Royalty**: 10% and up, depending on sales. First run: 2000+.

**Marketing Channels.** Distribution houses; cooperative distribution; direct mail; special sales. Subsidiary rights: none.

**Additional Information.** We are the only publisher specializing solely in the development of directories of financial aid. Tips: Be sure your project matches our stated interests. Catalog: upon request.

**REGAL BOOKS.** (Division of Gospel Light Publications). 2300 Knoll Dr. Ventura, CA 93003. Submissions Editor: Linda Holland. Number of titles published: 1988—28. Hardback 15%, softback 85%.

**Subjects of Interest.** **Nonfiction**—Bible studies; marriage and family; inspirational; teaching enrichment; young adult; evangelism; personal growth; contemporary issues.

**Initial Contact.** Query letter; or detailed outline and 2-3 sample chapters. No complete manuscripts.

**Acceptance Policies.** Unagented manuscripts: yes. Simultaneous submissions: yes. Disk submissions: no. Response time to initial inquiry: 3 months. Average time until publication: 11 months. **Advance**: none. **Royalty**: negotiable. First run: 5000.

**Marketing Channels.** Independent reps; telemarketing. Subsidiary rights: all.

**Additional Information.** Catalog: upon request.

**RE/SEARCH PUBLISHING.** 20 Romolo #B. San Francisco, CA 94133. (415) 362-1465. Submissions Editor: V. Vale or A. Juno. Founded: 1980. Number of titles published: cumulative—10, 1989—5. Hardback 10%, softback %90.

**Subjects of Interest.** **Nonfiction**—art; film; music; all books based on interviews with authors, directors, musicians, etc.; off beat, unusual subjects with emphasis on philosophy behind art, music and action. Recent publications: *Pranks; Incredibly Strange Films* (forgotten gems of '50s, '60s); *Interviews of J.G. Ballard*; *Industrial Culture Handbook*. **Fiction**—reprints of various out-of-print books varying from hard-boiled detective to literature. Recent publications: *High Priest of California* ('50s detective); *Torture Garden* (turn of century decadence). Do not want: poetry or fiction.

**Initial Contact.** book proposal.

**Acceptance Policies.** Unagented manuscripts: yes. Simultaneous submissions: yes. Disk submissions: PC compatible. Response time to initial inquiry: 1 month. Average time until publication: 1 year. **Advance**: none. **Royalty**: 8%. First run: 2000-3000.

**Marketing Channels.** Distribution houses; direct mail. Subsidiary rights: all.

**Additional Information.** Catalog: upon request.

**RESOURCE PUBLICATIONS, INC.** 160 E. Virginia St., Ste. 290. San Jose, CA 95112. (408) 286-850. Submissions Editor: Kenneth Guentert. Founded: 1973. Number of titles published: cumulative—75, 1987—13. Hardback 10%, softback 90%.

**Subjects of Interest. Nonfiction**—resources for secular and liturgical celebrations; myth and symbol. Recent publications: *Feeding the Spirit: How to Do Rites, Ceremonies and Celebrations at Home; Date Book Earth 1988; Symbols for All Seasons: Environmental Planning based on the Roman Catholic Lectionary. Fiction—Recent Publications: One Perfect Lover (first person telling of life of Christ after the resurrection). Do not want: inspirational fiction or poetry collections.*

**Initial Contact.** Query letter; book proposal with sample chapters. Indicate willingness of author to promote book; phone.

**Acceptance Policies.** Unagented manuscripts: yes. Simultaneous submissions: yes; inform us. Disk submissions: IBM PC; CP/M; MS-DOS; Wordstar; ASCII. First novels: yes. Response time to initial inquiry: 6 weeks for query. Average time until publication: 18 months. **Advance**: books often offered at wholesale. **Royalty**: 8% of net. First run: 2000. Subsidy basis: yes; some authors buy up to 500 copies at wholesale. However, we do not print any book we do not believe will sell.

**Marketing Channels.** Distribution houses; cooperative distribution; direct mail; independent reps; special sales. Subsidiary rights: all.

**Additional Information.** We are a communication company devoted to imaginative resources for celebrations. Tips: Call first. Write to fit our needs. Give us a book that represents your work so you have a stake in making it work. Catalog: SASE.

**RIDGE TIMES PRESS.** Box 90. Mendocino, CA 95460. (707) 964-8465. Submissions Editor: Jim and Judy Tarbell. Founded: 1981. Number of titles published: cumulative—2. Softback 100%.

**Subjects of Interest. Nonfiction**—only Northern California topics and authors. Recent publications: *Cash Crop*.

**Initial Contact.** Query letter.

**Acceptance Policies.** Unagented manuscripts: yes. Simultaneous submissions: yes. Disk submissions: Macintosh. First novels: perhaps. Response time to initial inquiry: n/i. Average time until publication: 6-12 months. **Advance**: none. **Royalty**: negotiable. First run: 5000. Subsidy basis: partnership.

**Marketing Channels.** Distribution houses; independent reps. Subsidiary rights: all.

**Additional Information.** Major focus is on quarterly magazine.

**RONIN PUBLISHING, INC.** PO Box 1035. Berkeley, CA 94701. (415) 540-6278. Submissions Editor: Sebastian Orfal. Founded: 1983. Number of titles published: 19898—6-8. Softback 100%.

**Subjects of Interest. Nonfiction**—business: how-to, management psychology (major focus); visionary; new age; underground comics; psychedelic. Recent publications: *The Way of the Ronin.*

**Initial Contact.** Query letter.

**Acceptance Policies.** Unagented manuscripts: yes. Simultaneous submissions: n/i. Disk submissions: query. Response time to initial inquiry: 2-3 months. Average time until publication: 1 year. **Advance**: some. **Royalty**: 10% net. First run: 5000-10000. Subsidy basis: some; inquire.

**Marketing Channels.** Distribution houses; direct mail. Subsidiary rights: all.

**ROSS BOOKS.** Box 4340. Berkeley, CA 94704. (415) 841-2474. Submissions Editor: Elizabeth Yerkes. Founded: 1977. Number of titles published: cumulative—32; 1989: 3. Hardback 33%, softback 66%.

**Subjects of Interest.** **Nonfiction**—popular science; holography; desktop publishing. Recent publications: *Holography Handbook; Holography Marketplace 1989* (sourcebook of the holography industry)*; How to Plan* and *Book Meetings and Seminars*. Do not want: dog or cat grooming; cosmotology; hairstyling.

**Initial Contact.** Query letter. Include SASE.

**Acceptance Policies.** Unagented manuscripts: yes. Simultaneous submissions: yes. Disk submissions: IBM; Macintosh. Response time to initial inquiry: 2-3 weeks. Average time until publication: 1-3 years. **Advance**: none. **Royalty**: 8%-10%. First run: 3500-5000.

**Marketing Channels.** Distribution houses; direct mail. Subsidiary rights: first serialization; second serialization; newspaper syndication; reprint rights; direct mail or direct sale; book club; translation and foreign; computer and magnet and electronic; commercial; English language publication outside United States and Canada.

**Additional Information.** Catalog: order (800) 367-0930.

**ROXBURY PUBLISHING CO.** Box 491044. Los Angeles, CA 90049. (213)653-1068. Submissions Editor: Claude Teweles. Founded: 1979. Number of titles published: cumulative—18, 1987—5. Hardback 15%, softback 85%.

**Subjects of Interest.** **Other**—only college texts. Recent publications: *Business Communication: Concepts, Applications and Strategies; The Answer Book; Speech Communication Workbook.*

**Initial Contact.** Query letter; book proposal with sample chapters.

**Acceptance Policies.** Unagented manuscripts: yes. Simultaneous submissions: yes. Disk submissions: no. Response time to initial inquiry: 2 months. Average time until publication: 6-12 months. **Advance**: negotiable. **Royalty**: varies. First run: 2000-5000.

**Marketing Channels.** Direct mail; independent reps; in-house staff. Subsidiary rights: all.

**SAN DIEGO PUBLISHING COMPANY.** Box 9222. San Diego, CA 92109-0060. (619) 295-9393. Submissions Editor: Thomas L. Thomson. Founded: 1981. Number of titles published: cumulative—4, 1989—1. Softback 100%.

**Subjects of Interest.** all. Do not want: incomplete manuscripts or manuscripts that aren't clean.

**Initial Contact.** Entire manuscript; $50,000 cashiers check.

**Acceptance Policies.** Unagented manuscripts: I do not deal with agents. Disk submissions: yes. Response time to initial inquiry: immediate. Average time until publication: 3 months maximum. **Advance:** n/a. **Royalty:** author keeps all revenues. First run: 10,000. Subsidy basis; $50,000 up-front fee. Publisher guarantees minimum $75,000 return from sales or $50,000 fee is returned prior to publication.

**Marketing Channels.** Distribution houses; direct mail; independent reps, in-house staff; special sales. Subsidiary rights: none; refer author to agent after publishing success as noted.

**Additional Information.** I subcontract all work and concentrate on promotion, distribution, and marketing. Author retains all rights and all profits. Tips: I guarantee sales or your money back. We'll rewrite or recompose manuscript for additional $25,000 and increase guaranteed return to $100,000.

**SAN DIEGO STATE UNIVERSITY PRESS.** San Diego State University. San Diego, CA 92182. (619) 594-6220. Submissions Editor: Ed Gordon. Founded: 1964. Number of titles published: cumulative—69; 1988: 19, 1989 —10. Hardback 12%, softback 88%.

**Subjects of Interest. Nonfiction**—athletics; Latin America; women's studies; gerontology; autobiography; history. Recent publications: *Eleanor Roosevelt: An American Journey; Chant the Names of God; Struggle to Be Borne.* **Fiction**—Journals: *Aethlon* (sport literature); *Fiction International* (fiction/literature).

**Initial Contact.** Query letter.

**Acceptance Policies.** Unagented manuscripts: yes. Simultaneous submissions: yes. Disk submissions: no. First novels: yes. Response time to initial inquiry: 1 month. Average time until publication: 6-18 months. **Advance**: none. **Royalty**: 10% of net; negotiable. First run: 1000. Subsidy basis: for monologues sponsored by departments of associations.

**Marketing Channels.** Distribution houses. Subsidiary rights: all.

**Additional Information.** Academic, generally. Tips: We are funded through the California State University System, therefore familiarity with state processes is helpful! Catalog: upon request.

**SAND RIVER PRESS.** 1319 14th St. Los Osos, CA 93402. (805) 543-3591. Submissions Editor: Mary C. Donnelly. Founded: 1987. Number of titles published: 1987—1; 1988: 1. Softback 100%.

**Subjects of Interest. Nonfiction**—history; cookbooks; literature. Recent publications: *Chumash, A Picture of Their World.* **Fiction**—novels.

**Initial Contact.** Query letter; book proposal with sample chapters. Include SASE.

**Acceptance Policies.** Unagented manuscripts: yes. Simultaneous submissions: yes. Disk submissions: yes. Response time to initial inquiry: 6 weeks. Average time until publication: 1 year. **Advance**: $1000. **Royalty**: standard. First run: 3000.

**Marketing Channels.** Distribution houses; independent reps. Subsidiary rights: first serialization; reprint rights; dramatization, motion picture and broadcast; video; sound and recording; book club; translation and foreign; English language publication outside the United States and Canada.

**Additional Information.** We are small but qualified. Tips: Query first. Catalog: upon request.

**SANTA CRUZ COUNTY HISTORICAL TRUST.** (Santa Cruz Historical Society). PO Box 246. Santa Cruz, CA 95061-0246. (408) 425-2450. Submissions Editor: Stanley D. Stevens. Founded: 1987. Number of titles published: cumulative—2, 1987—1. Hardback 33%, softback 66%.

**Subjects of Interest. Nonfiction**—Santa Cruz local history and related material. Recent publications: *Santa Cruz County Place Names: A Geographical Dictionary; Georgiana/ Feminist Reformer of the West: The Journal of Georgiana Bruce Kirby, 1852-1860, with Biography.* Do not want: fiction.

**Initial Contact.** Query letter; book proposal with sample chapters; abstract of central focus and table of contents. Material must not be under consideration by another publisher.

**Acceptance Policies.** Unagented manuscripts: yes.

Simultaneous submissions: no. Disk submissions: Macintosh II: Microsoft Word; IBM; ASCII. Response time to initial inquiry: 30 days. Average time until publication: 12 months. **Advance**: none. **Royalty**: 10%-12%. First run: varies.

**Marketing Channels.** Distribution houses; direct mail; special sales. Subsidiary rights: none.

**Additional Information.** This is a noncommercial operation by volunteers. Tips: Our annual journal is entitled: *Santa Cruz County Historical Review*. It is suitable for less than book-length articles of 20 double-spaced pages of text. Catalog: upon request.

**SANTA SUSANA PRESS.** CSUN Library. 18111 Nordhoff St. Northridge, CA 91330. (818) 885-2271. Submissions Editor: Norman Tanis. Founded: 1973. Number of titles published: cumulative—44, 1987—3; 1988: 1. Hardback 80%, softback 20%.

**Subjects of Interest.** **Nonfiction**—local history; history; biography. Recent publications: *Los Angeles: Dream of Reality; The Twilight of Orthodoxy in New England; The Last Good Kiss.*

**Initial Contact.** Query letter.

**Acceptance Policies.** Unagented manuscripts: yes. Simultaneous submissions: no. Disk submissions: no. Response time to initial inquiry: 1 month. Average time until publication: varies. **Advance**: 1/3 payment. **Royalty**: n/i. First run: 65-300.

**Marketing Channels.** Direct mail. Subsidiary rights: all.

**Additional Information.** We are a very specialized limited-edition, artistic literary press. Tips: Send for catalog before submitting material. Catalog: upon request.

**SCHEHERAZADE BOOKS.** PO Box 7573. Berkeley, CA 94707. (415) 526-8024. Submissions Editor: Mildred Messinger. Founded: 1986. Number of titles published: cumulative—2; 1988: 1. Softback 100%.

**Subjects of Interest.** **Nonfiction**—Multiple Sclerosis. Recent publications: *Sukey's Songbook of MS; Older Married Woman's Guide to Love and Happiness.* Do not want: any doctors, nurses, etc.; fiction.

**Initial Contact.** Query letter; book proposal with sample chapters; location.

**Acceptance Policies.** Unagented manuscripts: yes. Simultaneous submissions: yes. Disk submissions: no. Response time to initial inquiry: 4 weeks. Average time until publication: 1 year. **Advance**: none. **Royalty**: 10%. First run: n/i.

**Marketing Channels.** Direct mail. Subsidiary rights: none.

**Additional Information.** Catalog: upon request.

Serendipity *see* **PRICE STERN SLOAN.**

**DALE SEYMOUR PUBLICATIONS.** PO Box 10888. Palo Alto, CA 94303. (415) 324-2800. Submissions Editor: Beverly Cory. Founded: 1979. Number of titles published: cumulative—400+, 1989—30. Softback 100%.

**Subjects of Interest.** **Nonfiction**—supplementary educational materials, K-12, in areas of math, science, language arts, art education, gifted education. Recent Publications: *Mental Math in the Middle Grades; Critical Thinking Activities; Teaching Characterization; Logic Number Problems; Science Around Me.* Do not want: fiction; children's storybooks; poetry.

**Initial Contact.** Query letter; author's teaching affiliation.

**Acceptance Policies.** Unagented manuscripts: yes. Simultaneous submissions: yes. Disk submissions: Macintosh in MacWrite or Microsoft Word. Response time to initial inquiry: 6 weeks. Average time until publication: 12 months. **Advance**: none. **Royalty**: 8%. First run: 1500.

**Marketing Channels.** Independent reps; direct mail. Subsidiary rights: none.

**Additional Information.** Catalog: call (800) 222-0766.

SF West *see* **OCEAN VIEW PRESS.**

**LI KUNG SHAW.** PO Box 10427. San Francisco, CA 94116. (415) 731-0829. Submissions Editor: Li Kung Shaw. Founded: 1982. Number of titles published: cumulative—10, 1987—1. Hardback 50%, softback 50%.

**Subjects of Interest. Nonfiction**—biology; Chinese input system. Recent publications: *Purposive Biology; Shell-Corner Method.* Do not want: fiction.

**Initial Contact.** Query letter.

**Acceptance Policies.** Unagented manuscripts: yes. Simultaneous submissions: yes. Disk submissions: Apple III. Response time to initial inquiry: 30 days. Average time until publication: varies. **Advance**: varies. **Royalty**: varies. First run: 1000+. Subsidy basis: yes; to be negotiated.

**Marketing Channels.** Direct mail; independent reps; special sales. Subsidiary rights: none.

**Additional Information.** Catalog: upon request.

**SIERRA CLUB BOOKS.** 730 Polk St. San Francisco, CA 94109. (415) 776-2211. Submissions Editor: Daniel Moses. Founded: 1892. Number of titles published: cumulative—500+; 1988: 20. Hardback and softback.

**Subjects of Interest. Nonfiction**—natural history; environmental issues; animals; juveniles (ecology theme); philosophy; photography; recreation; travel; sports; science. Recent publications: *Adventuring in the Pacific; Adventuring in Alaska; The Best of Edward Abbey; A World of Watchers: An Informal History of the American Passion for Birds; Pesticide Alert.* **Fiction**—rarely, and only if it fits our themes of environmental protection and appreciation of the wilderness. Recent publications: *Adventuring in the Pacific.* Do not want: "coffee-table" books with little text; personal experiences with the "great outdoors"; travelling by motorized vehicles; observations of wildlife.

**Initial Contact.** Query first; summary and sample chapters; availability of photographs or artwork.

**Acceptance Policies.** Unagented manuscripts: yes. Disk Average time until publication: 12-18 months. **Advance**: $3000-$5000. **Royalty**: 7%-12.5%. First run: n/i.

**Marketing Channels.** Distribution houses. Subsidiary rights: all.

**Additional Information.** Catalog: upon request.

**SINGLEJACK BOOKS.** (Subsidiary of Writings about Work, Inc.). PO Box 1906. San Pedro, CA 90733. (213) 5488-5964. Submissions Editor: Stan Weir. Founded: 1977. Number of titles published: cumulative—15, 1989—4. Hardback 20%, softback 80%.

**Subjects of Interest. Nonfiction**—labor law for workers; fight against shutdowns; related to work. Recent publications: *Automation, Progress for Whom?* **Fiction**—writings by the people who have actually done it; in production: novel about a machinist whose job is exported. **Other**—poetry. Do not want: writings without direct relationship to work.

**Initial Contact.** Query letter.

**Acceptance Policies.** Unagented manuscripts: yes. Disk submissions: no. First novels: yes. Response time to initial inquiry: 2 weeks. Average time until publication: 14 months. **Advance**: n/i. **Royalty**: 9% of retail; wholesale scheduled. First run: 2500-5000.

**Marketing Channels.** Independent reps; in-house staff; special sales; review responses. Subsidiary rights: all.

**Additional Information.** Catalog: upon request.

**GENNY SMITH BOOKS.** 1304 Pitman Ave. Palo Alto, CA 94301. Submissions Editor: Genny Smith. Founded: 1976. Number of titles published: cumulative—7, 1987—7. Hardback and softback, most titles published in both.

**Subjects of Interest.** **Nonfiction**—natural history and history of the Eastern Sierra region of California. Recent publications: *The Lost Cement Mine; Old Mammoth; Autobiography of Helen MacKnight Doyle*. Do not want: anything other than the Eastern Sierra.

**Initial Contact.** Query letter; entire manuscript.

**Acceptance Policies.** Unagented manuscripts: n/i. Simultaneous submissions: no. Disk submissions: no. Response time to initial inquiry: 2 weeks. Average time until publication: varies. **Advance**: none. **Royalty**: 5-10%. First run: 5000+.

**Marketing Channels.** Direct mail; independent reps. Subsidiary rights: none.

**Additional Information.** Catalog: upon request.

**SPINSTERS/AUNT LUTE BOOKS.** PO Box 410687. San Francisco, CA 94141. (415) 558-9655. Submissions Editor: Lorraine Grassano. Founded: 1986. Number of titles published: cumulative—33. Softback 100%.

**Subjects of Interest.** **Nonfiction**—poetry, themes directed towards a saner world. Recent publications: *Borderlands/La Frontera* (history of the Mestiza in prose, poetry); *Lesbian Passion: Loving Ourselves and Each Other*. **Fiction**—by and about women, mainly lesbian, women of color. Recent publications: *Tight Spaces* (short stories from three black women from Detroit). Do not want: works by men; works supporting the status quo.

**Initial Contact.** Query letter. Include author information.

**Acceptance Policies.** Unagented manuscripts: yes. Simultaneous submissions: yes; inform us. Disk submissions: no. First novels: yes. Response time to initial inquiry: 2 weeks. Average time until publication: n/i. **Advance**: none. **Royalty**: 7 1/2%. First run: 5000.

**Marketing Channels.** Distribution houses; cooperative distribution; direct mail; in-house staff; special sales. Subsidiary rights: all.

**Additional Information.** Tips: Be patient. Catalog: upon request.

**SPIRIT PRESS.** 1499 Masonic Ave. San Francisco, CA 94117. (415) 863-8941. Submissions Editor: Christy Polk. Founded: 1986. Number of titles published: cumulative—4; 1989—1. Softback 100%.

**Subjects of Interest.** **Nonfiction**—Recent publications: *Bay Area Baby: The Essential Guide to Local Resources for Pregnancy, Childbirth and Parenthood; Clothe Your Spirit: Dressing for Self-Expression.* **Fiction**—*Mama, Daddy, Baby and Me.*

**Initial Contact.** Query letter; or book proposal with sample chapters; or phone call. Include market information and statistics or analysis and/or why it's a good idea.

**Acceptance Policies.** Unagented manuscripts: yes. Simultaneous submissions: no. Disk submissions: yes. First novels: not yet. Response time to initial inquiry: 1 month. Average time until publication: 6-12 months. **Advance**: negotiable. **Royalty**: negotiable. First run: negotiable.

**Marketing Channels.** Distribution houses. Subsidiary rights: first serialization; second serialization; book club.

**SQUIBOB PRESS, INC.** PO Box 421523. San Francisco, CA 94142-1523. (415) 525-3982. Submissions Editor: Richard D. Reynolds. Founded: 1987. Number of titles published: 1989—1. Softback 100%.

**Subjects of Interest.** **Nonfiction**—crime; photography; children's books. Recent publications: *Cry for War, The Story of Suzan and Michael Carson; The Ancient Art of Colima, Mexico.*

**Initial Contact.** Query letter.

**Acceptance Policies.** Unagented manuscripts: yes. Simultaneous submissions: yes. Disk submissions: yes. Response time to initial inquiry: 2 weeks. Average time until publication: n/i. **Advance**: $1000. **Royalty**: 10% net of retail. First run: 1000-3000. Subsidy basis: depends on cost estimates.

**Marketing Channels.** Distribution houses; in-house staff. Subsidiary rights: all.

**Additional Information.** We are a new press looking for product. Tips: We welcome your query letters. Catalog: write and request.

**STANFORD UNIVERSITY PRESS.** Stanford University. Stanford, CA 94305. (415) 723-9434. Submissions Editor: William W. Carver. Founded: 1925. Number of titles published: cumulative—1000+; 1989: 65+. Hardback and softback.

**Subjects of Interest.** **Nonfiction**—scholarly books in almost all academic fields; upper division texts; some for general audience.

**Initial Contact.** Query letter; prospectus; outline.

**Acceptance Policies.** Unagented manuscripts: yes. Disk submissions: query. Response time to initial inquiry: 3-5 weeks. Average time until publication: 1 year. **Advance**: sometimes. **Royalty**: 0%-15%. First run: n/i. Subsidy basis: 65% (nonauthor).

**Marketing Channels.** Distribution houses; direct sales. Subsidiary rights: all.

**Additional Information.** We are looking principally for works of academic scholarship with broad appeal. Catalog: upon request.

**STAR PUBLISHING COMPANY.** 940 Emmett Avenue. Belmont, CA 94002. (415) 591-3505. Submissions Editor: Stuart A. Hoffman. Founded: 1978. Number of titles published: cumulative—69, 1989—75. Softback 100%.

**Subjects of Interest.** **Nonfiction**—textbooks for higher education and reference books; California regional history. Recent publications: *California: The Golden Shore By the Sundown Sea; Essentials of Business Math; Wax and Casting Photography From Theory to Practice.* Do not want: fiction; non-textbooks.

**Initial Contact.** Book proposal with sample chapters.

**Acceptance Policies.** Unagented manuscripts: yes. Simultaneous submissions: yes; with reservations. Disk submissions: no. Response time to initial inquiry: 30 days. Average time until publication: 1 year. **Advance**: none usually. **Royalty**: 5-15%. First run: varies greatly.

**Marketing Channels.** Distribution houses; cooperative distribution; direct mail; independent reps; special sales. Subsidiary rights: all.

**Additional Information.** Tips: Be sure subject of proposals are for higher education texts, or "Californiana." Catalog: upon request.

**STAR ROVER HOUSE.** 1914 Foothill Blvd. Oakland, CA 94606. (415) 532-8408. Submissions Editor: Robert Martens. Founded: 1978. Number of titles published: cumulative—40, 1989—4. Softback 100%.

**Subjects of Interest.** **Fiction**—reprints of Jack London, Mark Twain, Bret Harte.

Storybook Special *see* **PRICE STERN SLOAN.**

**STRAWBERRY HILL PRESS.** (Imprints: Walnut Hill Books; Plain Jane Books; Irio I O). 2594 15th Avenue. San Francisco, CA 94127. (415) 848-8233. Submissions Editors: Joseph M. Lubow; Mary Castiglione; Sara Shopkow; Robin Witkin; Carolyn Soto, Anne Ingram (all work in all subject areas). Founded: 1973. Number of titles published: cumulative—120, 1989—15. Hardback 6%, softback 94%.

**Subjects of Interest.** **Nonfiction**—cookbooks; self-help; autobiography/biography; history; Third World; inspiration; health and nutrition; alternative lifestyles. Recent publications: *Dare To Dream: The Rose Resnick Story* (autobiography-inspirational); *Hang Tough!* (Basque cookbook). **Fiction**—some, general. Recent publications: *Sudden Ice* (literary mystery novel); *Angel Food* (psychological thriller). Do not want: poetry; plays; juveniles; short story collections; photography books.

**Initial Contact.** Query letter; book proposal. Include author's credentials. We neither read nor respond to anything not accompanied by a SASE.

**Acceptance Policies.** Unagented manuscripts: yes. Simultaneous submissions: never. Disk submissions: IBM compatible. First novels: sometimes. Response time to initial inquiry: 2-8 weeks. Average time until publication: 1-3 years. **Advance**: none at all—ever. **Royalty**: 10% of receipts. First run: 5,000 +/-.

**Marketing Channels.** Distribution houses; direct mail; independent reps; in-house staff; special sales. Subsidiary rights: all; very active with same.

**Additional Information.** We are extremely active in the promotion of our authors and their books. Tips: We already see some 6,000 unsolicited books projects each year. Catalog: appropriate SASE.

**STUDIO PRESS.** PO Box 1268. Twain Harte, CA 95383-1268. (209) 533-4222. Submissions Editor: Paul Castle. Founded: 1974. Number of titles published: cumulative—32, 1987—5. Hardback 40%, softback 60%.

**Subjects of Interest.** **Nonfiction**—books for professional studio photographers, books that tell how to take better pictures and sell more of them. Recent publications: *The Boudoir Portrait; Family Portraiture; Promoting Portraits; Successful Business Practices for Studio Photographers.* Do not want: anything but above, especially not books of pretty photos for the coffee table.

**Initial Contact.** Best is a phone call and a quick pitch of the idea. I can give a go-ahead in two minutes for the written proposal and sample chapters. Be sure to mention expertise in photography.

**Acceptance Policies.** Unagented manuscripts: prefer them. Simultaneous submissions: no. Disk submissions: no; maybe later. Response time to initial inquiry: phone, 2 minutes; proposal, 3 days; proposal with chapters, 7 days. Average time until publication: 3 months. **Advance**: none; most authors are photographers who will write just one book with a lot of help from us. **Royalty**: up to 15%; depends on work needed; potential sales. First run: 3000+. Subsidy basis: we have in the past and may in the future; but we don't look for it.

**Marketing Channels.** Direct mail (95%). Subsidiary rights: all; we have worldwide distribution by mail and overseas distributors.

**Additional Information.** Please read very carefully and only send us what we want. Tips: We are very easy to work with if you send us what we want. We work very closely with the author until we get the manuscript we want. Catalog: upon request.

Sufi Publishing *see* **HUNTER HOUSE PUBLISHERS.**

**SUN AND MOON PRESS.** (Subsidiary of The Contemporary Arts Educational Project, Inc.). 6148 Wilshire Blvd. Gertrude Stein Plaza. Los Angeles, CA 90048. (213) 857-1115. Submissions Editor: Ann Klefstad. Founded: 1978. Number of titles published: cumulative—55, 1989—11. Hardback 60%, softback 40 %.

**Subjects of Interest. Fiction**—literary. Recent publications: *Mrs. Reynolds* (an acute study of ordinary thought and life in wartime by Gertrude Stein); *Painted Turtle* (novel by noted experimentalist Clarence Major; story of an Indian folksinger, told with great generosity and insight). **Other**—poetry. Recent publications: *The Sophist* (poetry by Charles Bernstein, well-known New York "Language" poet). Do not want: new age; self-help.

**Initial Contact.** Book proposal with sample chapters or entire manuscript (if book is very long, sample chapters okay). Do not want query letters if unaccompanied by some part of the work.

**Acceptance Policies.** Unagented manuscripts: yes. Simultaneous submissions: yes; reluctantly. Disk submissions: no. First novels: yes. Response time to initial inquiry: 2 months. Average time until publication: 2 years. **Advance**: varies; small, but our royalties are good. **Royalty**: varies. First run: 2000 or larger.

**Marketing Channels.** Independent reps. Subsidiary rights: all.

**Additional Information.** We are a nonprofit literary press. We are committed to the books we publish and to their authors; we keep books in print. Tips: Let your work speak for itself. We read everything we get, and judge the work on its own merits. Resumés are meaningless as are punchy cover letters. Catalog: upon request.

**SUNBELT PUBLICATIONS.** 8622 Argent St., Ste. A. Santee, CA 92071. (619) 448-0884. Submissions Editor: William G. Hample. Founded: 1984. Number of titles published: cumulative—3; 1989—1. Softback 100%.

**Subjects of Interest. Nonfiction**—regional guidebooks to Southern California or Southwest; Baja, California; bicycle books; tourist guides; hiking and nature guides. Recent publications: *Bicycling Baja; Southwest America Bicycle Route*. Do not want: fiction; self-help; new age.

**Initial Contact.** Query letter; book proposal with one sample chapter. Include author background.

**Acceptance Policies.** Unagented manuscripts: yes. Simultaneous submissions: no. Disk submissions: yes. Response time to initial inquiry: 2 weeks. Average time until publication: 1 year. **Advance**: negotiable. **Royalty**: 10%. First run: 3000-5000.

**Marketing Channels.** Distribution houses; in-house staff. Subsidiary rights: none.

**Additional Information.** We are a book wholesaler (95%) and publisher (5%). Tips: Check our catalog. Catalog: upon request.

**SUNSET BOOKS.** 80 Willow Rd. Menlo Park, CA 94025. (415) 321-3600. Does mostly in-house publication.

Sun West *see* **ELYSIUM GROWTH PRESS.**

**SYBEX, INC.** (Imprints: Sybex). 2021 Challenger Dr. #100. Alameda, CA 94501. (415) 523-8233. Submissions Editor: Dianne King. Founded: 1976. Number of titles published: cumulative—375, 1989—78. Hardback 3%, softback 97%.

**Subjects of Interest. Nonfiction**—related to personal desktop or micro computer programs and equipment; mostly business and technical orientation. Recent publications: *Understanding dBASE IV; Mastering DOS; Mastering the Auto CAD; Programmer's Guide to OS/2*. Do not want: non-computer subjects.

**Initial Contact.** Book proposal with sample chapters. Include author background.

**Acceptance Policies.** Unagented manuscripts: yes. Simultaneous submissions: yes; not too multiple. Disk submissions: 5 1/4 IBM PC; WordStar; WordPerfect; ASCII, etc. Response time to initial inquiry: 1 month. Average time until publication: 6 months. **Advance**: $2500-$3000. **Royalty**: 10%. First run: 5000-10,000.

**Marketing Channels.** Distribution houses; in-house staff. Subsidiary rights: translation and foreign; English language publication outside United States and Canada.

**Additional Information.** Tips: Call and talk to our acquisitions editor. Catalog: upon request.

**JEREMY P. TARCHER, INC.** 9110 Sunset Blvd., Suite 250. Los Angeles, CA 90069. (213) 273-3274. Submissions Editor: Donna Zerner. Founded: 1964. Number of titles published: cumulative—175; 1989—45. Hardback 50%, softback 50%.

**Subjects of Interest.** **Nonfiction**—human potential; personal and social transformation; health; creativity; self-help; relationships; spirituality; leading edge psychology. Recent publications: *Age Wave; Women Who Love Too Much; Personal Mythology; The Agony of it All; A Time to Heal*. Do not want: art; children's; astrology; textbooks; cookbooks; exposés; game books; fiction; channeled material.

**Initial Contact.** Outline; summary; sample chapters. Include author bio stressing expertise in field; market survey of competing books; uniqueness of their book; clear picture of audience. Include SASE.

**Acceptance Policies.** Unagented manuscripts: yes. Simultaneous submissions: yes. Disk submissions: no. Response time to initial inquiry: 4-6 weeks. Average time until publication: 1 year. **Advance**: variable. **Royalty**: standard. First run: 7500-100,000.

**Marketing Channels.** Distribution houses; special sales. Subsidiary rights: all.

**Additional Information.** Catalog: 6x9 SASE, $1.05 postage.

**TEN SPEED PRESS.** (Imprints: Celestial Arts). Box 7123. Berkeley, CA 94705. (415) 845-8414. Submissions Editor: Mariah Bear. Founded: 1971. Number of titles published: cumulative—450, 1989—80. Hardback 5%, softback 95%, published simultaneously, if hardback edition published.

**Subjects of Interest.** **Nonfiction**—careers; cookbooks; humor; general Recent publications: *Publisher's Lunch; What Color is Your Parachute?; White Trash Cooking*. Do not want: poetry; fiction.

**Initial Contact.** Query letter. Tell briefly what the book is about, what makes it good, and who you are. Include SASE.

**Acceptance Policies.** Unagented manuscripts: yes. Simultaneous submissions: no. Disk submissions: no. Response time to initial inquiry: 2 months. Average time until publication: 1 1/2-2 years. **Advance**: varies. **Royalty**: varies. First run: varies.

**Marketing Channels.** Distribution houses; direct mail;independent reps; in-house staff; special sales. Subsidiary rights: all.

**Additional Information.** Tips: Our books have a high level of integrity. There is no substitute for good solid writing; it will always be the main reason for accepting a manuscript. Catalog: upon request.

**TIME WARP PUBLISHING.** 7956 White Oak Ave. Northridge, CA 91325. (818) 344-2286. Submissions Editor: Joseph Brosta IV. Founded: 1985. Number of titles published: cumulative—5, 1987—3. Softback 100%.

**Subjects of Interest. Nonfiction**—popular music; how-to for the entertainment industry. Recent publications: *1987 Key and BPM Guide to Dance Music; Spinning Gold; Off the Record.*

**Initial Contact.** Phone call.

**Acceptance Policies.** Unagented manuscripts: yes. Simultaneous submissions: no. Disk submissions: no. Response time to initial inquiry: 2 weeks. Average time until publication: 2 months. **Advance**: none. **Royalty**: 5%. First run: 1000.

**Marketing Channels.** Distribution houses; direct mail; in-house staff. Subsidiary rights: sound reproduction and recording; computer and other magnetic and electronic media rights; English language publication outside the United States and Canada.

**Additional Information.** Tips: Write about a topic not already published. Be timely and unique. Catalog: call.

**TIOGA PUBLISHING COMPANY** 150 Coquito Way. Portola Valley, CA 94025. (415) 854-2445. Submissions Editor: Karen Nilsson. Founded: 1979. Number of titles published: cumulative—21, 1989—1. Hardback 50%, softback 50%.

**Subjects of Interest. Nonfiction**—Western Americana. Recent publications: *Northwest Passages: From the Pen of John Muir; Gardens of Northern California.* Do not want: anything but Western nonfiction; no poetry.

**Initial Contact.** Query letter. Include experience of author, willingness to help market book, and funding ideas.

**Acceptance Policies.** Unagented manuscripts: yes. Simultaneous submissions: no. Disk submissions: any. Response time to initial inquiry: 3 months. Average time until publication: 1 1/2 years. **Advance**: none. **Royalty**: 10% net amount received. First run: 2000-5000.

**Marketing Channels.** Distribution houses; direct mail; special sales. Subsidiary rights: n/i.

**Additional Information.** Not likely to find a book this way; we work more through word of mouth. Tips: Explain why the world will be a better place if your book is published! Catalog: upon request.

**TRAVEL KEYS.** PO Box 160691. Sacramento, CA 95816. (916) 452-5200. Submissions Editor: Peter Manston. Founded: 1984. Number of titles published: cumulative—13, 1989—4. Hardback 10%, softback 90%.

**Subjects of Interest. Nonfiction**—travel; home; antiques; how-to (travel related). Recent publications: *Before You Leave on Your Vacation; Travel Key Europe '89; Manston's Travel Key Britain.*

**Initial Contact.** Sample chapters or entire manuscript. Include enough of subject and book so we can determine if: author is an authority in the field, if book topic and treatment fits our list.

**Acceptance Policies.** Unagented manuscripts: yes. Simultaneous submissions: yes; inform us. Disk submissions: IBM 5 1/4; ASCII; Word; Wordstar. Response time to initial inquiry: 1 month. Average time until publication: 3-9 months. **Advance**: variable. **Royalty**: we estimate royalty and pay fee for book, usually as work for hire. First run: 4000-10,000.

**Marketing Channels.** Distribution houses; cooperative distribution; direct mail; special sales. Subsidiary rights: all.

**Additional Information.** Catalog: SASE #10 envelope.

Treasure Books *see* **PRICE STERN SLOAN.**

Troubador Press *see* **PRICE STERN SLOAN.**

**TURKEY PRESS.** 6746 Sueno Rd. Isla Vista, CA 93117. Submissions Editor: Harry E. Reese. We publish hand-produced books in limited editions. We do not accept submissions of any kind.

**ULYSSES PRESS.** PO Box 4000-H. Berkeley, CA 94704. (415) 644-0915. Submissions Editor: Leslie Henriques. Founded: 1983. Number of titles published: cumulative—9, 1989—5. Softback 100%.

**Subjects of Interest.** **Nonfiction**—travel guide books. Recent publications: *Hidden Los Angeles and Southern California; Hidden San Francisco and Northern California; Hidden Hawaii; Hidden Mexico.*

**Initial Contact.** Query letter; book proposal with sample chapters.

**Acceptance Policies.** Unagented manuscripts: yes. Simultaneous submissions: yes. Disk submissions: n/i. Response time to initial inquiry: 6 weeks. Average time until publication: 1 year. **Advance**: work for hire. **Royalty**: n/i. First run: 10,000-15,000.

**Marketing Channels.** Distribution houses; direct mail. Subsidiary rights: all.

**Additional Information.** Catalog: upon request.

**UNITED RESOURCE PRESS.** 4521 Campus Dr., #388. Irvine, CA 92715. Submissions Editor: Sally Marshall Corngold. Founded: 1986. Number of titles published: cumulative—9. Softback 100%.

**Subjects of Interest.** **Nonfiction**—"how-to" personal finance; small business. Recent publications: *Clearing Your Credit: Financial Strategies During Divorce.* Do not want: fiction.

**Initial Contact.** Entire manuscript. Include photo availability; disk availability.

**Acceptance Policies.** Unagented manuscripts: yes. Simultaneous submissions: yes. Disk submissions: Wordstar (IBM or other). Response time to initial inquiry: 2-3 months. Average time until publication: 2-3 months. **Advance**: none. **Royalty**: 5%. First run: varies.

**Marketing Channels.** Distribution houses; cooperative distribution; direct mail; independent sales. Subsidiary rights: varies; direct mail or direct sales .

**Additional Information.** Our primary focus is books. Tips: All information must be well-documented. Send entire manuscript. Don't call. Catalog: 9x12 SASE, $1 postage.

**UNIVELT, INC.** (Imprints: American Astronautical Society; International Academy of Astronautics; National Space Society associated organizations). PO Box 28130. San Diego, CA 92128. (619) 746-4005. Submissions Editor: Horace Jacobs. Founded: 1970. Number of titles published: cumulative—160, 1989—12. Hardback 40%, softback 60%.

**Subjects of Interest.** **Nonfiction**—aerospace especially space and related; astronomy; technical communications/writing, editing, etc; veterinary first aid. Recent publications: *The NASA Mars Conference; Soviet Space Programs; Low-Gravity Sciences; The Human Quest in Space; Realm of the Long Eyes; General First Aid for Dogs.* Do not want: fiction.

**Initial Contact.** Query letter; book proposal with outline. Include biography.

**Acceptance Policies.** Unagented manuscripts: yes. Simultaneous submissions: yes; inform us. Disk submissions: after acceptance; IBM compatible. Response time to initial inquiry: 30-60 days. Average time until publication: 6-8 months. **Advance**: none. **Royalty**: 10%. First run: varies. Subsidy basis: yes; some organizations offer to buy a certain number of copies or provide funds to support editorial work or printing.

**Marketing Channels.** Distribution houses; cooperative distribution; direct mail. Subsidiary rights: all.

**Additional Information.** We are a small publisher but distribute worldwide—mostly technical books. Tips: Most of our titles deal with space or are space-related. We publish also in the field of technical communication. Catalog: upon request.

**UNIVERSITY ASSOCIATES, INC.** 8517 Production Ave. San Diego, CA 92121. (619) 578-5900. Submissions Editor: Richard L. Roe, Vice-President, Publications. Founded: 1968. Number of titles published: cumulative—220, 1989—30. Hardback 25%, softback 75%.

**Subjects of Interest. Nonfiction**—human resource development; management/leadership; consulting/training; strategic planning. Recent publications: *Training Technologies Series; Shaping Strategic Planning; The Abiline Paradox and Other Meditations for Managers; Change-Agent Skills.*

**Initial Contact.** Query letter; book proposal with 1 sample chapter.

**Acceptance Policies.** Unagented manuscripts: yes. Simultaneous submissions: yes. Disk submissions: PC-Write. Response time to initial inquiry: 60 days. Average time until publication: 6 months. **Advance**: varies. **Royalty**: varies. First run: n/i.

**Marketing Channels.** direct mail. Subsidiary rights: n/i.

**Additional Information.** Catalog: upon request.

**UNIVERSITY OF CALIFORNIA PRESS.** (Imprints: Philip E. Lilienthal Asian Studies Imprint). 2120 Berkeley Way. Berkeley, CA 94720. (415) 642-4247. Submissions Editor: send to attention of the subject editor. Founded: 1893. Number of titles published: cumulative—3500, 1987—230. Hardback 70%, softback 30%.

**Subjects of Interest. Nonfiction**—African studies; anthropology; art and architecture; Asian studies; biological sciences; classical studies; economics; film and theater; folklore and mythology; geography; history; labor relations; language and linguistics; Latin American studies; literature; medicine; music; natural history and ecology; Near Eastern studies; philosophy; political science; sociology; women's studies. Do not want: original fiction and poetry.

**Initial Contact.** Query letter. Include curriculum vitae.

**Acceptance Policies.** Unagented manuscripts: yes. Simultaneous submissions: preferably not. Disk submissions: no. Response time to initial inquiry: 2-6 weeks. Average time until publication: 1 year . **Advance**: n/i. **Royalty**: n/i. First run: n/i.

**Marketing Channels.** Cooperative distribution; direct mail; independent reps; in-house staff; special sales. Subsidiary rights: all.

**Additional Information.** Catalog: upon request.

**VALLEY OF THE SUN PUBLISHING.** (Subsidiary of Sutphen Corporation). Box 38. Malibu, CA 90265. (818) 889-1575. Submissions Editor: Sharon L. Boyd. Founded: 1972. Number of titles published: cumulative—16. Softback 100%.

**Subjects of Interest. Nonfiction**—metaphysical philosophy. Recent publications: *Master of Life Manual* (spiritual enlightenment principles); *Enlightenment Transcripts* (continues the spiritual enlightenment); *Lighting the Light Within* (collection of Dick Sutphen's writings). Do not want: fiction, metaphysical or otherwise; poetry; channeled information.

**Initial Contact.** Will only accept query letters; outline and sample chapters okay but not necessary. Include SASE.

**Acceptance Policies.** Unagented manuscripts: yes. Simultaneous submissions: no. Disk submissions: PC compatible; Microsoft Word. If not MS Word, then sample chapter to show formatting, with rest of manuscript in unformatted ASCII. Response time to initial inquiry: 3-6 months. Average time until publication: 3-4 months. **Advance**: negotiable. **Royalty**: negotiable. First run: 30,000.

**Marketing Channels.** Distribution houses; direct mail; independent reps. Subsidiary rights: none.

**Additional Information.** Catalog: upon request.

Valley Publishers *see* **WESTERN TANAGER PRESS.**

**VIEWPOINT PRESS.** (Subsidiary of Boxwood Press). 183 Ocean View Blvd. Pacific Grove, CA 93950. (408) 375-9110. Submissions Editor: Dr. Buchsbaum.

**Subjects of Interest.** **Nonfiction**—scholarly controversial books. Recent publications: *The Great Unwanted* (Mexican immigrants). For details *see* Boxwood Press.

**VINTAGE '45 PRESS.** PO Box 266. Orinda, CA 94563. (415) 254-7266. Submissions Editor: Susan Aglietti. Number of titles published: cumulative—1, 1990—1.

Publishes a literary anthology on specific themes related to women's issues by women writers only. Anthologies include poems, essays or short stories. Currently collecting mansucripts (poetry, essay, short story) by women about their grandmothers for forthcoming anthology. All submissions must be previously unpublished. Tip: A sample issue of *Vintage '45,* the uniquely supportive quarterly journal for women, is available for $2.50. This is the best indicator of the type of writing sought for the anthology.

**VOLCANO PRESS, INC.** (Imprints: Kazan Books, on Pacific Rim subjects). PO Box 270. Volcano, CA 95689. (209) 296-3445. FAX: (209) 296-4515. Submissions Editor: Ruth Gottstein. Founded: 1969. Number of titles published: 1989—4. Hardback 10%, softback 90%.

**Subjects of Interest.** **Nonfiction**—women's health; family violence; children's books; health books in Spanish; art books. Recent publications: *Goddesses; Learning to Live Without Violence: A Handbook for Men; A Kid's First Book About Sex; Visions of Coit Tower; Medical Self-Care Book of Women's Health.* **Fiction**: children's. Do not want: poetry; fiction.

**Initial Contact.** Query letter. Include SASE.

**Acceptance Policies.** Unagented manuscripts: yes. Simultaneous submissions: yes; inform us. Disk submissions: no. Response time to initial inquiry: 4-6 weeks. Average time until publication: varies. **Advance**: none. **Royalty**: varies. First run: 5000-7000.

**Marketing Channels.** Distribution houses; cooperative distribution; direct mail; in-house staff; special sales. Subsidiary rights: all.

**Additional Information.** See our catalog. Tips: Inquire first; include SASE. Catalog: SASE.

Walnut Hill Books *see* **STRAWBERRY HILL PRESS.**

Wee Sing *see* **PRICE STERN SLOAN.**

**WESTERN ASSOCIATION OF MAP LIBRARIES.** University of California. Santa Cruz, CA 95064. (408) 429-2364. Submissions Editor: Stanley Stevens. Founded: 1967. Number of titles published: cumulative—12, 1989—1. Softback 100%.

**Subjects of Interest.** **Nonfiction**—reference maps; bibliographies of maps; occasional papers. Recent publications: *Map Index to Topographic Quadrangles of the US, 1882-1940.*

**Initial Contact.** Book proposal. Include focus of the work; table of contents.

**Acceptance Policies.** Unagented manuscripts: no. Simultaneous submissions: no. Disk submissions: Microsoft Word for Macintosh. Response time to initial inquiry: 3 months. Average time until publication: 1 year. **Advance**: none. **Royalty**: none. First run: varies.

**Marketing Channels.** Special sales. Subsidiary rights: none.

**Additional Information.** Catalog: write and request.

**WESTERN MARINE ENTERPRISES INC.** 4051 Glencoe Ave., Ste. 14. Marina Del Rey, CA 90292. (213) 306-2094. Submissions Editor: Sue Artof. Founded: 1965. Number of titles published: cumulative—21, 1989—7. Hardback 15%, softback 85%.

**Subjects of Interest. Nonfiction**—marine how-to books.

**Initial Contact.** Book proposal with sample chapters; or entire manuscript.

**Acceptance Policies.** Unagented manuscripts: yes. Disk submissions: MS-DOS; Wordstar. Response time to initial inquiry: 30 days. Average time until publication: 5-6 months. **Advance**: hardly ever. **Royalty**: 15% net sales price. First run: 2000-10,000.

**Marketing Channels.** Distribution houses; direct mail; independent reps, in-house staff. Subsidiary rights: all.

**Additional Information.** Tips: Should be marine-oriented subjects or fun books. Catalog: upon request.

**WESTERN TANAGER PRESS.** 1111 Pacific Ave. Santa Cruz, CA 95060. (408) 425-1111. Submissions Editor: Hal Morris. Founded: 1979. Number of titles published: cumulative—30, 1989—3. Hardback 25%, softback 75%.

**Subjects of Interest. Nonfiction**—regional history and biography relating to California and the West; hiking and biking guides. Recent publications: *Guide to the Theodore Solomons Trail; History of Steinbeck's Cannery Row; The Palos Verdes Peninsula.* **Other**—*Miner's Christmas Carol* (a short story collection by Samuel Davis, 1886).

**Initial Contact.** Query letter; book proposal. Include table of contents.

**Acceptance Policies.** Unagented manuscripts: yes. Simultaneous submissions: yes. Disk submissions: not yet. Response time to initial inquiry: 1 month. Average time until publication: 6 months. **Advance**: varies. **Royalty**: 10%. First run: 3000-7000. Subsidy basis: contract.

**Marketing Channels.** Distribution houses; in-house staff; special sales. Subsidiary rights: all.

**Additional Information.** Tips: Research us first. Do we already publish books similar to the one you have submitted? Catalog: upon request.

**WILDERNESS PRESS.** 2440 Bancroft Way. Berkeley, CA 94704. (415) 843-8080. Submissions Editor: Thomas Winnett. Founded: 1967. Number of titles published: cumulative—75, 1989—7 Hardback 5%, softback 95%.

**Subjects of Interest. Nonfiction**—guidebooks and how-to books for self-propelled outdoor recreations such as hiking, backpacking, cross-country skiing, rock climbing, cycling. Recent publications: *Hiking the Big Sur Country; Emigrant Wilderness, Afoot and Afield in Orange County* (guidebook); *Backpacking and Camping in the Developing World* (how-to book); *Bicycling Across America* (guide and how-to). Do not want: fiction; poetry.

**Initial Contact.** Query letter; sample chapters; or entire manuscript. Include some photos if it is a guidebook; evidence that writer has personally covered all the places he writes about.

**Acceptance Policies.** Unagented manuscripts: yes. Simultaneous submissions: yes. Disk submissions: MS-DOS; any IBM compatible, except 1.44 megabyte high density. Response time to initial inquiry: 20 days. Average time until publication: 7-8 months. **Advance**: varies. **Royalty**: 8% if not previously published in our fields; 10% if so. First run: 5000.

**Marketing Channels.** Distribution houses; direct mail; independent sales reps. Subsidiary rights: all.

**Additional Information.** We seek to uphold a standard of English language that seems to be above most writers' abilities. Tips: Don't tell us the book is timely, well-written, or bound to sell well. Catalog: upon request.

**WILSHIRE BOOK COMPANY.** 12015 Sherman Rd. North Hollywood, CA 91605. (213) 875-1711. Submissions Editor: Melvin Powers. Founded: 1947. Number of titles published: cumulative—550, 1989—25. Softback 100%.

**Subjects of Interest.** **Nonfiction**—psychological; self-help; inspirational. Recent publications: *Psycho-Cybernetics; Magic of Thinking Big; Think and Grow Rich; Parent Survival Training; Magic of Thinking Success.* **Other**—adult fables. Recent publications: *The Knight in the Rusty Armor.*

**Initial Contact.** Query letter; phone call.

**Acceptance Policies.** Unagented manuscripts: yes. Simultaneous submissions: yes. Disk submissions: no. Response time to initial inquiry: 1 month. Average time until publication: 7 months. **Advance**: varies. **Royalty**: 5%. First run: 5000.

**Marketing Channels.** Distribution houses; direct mail; independent reps; in-house staff; special sales. Subsidiary rights: all.

**Additional Information.** Call for immediate response about manuscript. I welcome such phone calls to discuss your book proposal. Catalog: SASE (legal size).

B. L. Winch and Assoc. *see* **JALMAR PRESS.**

**WINTERBOURNE PRESS.** PO Box 7584. Berkeley, CA 94706. (415) 524-3067. Not currently accepting manuscripts.

**WIZARDS BOOKSHELF.** PO Box 6600. San Diego, CA 92106. (619) 297-9879. Submissions Editor: R. I. Robb. Founded: 1972. Number of titles published: cumulative—50, 1989—5. Hardback 95%, softback 5%.

**Subjects of Interest.** **Nonfiction**—Secret Doctrine references; philosophy; theosophy; antiquities. Recent publications: *Los Fragments of Proclus, 1824; Surya Siddhanta; Life of Paracelsus; Gnostics and Their Remains; Zohar; Esoteric Buddhism; Sacred Mysteries Mayas.* Do not want: anything except translations, or S.D. studies.

**Initial Contact.** Query letter; synopsis of manuscript.

**Acceptance Policies.** Unagented manuscripts: yes. Simultaneous submissions: no. Disk submissions: no; unless preceded by typed manuscript. Response time to initial inquiry: 1 week. Average time until publication: 9-12 months. **Advance**: none. **Royalty**: 20%. First run: varies.

**Marketing Channels.** Distribution houses; cooperative distribution; direct mail. Subsidiary rights: all.

**Additional Information.** We don't fit the standard mold. Tips: Contact us first. Catalog: upon request.

**ALAN WOFSY FINE ARTS.** Box 2210. San Francisco, CA 94126. Submissions Editor: Milton Goldbaum. Founded: 1969. Number of titles published: cumulative—50; 1988: 5. Hardback and softback.

**Subjects of Interest.** **Nonfiction**—art reference books; bibliographies related to art.

**Initial Contact.** Query.

**Acceptance Policies.** Unagented manuscripts: yes. Disk submissions: no. Response time to initial inquiry: 1 month. Average time until publication: 1 year. **Advance**: n/i. **Royalty**: negotiable. First run: n/i. Subsidy basis: about 15%.

**Marketing Channels.** Distribution houses; in-house reps; special sales.

**Additional Information.** Catalog: upon request.

**WOLCOTTS, INC.** 15124 Downey Ave. PO Box 467. Paramount, CA 90723. (213) 630-0911. Submissions Editor: Allen Hughes. Founded: 1893. Number of titles published—n/i. Hardback 5%, softback 95%.

**Subjects of Interest.** **Nonfiction**—mostly "how-to" legal books. Recent publications: *How To Evict a Tenant; Incorporation Made Easy; Divorce California Style; How To Deal With Contractors.* Do not want: fiction.

**Initial Contact.** Query letter.

**Acceptance Policies.** Unagented manuscripts: yes. Simultaneous submissions: no. Disk submissions: no. Response time to initial inquiry: 2 weeks. Average time until publication: n/i. **Advance**: n/i. **Royalty**: n/i. First run: n/i.

**Marketing Channels.** Distribution houses; direct mail. Subsidiary rights: n/i.

Wonder Books *see* **PRICE STERN SLOAN**.

**WOODBRIDGE PRESS.** PO Box 6189. Santa Barbara, CA 93160. (805) 965-7039. Submissions Editor: Howard Weeks. Founded: 1971. Number of titles published: cumulative—120+, 1989—4. Hardback 10%, softback 90%.

**Subjects of Interest.** **Nonfiction**—general; some emphasis on health, nutrition, food, gardening, cooking.

**Initial Contact.** Book proposal with sample chapters. Include author's credentials.

**Acceptance Policies.** Unagented manuscripts: yes. Disk submissions: no. Response time to initial inquiry: n/i. Average time until publication: n/i. **Advance**: usually none. **Royalty**: 10-15% of net receipts. First run: n/i.

**Marketing Channels.** Distribution houses; direct mail; independent reps; special sales. Subsidiary rights: all (at our discretion).

**Additional Information.** Catalog: write and request.

**WORMWOOD REVIEW PRESS.** PO Box 8840. Stockton, CA 95208-0840. (209) 466-8231. Submissions Editor: Marvin Malone Founded: 1959. Number of titles published: cumulative—14; 1988: 1. Softback %100.

**Subjects of Interest.** **Nonfiction**—contemporary poetry. Recent publications: *Beautiful and Other Long Poems; Children of a Lesser Demagogue.* Do not want: fiction or nonfiction.

**Initial Contact.** Entire manuscript.

**Acceptance Policies.** Unagented manuscripts: yes. Simultaneous submissions: no. Disk submissions: no. Response time to initial inquiry: 4-8 weeks. Average time until publication: 4-8 months. **Advance**: none. **Royalty**: variable. First run: 700.

**Marketing Channels.** Direct mail. Subsidiary rights: all.

**Additional Information.** Concentration on the prose-poem and contemporary concerns. Catalog: SASE.

Write to Sell *see* **COMMUNICATION UNLIMITED.**

Yes Press *see* **DOWN THERE PRESS.**

# Magazines

A single issue of a magazine is constructed from many different manuscripts, including articles, interviews, fiction, columns, reviews, poetry, etc. Some of this material is produced in-house by the publisher's staff, and some is purchased from freelance writers. We collected and organized the following information to help you find and approach those publishers most likely to accept your inquiry and your submission.

## How to Use the Information in This Section

The first paragraph of each entry identifies the magazine, lists its location, and identifies its type. Your initial contact should be directed to the submissions editor named in the entry. The percentage of freelance submissions used and the number of manuscripts purchased per year helps you evaluate your chances of selling to that particular market. If the number of manuscripts purchased is not mentioned, this means that the publisher doesn't pay for submissions, but may pay in copies or services described under Payment in the Acceptance Policies section of each listing.

## Editorial Needs

We divided editorial needs into three main fields: nonfiction, fiction, and other, with suggested formats and word lengths within each field. If you're writing nonfiction, one advantage is the option of selling your basic material several times over by slanting it to fit the themes of different publications. Use our magazine subject index to find various markets for your articles. In the fiction field there is a growing market for short stories—category to mainstream. Payment varies and is often nominal in the case of small literary magazines. However, an added perk is that your published short stories provide portfolio clips which establish your credibility as a writer when you query other markets.

## Initial contact

This information indicates how the editor wants you to contact him or her. You increase your chances for selling to a particular editor if you've followed the suggestions listed in this section. Whether stated or not, always include a SASE.

## Acceptance Policies

**Simultaneous submissions:** If the publisher information says "yes," you may submit your manuscript to several different publishers at the same time, but you must inform each publisher that the manuscript is being simultaneously submitted.

**Response time to initial inquiry:** Be patient and avoid phoning the editor unless you have an agreement with that individual to do so. Two to three weeks *after* the specified response time, you are entitled to send a written request for information concerning the status of your submission. As with any correspondence to a publisher or agent, remember to include your SASE.

**Average time until publication:** Always dependent upon a number of factors, this information provides an approximate idea of how long the publishing process takes after the editor has received and accepted the completed manuscript.

**Payment:** The amount of payment offered for your writing is dependent on length, subject matter, timeliness, your writing skill, and the magazine's current rates. Some of the smaller magazines offer contributor's copies and publish your byline as payment.

Most editors pay when an article is published. Some pay a kill fee if they accept an article and subsequently decide not to publish it. A small number of magazine publishers pay on acceptance, which is the ideal arrangement for authors because they will not have to wait until the magazine is published (often several months) to get paid.

**Writer's expenses on assignment:** Magazine editors rarely authorize the payment of expenses incurred on assignment for authors unknown (and unproven) to them. Assignments are generally reserved for writers with proven ability and reliability.

**Publishing rights:** Most magazine editors purchase first North American serial rights, which means they buy the right to publish your material first in their periodical for distribution in United States and Canada.

For information concerning other rights purchased we suggest that you consult one or more of the books listed in the Book Reference Section.

**Computer print-outs:** Most publishers will now accept computer print-outs but will usually accept dot matrix only if it is of near letter quality. While the majority of magazine publishers want your material submitted in the form of manuscript pages, many will now accept your finished submission on a disk compatible with their computer systems.

## Photography Submissions

We've included the magazine's preference for film type, format (prints or transparencies), and caption information. Payment for photographs may be made separately, or in conjunction with the article submitted. Photographic rights may also be handled in the same manner.

## Additional Information

This section of the entry reflects additional comments by the editor aimed specifically at the writer. Tips are suggestions to you to help insure your success in placing an article with a particular magazine. The best first step toward approaching any magazine is to obtain its writer's guidelines and a sample copy.

## Abbreviations

n/i means no information was given to us by the magazine.
n/a means that this particular question did not apply to the magazine.

---

**ADOLESCENCE.** 3089C Clairmont Dr., Ste. 383. San Diego, CA 92117. (619) 581-9449. Submissions Editor: William Kroll. Type: professional journal. Frequency of publication: quarterly. Circulation: 3000. Freelance submissions: all.

**Editorial Needs. Nonfiction**—articles dealing with adolescents (psychological, psychiatric, physiological, sociological, educational). Suggested word length—feature articles: 2400.

**Initial Contact.** Submission of abstract.

**Acceptance Policies.** Byline given: yes. Simultaneous submissions: no. Response time to initial inquiry: 3 weeks. Average time until publication: 1 year. **Payment:** none. Publishing rights: all. Computer print-outs: yes. Dot matrix: yes. Disk submissions: no.

**Additional Information.** Writer's guidelines: upon request.

**ALTADENA REVIEW.** PO Box 212. Altadena CA 91001. Submissions Editor: Address all mail to "The Editor." Type: poetry. Frequency of publication: irregular. Circulation: 250-300. Freelance submissions: 95-100%.

**Editorial Needs. Nonfiction**—reviews; interviews; book reviews; poetry. Suggested word length—feature articles: 700-1500; 3500 for interviews.

**Initial Contact.** Send 4 to 6 poems.

**Acceptance Policies.** Byline given: yes. Simultaneous submissions: no. Response time to initial inquiry: 3-6 weeks. Average time until publication: 8 months. **Payment:** 2 copies of magazine. Publishing rights: first North American serial rights. Computer print-outs: yes. Dot matrix: must be of very high quality. Disk submissions: no.

**Additional Information.** Writer's guidelines: sample copies $2.50.

**AMELIA.** 329 E Street. Bakersfield, CA 93304. (805) 323-4064. Submissions Editor: Frederick A. Raborg, Jr. Type: literary. Frequency of publication: quarterly. Circulation: 1250 print run. Freelance submissions: 100%. Number of manuscripts bought each year: 30-40 stories; 250-300 poems; 6-8 articles.

**Editorial Needs. Nonfiction**—book excerpts; book reviews; general interest; historical; humor; interview/profile; opinion; photo feature; poetry; travel. Suggested word length—feature articles: 2500. **Fiction**—literary; women's genre; mainstream. Short stories—number per issue: 6-8; per year: 24-40.

**Initial Contact.** Entire article; strong cover letter with bio or acknowledgments is helpful.

**Acceptance Policies.** Byline given: yes. Submit seasonal material 4 months in advance. Simultaneous submissions: yes; inform us. Response time to initial inquiry: 2 weeks to 3 months (latter for serious consideration). Average time until publication: 6 months. **Payment:** $35 on acceptance for fiction; $10 per 1000 words for nonfiction and fiction under 2000 words. Payment made: upon acceptance. Kill Fee: author keeps acceptance payment. Writer's expenses on assignment: no. Publishing rights: first North American serial rights. Computer print-outs: yes. Dot matrix: yes; rarely. Disk submissions: no.

**Photography Submissions.** Format: prints; no smaller than 5x7. Film: black and white; color (cover only). Photographs should include: captions; model releases. **Payment:** $10-$50 (latter for b/w cover); $100 (cover color). Photographic rights: first rights.

**Additional Information.** We also publish two smaller magazines: *Cicada* (Japanese poetry, fiction, essays, art); *SPSM&H* (sonnets, fiction, essays, art). Tips: Be professional and submit your best, neat, clean, polished work. Writer's guidelines: SASE.

**AMERICAN CLAY EXCHANGE.** PO Box 2674. La Mesa, CA 92044-0700. (619) 697-5922. Submissions Editor: Susan N. Cox. Type: American made pottery (china; earthenware, etc.); emphasis on collectables. Frequency of publication: biweekly. Circulation: n/i. Freelance submissions: 95%. Number of manuscripts bought each year: n/i.

**Editorial Needs. Nonfiction**—book reviews; historical; nostalgia; how-to; interview/profile. Suggested word length—feature articles: 1000 maximum; prefer 200-300.

**Initial Contact.** Query letter; or complete manuscript.

**Acceptance Policies:** Byline given: yes. Submit seasonal material 4 months in advance. Response time to initial inquiry: 1-2 months. Average time until publication: 2 months. **Payment:** up to $125. Payment made: upon acceptance. Kill Fee: n/i. Writer's expenses on assignment: n/i. Publishing rights: first North American serial rights. Computer print-outs: yes. Dot matrix: no. Disk submissions: no.

**Photography Submissions.** Format: prints. Film: black and white. Photographs should include: captions. **Payment:** $5. Photographic rights: one-time rights.

**Additional Information.** We are looking for articles dealing with companies operating between 1900-1950 and dinnerware produced during the same period. Tips: When discussing pieces, know the value and include the marks. Writer's guidelines: #10 SASE; sample copy $1.50.

**AMERICAN FITNESS MAGAZINE.** 15250 Ventura Blvd., Ste. 310. Sherman Oaks, CA 91403. (818) 905-0040. Submissions Editor: Susan Niver. Type: health and fitness. Frequency of publication: monthly. Circulation: 29,000. Freelance submissions: n/i. Number of manuscripts bought each year: n/i.

**Editorial Needs. Nonfiction**—general interest; health/fitness; how-to; inspiration; interviews/profile; opinion; photo feature; poetry; self-improvement; travel. Suggested word length—feature articles: 1500; columns: 1500. **Fiction**—fitness related. Short stories—number per issue: 1; per year: 9.

**Initial Contact.** Query letter. Include writing samples.

**Acceptance Policies.** Byline given: yes. Submit seasonal material 4 months in advance. Simultaneous submissions: no. Response time to initial inquiry: 1 month. Average time until publication: varies. **Payment:** n/i. Payment made: upon publication. Kill Fee: no. Writer's expenses on assignment: no. Publishing rights: first North American serial rights. Computer print-outs: yes. Dot matrix: yes. Disk submissions: yes.

**Additional Information.** Writer's guidelines: upon request.

**AMERICAN HANDGUNNER.** 591 Camino de La Reina, Ste. 200. San Diego, CA 92108. (619) 297-5352. Submissions Editor: Cameron Hopkins. Type: handguns; handgun sports; accessories. Frequency of publication: bimonthly. Circulation: 150,000. Freelance submissions: 90%. Number of manuscripts bought each year: 50-70.

**Editorial Needs. Nonfiction**—how to; interview/profile; travel; photo feature; new products. Suggested word length—feature articles: 500-3000; columns: 600-800.

**Initial Contact.** Query letter (include availability of photographs).

**Acceptance Policies.** Byline given: yes. Submit seasonal material 7 months in advance. Response time to initial inquiry: 1 week. Average time until publication: 5-9 months. **Payment:** $100-$400 for unsolicited; $175-$600 for assigned. Payment made: upon publication. Kill Fee: $50. Writer's expenses on assignment: sometimes. Publishing rights: First North American serial rights. Computer print-outs: yes. Dot matrix: letter quality. Disk submissions: n/i.

**Photography Submissions.** Format: slides; contact sheets; 4x5 transparencies; 5x7 prints. Film: black and white; color. Photographs should include: captions; identification of subjects. **Payment:** none for black and white with article; $50-$250 for color. Photographic rights: first North American serial rights.

**Additional Information.** Tips: Writer must have technical knowledge of handguns as well as knowledge of the sport. Writer's guidelines: upon request.

**AMERICAN TRUCKER MAGAZINE.** PO Box 9159. Brea, CA 92622. (714) 528-6600. Submissions Editor: Tom Berg. Type: for professional truck drivers, owners, etc. Frequency of publication: monthly. Circulation: 80,000. Freelance submissions: 10%. Number of manuscripts bought each year: 60+\-.

**Editorial Needs. Nonfiction**—articles which promote positive aspects of trucking industry and owner-operators; humor; fillers. Suggested word length—feature articles: 450-500.

**Initial Contact.** Query letter; availability of photos; phone queries okay.

**Acceptance Policies.** Byline given: yes. Submit seasonal material 3 months in advance. Response time to initial inquiry: 6 weeks. Average time until publication: 3 months. **Payment:** standard. Payment made: upon publication. Kill Fee: n/i. Writer's expenses on assignment: sometimes. Publishing rights: first rights. Computer print-outs: yes. Dot matrix: n/i. Disk submissions: query.

**Photography Submissions.** Format: prints. Film: black and white; color. Photographs should include: captions; model releases. **Payment:** upon publication. Photographic rights: first rights.

**Additional Information.** We look for articles which are conservative in nature and enhance the trucker image. Writer's guidelines: SASE.

**AMPERSAND'S ENTERTAINMENT GUIDE.** 303 N. Glenoaks Blvd., Ste. 600. Burbank, CA 91502. (818) 848-4666. Submissions Editor: Charlotte Wolter. Type: entertainment for the college audience, ages 18-26. Frequency of publication: quarterly. Circulation: 1.3 million. Freelance submissions: 100%. Number of manuscripts bought each year: 15-20.

**Editorial Needs. Nonfiction**—book reviews; trends; profile/interviews; humor; short subjects—on campus, of general entertainment interest. Suggested word length—feature articles: 600-2500; columns: 50-250.

**Initial Contact.** Query letter. State availability of photos.

**Acceptance Policies.** Byline given: yes. Simultaneous submissions: no. Response time to initial inquiry: 2 months. Average time until publication: 3 months. **Payment:** $250-$1000; columns $25-$100. Payment made: upon acceptance. Kill fee: 50%. Writer's expenses on assignment: sometimes. Publishing rights: first-time. Computer print-outs: yes. Dot matrix: letter quality. Disk submissions: no.

**Photography Submissions.** Format: prints. Film: black and white; color. Photographs should include: identification of subjects. **Payment**: $25-material: write or call for next100. Photographic rights: one-time.

**Additional Information.** We prefer professional, experienced writers who have access to entertainment personalities. Tips: Have an interesting, lively style with a new viewpoint directed toward the college audience on a relevant topic. Writer's guidelines: upon request.

## ATHELON, THE JOURNAL OF SPORTS LITERATURE.

San Diego State Univ. San Diego, CA 92182. (619) 265-6220. Submissions Editor: Fred Boe. Type: sports literature. Frequency of publication: biannual. Circulation: 800. Freelance submissions: yes. Number of manuscripts bought each year: n/i.

**Editorial Needs. Nonfiction**—book reviews. **Fiction**—genre; sports literature. Short stories—number per issue: 20.

**Initial Contact.** Query letter.

**Acceptance Policies.** Byline given: yes. Response time to initial inquiry: 4 weeks. Average time until publication: 6 months. **Payment**: $50 honorarium. Payment made: upon publication. Kill fee: no. Writer's expenses on assignment: no. Publishing rights: first rights. Computer print-outs: yes. Dot matrix: yes. Disk submissions: no.

**Additional Information.** *Athelon* (formerly known as *ARETE*) is the journal of the Sports Literature Association. Writer's guidelines: upon request.

## ATHENA INCOGNITO MAGAZINE.

702A Moultrie St. San Francisco, CA 94110. (415) 826-5355. Submissions Editor: Chris Custer, Editor; Ronn Rosen, Associate Editor. Type: literary, experimental. Frequency of publication: quarterly. Circulation: 1100. Freelance submissions: 92%.

**Editorial Needs. Nonfiction**—book reviews; general interest; interviews/profile; poetry; photo essay. Suggested word length—feature articles: 1500. **Fiction**—literary; avant-garde; surrealism; experimental. Short stories—number per issue: 4; per year: 8.

**Initial Contact.** Query letter; entire article. Give a general statement of your writing process. Submissions must accompany a purchase order of either a current issue or back issue ($3 postpaid, SASE); or a year subscription ($6.50). Include SASE.

**Acceptance Policies.** Byline given: no. Submit seasonal material 2 months in advance. Simultaneous submissions: yes. Response time to initial inquiry: 2 weeks-2 months. Average time until publication: 3 months. **Payment**: copies. Publishing rights: simultaneous. Computer print-outs: yes. Dot matrix: yes. Disk submissions: yes.

**Photography Submissions.** Format: prints (any size); negatives; contact sheets. Film: black and white. Photographs should include: captions; model releases. **Payment**: copies. Photographic rights: simultaneous.

**Additional Information.** Prose should be single spaced, under three pages and recognizably surreal or about surrealism. Please, no metric poems, end-rhymes or writings belonging to religions or family albums. Tips: Unpublished/unpopular writers are strongly encouraged to submit. We allow madness in light of the genuine. Writer's guidelines: SASE.

**AUTOMATED BUILDER.** PO Box 120. Carpinteria, CA 93013. (805) 684-7659. Submissions Editor: Don Carlson. Type: managing manufactured and volume home building. Frequency of publication: monthly. Circulation: 25,000. Freelance submissions: 15%. Number of manuscripts bought each year: 15.

**Editorial Needs. Nonfiction**—profile/interview; photo feature; technical aspects; in areas of large volume home builders, manufacturers of mobile homes, modular homes, prefabs, house components. Suggested word length—feature articles: 500-1000.

**Initial Contact.** Query letter; or query by phone (preferred).

**Acceptance Policies.** Byline given: yes. Response time to initial inquiry: 2 weeks. Average time until publication: 3 months. **Payment**: $300+. Payment made: upon acceptance. Kill fee: n/i. Writer's expenses on assignment: n/i. Publishing rights: first North American serial rights. Computer print-outs: yes. Dot matrix: no. Disk submissions: no.

**Photography Submissions.** Format and film: 4x5, 5x7, 8x10 glossy prints (black and white); 35mm transparencies (color). Photographs should include: captions. **Payment**: included with article. Photographic rights: same as article.

**Additional Information.** Projects must be under construction or finished. Tips: Keep articles short and succinct. Writer's guidelines: upon request.

**AXIOS.** 806 S. Euclid St. Fullerton, CA 92632. (714) 526-4952. Submissions Editor: Daniel Gorham. Type: literary. Frequency of publication: monthly. Circulation: 8587. Freelance submissions: 50%. Number of manuscripts bought each year: 24-50.

**Editorial Needs. Nonfiction**—book excerpts; book reviews; historical; inspiration; interview/profile; opinion. Suggested word length—feature articles: 2000.

**Initial Contact.** Query letter.

**Acceptance Policies.** Byline given: yes. Submit seasonal material 5 months in advance. Simultaneous submissions: yes. Response time to initial inquiry: 3-4 months. Average time until publication: 2 months. **Payment**: $.05 a word, depending on quality of the work. Payment made: upon acceptance. Kill fee: yes. Writer's expenses on assignment: no. Publishing rights: first North American serial rights; work-for-hire assignments. Computer print-outs: yes. Dot matrix: yes. Disk submissions: Microsoft Word.

**Additional Information.** We are an international publication of high quality for the serious reader, mostly religious minded. Tips: Be honest.

**BAY AND DELTA YACHTSMAN.** 2019 Clement Ave. Alameda, CA 94501. (415) 865-7500. Submissions Editor: Bill Parks. Type: Northern California recreational boating for owners of small boats and yachts. Frequency of publication: monthly. Circulation: 22,000. Freelance submissions: 45%. Number of manuscripts bought each year: 20+/-.

**Editorial Needs. Nonfiction**—historical; how-to; interview/profile; photo feature; government legislation; personal experience; travel; tips on boating. Suggested word length—feature articles: 2500.

**Initial Contact.** Query letter.

**Acceptance Policies.** Byline given: yes. Simultaneous submissions: yes, if to non-competitive market. Submit seasonal material 3 months in advance. Response time to initial inquiry: 2 month. Average time until publication: 1 month. **Payment**: $1 per column inch. Payment made: upon publication. Kill fee: no. Writer's expenses on assignment: no. Publishing rights: first rights. Computer print-outs: yes. Dot matrix: n/i. Disk submissions: Macintosh; Microsoft Word.

**Photography Submissions.** Format: 8x10 glossy or matte prints. Film: black and white. Photographs should include: captions. **Payment:** $5 per photo. Photographic rights: same as article.

**Additional Information.** Tips: Our readers are knowledgeable about boating. Think of unique ways in which they could increase their knowledge and pleasure of the Northern California waterways and their boats. Writer's guidelines: upon request.

## BAY AREA BABY NEWS MAGAZINE. BAY AREA PARENT NEWS MAGAZINE.

455 Los Gatos, #103. Los Gatos, CA 95032. (408) 356-4121. Submissions Editor: Lynn Berardo.

*Bay Area Baby Magazine.* Type: pregnancy. Frequency of publication: twice yearly. Circulation. 60,000 annually.

*Bay Area Parent News Magazine.* Type: parenting. Frequency of publication: monthly. Circulation: 56,000 monthly.

Freelance submissions: 100%. Number of manuscripts bought each year: 140.

**Editorial Needs.** **Nonfiction**—book excerpts; book reviews; general interest; health/fitness; how-to; humor; inspiration; interview/profile; photo feature; self-improvement; travel; local adventure trips for families, etc.; education issues. Suggested word length—feature articles: 1200-2000; columns: 800.

**Initial Contact.** Query letter; article proposal or entire article. Include samples of previous work.

**Acceptance Policies.** Byline given: yes. Submit seasonal material 4 months in advance. Simultaneous submissions: yes; prefer first time local printing. Response time to initial inquiry: 3 months. Average time until publication: 3 months. **Payment:** $.05 per word. Payment made: upon publication. Kill fee: no. Writer's expenses on assignment: phone expenses. Publishing rights: first rights; simultaneous rights. Computer print-outs: yes. Dot matrix: yes. Disk submissions: IBM or Macintosh; Microsoft Word.

**Photography Submissions.** Format: prints (any size); contact sheets. Film: black and white; color. Photographs should include: model releases; identification of subjects. **Payment:** $10-$35. Photographic rights: one-time use.

## BIRD TALK,

Dedicated to Better Care for Pet Birds. PO Box 6050. Mission Viejo, CA 92690. (714) 855-8822. Submissions Editor: Karyn New. Type: care and training of cage birds. Frequency of publication: monthly. Circulation: 170,000. Freelance submissions: 85%. Number of manuscripts bought each year: 150.

**Editorial Needs.** **Nonfiction**—general interest; historical; nostalgia; how-to; humor; interview/profile; photo feature; medical and legal information; personal experience. Suggested word length—feature articles: 500-3000; columns: editorial; short news items; 300-1200. **Fiction**—pet birds in any genre (talking birds only if its their vocabulary); 2000-3000 words.

**Initial Contact.** Query letter or complete manuscript (nonfiction); complete manuscript (fiction). Include availability of photos.

**Acceptance Policies.** Byline given: yes. Submit seasonal material 7 months in advance. Simultaneous submissions: no. Response time to initial inquiry: 3 weeks. Average time until publication: 6 months. **Payment:** $.10-$.15 nonfiction; $.07+ fiction and columns. Payment made: after publication. Kill fee: n/i. Writer's expenses on assignment: n/i. Publishing rights: first North American serial rights. Computer print-outs: yes. Dot matrix: letter quality. Disk submissions: no.

**Photography Submissions.** Format: contact sheets; prints (preferred); transparencies (color). Film: black and white; color. Photographs should include: model releases;

identification of subjects. **Payment:** $15 (black and white); $50-$150 (color). Photographic rights: one-time rights.

**Additional Information.** We also need articles on building bird-related items; crafts; safe plants; health; nutrition; and human interest. Tips: Read back issues. Writer's guidelines: #10 SASE, 1 first class stamp.

**BLITZ MAGAZINE.** PO Box 48124. Los Angeles, CA 90048-0124. (818) 705-4163. Submissions Editor: Mike McDowell. Type: music (emphasis on early rock and roll). Frequency of publication: bimonthly. Circulation: 5000. Freelance submissions: 40%.

**Editorial Needs.** **Nonfiction**—book reviews; entertainment reviews; historical; opinion; musician interviews. Suggested word length—feature articles: 8 page, double-spaced.

**Initial Contact.** Query letter; entire article; proposed ideas.

**Acceptance Policies.** Byline given: yes. Submit seasonal material 4 months in advance. Simultaneous submissions: yes. Response time to initial inquiry: 1 month. Average time until publication: 6-12 months. **Payment:** copies. Publishing rights: n/a. Computer print-outs: yes. Dot matrix: yes. Disk submissions: no.

**Photography Submissions.** Format: prints, 8 1/2x11 or 5x8. Film: black and white. Photographs should include: identification of subjects. **Payment:** cost of film or developing. Photographic rights: exclusive.

**Additional Information.** Journalistic slant is strictly academic—no sensationalism. We plan to start book publishing in the near future. Tips: Understand the subject matter; not interested in superficial stories. Writer's guidelines: upon request.

**BLUE UNICORN.** 22 Avon Rd. Kensington, CA 94707. (415) 526-8439. Submissions Editor: Ruth G. Iodices; Robert L. Bradley (art editor). Type: literary; we publish only poetry, and use a limited amount of art. Frequency of publication: 3 issues per year. Circulation. 500 Freelance submissions: 100%. Number of manuscripts bought each year: 300.

**Editorial Needs.** **Nonfiction**—poetry.

**Initial Contact.** The poem alone is sufficient, but we do not object to brief query or bio letters.

**Acceptance Policies.** Byline given: yes. Simultaneous submissions: no. Response time to initial inquiry: 3-4 months. Average time until publication: 1 year. **Payment:** copy of issue in which work appears. Payment made: upon publication. Publishing rights: first North American serial rights; we hope poets will give credit to BU for first publication. Computer print-outs: yes. Dot matrix: no. Disk submissions: no.

**Additional Information.** It is a good idea for poets to have read our magazine so they can see what we are looking for. Lacking that, they may send a SASE for brochure. Tips: Write good, well-crafted poetry. Writer's guidelines: SASE.

**BOW AND ARROW HUNTING.** PO Box HH, 34249 Camino Capistrano. Capistrano Beach, CA 92624. Submissions Editor: Roger Combs. Type: bow hunters. Frequency of publication: bimonthly. Circulation: n/i. Freelance submissions: 80%. Number of manuscripts bought each year:

**Editorial Needs.** **Nonfiction**—how-to; techniques; first-person. Suggested word length—feature articles: 1500-2500.

**Initial Contact.** Complete manuscript.

**Acceptance Policies.** Byline given: yes. Response time to initial inquiry: 2 months. Average time until publication: 6 months. **Payment:** $150-$300. Payment made: upon acceptance. Kill fee: n/i. Writer's expenses on assignment: n/i. Publishing rights:n/i. Computer print-outs: yes. Dot matrix: letter quality. Disk submissions: no.

**Photography Submissions.** Good black and white photos are very important; no color. Format: 5x7 or larger. Film: black and white. Photographs should include: n/i. **Payment**: included with article. ($100 for cover transparencies, 35mm). Photographic rights: same as article.

**Additional Information.** Tips: Write with humor and know your archery terms and subject. We will help edit. Writer's guidelines: n/i.

**BREAKFAST WITHOUT MEAT.** 1827 Haight St. #188. San Francisco, CA 94117. Submissions Editor: Gregg Turkington. Type: humor; anti-general interest. Frequency of publication: 3 times per year. Circulation: 1000. Freelance submissions: 6%.

**Editorial Needs.** **Nonfiction**—entertainment reviews; fillers; humor; interview; profile; poetry. Suggested word length—feature articles: 600. **Fiction**—genre; unusual humor. Short stories—number per issue: 1+/-; per year: 3.

**Initial Contact.** Query letter; article.

**Acceptance Policies.** Byline given: yes. Submit seasonal material 6 months in advance. Response time to initial inquiry: 2-6 weeks. Average time until publication: 2-6 months. **Payment**: copies. Publishing rights: first rights. Computer print-outs: yes. Dot matrix: no. Disk submissions: Apple IIe; PIEwriter.

**Additional Information.** Writers should see a copy of the magazine before submitting material. Sample copy: $1.25 ppd. Tips: Don't waste your time sending us stories that are supposed to indicate how cool you are. Writer's guidelines: SASE.

**CA CRAFT CONNECTION NEWSPAPER.** PO Box 1280. Pine Grove, CA 95665-1280. (209) 295-4644. Submissions Editor: E. S. Matz. Type: professional crafters (not for hobbyists). Frequency of publication: bimonthly. Circulation: 6000. Freelance submissions: 90%. Number of manuscripts bought each year: n/i.

**Editorial Needs.** **Nonfiction**—book reviews; how-to; interview/profile; marketing crafts; homebased crafts business. Suggested word length—feature articles: up to 1000.

**Initial Contact.** Entire article.

**Acceptance Policies.** Byline given: yes. Submit seasonal material 2 months in advance. Simultaneous submissions: yes. Response time to initial inquiry: 1 week. Average time until publication: n/i. **Payment**: $.05 for original article; $.03 for reprint. Payment made: upon publication. Kill fee: no. Writer's expenses on assignment: no. Publishing rights: n/i. Computer print-outs: yes. Dot matrix: yes. Disk submissions: no.

**Photography Submissions.** Format: prints. Film: black and white; color. Photographs should include: identification of subjects. **Payment**: n/i. Photographic rights: n/i.

**Additional Information.** We are a trade publication for professional craftspeople. We include a show calendar. Writer's guidelines: call or write.

**CALIFORNIA.** 11601 Wilshire Blvd., Ste. 1800. Los Angeles, CA 90025. (213) 479-6511. Submissions Editor: Rebecca Levy. Type: any subject with a California slant. Frequency of publication: monthly. Circulation: n/i. Freelance submissions: 90%. Number of manuscripts bought each year: a large number.

**Editorial Needs.** **Nonfiction**—book excerpts; book reviews; entertainment reviews; fillers; general interest; health/fitness; historical; how-to; humor; inspiration; interview/profile; photo feature; poetry; self-improvement; travel. Suggested word length—feature articles: we read anything, any length. **Fiction**—state of California. Short stories—per year: 2-3.

**Initial Contact.** Query letter.

**Acceptance Policies.** Byline given: yes. Submit seasonal material 2 months in advance. Simultaneous submissions: yes. Response time to initial inquiry: 6 weeks. Average time until publication: 3-5 months. **Payment**: varies. Payment made: upon publication. Kill fee: 25%. Writer's expenses on assignment: sometimes. Publishing rights: first rights.

Computer print-outs: yes. Dot matrix: yes. Disk submissions: no.

**Photography submissions.** Format and film: black and white prints; color transparencies. Photographs should include: captions; model releases; identification of subjects. **Payment:** varies. Photographic rights: first-time rights.

**Additional Information.** Tips: Be sure your article involves California and read the magazine before making a submission. Writer's guidelines: none.

**CALIFORNIA BUSINESS.** 4221 Wilshire Blvd., Ste. 400. Los Angeles, CA 90010. (213) 937-5820. Submissions Editor: Joan Yee. Type: business in California, Mexico and the Pacific Rim. Frequency of publication: monthly. Circulation: 130,000. Freelance submissions: 80%. Number of manuscripts bought each year: 90+/-.

**Editorial Needs. Nonfiction**—book excerpts; interview/profile; business exposé. Suggested word length—feature articles: 2000-4000.

**Initial Contact.** Query letter. State availability of photos.

**Acceptance Policies.** Byline given: yes. Submit seasonal material 6 months in advance. Response time to initial inquiry: 1 month. Average time until publication: 3 months. **Payment**: $1500-$4000 (assigned). Payment made: upon acceptance. Kill fee: 30%. Writer's expenses on assignment: yes. Publishing rights: first North American serial rights. Computer print-outs: yes. Dot matrix: letter quality. Disk submissions: query.

**Photography Submissions.** Format: transparencies. Film: Photographs should include: captions; model releases. **Payment**: Photographic rights: one-time rights.

**Additional Information.** Writer's guidelines: #10 SASE, 4 first class stamps.

**CALIFORNIA FARMER.** 731 Market St. San Francisco, CA 94103. (415) 495-3340. Submissions Editor: Richard Smoley. Type: agricultural (California only). Frequency of publication: semimonthly. Circulation: 53,000. Freelance submissions: 60%. Number of manuscripts bought each year: 80.

**Editorial Needs. Nonfiction**—how-to. Suggested word length—feature articles: 1500-2000.

**Initial Contact.** Query letter. Include resumé; published clips.

**Acceptance Policies.** Byline given: yes. Simultaneous submissions: no. Response time to initial inquiry: 4 weeks. Average time until publication: 1-3 months. **Payment:** $400 plus expenses for a 1500-2000 word article. Payment made: upon acceptance. Kill fee: only for assigned stories. Writer's expenses on assignment: yes. Publishing rights: first North American serial rights. Computer print-outs: yes. Dot matrix: yes. Disk submissions: no.

**Photography Submissions.** Format: transparencies. Film: black and white; color. Photographs should include: captions; identification of subjects. **Payment:** $50-125 for color (depending upon size used in magazine); $35-$100 for black and white. Photographic rights: first rights.

**CALIFORNIA HIGHWAY PATROLMAN.** 2030 V Street. Sacramento, CA 95818. (916) 452-6751. Submissions Editor: Carol Perri. Type: general interest. Frequency of publication: monthly. Circulation: 18,000. Freelance submissions: 80%. Number of manuscripts bought each year: 100-150.

**Editorial Needs.** **Nonfiction**—general interest; health/fitness; historical; humor; interview/profile; photo feature; self-improvement; travel; safety. Suggested word length—feature articles: as long as necessary. Short stories—yes. number per issue: n/i.

**Initial Contact.** Query letter; outline. Include author's expertise in area; SASE.

**Acceptance Policies.** Byline given: yes. Submit seasonal material 3-6 months in advance. Simultaneous submissions: yes; inform us where else submitted or previously published. Response time to initial inquiry: 2 months. Average time until publication: varies. **Payment**: $.025 per word. Payment made: upon publication. Kill fee: no. Writer's expenses on assignment: no. Publishing rights: one-time use. Computer print-outs: yes. Dot matrix: yes. Disk submissions: no.

**Photography Submissions.** Format: any size, but very clear. Film: black and white. Photographs should include: captions; identification of subjects; credit line. **Payment**: $5 each. Photographic rights: one-time use.

**Additional Information.** We are a two-person staff, so rejects are sent back immediately, but patience is requested for others. Tips: Good writing! Writer's guidelines: upon request.

**CALIFORNIA HORSE REVIEW.** PO Box 2437. Fair Oaks, CA 95628. (916) 638-1519. Submissions Editor: Jennifer F. Meyer. Type: all breeds horse magazine. Frequency of publication: monthly. Circulation: 6500. Freelance submissions: 70%. Number of manuscripts bought each year: 24.

**Editorial Needs.** **Nonfiction**—book reviews; fillers; how-to; humor; interview/profile; video reviews. Suggested word length—feature articles: 500-1500.

**Initial Contact.** Entire article.

**Acceptance Policies.** Byline given: yes. Simultaneous submissions: yes; inform us, specific details. Response time to initial inquiry: 6-8 weeks. Average time until publication: 2-3 months. **Payment**: $25-$125. Payment made: upon publication. Kill fee: no. Writer's expenses on assignment: no. Publishing rights: first North American serial rights. Computer print-outs: yes. Dot matrix: no. Disk submissions: no.

**Photography Submissions.** Format: prints, 5x7. Film: black and white. Photographs should include: captions; identification of subjects. **Payment**: purchased with article only. Photographic rights: first-time rights.

**Additional Information.** Writer's guidelines: SASE.

**CALIFORNIA JOURNAL.** 1714 Capitol Ave. Sacramento, CA 95814. (916) 444-2840. Submissions Editor: Richard Zeiger. Type: politics and government. Frequency of publication: monthly. Circulation: 19,000. Freelance submissions: 75%. Number of manuscripts bought each year: 50+.

**Editorial Needs.** **Nonfiction**—politics and government. Suggested word length—feature articles: open.

**Initial Contact.** Query letter; entire article. Include background of author; clips.

**Acceptance Policies.** Byline given: yes. Simultaneous submissions: no. Response time to initial inquiry: 1 month. Average time until publication: 1-2 months. **Payment**: negotiable. Payment made: upon publication. Kill fee: no. Writer's expenses on assignment: no. Publishing rights: all. Computer print-outs: yes. Dot matrix: yes. Disk submissions: IBM PC.

**Additional Information.** Writer's guidelines: upon request.

## CALIFORNIA LAWYER.
1390 Market St., Ste. 10106. San Francisco, CA 94102. (415) 558-9888. Submissions Editors: Thomas K. Brom; Gordon Smith (illustrations). Type: trade. Frequency of publication: monthly. Circulation: 120,000. Freelance submissions: 80%. Number of manuscripts bought each year: 60.

**Editorial Needs. Nonfiction**—current legal affairs; in-depth legal features and profiles; book reviews; interview/profile; current legal affairs reporting. Suggested word length—feature articles: 3000; news articles 750-1000; columns: 2000.

**Initial Contact.** Query letter; article proposal with subject outline; entire article. Include previously published work.

**Acceptance Policies.** Byline given: yes. Simultaneous submissions: no. Response time to initial inquiry: 2 weeks. Average time until publication: 2 months. **Payment:** news section to $200; departments $300-$400; features $600-$1000. Payment made: upon acceptance. Kill fee: 1/3 article fee. Writer's expenses on assignment: yes. Publishing rights: first North American serial rights; reprints by nonprofit, educational organizations. Computer print-outs: yes. Dot matrix: yes. Disk submissions: 3 1/2" IBM.

**Photography Submissions.** Format: slides; prints; contact sheets. Film: black and white. Photographs should include: model releases; identification of subjects. **Payment:** varies by assignment.

**Additional Information.** Tips: Knowledge of the law and legal practice vital. Writer's guidelines: SASE.

## CALIFORNIA NURSING REVIEW.
1470 Halford Ave. Santa Clara, CA 95051. (408) 249-5877. Submissions Editor: Cledith Rice. Type: nursing. Frequency of publication: every 2 months. Circulation: 180,000 California RNs. Freelance submissions: n/i. Number of manuscripts bought each year: n/i.

**Editorial Needs. Nonfiction**—articles related to nursing. Suggested word length—feature articles: n/i.

**Initial Contact.** Article proposal with subject outline. Include resumé of writer.

**Acceptance Policies.** Byline given: n/i. Submit seasonal material 4 months in advance. Simultaneous submissions: no. Response time to initial inquiry: 6 weeks. Average time until publication: 2-4 months. **Payment:** varies. Payment made: upon publication. Kill fee: no. Writer's expenses on assignment: no. Publishing rights: all rights. Computer print-outs: yes. Dot matrix: no. Disk submissions: yes.

**Photography Submissions.** Format: prints. Film: color. Photographs should include: captions; model releases; identification of subjects. **Payment:** n/i. Photographic rights: n/i.

**Additional Information.** Writer's guidelines: upon request.

## CALIFORNIA STATE POETRY QUARTERLY (CQ).
1200 E. Ocean Blvd., #64. Long Beach, CA 90802. (213) 495-0925. Submissions Editor: John M. Brander. Type: poetry. Frequency of publication: weekly. Circulation: 700. Freelance submissions: n/i.

**Editorial Needs. Nonfiction**—poetry.

**Initial Contact.** Entire article.

**Acceptance Policies.** Byline given: n/i. Simultaneous submissions: no. Response time to initial inquiry: 3 months. Average time until publication: 3-6 months. **Payment:** copies. Publishing rights: n/i. Computer print-outs: yes. Dot matrix: no. Disk submissions: no.

**Additional Information.** Writer's guidelines: upon request.

**CAR CRAFT.** 8490 Sunset Blvd. Los Angeles, CA 90069. (213) 657-5100, ext 345. Submissions Editor: Cam Benty. Type: audience 18-34, owners of 1949 and newer muscle cars. Frequency of publication: monthly. Circulation: 400,000. Number of manuscripts bought each year: 2-10.

**Editorial Needs.** **Nonfiction**—how-to; drag features; do-it-yourself. Suggested word length—feature articles: any.

**Initial Contact.** Query letter.

**Acceptance Policies.** Byline given: yes. Response time to initial inquiry: n/i. Average time until publication: n/i. **Payment**: $100-$200 page; rate higher for complete submissions (photos, captions, titles, etc.). Payment made: upon publication. Kill fee: n/i. Writer's expenses on assignment: n/i. Publishing rights: all rights. Computer print-outs: yes. Dot matrix: n/i. Disk submissions: no.

**Photography Submissions.** Will purchase separate photos. Format and film: 8x10 glossy (black and white); 35mm or 2 1/4x2 1/4 (color). Photographs should include: caption. **Payment**: $30 black and white; color, negotiable. Photographic rights: n/i.

**Additional Information.** Tips: Review past issues before coming up with ideas or making submissions.

**CAT FANCY.** PO Box 6050. Mission Viejo, CA 92690. (714) 855-8822. Submissions Editor: Linda Lewis. Type: for cat owners. Frequency of publication: monthly. Circulation: 200,000. Freelance submissions: 80-90%. Number of manuscripts bought each year: 80.

**Editorial Needs.** **Nonfiction**—fillers; historical; how-to; photo feature; personal experience; medical; technical. Suggested word length—feature articles: 500-3000. columns: unique items; cartoons. 100-500 words. **Fiction**—cats in any genre (none that speak).

**Initial Contact.** Query letter or complete manuscript (nonfiction); complete manuscript (fiction).

**Acceptance Policies.** Byline given: yes. Submit seasonal material 4 months in advance. Response time to initial inquiry: 6 weeks. Average time until publication: n/i. **Payment**: $.05 per word (more for complete story/photo submission); $25-$30 (fillers). Payment made: after publication. Kill fee: n/i. Writer's expenses on assignment: n/i. Publishing rights: first North American serial rights. Computer print-outs: yes. Dot matrix: n/i. Disk submissions: no.

**Photography Submissions.** will also purchase separate photos. Format and film: 8x10 glossy prints (black and white); 35mm or 2 1/4 x 2 1/4 transparencies (color). Photographs should include: model release. **Payment**: $15 (black and white); $50-$150 (color). Photographic rights: n/i.

**Additional Information.** Tips: We need the longer well-researched article rather than fillers. Writer's guidelines: SASE.

**CHIC.** 9171 Wilshire Blvd. Ste. 300. Beverly Hills, CA 90210. Submissions Editor: Doug Oliver. Type: men's. Frequency of publication: monthly. Circulation: 100,000. Freelance submissions: 40%. Number of manuscripts bought each year: 18+/-.

**Editorial Needs.** **Nonfiction**—interview/profile (celebrities and personalities); national items of interest. Suggested word length—feature articles: 4500. Columns: Odds and Ends (refer to publication), 100-300 words; Third Degree, 2000 words. **Fiction**—must involve sex and eroticism which evolves naturally from the plot and is predominate; any genre. No stories with drugs, sex with minors, incest and cruelty.

**Initial Contact.** Query letter.

**Acceptance Policies.** Byline given: yes (unless requested otherwise). Simultaneous submissions: no. Response time to initial inquiry: 2 months. Average time until publication: 3

months. **Payment**: $750 (nonfiction); $50-$350 (columns). Payment made: 1 month after acceptance. Kill fee: 20%. Writer's expenses on assignment: sometimes. Publishing rights: all rights. Computer print-outs: yes. Dot matrix: letter quality. Disk submissions: no.

**Additional Information.** Our audience are men who are college-educated and have sophisticated tastes in the general areas of politics, entertainment and sports. Writer's guidelines: #10 SASE.

**CHURCH EDUCATOR.** 2861-C Saturn St. Brea, CA 92621. (714) 961-0622. Submissions Editors: Robert G. Davidson (youth and adult); Linda Davidson (children's). Type: Christian education. Frequency of publication: monthly. Circulation: 4000. Freelance submissions: 60%. Number of manuscripts bought each year: 120.

**Editorial Needs. Nonfiction**—book reviews; how-to's on church educator programs. Suggested word length—feature articles: 700-2000. **Fiction**—children's.

**Initial Contact.** Entire article.

**Acceptance Policies.** Byline given: yes. Submit seasonal material 6 months in advance. Simultaneous submissions: yes. Response time to initial inquiry: 2-3 months. Average time until publication: 4-5 months. **Payment**: $.03 per word. Payment made: upon publication. Kill fee: no. Writer's expenses on assignment: no. Publishing rights: all rights. Computer print-outs: yes. Dot matrix: yes. Disk submissions: no.

**Photography Submissions.** Format: prints, 3 1/2x5. Film: black and white. Photographs should include: captions; model releases; identification of subjects. **Payment**: $5-$10. Photographic rights: n/i.

**Additional Information.** Our readers are mostly main-line Christian protestants, so do not submit conservative, fundamental type articles. Writer's guidelines: upon request to Linda Davidson.

**CINEMASCORE: THE FILM MUSIC JOURNAL.** PO Box 70868. Sunnyvale, CA 94086. (408) 247-4289. Submissions Editor: Randall D. Larson. Type: arts and entertainment. Frequency of publication: irregular/annual. Circulation: 2000. Freelance submissions: 5% but growing. Number of manuscripts bought each year: 1-2.

**Editorial Needs. Nonfiction**—book reviews; entertainment reviews; interview/profile. Suggested word length—feature articles: 3000-4000.

**Initial Contact.** Query letter.

**Acceptance Policies.** Byline given: yes. Simultaneous submissions: no. Response time to initial inquiry: 1-4 weeks. Average time until publication: 6-24 months or more. **Payment**: flat rate $15-$100 for major research pieces/ interviews, with approval. Usual payment is in copies/subscriptions for most material. Payment made: half on acceptance/ balance on publication. Kill fee: the half payment author received on acceptance. Writer's expenses on assignment: no (with certain exceptions). Publishing rights: first North American serial rights. Computer print-outs: yes. Dot matrix: yes. Disk submissions: ASCII for IBM PC or Microsoft Word.

**Photography Submissions.** Format: 35mm or 8x10 glossy. Film: black and white; color. Photographs should include: identification of subjects. **Payment**: Inclusive with text; or in copies for file photos. Photographic rights: n/i.

**Additional Information.** We feature behind-the-scenes interviews and historical analysis of music for motion pictures. Tips: Be familiar with film music, our magazine, and be able to contact film music professionals. Writer's guidelines: Best way is to look at a copy of magazine.

**COYDOG REVIEW.** PO Box 2608. Aptos, CA 95001. (408) 761-1824. Submissions Editor: Candida Lawrence. Type: literary—poems, essays, stories, art. Frequency of publication: annual. Circulation: 500. Freelance submissions: 100%.

**Editorial Needs. Nonfiction**— interview; poetry; satire; criticism; articles; art. **Fiction**—book excerpts; women's; literary (must be excellent). Short stories—number per issue: 4; per year: 4.

**Initial Contact.** n/i.

**Acceptance Policies.** Byline given: n/i. Simultaneous submissions: yes. Response time to initial inquiry: 1 month. Average time until publication: 6 months. **Payment**: 2 copies. Publishing rights: copyright reverts to author. Computer print-outs: yes. Dot matrix: n/i. Disk submissions: no.

**Additional Information.** Editors at present like narrative poetry, strange stories—no easy/happy life stories.

**CRAZY QUILT LITERARY QUARTERLY.** 3141 Adams Ave. San Diego, CA 92116. (619) 576-0104. Submissions Editors: Marsh Cassady, Steve Smith (fiction); Nancy Churnin (drama); Jackie Cicchetti (poetry); Edee Suslick (art); Leif Fearn (nonfiction). Type: literary. Frequency of publication: quarterly. Circulation: 150. Freelance submissions: 100%.

**Editorial Needs. Nonfiction**—about writers; literary criticism. **Fiction**—literary; science fiction. Short stories—number per issue: 3-4; per year: 12-15. Drama (one act plays): 1-4. Poetry: 15-60.

**Initial Contact.** Entire article.

**Acceptance Policies.** Byline given: yes. Simultaneous submissions: yes. Response time to initial inquiry: 8-10 weeks. Average time until publication: 9-12 months. **Payment**: 2 copies per accepted submission. Payment made: upon publication. Publishing rights: first North American serial rights. Computer print-outs: yes. Dot matrix: yes. Disk submissions: no.

**Photography Submissions.** Format: n/i. Film: black and white. Photographs should include: n/i. **Payment**: 2 copies per photo. Photographic rights: first North American serial rights.

**Additional Information.** Writer's guidelines: SASE.

**CREATIVE WITH WORDS PUBLICATIONS.** PO Box 223226. Carmel, CA 93922. (408) 649-1862. Submissions Editor: Brigitta Geltrich. Type: general interest; children (for and by); senior citizens (for and by); folklore; poetry and prose. Frequency of publication: 2-3 times yearly. Circulation: varies. Freelance submissions: 100%.

**Editorial Needs. Nonfiction**—varies. Suggested word length—feature articles: 1000. **Fiction**—children's; folklore. Short stories—number per issue: depends on topic; publish according to theme.

**Initial Contact.** Query letter. Writer should state his/her age.

**Acceptance Policies.** Byline given: yes. Submit seasonal material 2-6 months in advance. Simultaneous submissions: no. Response time to initial inquiry: 2 months. Average time until publication: depends on theme and deadline. **Payment**: 20% reduction in cost of copies. Publishing rights: first rights. Computer print-outs: yes. Dot matrix: yes. Disk submissions: TR-80 (TRSDOS: Radio Shack).

**Additional Information.** Tips: Be proficient, yet brief. Include SASE. Accept set rules. Writer's guidelines: SASE.

**CRITIQUE.** PO Box 11368. Santa Rosa, CA 95406. (707) 525-9401. Submissions Editor: Bob Banner. Type: exposing consensus reality. Frequency of publication: 3 times per year. Circulation: 5000. Freelance submissions: 95%; 40% solicited freelance. Number of manuscripts bought each year: 80.

**Editorial Needs. Nonfiction**—book excerpts; book reviews; fillers; historical; humor; inspiration; interview/profile; opinion; political analysis. Suggested word length—feature articles: 3000; columns: 1000. **Fiction**—science fiction; fantasy; avant-garde; relating to our purpose of exposing consensus reality.

**Initial Contact.** Query letter; article proposal with subject outline. Include brief bio; SASE.

**Acceptance Policies.** Byline given: yes. Simultaneous submissions: yes. Response time to initial inquiry: 2 months. Average time until publication: 3 weeks to 3 months. **Payment:** 3 free copies; to $100; ad exchange. Payment made: upon publication. Kill fee: no. Writer's expenses on assignment: no. Publishing rights: n/i. Computer print-outs: yes. Dot matrix: yes. Disk submissions: Macintosh (preferable).

**Photography Submissions.** Format: prints. Film: black and white. Photographs should include: captions; identification of subjects. **Payment:** $10-$20. Photographic rights: none.

**Additional Information.** Tips: Be sure to see a copy of our publication. Writer's guidelines: upon request.

**CUM NOTIS VARIORUM.** Music Library, 240 Morrison Hall. Berkeley, CA 94720. (415) 642-2624. Submissions Editor: Ann Basart. Type: music library newsletter. Frequency of publication: 10 issues per year. Circulation: 675. Freelance submissions: 20-30%.

**Editorial Needs. Nonfiction**—book reviews; humor; bibliographies; indexes; discographies; reports of music and library conferences, festivals.

**Initial Contact.** Query letter; or article proposal with subject outline; or entire article. Include brief autobiographical statement, if author unknown to us.

**Acceptance Policies.** Byline given: yes. Submit seasonal material 2 months in advance. Simultaneous submissions: yes; inform us. Response time to initial inquiry: 1 month. Average time until publication: 2 months. **Payment:** none. Publishing rights: author holds copyright. Computer print-outs: yes. Dot matrix: yes. Disk submissions: IBM compatible.

**Additional Information.** Writer's guidelines: upon request.

**CURRENT WORLD LEADERS.** 800 Garden St., Ste. D. Santa Barbara, CA 93101. (805) 965-5010. Submissions Editor: Thomas S. Garrison. Type: international relations; comparative politics. Frequency of publication: 8 issues per year. Circulation: 1000. Freelance submissions: 25%. Number of manuscripts bought each year: 10-15.

**Editorial Needs. Nonfiction**—historical; political, especially international politics. Suggested word length—feature articles: 3500-6000.

**Initial Contact.** Article proposal with subject outline. Include evidence of author's expertise in subject area.

**Acceptance Policies.** Byline given: yes. Simultaneous submissions: no. Response time to initial inquiry: 2 weeks. Average time until publication: 6 months. **Payment:** $25-$100 per article. Payment made: upon publication. Kill fee: no. Writer's expenses on assignment: no. Publishing rights: first rights. Computer print-outs: yes. Dot matrix: yes. Disk submissions: Word Perfect 4.2 or 5.0.

**Additional Information.** Writer's guidelines: upon request.

**DANCE TEACHER NOW.** 3020 Beacon Blvd. West Sacramento, CA. 95691. (916) 373-0201. Submission Editor: Martin A. David. Type: trade publication for dance. Frequency of publication: 9 times per year. Circulation: 7000. Freelance submissions: n/i. Number of manuscripts bought each year: 30.

**Editorial Needs.** **Nonfiction**—book reviews; health/fitness; how-to; humor; inspiration; interview/profile; self-improvement; travel. Suggested word length—feature articles: 2500.

**Initial Contact.** Query letter; article proposal with subject outline; entire article.

**Acceptance Policies.** Byline given: yes. Submit seasonal material 4-6 months in advance. Simultaneous submissions: yes; if not being submitted in dance industry. Response time to initial inquiry: 4 weeks. Average time until publication: 4-6 months. **Payment**: $150-$300; varies with length, complexity. Payment made: upon publication. Kill fee: usually 50%. Writer's expenses on assignment: some; usually telephone. Publishing rights: all rights; released back to author, on request, in most cases. Computer print-outs: yes. Dot matrix: letter quality. Disk submissions: IBM compatible; Word Star, Word Perfect; ASCII.

**Photography Submissions.** Format and film: 5x7 prints, black and white; color transparencies for cover. Photographs should include: captions; model releases; identification of subjects. **Payment**: $20. Photographic rights: one-time.

**Additional Information.** Tips: Prefer no phone queries. Writer's guidelines: upon request.

**DOG FANCY.** PO Box 6050. Mission Viejo, CA 92690. Submissions Editor: Linda Lewis. *See* information under **CAT FANCY**.

**THE DOLPHIN LOG.** (The Cousteau Society). 8440 Santa Monica Blvd. Los Angeles, CA 90069. (213) 656-4422. Submissions Editor: Pamela Stacey. Type: (for children) ecology; marine biology; environment; natural history. Frequency of publication: bimonthly. Circulation: 85,000. Freelance submissions: 50%.

**Editorial Needs.** **Nonfiction**—any area (including games, experiments, humor, jokes, crafts and articles) directly related to the ecological global water system which will encourage young people to understand and respect the environment. Suggested word length—feature articles: 500-1000.

**Initial Contact.** Query letter; or complete manuscript.

**Acceptance Policies.** Byline given: yes. Submit seasonal material 4 months in advance. Response time to initial inquiry: 2 months. Average time until publication: n/i. **Payment**: $50-$150. Payment made: upon publication. Kill fee: no. Writer's expenses on assignment: no. Publishing rights: one-time; translation. Computer print-outs: yes. Dot matrix: letter quality. Disk submissions: IBM-PC (ASCII).

**Photography Submissions.** Send with manuscript. Only duplicates accepted, no originals. Format: n/i. Film: n/i. Photographs should include: identification of subject. **Payment**: $25-$100 per photo. Photographic rights: one-time; translation.

**Additional Information.** Writers should be current in their knowledge and able to write in a lively style appropriate for an audience ages 7-15. Tips: Make sure material is accurate. Feature an interesting marine animal, and make it interesting. No fiction or talking animals. Writer's guidelines: SASE; sample copy $2, SASE.

**DR. DOBB'S JOURNAL.** 501 Galveston Dr. Redwood City, CA 94061. (415) 366-3600. Submissions Editor: Jon Erickson, Kent Porter, or Michael Floyd (proposals); Kathleen Evans Ralston (manuscripts). Type: for computer programmers. Frequency of publication: monthly; plus 2 special issues a year. Circulation: 75,000. Freelance submissions: 90%. Number of manuscripts bought each year: 100+/-.

**Editorial Needs. Nonfiction**—book reviews; product reviews; opinion; articles for programers, often including listings. Suggested word length—feature articles: 2500+/-; reviews: 500-1000.

**Initial Contact.** Article proposal with outline. Include author's address, home and work phone; social security number.

**Acceptance Policies.** Byline given: yes. Submit seasonal material 3 months in advance. Simultaneous submissions: only in proposal form rather than full manuscript. Response time to initial inquiry: 1 month. Average time until publication: 6 months. **Payment**: varies, depending on length of article, completeness, and author skill and knowledge. Payment made: $50 on acceptance; remainder upon publication. Kill fee: $50. Writer's expenses on assignment: depends. Publishing rights: all. Computer print-outs: yes; double spaced. Dot matrix: yes. Disk submissions: pure ASCII unformatted with control codes on either PC compatible (5 1/4 DS/DD) or Macintosh disk.

**Photography Submissions.** We encourage charts, listings, etc.

**Additional Information.** *DDJ* readers are advanced programmers, and *DDJ* is primarily a software magazine. Tips: If you submit an article but don't hear from us for a while, call us. Writer's guidelines: write or call Kathleen Evans Ralston.

**DVORAK DEVELOPMENTS.** (Publication of Freelance Communications). PO Box 1895. Upland, CA 91785. (714) 985-3465. Submissions Editor: Randy Cassingham. Type: promotion of Dvorak keyboard. Frequency of publication: quarterly. Circulation: 1000+. Freelance submissions: 30%. Number of manuscripts bought each year: 10.

**Editorial Needs. Nonfiction**—case studies of Dvorak users (area most open to freelancers); book reviews; historical; interview/profile; application notes; software/hardware reviews; current research on our field. Suggested word length—feature articles: 1000.

**Initial Contact.** Query letter.

**Acceptance Policies.** Byline given: yes. Submit seasonal material 6 months in advance. Simultaneous submissions: no. Response time to initial inquiry: 2 weeks. Average time until publication: 2 months. **Payment**: $24-$50. Payment made: upon acceptance. Kill fee: 33%. Writer's expenses on assignment: no. Publishing rights: first North American serial rights; second serial rights (sometimes). Computer print-outs: yes. Dot matrix: yes. Disk submissions: prefer IBM 5 1/4 ; Word Perfect.

**Photography Submissions.** Format: contact sheets. Film: black and white. Photographs should include: captions; identification of subjects. **Payment**: negotiable. Photographic rights: one-time use and reprint.

**Additional Information**: Writers guidelines: SASE.

**EASYRIDERS MAGAZINE.** 28210 Dorothy Ave. Agoura Hills, CA 91301. (818) 889-8740. Submissions Editor: Keith Ball. Type: men's magazine for riders of Harley-Davidsons. Frequency of publication: monthly. Circulation: 300,000. Freelance submissions: 40%. Number of manuscripts bought each year: 24-30.

**Editorial Needs. Nonfiction**—how-to; humor; interview/profile; opinion; photo feature. Suggested word length—feature articles: 3000-5000. **Fiction**—motorcycle (Harley-Davidson) related. Short stories—number per issue: 2. per year: 24.

**Initial Contact.** Query letter; article proposal with subject outline.

**Acceptance Policies.** Byline given: yes. Submit seasonal material 4 months in advance. Simultaneous submissions: yes. Response time to initial inquiry: 4-6 weeks. Average time until publication: 3-4 months. **Payment**: $.10-$.15 per word. Payment made: upon publication. Kill fee: n/i. Writer's expenses on assignment: yes. Publishing rights: all rights; work-for-hire assignments. Computer print-outs: yes. Dot matrix: yes. Disk submissions: n/i.

**Photography Submissions.** Format: negatives; transparencies. Film: black and white; color. Photographs should include: identification of subjects. **Payment**: $40 (color); $30 (black and white). Photographic rights: first rights.

**Additional Information.** Our magazine has a macho male audience who rides Harley-Davidson motorcycles only. Writer's guidelines: upon request.

**ECPHORIZER.** 481 Century Dr. Campbell, CA 95008. (408) 378-8820. Submissions Editor: Michael J. Eager. Type: Literary and idea oriented. The name means to take a concept from a latent form to a real state. Frequency of publication: 6 times per year. Circulation: 350. Freelance submissions: 85%.

**Editorial Needs. Nonfiction**—book excerpts; book reviews; fillers; general interest; historical; humor; interview/profile; opinion; poetry; travel. Suggested word length—feature articles: 1000-3000. **Fiction**—literary; women's; genre. Short stories—number per issue: 5.

**Initial Contact.** Query letter; article proposal with subject outline; entire article.

**Acceptance Policies.** Byline given: yes. Submit seasonal material 4 months in advance. Simultaneous submissions: yes. Response time to initial inquiry: 2 weeks. Average time until publication: 2-3 months. **Payment**: copies. Publishing rights: n/i. Computer print-outs: yes. Dot matrix: yes. Disk submissions: IBM PC; ASCII; Macintosh MacWrite.

**Photography Submissions.** Format: prints, 5x7 or larger. Film: black and white. Photographs should include: captions; model releases; identification of subjects. **Payment**: none. Photographic rights: n/i.

**Additional Information.** Ecphorize means to evoke ideas. We are a magazine oriented toward the Mensa community, with interest in articles which are interesting, provocative, or humorous.

**ELLIPSIS.** 1176 E. Campbell Ave. Campbell, CA 95008. (408) 559-7283, 354-1481. Submissions Editor: Jonathan Ther. Type: literary. Frequency of publication: quarterly. Circulation: 200, and growing. Freelance submissions: 100%. Number of manuscripts bought each year: 70-80.

**Editorial Needs. Nonfiction**—humor; poetry; opinion section is open to essays of a philosophical bent. Suggested word length—feature articles: 1500-5000. **Fiction**—literary; women's genre; avant-garde. Short stories—number per issue: 4; per year: 16.

**Initial Contact.** Query letter; entire article.

**Acceptance Policies.** Byline given: yes. Simultaneous submissions: yes; inform us. Response time to initial inquiry: 1 month. Average time until publication: 3 months. **Payment**: $5 minimum; $.01 per word; 2 copies of issue and discount for additional copies. Payment made: upon publication. Kill fee: $5 minimum or 50%. Writer's expenses on assignment: no. Publishing rights: first North American serial rights; second serial rights (on occasion). Computer print-outs: yes. Dot matrix: yes. Disk submissions: Macintosh.

**Additional Information.** We are new. We are interested in unpublished writers. We are looking for unique use of language—stories and poetry which reflects the human condition with sensitivity, grace, depth and humor. Tips: Do not send personally cathartic writing unless it is prize-winning material! Writer's guidelines: SASE.

**EMMY MAGAZINE.** Academy of Television Arts & Sciences). 3500 W. Olive, Ste. 700. Burbank, CA 91505-4628. Editor/Publisher: Hank Rieger. Type: focus on thoughtful analysis of television's impact on society. Magazine in read by TV industry as well as general subscribers, so articles must be appropriate for both. Frequency of publication: bimonthly. Circulation: 12,000. Freelance submissions: 100%. Number of manuscripts bought each year: 40.

**Editorial Needs. Nonfiction**—interview/profile; opinion; current topics; humor; nostalgia. Suggested word length—feature articles: columns: 800-1500 words (opinion column).

**Initial Contact.** Query. Include clips.

**Acceptance Policies.** Byline given: yes. Response time to initial inquiry: 3-4 weeks. Average time until publication: 3 months. **Payment:** $450-$800 (articles); $250-$550 (columns). Payment made: upon publication. Kill fee: 20%. Writer's expenses on assignment: sometimes. Publishing rights: first North American serial rights. Computer print-outs: yes. Dot matrix: letter quality. Disk submissions: no.

**Additional Information.** *Emmy* is not a fan magazine; do not send these types of articles. Tips: Make sure your query letter accurately describes your article. Do not call. Read the magazine first (9x12 SASE, 5 first class stamps).

**ENTREPRENEUR.** 2392 Morse Ave. Irvine, CA 92714. Submissions Editor: Rieva Lesonsky. Type: business. Frequency of publication: monthly. Circulation: 250,000. Freelance submissions: 10-20%. Number of manuscripts bought each year: 30-40.

**Editorial Needs. Nonfiction**—how-to; interview/profile. Suggested word length—feature articles: 500-750; 1750-2000.

**Initial Contact.** Query letter; article proposal with subject outline; outline specifically who/what you plan to write about and why. Get to the point immediately in the submission.

**Acceptance Policies.** Byline given: yes. Submit seasonal material 6-7 months in advance. Simultaneous submissions: no. Response time to initial inquiry: 6-8 weeks. Average time until publication: varies. **Payment:** $200-$400. Payment made: upon acceptance. Kill fee: yes; 20%. Writer's expenses on assignment: varies. Publishing rights: all rights. Computer print-outs: yes. Dot matrix: yes. Disk submissions: no.

**Photography Submissions.** Format: transparencies. Film: color. Photographs should include: model releases; identification of subjects. **Payment:** n/i. Photographic rights: n/i.

**Additional Information.** We are a national magazine, aimed at the person wanting to start a business or already in business and seeking additional guidance and assistance. Tips: Read the magazine before querying. Put address and phone on every page of query. Writer's guidelines: SASE. For sample of magazine send $3.

**FAMILY MAGAZINE.** PO Box 4993. Walnut Creek, CA 94596. (415) 284-9093. Submissions Editor: Janet Venturino. Type: military magazine for women. Frequency of publication: monthly. Circulation: 600,000. Freelance submissions: 100% Number of manuscripts bought each year: 30.

**Editorial Needs. Nonfiction**—general interest; health/fitness; how-to; humor; interview/profile; photo feature; self-improvement; travel. Suggested word length—feature articles: 1000. **Fiction**—women's. Short stories—number per issue: 1; per year: 8.

**Initial Contact.** Query letter; entire article.

**Acceptance Policies.** Byline given: yes. Submit seasonal material 6 months in advance. Response time to initial inquiry: 1 month. Average time until publication: 6 months. **Payment:** $75-$200, depending on length. Payment made: upon publication. Kill fee: yes; 25%. Writer's expenses on assignment: no. Publishing rights: first North American serial rights. Computer print-outs: yes. Dot matrix: no. Disk submissions: no.

**Photography Submissions.** Format and film: black and white prints, 8x10; color transparencies. Photographs should include: captions; model releases; identification of subjects. **Payment:** $25 (black and white); $50 (color); $150 (cover). Photographic rights: one-time use.

**Additional Information.** We are looking for articles/photos aimed at young women, high school educated, who move often. Writer's guidelines: SASE.

## FAMILY THERAPY. (Subsidiary of Libra Publishers, Inc.)

3089C Clairemont Dr., Ste. 383. San Diego, CA 92117. (619) 581-9449. Submissions Editor: Martin Blinder, M.D. Type: professional journal. Frequency of publication: 3 times per year. Circulation: 1000. Freelance submissions: 100%.

**Editorial Needs. Nonfiction**—articles on marital and family therapy. Suggested word length—feature articles: 2400.

**Initial Contact.** Submission of abstract.

**Acceptance Policies.** Byline given: yes. Simultaneous submissions: no. Response time to initial inquiry: 3 weeks. Average time until publication: 6-12 months. **Payment:** none. Publishing rights: all. Computer print-outs: yes. Dot matrix: yes. Disk submissions: no.

**Additional Information.** Writer's guidelines: upon request.

## FAMILY TRAVEL GUIDES (catalog). PO Box 6061. Albany, CA 94706.

(415) 527-5849. Submissions Editor: Carole T. Meyers. Type: family travel. Frequency of publication: annual. Circulation: 25,000. Freelance submissions: n/i. Number of manuscripts bought each year: 5-10.

**Editorial Needs. Nonfiction**—travel. Suggested word length—feature articles: 1000-2500.

**Initial Contact.** Outline. Reprints are okay.

**Acceptance Policies.** Byline given: yes. Simultaneous submissions: yes. Response time to initial inquiry: 1 month. Average time until publication: next annual catalog. **Payment:** 10% of article price. Payment made: at end of year. Kill fee: no. Writer's expenses on assignment: no. Publishing rights: second serial rights. Computer print-outs: yes. Dot Matrix: yes. Disk submissions: no.

**Additional Information.** Writer's guidelines: #10 SASE; $.45 postage.

## FEMINIST BOOKSTORE NEWS. PO Box 882554. San Francisco, CA

94188. (415) 626-1556. Submissions Editor: Carol Seajay. Type: feminist publishing and bookselling. Frequency of publication: bimonthly. Circulation: 500. Freelance submissions: n/i.

**Editorial Needs. Nonfiction**—book excerpts; book reviews; interview/profile. Suggested word length—feature articles: 500.

**Initial Contact.** Query letter. Include your experience in the book trade.

**Acceptance Policies.** Byline given: yes. Simultaneous submissions: no. Response time to initial inquiry: 6 weeks. Average time until publication: 3 months. **Payment:** subscription or issues. Publishing rights: n/i. Computer print-outs: yes. Dot matrix: yes. Disk submissions: yes; must be accompanied by hard copy.

**Photography Submissions.** Format: prints, 4x6. Film: black and white. Photographs should include: captions; model releases; identification of subjects. Payment: copies. Photographic rights: n/i.

**Additional Information.** We publish only nonfiction articles about the feminist book trade. Ninety-five percent of our articles are written by women working in the book trade.

**FESSENDEN REVIEW.** PO Box 7272. San Diego, CA 92107. (619) 488-4991. Submissions Editor: Mike Jennings. Type: literary book review. Frequency of publication: quarterly. Circulation: Freelance submissions: 20%. Number of manuscripts bought per year: 50.

**Editorial Needs. Nonfiction**—book reviews, most with illustrations. Suggested word length—feature articles: 200-2000; columns 200-500 (brief reviews, nontraditional, humorous).

**Initial Contact.** Complete manuscript. Include availability of photos.

**Acceptance Policies.** Byline given: no. Simultaneous submissions: Response time to initial inquiry: 3 months. Average time until publication: 3-6 months. **Payment**: $30 (articles); $15 (column). Payment made: upon publication. Kill fee: no. Writer's expenses on assignment: no. Publishing rights: one-time. Computer print-outs: yes. Dot matrix: no. Disk submissions: query.

**Photography Submissions.** State availability with manuscript submission.

**Additional Information.** Tips: Know your subject; send for sample copy 9x12 SASE, 9 first class stamps.

**FICTION INTERNATIONAL.** San Diego State University Press. San Diego, CA 92182. (619) 265-6220. Submissions Editor: Hal Jaffe and Larry McCaffery. Type: literary. Frequency of publication: semiannual. Circulation: 500.

**Editorial Needs. Nonfiction**—book reviews; interview/profile; poetry. Suggested word length—feature articles: n/i. **Fiction**—literary; genre. Short stories—number per issue: 25.

**Initial Contact.** Entire article.

**Acceptance Policies.** Byline given: yes. Response time to initial inquiry: 4 weeks. Average time until publication: 6 months. **Payment**: $50 honorarium. Payment made: upon publication. Kill fee: no. Writer's expenses on assignment: no. Publishing rights: first rights. Computer print-outs: yes. Dot matrix: yes. Disk submissions: no.

**Additional Information.** Writer's guidelines: upon request.

**FICTION NETWORK MAGAZINE.** PO Box 5651. San Francisco, CA 94101. (415) 391-6610. Submissions Editor: Jay Schaefer. Type: short stories. Frequency of publication: 2 times per year. Circulation: 6000. Freelance submissions: 100%. Number of manuscripts bought each year: 50.

**Editorial Needs.** (within stated interest areas) **Fiction**—very short, all types; novel excerpts must stand alone. Only unpublished works accepted.

**Initial Contact.** Complete manuscript; SASE. Submit one at a time.

**Acceptance Policies.** Byline given: yes. Response time to initial inquiry: 4 months. Average time until publication: 6 months. **Payment**: $25; 50% syndicate sales. Payment made: upon publication. Kill fee: no. Writer's expenses on assignment: no. Publishing rights: first serial. Computer print-outs: yes. Dot matrix: letter quality. Disk submissions: no.

**Additional Information.** We are interested in opening new markets for fiction, and we will also submit your short stories to newspapers, magazines and place them in syndication. No children's, interviews, essays. Tips: Sample copy $5. Writer's guidelines: #10 SASE.

**FILM QUARTERLY.** Univ. of California Press. 2120 Berkeley Way. Berkeley, CA 94720. (415) 642-6333. Submissions Editor: Ernest Callenbach. Type: film criticism. Frequency of publication: quarterly. Circulation: 6500. Freelance submissions: 100%. Number of manuscripts bought each year: 50.

**Editorial Needs. Nonfiction**—book reviews; film reviews; critical articles; some history and theory. Suggested word length—feature articles: 5000-6000; columns: 1500 (film reviews).

**Initial Contact.** Query letter; entire article or sample page for proposed or another article.

**Acceptance Policies.** Byline given: yes. Simultaneous submissions: yes; inform us. Response time to initial inquiry: 2 weeks. Average time until publication: 2 months. **Payment**: $.02+ per word; two gratis copies. Payment made: upon publication. Kill fee: no. Writer's expenses on assignment: no. Publishing rights: all rights; we then split subsidiary (reprint) payments 50/50. Computer print-outs: yes. Dot matrix: a real handicap. Disk submissions: no.

**Photography Submissions.** Only if free with article. Format: prints, 4x5. Film: black and white. Photographs should include: captions.

**Additional Information.** We are extremely specialized and writers must have a serious knowledge of film to have much chance of acceptance. We don't have a substantial backlog like many other scholarly journals. Tips: Would-be contributors must study back issues carefully and have a good film background.

**FITNESS MANAGEMENT, THE MAGAZINE FOR PROFESSIONALS IN ADULT PHYSICAL FITNESS.** PO Box 1198. Solano Beach, CA 92075. (619) 481-4155. Submissions Editor: Edward H. Pitts. Type: fitness centers. Frequency of publication: monthly. Circulation: 21,000. Freelance submissions: 50%. Number of manuscripts bought each year: 30.

**Editorial Needs. Nonfiction**—book excerpts; how-to; new product; photo feature; technical; health and research in industry. Suggested word length—feature articles: 750-2000.

**Initial Contact.** Query letter.

**Acceptance Policies.** Byline given: yes. Submit seasonal material 6 months in advance. Simultaneous submissions: no. Response time to initial inquiry: 1 month. Average time until publication: 5 months. **Payment**: $60-$300 (assigned); $160 (unsolicited). Payment made: upon publication. Kill fee: 50%. Writer's expenses on assignment: yes. Publishing rights: all. Computer print-outs: yes. Dot matrix: letter quality. Disk submissions: query.

**Photography Submissions.** Send with manuscript. Format: contact sheets; 2x2, 4x5 transparencies; 5x7 prints. Film: black and white; color. Photographs should include: captions; model releases. **Payment**: $10. Photographic rights: same as article.

**Additional Information.** Helps owners, managers and program directors to better run their establishment. Tips: Author should be current with new happenings in the field; include quotes from people concerned with your subject. Writer's guidelines: #10 SASE; sample copy $5.

**FLOWERS &, THE BEAUTIFUL MAGAZINE ABOUT THE BUSINESS OF FLOWERS.** 12233 W. Olympic Blvd., Ste. 260. Los Angeles, CA 90064. (213) 826-5253. Submissions Editor: Marie Monysmith. Type: retail florist industry. Frequency of publication: monthly. Circulation: 28,000+/-. Freelance submissions: 40%. Number of manuscripts bought each year: 20.

**Editorial Needs. Nonfiction**—book excerpts; historical; nostalgia; how-to; interview/profile; new product; technical. Suggested word length—feature articles: 1000-3000.

**Initial Contact.** Query. Include clips.

**Acceptance Policies.** Byline given: yes. Submit seasonal material 4 months in advance. Simultaneous submissions: yes. Response time to initial inquiry: 1 month. Average time until publication: 4 months. **Payment:** $250-$500. Payment made: upon acceptance. Kill fee: 20%. Writer's expenses on assignment: sometimes. Publishing rights: first North American serial rights; second serial rights. Computer print-outs: yes. Dot matrix: letter quality. Disk submissions: query.

**Photography Submissions.** Format: contact sheets; 4x5 transparencies. Film: black and white; color. Photographs should include: captions; model releases; identification of subjects. **Payment:** #25-100 per photo. Photographic rights: one-time rights.

**Additional Information.** Geared to the small business owner's daily problems and solutions as they apply to the floral industry. Tips: Make sure query letter is direct and covers both your approach to the problem and the solution. Writer's guidelines: #10 SASE; sample copy 9 1/2x11 SASE.

**FOUR WHEELER.** 6728 Eton Ave. Canoga Park, CA 91306. (818) 992-4777. Submissions Editor: John Stewart. Type: hobbyist-enthusiasts for 4x4 vehicles. Frequency of publication: monthly. Circulation: 275,000. Freelance submissions: 30%. Number of manuscripts bought each year: 12-15.

**Editorial Needs. Nonfiction**—how-to; humor; photo feature; travel; truck features. Suggested word length—feature articles: 2000, columns: 750.

**Initial Contact.** Entire article.

**Acceptance Policies.** Byline given: yes. Submit seasonal material 4 months in advance. Simultaneous submissions: no. Response time to initial inquiry: 3-4 weeks. Average time until publication: n/i. **Payment:** $100-$1000. Payment made: upon acceptance. Kill fee: n/i. Writer's expenses on assignment: no. Publishing rights: n/i. Computer print-outs: yes. Dot matrix: yes. Disk submissions: yes.

**Photography Submissions.** Format: prints, 5x7. Film: black and white. Photographs should include: captions; model releases; identification of subjects. **Payment:** n/i. Photographic rights: n/i.

**Additional Information.** Writer's guidelines: SASE.

**FRETS.** 20085 Stevens Creek Blvd. Cupertino, CA 95014. (408) 446-1105. Submissions Editor: Phil Hood. Type: acoustic music instruction; interviews; instrument repair and construction (lutherie). Frequency of publication: monthly. Circulation: n/i. Freelance submissions: n/i.

**Editorial Needs. Nonfiction**—book reviews; historical; how-to; interview/profile; short interviews or articles; anything related to acoustic music. Suggested word length—feature articles: varies.

**Initial Contact.** Query letter.

**Acceptance Policies.** Byline given: yes. Simultaneous submissions: yes. Response time to initial inquiry: 2-3 weeks. Average time until publication: 2-12 months. **Payment:** $100-$350. Payment made: upon acceptance. Publishing rights: n/i. Computer print-outs: yes. Dot matrix: yes. Disk submissions: yes.

**Photography Submissions.** Format: prints, 5x7, 8x10; transparencies. Film: black and white; color. Photographs should include: identification of subjects; identification of photographer. **Payment:** $35+. Photographic rights: n/i.

**Additional Information.** Writer's guidelines: SASE to Diane Gershuny, Office Coordinator.

**GALACTIC DISCOURSE.** 1111 Dartmouth, #214. Claremont, CA 91711. Submissions Editor: Laurie Huff. Type: arts and entertainment. Frequency of publication: irregular. Circulation: 1000+. Freelance submissions: 100%.

**Editorial Needs. Fiction**—science fiction; fantasy; "Star Trek." Short stories—number per issue: 10+/-.

**Initial Contact.** Query letter.

**Acceptance Policies.** Byline given: yes. Simultaneous submissions: yes. Response time to initial inquiry: 6-8 weeks. Average time until publication: 18 months. **Payment**: gratis contributor copy. Publishing rights: second serial rights. Computer print-outs: yes. Dot matrix: very legible. Disk submissions: IBM compatible; Wordstar; Microsoft Word.

**Additional Information.** Writer's guidelines: SASE.

**GAMBLING TIMES.** 1018 N. Cole Ave. Hollywood, CA 90038. Submissions Editor: Len Miller. Type: gambling related. Frequency of publication: monthly. Circulation: 70,000. Freelance submissions: 50%. Number of manuscripts bought each year: 100.

**Editorial Needs. Nonfiction**—how-to; humor; photo feature; legal issues; travel. Suggested word length—feature articles: 10 pages. **Fiction**—gambling related; humorous.

**Initial Contact.** Query letter. Prefer photos with manuscript. Manuscripts must be double-spaced.

**Acceptance Policies.** Byline given: yes. Submit seasonal material 5 months in advance. Response time to initial inquiry: 4-6 weeks. Average time until publication: 5 months. **Payment**: $50-$150. Payment made: upon publication. Kill fee: no. Writer's expenses on assignment: n/i. Publishing rights: first North American serial rights. Computer print-outs: yes. Dot matrix: letter quality. Disk submissions: after acceptance; query for format.

**Photography Submissions.** Action shots involving people. **Payment**: $50. Photographic rights: same as article.

**Additional Information.** Tips: Know your subject thoroughly. Style should be clean and concise; hard-edged humor appreciated. Writer's guidelines: upon request.

**GAS.** PO Box 397. Marina, CA 93933. (408) 384-2768 (leave message). Submissions Editor: Jeanette M. Hopper. Type: humorous horror, horrible humor and a touch of the serious to keep you regular. Frequency of publication: quarterly. Circulation: 250. Freelance submissions: 100%. Number of manuscripts bought each year: 50.

**Editorial Needs. Nonfiction**—book excerpts; book reviews; entertainment reviews; fillers; how-to; humor; interview/profile; opinion; poetry; puzzles; quizzes (with answers); cartoons; classified advertising. Suggested word length—feature articles: as needed; columns: 1500 words. **Fiction**—women's; mystery; humorous horror (serious considered, if very strong). Short stories—number per issue: 4+ per year: 20+/-. No fiction over 1500 words considered.

**Initial Contact.** Query letter; entire article. Include brief personal information; past publications if applicable; indication you have read the magazine.

**Acceptance Policies.** Byline given: yes. Submit seasonal material 6 months in advance. Simultaneous submissions: no. Response time to initial inquiry: 1-2 weeks. Average time until publication: 6 months. **Payment**: $.025 cents per word, with $2 minimum for fiction and nonfiction (may be credited toward next issue). $1 per poem. Willing to consider any form of barter trade. Payment made: upon publication. Kill fee: same as payment. Writer's expenses on assignment: no. Publishing rights: first rights. Computer print-outs: yes. Dot matrix: if dark and clearly readable. Disk submissions: no.

**Photography Submissions.** Format: prints. Film: black and white (screened). Photographs should include: model releases; identification of subjects. **Payment**: $3 per full-page; $1.50 per half page; $1 per quarter page or spot; cover pays $5 plus 3 copies. (Art work is acceptable according to guidelines, and pays the same). Photographic rights: one-time use.

**Additional Information.** Potential submitters must be familiar with *GAS*, due to its unique slant on the horror/humor genres. Tips: Write well, do not assume that because *GAS* dwells on the strange and forbidden, inferior writing is acceptable. Writer's guidelines: #10 SASE; sample copy $3.50.

## GREEN FUSE.

10790 Bodega Hwy. Sebastopol, CA 95472. (707) 823-1275. Submissions Editor: Ralph Smith. Type: dedicated to pursuit of peace and preservation of the planet. Frequency of publication: twice yearly. Circulation: 275.

**Editorial Needs. Nonfiction**—poetry. Suggested word length—60 lines of poetry maximum.

**Initial Contact.** Entire manuscript.

**Acceptance Policies.** Byline given: yes. Submit seasonal material 4 months in advance. Response time to initial inquiry: 4 months. Average time until publication: 2 months. **Payment**: 1 copy. Publishing rights: n/i. Computer print-outs: yes. Dot matrix: n/i. Disk submissions: no.

**Additional Information.** Deadlines are July 15 and January 15. Writer's guidelines: SASE.

## GUITAR PLAYER MAGAZINE.

20085 Stevens Creek Blvd. Cupertino, CA 95014. (408) 446-1105. Submissions Editor: Tom Wheeler. Type: all phases of guitar (for musicians). Frequency of publication: monthly. Circulation: 180,000. Freelance submissions: 70%. Number of manuscripts bought each year: 35+/-.

**Editorial Needs. Nonfiction**—how-to; interview/profile; techniques. Suggested word length—feature articles: open.

**Initial Contact.** Query letter.

**Acceptance Policies.** Byline given: yes. Response time to initial inquiry: 6 weeks. Average time until publication: 3 months. **Payment**: $100-$300. Payment made: upon acceptance. Kill fee: n/i. Writer's expenses on assignment: sometimes. Publishing rights: first North American serial rights; second serial rights (limited). Computer print-outs: yes. Dot matrix: letter quality. Disk submissions: IBM compatible; ASCII.

**Photography Submissions.** Format and film: black and white glossy prints; color transparencies. Photographs should include: n/i. **Payment**: $35-$50 (black and white); $75-$250 (color transparencies, cover shot). Photographic rights: one-time rights.

**Additional Information.** Writer's guidelines: #10 SASE.

## HIBISCUS MAGAZINE.

PO Box 22248. Sacramento, CA 95822. Submissions Editors: Margaret Wensrich (fiction, art); Joyce Odam (poetry). Type: literary. Frequency of publication: 3 times per year. Circulation: 1000. Freelance submissions: 100%+/-. Number of manuscripts bought each year: 10-12 short stories; 40-60 poems; art on commission.

**Editorial Needs. Fiction**—mystery; romance; western; science fiction; fantasy; slice of life. Short stories—number per issue: 2-3; per year: 6-10. **Other**—poetry.

**Initial Contact.** n/i.

**Acceptance Policies.** Byline given: yes. Submit seasonal material 12 months in advance. Simultaneous submissions: yes. Response time to initial inquiry: 2-4 months. Average time until publication: 1-2 years. **Payment**: n/i. Payment made: on publication. Kill fee: no.

Writer's expenses on assignment: no. Publishing rights: first North American serial rights. Computer print-outs: yes. Dot matrix: new black ribbon, double strike. Disk submissions: no.

**Additional Information.** We do not answer any letter unless accompanied by a SASE. We often cannot return Canadian or overseas manuscripts because author does not include sufficient IRC. Writer's guidelines: SASE with first class postage. Two IRC for each 4 pages of Canadian of foreign manuscripts to pay for return postage. Sample copy $4.

## HIGH TECHNOLOGY CAREERS. c/o Writers Connection.

1601 Saratoga-Sunnyvale Rd., Ste. 180. Cupertino, CA 95014. (408) 973-0227. Submissions Editor: Meera Lester. *High Technology Careers* is circulated in the Sunday edition of the San Jose *Mercury News. Professional Careers* is circulated in Southern California. Type: high technology (biotechnology, computers, space, robotics) and its impact on our lives directed to engineers, electronic, aerospace and defense professionals. Frequency of publication: monthly. Circulation: 348,000. Freelance submissions: 100%. Number of manuscripts bought each year: 36.

**Editorial Needs.** **Nonfiction**—biotechnology; computers; electronics; aerospace; defense; technology; transportation; science; marketing; management; futuristic high technology; new technology applications. Suggested word length—feature articles: 1000-1500; sidebar for article: 500.

**Initial Contact.** Query letter; published clips; or completed manuscript.

**Acceptance Policies.** Byline given: yes. Simultaneous submissions: no. Response time to initial inquiry: 2-4 weeks. Average time until publication: 3 months. **Payment**: $.175 based on edited, final count. Payment made: upon publication. Kill fee: 25%. Writer's expenses on assignment: sometimes. Publishing rights: all rights. Computer print-outs: yes. Dot matrix: letter quality. Disk submissions: query for electronic submissions.

**Additional Information.** Our audience includes managers, engineers, and other professional working in high technology industries. Writer's guidelines: upon request; SASE. Sample copy $2.

## HORROR SHOW, THE. 14848 Misty Springs Lane. Oak Run, CA 96069.

(916) 472-3540. Submissions Editor: David B. Silva. Type: horror fiction. Frequency of publication: quarterly. Circulation: 44,000. Freelance submissions: 75%. Number of manuscripts bought each year: n/i.

**Editorial Needs.** **Nonfiction**—book excerpts; interview/profile. Suggested word length—feature articles: 2000-4000. **Fiction**—horror. Short stories—number per year: 40.

**Initial Contact.** Article proposal with subject outline.

**Acceptance Policies.** Byline given: yes. Submit seasonal material 5 months in advance. Simultaneous submissions: yes. Response time to initial inquiry: 3 weeks. Average time until publication: 3 months. **Payment**: $.01-$.02 per word. Payment made: upon acceptance. Kill fee: no. Writer's expenses on assignment: no. Publishing rights: first rights. Computer print-outs: yes. Dot matrix: yes. Disk submissions: no.

**Photography Submissions.** Format: prints. Film: black and white. **Payment**: varies. Photographic rights: one-time.

**Additional Information.** Writer's guidelines: SASE.

## HOSPITAL GIFT SHOP MANAGEMENT. 7628 Densmore. Van Nuys, CA

91406. (818) 782-7232. Submissions Editor: Barbara Feiner. Type: hospital gift shop management. Frequency of publication: monthly. Circulation: 15,000. Freelance submissions: 25%. Number of manuscripts bought each year: 12-25.

**Editorial Needs.** **Nonfiction**—how-to; interview/profile; photo feature; cartoons; management. Suggested word length—feature articles: 750-2500.

**Initial Contact**. Query first; double-spaced submissions. State availability of photos.

**Acceptance Policies**. Byline given: yes. Submit seasonal material 8 months in advance. Simultaneous submissions: no. Response time to initial inquiry: 1 month. Average time until publication: 4 months. **Payment**: $10-$100; $20 (cartoons). Payment made: upon acceptance. Kill fee: no. Writer's expenses on assignment: no. Publishing rights: first North American serial rights. Computer print-outs: yes. Dot matrix: must be readable. Disk submissions: yes.

**Photography Submissions**. Format: 5x7 prints. Film: black and white; color. Photographs should include: captions; model release; identification of subjects. **Payment**: varies.

**Additional Information**. We are interested in articles dealing with how to expand the hospital gift shop into a very profitable venture. Tips: Make sure your query is direct and exciting. That will help convince me your story will be also. Writer's guidelines: and sample copy $4 postage.

**HOUSEWIFE-WRITER'S FORUM.** Drawer 1518. Lafayette, CA 94549. (415) 932-1143. Submissions Editor: Deborah Haeseler. Type: literary; for and by women running a house and writing. Frequency of publication: bimonthly. Circulation: 600+. Freelance submissions: 100%. Number of manuscripts bought each year: 300.

**Editorial Needs**. **Nonfiction**—excerpts; essays; how-to; humor; interview/profile; opinion; personal experience; poetry; fillers. Suggested word length—feature articles: 1500. Columns—Confession of Housewife-Writers (lifestyle, reminiscences); suggested word length—25-800. Book reviews; suggested word length—25-800. **Fiction**—humorous; experimental; mainstream; mystery; etc. Suggested word length—2000 maximum.

**Initial Contact**. Query letter or complete manuscript for nonfiction; complete manuscript for fiction, poetry, (maximum of 10 poems), and columns.

**Acceptance Policies**. Byline given: yes. Submit seasonal material 6 months in advance. Simultaneous submissions: yes. Response time to initial inquiry: 2-4 weeks. Average time until publication: 6-12 months. **Payment**: $1-$10 (nonfiction; fiction); $.25-$1 (columns; poetry; fillers, etc). Payment made: on acceptance. Publishing rights: one-time rights. Computer print-outs: yes. Dot matrix: yes. Disk submissions: no.

**Additional Information**. We encourage beginning writers, try to get to know you, and help you be the best writer you can be. Writer's guidelines: #10 SASE; sample copy $3.

**"HOWTO" BETTER HEALTH NEWSLETTER.** 815 N. La Brea Ave., Ste. 342. Inglewood, CA 90302. (213) 385-2797. Submissions Editor: Walter L. Foster. Type: health and fitness. Frequency of publication: quarterly. Circulation: 10,364. Freelance submissions: 50%. Number of manuscripts bought each year: 12.

**Editorial Needs**. **Nonfiction**—health/fitness; how-to; self-improvement; cartoons. Suggested word length—feature articles: 100-150.

**Initial Contact**. Article proposal with subject outline; or entire article (must include SASE if author wants manuscript returned). Include photos that harmonize with the article.

**Acceptance Policies**. Byline given: yes. Submit seasonal material 2 months in advance. Simultaneous submissions: yes. Response time to initial inquiry: 3 weeks. Average time until publication: 3 months. **Payment**: $.30 per word/150 words maximum; $5 (cartoons). Payment made: upon publication. Kill fee: no. Writer's expenses on assignment: no. Publishing rights: all. Computer print-outs: yes. Dot matrix: n/i. Disk submissions: n/i.

**Photography Submissions**. Format: 3x5 glossies. Film: black and white. Photographs should include: captions; model releases. **Payment**: $5. Photographic rights: all.

**Additional Information**. Published in February, May, August and November. Articles must have a "listed" 1-2-3 format telling "how-to" achieve a certain health, fitness, or diet problem. Tips: Send for sample copy $2. Writer's guidelines: upon request.

**HUSTLER.** 9171 Wilshire Blvd., Ste. 300. Beverly Hills, CA 90210. (213) 858-7100. Submissions Editors: Allan MacDonell (articles, nonfiction feature articles); Mike Di Gregorio (fiction, columns). Type: men's. Frequency of publication: monthly. Circulation: 800,000. Freelance submissions: 2 features, 2 columns monthly. Number of manuscripts bought each year: 30-35.

**Editorial Needs. Nonfiction**—how-to; general interest; interview/profile; work must have sex angle related to current sexual topic; or strong political angle. Suggested word length—feature articles: 4000; columns: 1500-2000. **Fiction**—strong adventure/mystery story with sex scenes. Short stories—number per issue: n/i. per year: 6.

**Initial Contact.** Article proposal with subject outline. State how the article fits our specific approach.

**Acceptance Policies.** Byline given: yes. Average time until publication: varies. **Payment**: $1500 (features); $1000 (fiction); $600-$800 (sex play); $300 (AIDSWatch). Simultaneous submissions: no. Response time to initial inquiry: 2-3 weeks. Payment made: upon acceptance. Kill fee: 20% of commissioned fee. Writer's expenses on assignment: yes. Publishing rights: all rights. Computer print-outs: yes. Dot matrix: no. Disk submissions: ASCII (MS-DOS/APPLE).

**Additional Information.** We expect articles that take a deeper look at sex/politics/social issues than other media. Writer's guidelines: write "Guidelines" in care of above address.

**IMAGE.** (San Francisco Examiner). 925 Mission St. San Francisco, CA 94103. (415) 777-2424. Submissions Editor: Bruce Adams. Type: general interest. Frequency of publication: weekly. Circulation: 800,000. Freelance submissions: 10-20%. Number of manuscripts bought each year: few; magazine written mostly in-house.

**Editorial Needs. Nonfiction**—general interest; historical; humor (when a part of the approach); interview/profile; opinion. Suggested word length—feature articles: 100-1500.

**Initial Contact.** Query (by mail only).

**Acceptance Policies.** Byline given: yes. Submit seasonal material 2 months in advance. Simultaneous submissions: yes. Response time to initial inquiry: 6 weeks. Average time until publication: 2 months. **Payment**: varies with assignment. Payment made: upon publication. Kill fee: 25%. Writer's expenses on assignment: within reason. Publishing rights: first North American serial rights. Computer print-outs. yes. Dot matrix: yes. Disk submissions: no.

**Additional Information.** Freelance material is rarely accepted. Writer's guidelines: upon request.

**INTERNATIONAL OLYMPIC LIFTER.** PO Box 65855. Los Angeles, CA 90065. (213) 257-8762. Submissions Editor: Bob Hise. Type: Olympic sport of weight lifting. Frequency of publication: 6 issues per year. Circulation: 10,000. Freelance submissions: 5%. Number of manuscripts bought each year: 4.

**Editorial Needs. Nonfiction**—training; diet; contest reports; poetry. Suggested word length—feature articles: 250-2000.

**Initial Contact.** Query letter. State availability of photos.

**Acceptance Policies.** Byline given: yes. Submit seasonal material 5 months in advance. Simultaneous submissions: no. Response time to initial inquiry: 6 weeks. Average time until publication: 2 months. **Payment**: variable. Payment made: upon publication. Kill fee: $25. Writer's expenses on assignment: n/i. Publishing rights: one-time rights; negotiable. Computer print-outs: yes. Dot matrix: letter quality. Disk submissions: no.

**Photography Submissions.** action; training. Format: 5x7 prints. Film: black and white. Photographs should include: identification of subjects. **Payment**: $5. Photographic rights: n/i.

**Additional Information.** Writing must be apolitical. Writer's guidelines: 9x12 SASE, 5 first class stamps; sample copy $4.

**ISLANDS.** 3886 State Street. Santa Barbara, CA 93105. (805) 682-7177. Submissions Editor: Joan Tapper (manuscript and story idea queries); Zorah Kruger (photo stock lists). Type: travel. Frequency of publication: twice monthly. Circulation: 14,000. Freelance submissions: 100%. Number of manuscripts bought each year: 75.

**Editorial Needs. Nonfiction**—book reviews; general interest; interview/profile; historical; nature; sports; art; travel. Suggested word length—feature articles: 2000-3000; columns: 1200-1700.

**Initial Contact.** Query letter; article proposal with subject outline. Include tear sheets of previously published manuscripts; support materials, and tear sheets for photographers.

**Acceptance Policies.** Byline given: yes. Submit seasonal material 6+ months in advance. Simultaneous submissions: no. Response time to initial inquiry: 4-6 weeks. Average time until publication: 3-6 months. **Payment:** $.25 per word and up. Payment made: 1/2 on acceptance; 1/2 on publication. Kill fee: 1/4. Writer's expenses on assignment: yes. Publishing rights: first rights. Computer print-outs: yes. Dot matrix: yes. Disk submissions: ASCII; modem.

**Photography Submissions.** Format: transparencies. Film: color. Photographs should include: captions; model releases; identification of subjects. **Payment:** $75-$300 depending on usage. Photographic rights: one-time use.

**Additional Information.** Writer's guidelines: upon request, SASE.

**JOTS (JOURNAL OF THE SENSES).** (Subsidiary of Elysium Growth Press). 814 Robinson Rd. Topanga, CA 90290. (213) 455-1000. Submissions Editor: Ed Lange. Type: clothing optional lifestyle; body self-esteem. Frequency of publication: quarterly. Circulation: 14,000. Freelance submissions: 10% Number of manuscripts bought each year: 4.

**Editorial Needs. Nonfiction**—book reviews; inspiration; photo feature; self-improvement. Suggested word length—feature articles: 700. Short stories—number per year: 1.

**Initial Contact.** Query letter.

**Acceptance Policies.** Byline given: yes. Simultaneous submissions: yes. Response time to initial inquiry: 6 weeks. Average time until publication: 6 months. **Payment:** $100. Payment made: upon publication. Kill fee: no. Writer's expenses on assignment: n/i. Publishing rights: all. Computer print-outs: yes. Dot matrix: yes. Disk submissions: Macintosh.

**Photography Submissions.** Format: 8x10 35mm transparencies; contact sheets. Film: black and white; color. Photographs should include: captions; model releases; identification of subjects. **Payment:** $25. Photographic rights: all.

**Additional Information.** Writer's guidelines: upon request.

**JOURNAL OF WISDOM.** (Subsidiary of Li Kung Shaw). PO Box 16427. San Francisco, CA 94116. (415) 731-0829. Submissions Editor: Li Kung Shaw. Type: philosophy. Frequency of publication: monthly. Circulation: 100. Freelance submissions: 50%. Number of manuscripts bought each year: 1-2.

**Editorial Needs. Nonfiction**—philosophy. Suggested word length—feature articles: 3000.

**Initial Contact.** Query letter.

**Acceptance Policies.** Byline given: n/i. Simultaneous submissions: yes; we negotiate. Response time to initial inquiry: 30 days. Average time until publication: 6 months. **Payment**: yes. Payment made: upon publication. Kill fee: no. Writer's expenses on assignment: no. Publishing rights: first rights. Computer print-outs: yes. Dot matrix: no. Disk submissions: Apple 3 (Three Easy Pieces).

**KEYBOARD MAGAZINE.** 20085 Stevens Creek Blvd. Cupertino, CA 95014. (408) 446-1105. Submissions Editor: Dominic Milano. Type: keyboard players, all styles, all abilities. Frequency of publication: monthly. Circulation: 82,000. Freelance submissions: 25%. Number of manuscripts bought each year: 20.

**Editorial Needs. Nonfiction**—interviews; historical; how-to. Suggested word length—feature articles: 1000-5000.

**Initial Contact.** Phone query; or query letter.

**Acceptance Policies.** Byline given: yes. Response time to initial inquiry: 2 weeks. Average time until publication: 6 months. **Payment**: $150-$500. Payment made: upon acceptance. Kill fee: n/i. Writer's expenses on assignment: sometimes. Publishing rights: first serial rights; second serial rights. Computer print-outs: yes. Dot matrix: letter quality. Disk submissions: query.

**Additional Information.** We are looking for anything that amateur of professional keyboard players would find helpful, new, or interesting. Writer's guidelines: upon request.

**KINGFISHER.** PO Box 9783. North Berkeley, CA 94709. (415) 893-2425. Submissions Editor: c/o Editor. Type: literary magazine focusing on short fiction. Frequency of publication: twice yearly. Circulation: 1000. Freelance submissions: 100%.

**Editorial Needs. Nonfiction**—occasional essays. **Fiction**—literary. Short stories—number per year: 20.

**Initial Contact.** Cover letter with fiction or poetry. Include previous publication credits and SASE.

**Acceptance Policies.** Byline given: yes. Simultaneous submissions: yes if previously published or translated include release from original publisher or author). Response time to initial inquiry: 2-3 months. Average time until publication: 6-12 months. **Payment**: 2 copies. Publishing rights: first North American serial rights. Computer print-outs: yes. Dot matrix: no. Disk submissions: n/i.

**Additional Information.** Writer's guidelines: upon request; SASE.

**KITPLANES.** PO Box 6050. Mission Viejo, CA 92690. (714) 885-8822. Submissions Editor: Dave Martin. Type: for designers, builders, and pilots of experimental aircraft. Frequency of publication: monthly. Circulation: 53,000. Freelance submissions: 70%. Number of manuscripts bought each year: 80.

**Editorial Needs. Nonfiction**—how to; interview/profile; new product; personal experience; photo feature; technical; general interest. Suggested word length—feature articles: 500-5000.

**Initial Contact.** Query letter; availability of photos.

**Acceptance Policies.** Byline given: yes. Submit seasonal material 6 months in advance. Simultaneous submissions: no. Response time to initial inquiry: 2 weeks. Average time until publication: 3 months. **Payment**: $100-$400. Payment made: upon publication. Kill fee: negotiable. Writer's expenses on assignment: n/i. Publishing rights: first North American serial rights. Computer print-outs: yes. Dot matrix: caps and lower case. Disk submissions: query.

**Photography Submissions.** Format: prints; transparencies. Film: black and white; color. Photographs should include: captions; identification of subjects. **Payment**: $10-$75 (black and white); $20-$150 (color). Photographic rights: one-time rights.

**Additional Information.** Tips: Article must be directed to the individual craftsperson. We are looking for photo features. Writer's guidelines: #10 SASE; sample copy $3.

**LA GENTE de AZTLAN.** (Chicano student newspaper published at UCLA). 112D Kerchoff Hall. 308 Westwood Plaza. Los Angeles, CA 90024. (213) 825-9836, 206-3757. Submissions Editor: Ronald W. Lopez II. Type: Chicano student newspaper. Frequency of publication: 6 times during the academic year. Circulation: 10,000. Freelance submissions: 10%.

**Editorial Needs. Nonfiction**—book reviews; entertainment reviews; fillers; general interest; health/fitness; historical; how-to; humor; interview/profile; opinion; photo feature; poetry; self-improvement. Suggested word length—feature articles: 1000; columns: 500. **Fiction**—literary; women's; Chicano/Latino issues, etc. Short Stories—number per year: 2.

**Initial Contact.** Query letter; article proposal; entire article. Include background of the author.

**Acceptance Policies.** Byline given: yes. Submit seasonal material 1 month in advance. Simultaneous submissions: yes. Response time to initial inquiry: 2 weeks. Average time until publication: 3 weeks. **Payment**: none. Publishing rights: n/i. Computer print-outs: yes. Dot Matrix: yes. Disk submissions: Macintosh 3.5 disk; Macwrite or Microsoft Word (preferred).

**Photography Submissions.** Format: 8x10 prints; contact sheets. Film: black and white. Photographs should include: captions; identification of subjects; place, time, and event. **Payment**: none. Photographic rights: n/i.

**Additional Information.** We deal with issues of relevance to the Latino community. If possible, send a Spanish version also. Writer's guidelines: call or write.

**L.A. WEST.** 919 Santa Monica Blvd. #245. Santa Monica, CA 90401. (213) 458-3376. Submissions Editor: Mary Daily. Type: service/lifestyle for West Los Angeles. Frequency of publication: monthly. Circulation: 62,000. Freelance submissions: 95%. Number of manuscripts bought each year: 45.

**Editorial Needs. Nonfiction**—general interest; health/fitness; historical; how-to; humor; interview/profile; opinion; travel. Suggested word length—feature articles: 800-1000; columns: 550.

**Initial Contact.** Query letter; entire article; clips.

**Acceptance Policies.** Byline given: yes. Simultaneous submissions: no. Response time to initial inquiry: 6-8 weeks. Average time until publication: 6-8 months. **Payment**: $75-1000. Payment made: upon acceptance. Kill fee: no. Writer's expenses on assignment: no. Publishing rights: all. Computer print-outs: yes. Dot matrix: yes. Disk submissions: yes.

**Photography Submissions.** Format: transparencies. Film: color. Photographs should include: captions; model releases; identification of subjects. **Payment**: $45. Photographic rights: all.

**Additional Information.** Writer's guidelines: SASE.

**LECTOR.** 16161 Ventura Blvd., Ste. 830. Encino, CA 91436. (818) 990-1885. Submissions Editor: Roberto Cabello-Argandona. Type: Hispanic book review media. Frequency of publication: biannual. Circulation: 3000. Freelance submissions: 90%. Number of manuscripts bought each year: 4.

**Editorial Needs. Nonfiction**—book excerpts; book reviews; entertainment reviews; humor; interview/profile; literary opinion; photo feature; poetry. Suggested word length—feature articles: 2000; columns: 1000. **Fiction**—Hispanic literary and women's. Short stories—number per issue: 2; per year: 4.

**Initial Contact.** Query letter; article proposal with written subject outline. Include resumé and clips.

**Acceptance Policies.** Byline given: yes. Submit seasonal material 12 months in advance. Simultaneous submissions: yes. Response time to initial inquiry: 60-90 days. Average time until publication: 60-90 days. **Payment**: $50, negotiable. Payment made: within 90 days after publication. Kill fee: no. Expenses of writers on assignment: no. Publishing rights: all. Computer print-outs: yes. Dot matrix: yes. Disk submissions: prefer MS-DOS with hard copy, other accepted.

**Photography Submissions.** Call about color ar submissions. Format: transparencies, call about size. Film: black and white; color. Photographs should include: caption. **Payment**: photographic essay paid separately. Photographic rights: one-time rights.

**Additional Information.** Publication provides literary articles with Hispanic cultural and humanistic focus. Tips: Writing should be in a creative, literary style. Writer's guidelines: SASE, include $5.

**LEFT CURVE.** PO Box 472. Oakland, CA 94604. (415) 763-7193. Submissions Editor: CSABA Polony. Type: progressive art and culture. Frequency of publication: irregular. Circulation: 1000. Freelance submissions: 100%.

**Editorial Needs.** **Nonfiction**—book reviews; historical; interview/profile; opinion; photo feature; poetry; progressive culture. Suggested word length—feature articles: 2500. **Fiction**—literary; science-fiction; avant-garde; progressive culture; minority; activist; experimental. Short stories—number per year: 1.

**Initial Contact.** Article proposal with subject outline. State author's purpose. Include SASE.

**Acceptance Policies.** Byline given: yes. Simultaneous submissions: no. Response time to initial inquiry: 3 months. Average time until publication: 6 months. **Payment**: 5 copies of issue. Publishing rights: rights revert to author with written permission. Computer print-outs: yes. Dot matrix: n/i. Disk submissions: no.

**Photography Submissions.** Format: 5x7, or less. Film: black and white. Photographs should include: captions as necessary for story. **Payment**: none. Photographic rights: none.

**Additional Information.** Writer's guidelines: no.

**LET'S LIVE MAGAZINE.** 444 N. Larchmont Blvd. PO Box 74908. Los Angeles, CA 90004. (213) 469-8379. Submissions Editors: Debra A. Jenkins (print editor); Linda McMakin (photo editor). Type: health and fitness. Frequency of publication: monthly. Circulation: 140,000. Freelance submissions: 10%. Number of manuscripts bought each year: 12-30.

**Editorial Needs.** **Nonfiction**—book excerpts; book reviews; health/fitness; interview/profile; self-improvement. Suggested word length—feature articles: 1000-1500.

**Initial Contact.** Query letter. State photo availability.

**Acceptance Policies.** Byline given: yes. Submit seasonal material 9 months in advance. Simultaneous submissions: no. Response time to initial inquiry: 6 weeks. Average time until publication: n/i. **Payment**: $150 per article. Payment made: upon publication. Kill fee: no. Writer's expenses on assignment: no; some exceptions. Publishing rights: first North American serial rights. Computer print-outs: yes. Dot matrix: n/i. Disk submissions: IBM PC.

**Photography Submissions.** Format: transparencies. Film: black and white; color. Photographs should include: model releases; identification of subjects. **Payment**: $35 per photo. Photographic rights: one-time use.

**Additional Information.** Writer's guidelines: SASE.

**LLAMAS.** PO Box 100. Herald, CA 95638. (209) 748-2620. Submissions Editor: Assistant Editor, Susan Jones-Ley. Type: livestock. Frequency of publication: 8 times per year. Circulation: 5500. Freelance submissions: 30% and growing. Number of manuscripts bought each year: 25.

**Editorial Needs. Nonfiction**—book excerpts; fillers; general interest; photo feature; travel. Suggested word length—feature articles: 1000-4000. Short stories—number per issue: 4; per year: 24-30.

**Initial Contact.** Query letter; article proposal with subject outline; entire article. Include sample work.

**Acceptance Policies.** Byline given: yes. Submit seasonal material 5 months in advance. Simultaneous submissions: yes. Response time to initial inquiry: 30 days. Average time until publication: varies. **Payment**: $50-$400. Payment made: upon publication. Kill fee: per contract agreement. Writer's expenses on assignment: on occasion. Publishing rights: first and second North American serial rights; first rights. Computer print-outs: yes. Dot matrix: no. Disk submissions: no.

**Photography Submissions.** Format: prints, any size. Film: black and white; color. Photographs should include: captions; model releases; identification of subjects. **Payment**: $25-$50 for color; $10-$15 black and white. Photographic rights: varies. Please do not write on photograph!

**Additional Information.** Sample magazine sent upon request. Tips: Know our magazine and its needs. Writer's guidelines: SASE.

**LOS ANGELES LAWYER.** PO Box 55020. Los Angeles, CA 90055. (213) 627-2727. Submissions Editor: Susan Pettit. Type: Law. Directed to the membership of the Los Angeles County Bar Association. Consists of scholarly legal articles, legal features and profiles; practice tips and tax tips. Frequency of publication: monthly. Circulation: 21,000. Freelance submissions: 20%. Number of manuscripts bought each year: 8-10.

**Editorial Needs. Nonfiction**—book reviews; historical; interviews/profile; legal education. Suggested word length—feature articles: 4000.

**Initial Contact.** Query letter. Include brief biography of writer; clips.

**Acceptance Policies.** Byline given: yes. Simultaneous submissions: yes; if manuscript is accepted by another publication, we must be notified immediately. Response time to initial inquiry: 8 weeks. Average time until publication: varies. **Payment**: $300-$800. Payment made: upon acceptance. Kill fee: yes. Writer's expenses on assignment: no. Publishing rights: first North American serial rights; work-for-hire assignments. Computer print-outs: yes. Dot matrix: n/i. Disk submissions: no.

**Photography Submissions.** Format: prints, 5x7. Film: black and white; color. Photographs should include: captions; model releases; identification of subjects. **Payment**: varies. Photographic rights: one-time use; work for hire.

**Additional Information.** Emphasis on scholarly legal articles of interest to Southern California attorneys. Tips: Footnotes must be typed double-spaced on separate pages at the end of article. Writer's guidelines: upon request; sample copies $2.

**LOS ANGELES MAGAZINE.** 1888 Century Park East, Ste. 920. Los Angeles, CA 90067. (213) 557-1212. Submissions Editors: Rodger Claire, Managing Editor; Lew Harris, Executive Editor. Type: articles of general interest pertaining to the Los Angeles and Southern California area. Frequency of publication: monthly. Circulation: 172,000. Freelance submissions: 90%. Number of manuscripts bought each year: n/i.

**Editorial Needs. Nonfiction**—book excerpts; book reviews; historical; interview/profile; travel; business; politics. Suggested word-length—feature articles: 1500.

**Initial Contact.** Query letter. Include clips.

**Acceptance Policies.** Byline given: Submit seasonal material 2-3 months in advance. Simultaneous submissions: yes. Response time to initial inquiry: 3-4 weeks. Average time until publication: varies. **Payment**: individually based. Payment made: upon acceptance. Kill fee: 30%. Writer's expenses on assignment: mostly. Publishing rights: first North American serial rights. Computer print-outs. yes. Dot matrix: yes. Disk submissions: no.

**Additional Information.** All articles should have a local angle. Tips: Research the magazine and be sure to address our audience which is sophisticated and upscale. Writer's guidelines: request by mail with SASE.

**LOS ANGELES READER.** 12224 Victory Blvd. North Hollywood, CA 91606. (213) 655-8810. (818) 763-3555. Submissions Editors: Heidi Dvorak (cityside); James Vowell (features). Type: general interest; arts and entertainment (especially reviews and listings). Frequency of publication: weekly. Circulation: 65,000. Freelance submissions: 100%. Number of manuscripts bought each year: 100.

**Editorial Needs. Nonfiction**—book excerpts; book reviews; entertainment reviews; general interest; humor; interview/profile. Suggested word length—feature articles: 3500; columns: 1000. **Fiction**—literary (rarely use fiction).

**Initial Contact.** Query letter.

**Acceptance Policies.** Byline given: yes. Simultaneous submissions: no. Response time to initial inquiry: 1 month. Average time until publication: a few weeks. **Payment**: $300 for major features of 3500 words or more; graduated down for shorter pieces. Payment made: upon publication. Kill fee: no. Writer's expenses on assignment: no. Publishing rights: first North American serial rights. Computer print-outs: yes. Dot matrix: yes. Disk submissions: MS-DOS; IBM.

**Photography Submissions.** Format: n/i. Film: n/i. Photographs should include: n/i. **Payment**: $30 per published photo. Photographic rights: first.

**Additional Information.** Writer's guidelines: upon request.

**LOS ANGELES TIMES BOOK REVIEW.** Times Mirror. Times Mirror Square. Los Angeles, CA 90053. (213) 237-7777. Submissions Editor: Jack Miles. Type: review of current books. Frequency of publication: weekly. Circulation: 1.3 million. Freelance submissions: 70%. Number of manuscripts bought each year: 500.

**Editorial Needs. Nonfiction**—book reviews. Suggested word length—feature articles: 200-1500.

**Initial Contact.** Query letter. Include published samples of pertinent works.

**Acceptance Policies.** Byline given: yes. Simultaneous submissions: no. Response time to initial inquiry: immediate. Average time until publication: 3 weeks. **Payment**: $75-$500. Payment made: upon publication. Kill fee: variable. Writer's expenses on assignment: n/a. Publishing rights: first North American serial rights. Computer print-outs: yes. Dot matrix: letter quality. Disk submissions: no.

**Additional Information.** We will not accept requests for specific titles to review or unsolicited reviews without query first.

**LOS ANGELES TIMES MAGAZINE.** Times Mirror Square. Los Angeles, CA 90053. (213) 237-7811. Submissions Editors: Leslie Allyson Ware (freelance and excerpts); John Lindsay (projects editor). Type: Sunday magazine. Frequency of publication: weekly. Circulation: 1,421,711. Freelance submissions: 70-80%. Number of manuscripts bought each year: 260.

**Editorial Needs. Nonfiction**—book excerpts; general interest; health/fitness; historical; interview/profile; photo feature. Suggested word length—feature articles: 1500-4000.

**Initial Contact.** Query letter for each article to be submitted; clips; resumé.

**Acceptance Policies.** Byline given: yes. Submit seasonal material 2 months in advance. Simultaneous submissions: yes. Response time to initial inquiry: 6 weeks. Average time until publication: 1 month. **Payment:** $1 per word, on average. Payment made: upon acceptance. Kill fee: yes. Writer's expenses on assignment: yes. Publishing rights: first North American serial rights; first rights. Computer print-outs: yes. Dot matrix: n/i. Disk submissions: no.

**Additional Information.** Looking for Los Angeles, Southern California, Pacific Rim-oriented stories. Tips: Have a concise query letter; include writing samples if no clips. Writer's guidelines: SASE.

**MACWEEK.** 525 Brannan St. San Francisco, CA 94107. (415) 882-7370. Submissions Editors: Henry Norr (news); Bernard Ohanian (opinions and features); Anita Malnig (graphic arts); Rochelle Garner (Window On, product overviews); Rebecca Waring (reviews). Type: computer. Frequency of publication: weekly. Circulation: n/i. Freelance submissions: most features; some news. Number of manuscripts bought each year: hundreds.

**Editorial Needs. Nonfiction**—opinion; computer industry news; profiles of Macintosh users in big business. Suggested word length—feature articles: 300-1200; columns: variable.

**Initial Contact.** Query letter. State computer expertise of writer.

**Acceptance Policies.** Byline given: yes. Simultaneous submissions: no. Response time to initial inquiry: 4 weeks. Average time until publication: 1 month. **Payment:** $.40 per word is typical. Payment made: upon acceptance. Kill fee: varies according to contract. Writer's expenses on assignment: yes. Publishing rights: all rights. Computer print-outs: We want all submissions on disk or electronic file via MCI or other e-mail services. Disk submissions: Macintosh (3.5) only; Word format.

**Photography Submissions.** Photographers wishing assignments should contact Photo Editor John Hornstein.

**Additional Information.** We are the preeminent service publication for "volume buyers" of Apple Macintosh computers and accompanying software and peripherals. Tips: Don't call us; send query. Writer's guidelines: written request.

**MAGICAL BLEND, A TRANSFORMATIVE JOURNEY.** PO Box 11303. San Francisco, CA 94101. (415) 673-1001. Submissions Editor: Jerry Snider. Type: new age spirituality. Frequency of publication: quarterly. Circulation: 75,000. Freelance submissions: 70%. Number of manuscripts bought each year: 40.

**Editorial Needs. Nonfiction**—book excerpts; essays; general interest; how-to; humor; interview/profile; photo feature; new product; religious; technical; travel; columns (crystals; Magic In Your Life; astrology; spiritual travel). Suggested word length—feature articles: 900-4000; columns: 100-3000. **Fiction**—adventure; book selections; erotica; experimental; fantasy; science fiction; novels (condensed and serialized). Suggested word length—100-3000.

**Initial Contact.** Complete manuscript. Send photos.

**Acceptance Policies.** Byline given: yes. Submit seasonal material 6 months in advance. Response time to initial inquiry: 5 months. Average time until publication: n/i. **Payment**: $1-$100. Payment made: upon publication. Kill fee: no. Writer's expenses on assignment: no. Publishing rights: all. Computer print-outs: yes. Dot matrix: letter quality. Disk submissions: query first.

**Photography Submissions.** Format: n/i. Film: n/i. Photographs should include: captions; model releases; identification of subjects. **Payment**: $1-100. Photographic rights: all.

**Additional Information.** Tips: Be positive in your approach. Read the journal before submitting material. Writer's guidelines: #10 SASE; sample copy $4.

## MAINSTREAM, MAGAZINE OF THE ABLE-DISABLED.

2973 Beech St. San Diego, CA 92102. (619) 234-3138. Submissions Editor: Cyndi Jones. Type: audience is disabled consumers. Frequency of publication: 10 times yearly. Circulation: 15,500. Freelance submissions: 100%. Number of manuscripts bought each year: 50.

**Editorial Needs. Nonfiction**—book excerpts; how-to; humor; interview/profile; photo feature; travel; legislation; personal experience; columns (Creative Solutions; Personal Page). Suggested word length—feature articles: 6-12 pages; columns: 500-800. **Fiction**—humor, disability related. Suggested word length—800-1200 words.

**Initial Contact.** Query letter; or complete manuscript. Include clips; availability of photos.

**Acceptance Policies.** Byline given: yes. Submit seasonal material 4 months in advance. Response time to initial inquiry: 2 months. Average time until publication: 3 months. **Payment**: $50-$100; $25-$50 (columns). Payment made: upon publication. Kill fee: no. Writer's expenses on assignment: no. Publishing rights: all. Computer print-outs: yes. Dot matrix: letter quality. Disk submissions:

**Photography Submissions.** Format: contact sheets; 1 1/2 x 3/4 transparencies; 5x7 + prints. Film: black and white; color. Photographs should include: captions; identification of subjects. **Payment:** $5-$25 (black and white). Photographic rights: all.

**Additional Information.** Writer's guidelines: #10 SASE.

## MERCURY. (Astronomical Society of the Pacific). 390 Ashton Ave.

San Francisco, CA 94112. Submissions Editor: Andrew Fraknoi. Type: astronomy. Frequency of publication: twice monthly. Circulation: 7500.

**Editorial Needs. Nonfiction**—book excerpts; book reviews; general interest; historical; interview/profile; opinion; photo feature. Suggested word length—feature articles: varies.

**Initial Contact.** Query letter.

**Acceptance Policies.** Byline given: yes. Submit seasonal material 5-6 months in advance. Simultaneous submissions: no. Response time to initial inquiry: 2-5 months. Average time until publication: 2 months. **Payment**: We do not pay for manuscripts. All are written by scientists or science writers who believe in our international program of science education. Publishing rights: first North American serial rights. Computer print-outs: yes. Dot matrix: yes. Disk submissions: IBM or Macintosh.

**Photography Submissions.** Format: n/i. Film: black and white. Photographs should include: captions.

**Additional Information.** *Mercury* is a magazine on popular astronomy, published by the nonprofit Astronomical Society of the Pacific, founded in 1889.

**MEXICO WEST.** PO Box 1646. Bonita, CA 92002. (619) 585-3033. Submissions Editor: Shirley Miller. Type: Baja (Mexico) travel information. Frequency of publication: monthly. Circulation: 2500. Freelance submissions: 100%. Number of manuscripts bought each year: 60.

**Editorial Needs. Nonfiction**—book reviews; travel. Suggested word length—feature articles: 900-1200.

**Initial Contact.** Article proposal with subject outline; story as information.

**Acceptance Policies.** Byline given: yes. Simultaneous submissions: yes. Response time to initial inquiry: 2 weeks. Average time until publication: 1 month. **Payment**: $50. Payment made: upon publication. Kill fee: yes. Writer's expenses on assignment: n/i. Publishing rights: first North American serial rights. Computer print-outs: yes. Dot matrix: yes. Disk submissions: Microsoft Word; Macintosh Plus.

**Photography Submissions.** Format: print, 3x5. Film: black and white; color. Photographs should include: captions. **Payment**: include with story. Photographic rights: one-time use.

**Additional Information.** We are very specialized. Informational material. No "Me and Joe went . . . ." Tips: Know something about area. Writer's guidelines: write and request.

**MIND IN MOTION, A MAGAZINE OF POETRY AND SHORT PROSE.** PO Box 1118. Apple Valley, CA 92307. (619) 248-6512. Submissions Editor: Celeste Goyer. Type: literary. Frequency of publication: quarterly. Circulation: 250. Freelance submissions: 100%. Number of manuscripts bought each year: 160.

**Editorial Needs. Nonfiction**—might consider essays. **Fiction**—literary; science fiction; fantasy; avant-garde; satire; philosophy; surrealism. **Other**—poetry. Suggested word length—250-3000. Short stories—number per issue: 10; per year: 40.

**Initial Contact.** Entire manuscript; cover letter or bio with published credits not necessary.

**Acceptance Policies.** Byline given: initials follow piece; full name appears in index in back of each issue. Simultaneous submissions: yes; inform us. Response time to initial inquiry: 1 week-3 months. Average time until publication: 1 week to 3 months. **Payment**: one copy, when financially feasible. Publishing rights: first North American serial rights; or first rights. Computer print-outs: yes. Dot matrix: yes. Disk submissions: no.

**Additional Information.** Tips: Send your works of inspired brilliance. Please include dates of composition (if available) for all works. Writer's guidelines: #10 SASE.

**MODERN MATURITY.** (American Association of Retired Persons). 3200 E. Carson. Lakewood, CA 90712. Submissions Editor: Ian Ledgerwood. Type: for persons aged 50 and over. Frequency of publication: bimonthly. Circulation: 20 million. Freelance submissions: 50%. Number of manuscripts bought each year: n/i.

**Editorial Needs. Nonfiction**—practical information; health; legal; consumer; profiles; fillers (jokes, short anecdotes and humor; word-search puzzles). Suggested word length—feature articles: up to 2000. **Fiction**—write for information.

**Initial Contact.** Query first.

**Acceptance Policies.** Byline given: yes. Submit seasonal material 6 months in advance. Response time to initial inquiry: 6-8 weeks. Average time until publication: 4-6 months. **Payment**: up to $3000 (nonfiction); $50 (fillers, humor, etc). Payment made: upon acceptance. Kill fee: yes. Writer's expenses on assignment: sometimes. Publishing rights: first North American serial rights. Computer print-outs: yes. Dot matrix: no. Disk submissions: query first.

**Additional Information.** Writer's guidelines: upon request.

**MOTHER JONES MAGAZINE.** 1663 Mission Street. San Francisco, CA 94103. (415) 558-8881. Submissions Editors: Peggy Orenstein (general submissions); David Beers (profiles; shorter articles). Type: political. Frequency of publication: monthly. Circulation: 180,000. Freelance submissions: 100%.

**Editorial Needs. Nonfiction**—book excerpts; general interest. Suggested word length—feature articles: 3500; columns: 1000. **Fiction**—political. Short stories—number per year: 2-3.

**Initial Contact.** Query letter. Include clips.

**Acceptance Policies.** Byline given: yes. Submit seasonal material 3 months in advance. Simultaneous submissions: no. Response time to initial inquiry: 4-6 weeks. Average time until publication: 4 weeks. **Payment**: per text. Payment made: upon publication. Kill fee: 1/4. Writer's expenses on assignment: yes. Publishing rights: all rights. Computer print-outs: yes. Dot matrix: n/i. Disk submissions: yes.

**Additional Information.** Politically to the left. Writer's guidelines: request by mail.

**MOTORCYCLIST.** 8490 Sunset Blvd. Los Angeles, CA 90069. (213) 854-2230. Submissions Editor: Art Friedman. Type: motorcycle enthusiasts. Frequency of publication: monthly. Circulation: n/i. Freelance submissions: n/i.

**Editorial Needs. Nonfiction**—how-to; interview/profile; travel; timely news items; humor; cartoons. Suggested word length—feature articles: 2000-2500. **Fiction**—only the best humorous; philosophical; suspenseful or science fiction-type pieces involving motorcycles. Suggested word length—1500-2000.

**Initial Contact.** Entire article. Include SASE.

**Acceptance Policies.** Byline given: yes. Submit seasonal material 3-4 months in advance. Simultaneous submissions: no. Response time to initial inquiry: 4-6 weeks. Average time until publication: varies. **Payment**: $75-$100 per published page. Payment made: upon publication. Kill fee: n/i. Writer's expenses on assignment: n/i. Publishing rights: all rights. Computer print-outs: yes. Dot matrix: n/i. Disk submissions: no.

**Photography Submissions.** Format and film: color, 35mm or 2 1/4x2 1/4 transparencies; black and white, 8x10 glossy or matte prints. Photographs should include: captions. **Payment**: according to quality and published size. Photographic rights: n/i.

**Additional Information.** Our audience is young, affluent and educated. Tips: Typed, double-spaced, single side only. Material is subject to condensation or editing. Writer's guidelines: upon request.

**MOTORHOME.** 29901 Agoura Rd. Agoura, CA 91301. (818) 991-4980. Submissions Editord: Gail Harrington; Barbara Leonard. Type: travel and technical publication for motorhome owners. Frequency of publication: monthly. Circulation: 130,000. Freelance submissions: 75%. Number of manuscripts bought each year: 75.

**Editorial Needs. Nonfiction**—general interest; historical; how-to; humor; interview/profile; photo feature; travel.

**Initial Contact.** Query letter.

**Acceptance Policies.** Byline given: yes. Submit seasonal material 6-9 months in advance. Simultaneous submissions: yes. Response time to initial inquiry: 30 days. Average time until publication: 6-12 months. **Payment**: $200-$500. Payment made: upon acceptance. Kill fee: 1/3 of payment. Writer's expenses on assignment: yes. Publishing rights: first North American serial rights. Computer print-outs: yes. Dot matrix: n/i. Disk submissions: yes.

**Photography Submissions.** Format: transparencies. Film: color. Photographs should include: captions; model releases; identification of subjects. **Payment**: $75-$250. Photographic rights: one-time rights.

**Additional Information.** Tips: Understand our subject and travel needs and interests of motorhome travelers. Writer's guidelines: send letter to reader correspondent.

**MOTORLAND.** Not accepting manuscripts.

**MOTOR TREND.** 8490 Sunset Blvd. Los Angeles, CA 90069. (213) 854-2222. Submissions Editor: Jack Nerad. Type: automotive and related subjects of national interest. Frequency of publication: monthly. Circulation: 75,000. Freelance submissions: 20%. Number of manuscripts bought each year: n/i.

**Editorial Needs. Nonfiction**—new products; impressions; domestic and imported cars; classics; travel; racing. Suggested word length—feature articles: columns:

**Initial Contact.** Query letter (be specific).

**Acceptance Policies.** Byline given: n/i. Simultaneous submissions: no. Response time to initial inquiry: 1 month. Average time until publication: 3 months. **Payment**: n/i. Publishing rights: all. Computer print-outs: yes. Dot matrix: letter quality. Disk submissions: no.

**Photography Submissions.** Format and film: black and white glossy prints; color transparencies. Photographs should include: n/i. **Payment**: $25. Photographic rights: n/i.

**Additional Information.** Tips: Concentrate on the facts.

**MYSTERY READERS JOURNAL.** PO Box 8116. Berkeley, CA 94707. (415) 548-5799. Submissions Editor: Janet A. Rudolph. Type: literary/mystery review. Frequency of publication: quarterly. Circulation: 750. Freelance submissions: 100%.

**Editorial Needs. Nonfiction**—book reviews; entertainment reviews; interview/profile. Suggested word length—feature articles: 500-2500; columns: 500.

**Initial Contact.** Article proposal with subject outline. Include background of writer.

**Acceptance Policies.** Byline given: yes. Submit seasonal material 2 months in advance. Simultaneous submissions: no. Response time to initial inquiry: 2-3 weeks. Average time until publication: 1-2 months (depending on theme). **Payment**: issue of journal. Publishing rights: negotiable. Computer print-outs: yes. Dot matrix: yes. Disk submissions: Macintosh.

**Additional Information.** Each issue is thematic; articles pertaining to that issue only, i.e. 1989 Theatrical Mysteries; Murder on the Job; Legal Mysteries; and Bibliomysteries. Writer's guidelines: upon request.

**NATIONAL MASTERS NEWS.** PO Box 2372. Van Nuys, CA 91404. (818) 785-1895. Submissions Editors: Steve Lewallen (stories, photos); Jerry Wojcik (all track and field). Type: running, racewalking; track and field for age 40+. Frequency of publication: monthly. Circulation: 4800. Freelance submissions: 100%.

**Editorial Needs. Nonfiction**—general interest; health/fitness; interview/profile; opinion; coverage of races or meets. Suggested word length—feature articles: 1000; columns: 1000.

**Initial Contact.** Query letter.

**Acceptance Policies.** Byline given: yes. Submit seasonal material 1 month in advance. Simultaneous submissions: yes. Response time to initial inquiry: 2 weeks. Average time until publication: 2-4 weeks. **Payment**: none. Publishing rights: n/i. Computer print-outs: yes. Dot matrix: no. Disk submissions: no.

**Photography Submissions.** Format: prints, any size. Film: black and white. Photographs should include: identification of subjects; age of runner; event; finishing time. **Payment:** $7.50. Photographic rights: we keep photos.

**Additional Information.** Tips: Brevity is appreciated. Writer's guidelines: write and request.

**NATURE'S IMAGE.** PO Box 255. Davenport, CA 95017. (408) 426-8205. Submissions Editor: Frank S. Balthis. As photographers we seek science, history and travel writers for joint submissions to magazine and book publishers mainly in the areas of natural history and travel with a California emphasis.

**NEW bLOOD MAGAZINE.** 540 W. Foothill Blvd., Ste. 3730. Glendora, CA 91740. Submissions Editor: Chris Lacher. Type: horror/dark fantasy; science fiction; publishes fiction and other considered too strong by other periodicals. Frequency of publication: quarterly. Circulation: 10,000. Freelance submissions: 90% Number of manuscripts bought each year: 100-150.

**Editorial Needs.** **Nonfiction**—fillers; general interest; historical; humor; interview/profile; opinion; poetry; Suggested word length—feature articles: 3000. **Fiction**—no restrictions, as long as themes are strong or bizarre. Short stories—number per issue: 12; per year: 48-50.

**Initial Contact.** Any method is acceptable. Include publishing background, if any; brief bio. Can submit 3 stories under 1500 words; up to 10 poems.

**Acceptance Policies.** Byline given: yes. Submit seasonal material 6 months in advance. Response time to initial inquiry: 2 weeks, or less, on dated correspondence. Average time until publication: 3-6 months. **Payment:** $.03-$.06 per word; higher for special. Payment made: 1/2 upon acceptance; 1/2 upon publication. Kill fee: 1/2 of offered payment. Writer's expenses on assignment: no. Publishing rights: all rights revert back to author upon publication. Computer print-outs: yes. Dot matrix: yes. Disk submissions: no.

**Photography Submissions.** Format: prints, any size. Film: black and white. Photographs should include: n/i. Payment: negotiable. Photographic rights: all rights revert back to photographer on publication.

**Additional Information.** As a writer myself, I treat all contributors as family; I support you, and I ask you to support your magazine. Tips: Becoming familiar with the unique type of fiction and features before submitting by purchasing a subscription is crucial. Writer's guidelines: SASE; I always respond personally.

**NEW METHODS, JOURNAL OF ANIMAL HEALTH TECHNOLOGY.** PO Box 22605. San Francisco, CA 94122-0605. (415) 664-3469. Submissions Editor: Ronald S. Lippert. Type: animal professional's industry journal. Frequency of publication: irregular. Circulation: 5400+. Freelance submissions: 25%. Number of manuscripts bought each year: 2.

**Editorial Needs.** **Nonfiction**—book reviews; fillers; how-to; interview/profile; photo feature; animal field on an information level. Suggested word length—feature articles: varies; columns: varies.

**Initial Contact.** Query letter. Include name, address, phone. State minimum acceptable fee; turn around for specific work submitted.

**Acceptance Policies.** Byline given: yes. Submit seasonal material 2 months in advance. Response time to initial inquiry: 1 month or less. Average time until publication: 2 months +/-. **Payment:** varies, but low; products; trips; vacation spots,etc. Payment made: upon publication. Kill fee: no. Writer's expenses on assignment: yes. Publishing rights: author retains all rights. Computer print-outs: yes. Dot matrix: yes. Disk submissions: no.

**Photography Submissions.** Don't submit unless we request. Format: prints, 3x5. Film: black and white. Photographs should include: whatever you think is necessary. **Payment**: low. Photographic rights: photographer retains rights.

**Additional Information.** Tips: Write first please; include SASE. Writer's guidelines: write; enclose SASE.

**NEW WORLD TRAVELER; WEST COAST TRAVELER; EASY TRAVELER.** 1449 Grant St. Berkeley, CA 94705. (415) 524-8383. Submissions Editors: Selma Exton; Peter Von Blum. All writing in done in-house at this time.

**NORTHCOAST VIEW.** PO Box 1374. Eureka, CA 95502. (707) 443-4887. Submissions Editors: Scott K. Ryan and Damon Maguire (general); Stephen P. Miller (poetry). Type: regional-Humboldt County, CA. Frequency of publication: monthly. Circulation: 22,500. Freelance submissions: 100%. Number of manuscripts bought each year: 200.

**Editorial Needs. Nonfiction**—book reviews; general interest; health/fitness; historical; interview/profile; opinion; photo feature; poetry. Suggested word length—feature articles: 2250; columns: 600. **Fiction**—literary; genre. Short stories—number per issue: 1; per year: 8.

**Initial Contact.** Query letter; entire article. Include author bio.

**Acceptance Policies.** Byline given: yes. Submit seasonal material 6 months in advance. Simultaneous submissions: no. Response time to initial inquiry: 4-6 months. Average time until publication: 2 months. **Payment**: $.02-$.10 per word. Payment made: upon publication. Kill fee: no. Writer's expenses on assignment: no. Publishing rights: all rights. Computer print-outs: yes. Dot matrix: no. Disk submissions: no.

**Photography Submissions.** Format: prints, 5x7. Film: black and white. Photographs should include: model releases; identification of subjects. **Payment**: $20. Photographic rights: all.

**Additional Information.** Tips: Most submissions must have Humboldt County angle. Writer's guidelines: SASE. Sample copy $1.

**NOTEBOOK: A LITTLE MAGAZINE.** PO Box 170. Barstow, CA 92312. Submissions Editor: Yoly Zentella. Type: literary; women; humanism; Latino-American. Frequency of publication: semi-annual. Circulation: 100. Freelance submissions: 100%.

**Editorial Needs. Nonfiction**—book reviews; entertainment reviews; historical; interview/profile; opinion; photo feature; travel; Latino-American perspectives. Suggested word length—feature articles: 3000. **Fiction**—literary; women's; children's; avant-garde; Ethnic-American perspectives. Short stories—number per issue: 4/5; per year: 10-12.

**Initial Contact.** Query letter; entire article; SASE; source for contact with our press.

**Acceptance Policies.** Byline given: sometimes. Simultaneous submissions: yes; if we accept first, author withdraws manuscripts from other presses and guarantees us first rights. Response time to initial inquiry: 4-6 weeks. Average time until publication: varies. **Payment**: copies. Writer's expenses on assignment: no. Publishing rights: first North American serial rights. Computer print-outs: yes. Dot matrix: yes. Disk submissions: no.

**Photography Submissions.** Format: prints, 3x5 or larger; and contact sheets. Film: black and white. Photographs should include: identification of subjects; name, address of photographer; date. **Payment**: none if published with story; if separate, paid in copies. Photographic rights: first.

**Additional Information.** We stress writing by Latinos, Native Americans, Black-Americans, Arab-Americans and Asian Americans. We encourage writers to submit manuscripts to us. Tips: Just send it; include SASE. Writer's guidelines: SASE.

**OFF DUTY MAGAZINE.** 3303 Harbor Blvd., Ste. C-2. Costa Mesa, CA 92626. Submissions Editors: Bruce Thorstad (general; travel); Gary Birch (photo; audio/video; home computers); Joy Vandenberg (food; finance; lifestyle; home). Type: general interest for active duty military and their families. Frequency of publication: bimonthly. Circulation: 525,000. Freelance submissions: 40% +/-. Number of manuscripts bought each year: 25-30.

**Editorial Needs. Nonfiction**—general interest; health/fitness; interview/profile; photo feature; self-improvement; travel (often, we like to deal with the how of travel rather than the where); off-duty concerns of today's military people. Suggested word length—feature articles: 800, 1400, 1800 words. **Fiction**—We use one piece of fiction a year. It must be military and holiday themed. Query first.

**Initial Contact.** Query letter (first); article proposal with subject outline.

**Acceptance Policies.** Byline given: yes. Submit seasonal material 6 months in advance. Simultaneous submissions: yes; if they aren't offered elsewhere to our special audience. Response time to initial inquiry: We're flooded. Often, we can't respond at all to unsuitable queries. Average time until publication: n/i. **Payment**: $.13 per word; or by arrangement. Payment made: upon acceptance. Kill fee: n/i. Writer's expenses on assignment: sometimes phone and mileage. Publishing rights: first rights. Computer print-outs: yes. Dot matrix: yes. Disk submissions: no.

**Photography Submissions.** Format: prints; slides; transparencies. Film: black and white (depends on subject). Photographs should include: model releases; identification of subjects. **Payment**: depends on use. Photographic rights: first rights.

**Additional Information.** We're in California, but not *of* it. Our "beat" is 50 states. We are national. We assign half our stories to freelancers who work with us constantly. "On spec" stories are rarely for us. Tips: Query first. Writer's guidelines: $1; SASE.

**OPERA COMPANION.** 40 Museum Way. San Francisco, CA 94114. (415) 626-2741. Submissions Editor: James Keolker. Type: opera; music. Frequency of publication: 14 times yearly. Circulation: 8000. Freelance submissions: 25%. Number of manuscripts bought each year: 10.

**Editorial Needs. Nonfiction**—essay; historical; nostalgic; humor; interview/profile; fillers (humor; anecdotes). Suggested word length—feature articles: 500-5000; fillers: 150-500.

**Initial Contact.** Query. Include clips.

**Acceptance Policies.** Byline given: yes. Response time to initial inquiry: 1-4 weeks. Average time until publication: 2 months. **Payment**: $50-$250 (fillers). Payment made: upon acceptance. Kill fee: n/i. Writer's expenses on assignment: n/i. Publishing rights: first rights. Computer print-outs: yes. Dot matrix: letter quality. Disk submissions: no.

**Additional Information.** Each issue highlights a specific opera and composer. Contact us for which composers and operas will be featured in upcoming issues. Writer's guidelines: 8 1/2x11 SASE, 3 first class stamps.

**OUT WEST.** PO Box 19894. Sacramento, CA 95819. (916) 457-4006. Submissions Editor: Chuck Woodbury. Type: American West, general interest. Frequency of publication: quarterly. Circulation: 5000 and growing fast. Freelance submissions: 25%. Number of manuscripts bought each year: 40-50.

**Editorial Needs. Nonfiction**—book reviews; fillers; general interest; historical; interview/profile; photo feature; travel; columns; fillers. Suggested word length—feature articles: 400-900; columns: 350-600.

**Initial Contact.** Query letter; entire article.

**Acceptance Policies.** Byline given: yes. Submit seasonal material 3 months in advance. Simultaneous submissions: yes. Response time to initial inquiry: 1-7 weeks. Average time until publication: 1-4 months. **Payment:** $.04-$.06 per word; more on occasion. Payment made: upon acceptance; or upon publication. Kill fee: 50%. Writer's expenses on assignment: no. Publishing rights: second serial rights; usually one-time rights. Computer print-outs: yes. Dot matrix: yes. Disk submissions: no.

**Photography Submissions.** Format: 5x7 or 8x10 prints. Film: black and white. Photographs should include: captions; identification of subjects. **Payment:** $6-$15. Photographic rights: one-time.

**Additional Information.** We are looking for the offbeat "little" story; out-of-the way travel places; humor always a plus. Tips: Be sure and read the publication first; $6 for yearly subscription. Writer's guidelines: #10 SASE.

**OWLFLIGHT.** 1025 55th St. Oakland, CA 94608. (415) 655-3024. Submissions Editor: Millea Kenin. Type: science fiction and fantasy. Frequency of publication: 1-3 per year. Circulation: 1000. Freelance submissions: 100%. Number of manuscripts bought each year: 10-45.

**Editorial Needs. Nonfiction**—no unsolicited nonfiction. Short stories—number per issue: 10-15; per year: 10-45. **Fiction**—science fiction; fantasy. Suggested word length—3000-8000. **Other**—line art; poems (same genre as fiction).

**Initial Contact.** Query letter (only to learn if we're overstocked); entire story. Include cover letter with pertinent information. No descriptions of story or lengthy author credit sheet. Send only 1 story, up to 6 poems or art samples per submission.

**Acceptance Policies.** Byline given: yes. Simultaneous submissions: yes; must be identified; will only take second options on them. Response time to initial inquiry: 1 week to 2 months. Average time until publication: 1-2 years. **Payment:** $.01 per word, $1 minimum up to $10. Payment made: 1/2 on acceptance; 1/2 on publication. Kill fee: all or $10, whichever is smaller. Writer's expenses on assignment: no. Publishing rights: first North American serial rights; second serial rights (send for reprint guidelines-1 stamp SASE). Computer print-outs: yes. Dot matrix: black, letter quality. Disk submissions: only after acceptance of hard copy; Macintosh or IBM compatible text format.

**Photography Submissions.** Query first.

**Additional Information.** We have won Small Press Writers and Artists Association award twice. Tips: Get Guidelines first. They are detailed and let you know what lengths, what themes are overstocked. Writer's guidelines: #10 SASE with postage to cover 2 ounces .

**PAN-EROTIC REVIEW.** PO Box 2992. Santa Cruz, CA 95063. (408) 426-7082. Submissions Editor: David Steinberg. Type: erotica—high quality, provocative, non-pornographic erotic fiction, poetry and photography. Frequency of publication: quarterly. Circulation: n/i. Freelance submissions: most. Number of manuscripts bought each year: varies.

**Editorial Needs. Nonfiction**—poems; photo feature. **Fiction**—quality erotica, sexually explicit is fine. Short stories—number per issue: varies.

**Initial Contact.** Query letter. Include samples of work.

**Acceptance Policies.** Byline given: yes. Submit seasonal material 3 months in advance. Simultaneous submissions: yes. Response time to initial inquiry: 2-4 weeks. Average time until publication: varies. **Payment:** varies. Payment made: varies. Kill fee: no. Writer's expenses on assignment: no. Publishing rights: first North American serial rights; first rights; second serial rights. Computer print-outs: yes. Dot matrix: yes. Disk submissions: Macintosh.

**Photography Submissions.** Format: prints, 8x10. Film: black and white. Photographs should include: n/i. **Payment**: varies. Photographic rights: one-time or all.

## PANGLOSS PAPERS.

PO Box 18917. Los Angeles, CA 90018. (213) 663-1950. Submissions Editor: Bard Dahl. Type: literary. Frequency of publication: quarterly. Circulation: 600. Freelance submissions: 100%.

**Editorial Needs. Nonfiction**—poetry; articles; cartoons; satire; reviews. **Fiction**—satirical, but not exclusively. Our magazine is only 50 pages, therefore fiction must be kept short.

**Initial Contact.** Entire manuscript.

**Acceptance Policies.** Byline given: yes. Response time to initial inquiry: 3 weeks. Average time until publication: 3 months. **Payment**: 2 copies. Publishing rights: remain with author. Computer print-outs: no. Dot matrix: n/i. Disk submissions: no.

**Additional Information.** Suspending publication in Fall of 1989.

## PENINSULA MAGAZINE.

656 Bair Island Raod. Redwood City, CA 94063. (415) 368-8800. Submissions Editor: David Gorn, Dale Conour. Type: general-interest local magazine covering San Francisco Peninsula (not including San Francisco). Frequency of publication: monthly. Circulation: 40,000. Freelance submissions: 50%. Number of manuscripts bought each year: 100.

**Editorial Needs. Nonfiction**—entertainment reviews; general interest; health/fitness; historical; interview/profile; photo feature; investigative pieces; environment. Suggested word length—feature articles: 2500-4000; columns: 750.

**Initial Contact.** Query letter.

**Acceptance Policies.** Byline given: yes. Submit seasonal material 2-3 months in advance. Simultaneous submissions: no. Response time to initial inquiry: 1 month. Average time until publication: 4 months. **Payment**: varies. Payment made: upon acceptance. Kill fee: 30% of purchase price. Writer's expenses on assignment: yes. Publishing rights: first rights; rights of re-use without further compensation. Computer print-outs: yes. Dot matrix: yes. Disk submissions: ASCII.

**Photography Submissions.** Format: contact sheets; transparencies. Film: black and white; color. Photographs should include: captions; model releases; identification of subjects. **Payment**: varies. Photographic rights: first rights.

**Additional Information.** Tips: Use local angle. Writer's guidelines: write and request.

## PETERSEN'S PHOTOGRAPHIC MAGAZINE.

8490 Sunset Blvd. Los Angeles, CA 90069. (213) 854-2200. Submissions Editor: Bill Hurter. Type: how-to photography. Frequency of publication: monthly. Circulation: 275,000. Freelance submissions: 40%. Number of manuscripts bought each year: 50+.

**Editorial Needs. Nonfiction**—how-to. Suggested word length—feature articles: n/i.

**Initial Contact.** Complete manuscript. Include captioned photos.

**Acceptance Policies.** Byline given: n/i. Submit seasonal material 5 months in advance. Response time to initial inquiry: 2 months. Average time until publication: 9 months. **Payment**: $60 per printed page. Payment made: upon publication. Kill fee: no. Writer's expenses on assignment: no. Publishing rights: all. Computer print-outs: yes. Dot matrix: n/i. Disk submissions: IBM PC compatible only.

**Photography Submissions.** Cover shots purchased separately. Format: n/i. Film: black and white; color. Photographs should include: model releases; technical details. **Payment**: $25-$35; cover, negotiable. Photographic rights: all. Writer's guidelines: #10 SASE; sample copy $3.

**PLAYERS PRESS, INC.** PO Box 1132. Studio City, CA 91604. (818) 789-4980. Submissions Editor: Robert W. Gordon.

Publishes plays and scripts. Send for writer's guidelines; has very specific and unusual requirements.

**PM/PEDANTIC MONTHLY.** (Subsidiary of Numedia). 1383 Idaho St. Santa Clara, CA 95050. (408) 985-9208. Submissions Editors: Lydia Renay (fiction); Erik Johnson (all other entries). Type: humor/satire. Frequency of publication: 5 times per year. Circulation: 500. Freelance submissions: 60-70%.

**Editorial Needs. Nonfiction**—book reviews; entertainment reviews; fillers; humor; poetry; spoofs; parodies; drawings;cartoons. Suggested word length—feature articles: 1500-2000; columns: 500-1000. **Fiction**—fantasy; humor. Short stories—number per issue: 2-3; per year: 10-15. Art—black and white photos, drawings, cartoons, etc. to maximum print area of 4x5. We can scale/scan larger pieces (to 12x20).

**Initial Contact.** Entire article.

**Acceptance Policies.** Byline given: yes. Simultaneous submissions: yes; inform us. Response time to initial inquiry: 1-2 months. Average time until publication: 1-2 months. **Payment**: copies; subscription. Publishing rights: first North American serial rights. Computer print-outs: yes. Dot matrix: yes. Disk submissions: Macintosh, MacWrite or Word; 3 1/2" disks.

**Additional Information.** Every possible subject is appropriate, if treated humorously. We're original. Tips: You be original. Writer's guidelines: SASE.

**POETRY/LA.** PO Box 84271. Los Angeles, CA 90073. (213) 472-6171. Submissions Editor: Helen Friedland. Type: literary, poetry only. Frequency of publication: twice yearly. Circulation: 500. Freelance submissions: 100%. Number of manuscripts bought each year: about 200 poems.

**Editorial Needs. Nonfiction**—poetry. Suggested word length—any.

**Initial Contact.** Submit poems.

**Acceptance Policies.** Byline given: yes. Simultaneous submissions: no. Response time to initial inquiry: n/i. Average time until publication: 6 months. **Payment**: 1-5 copies depending on length and number of poems. Publishing rights: all rights; will release on request for reprint. Computer print-outs: yes. Dot matrix: no. Disk submissions: no.

**Additional Information.** We publish only Los Angeles area poets (Santa Barbara to Irvine). Tips: Send a SASE for writer's guidelines; or $3.50 for sample copy.

**POLICE.** 6300 Yarrow Dr. Carlsbad, CA 92009. (619) 438-2511. Submissions Editor: Jennifer Mencher. Type: professional trade journal for law enforcement officers. Frequency of publication: monthly. Circulation: 50,000. Freelance submissions: 90% Number of manuscripts bought each year: 100.

**Editorial Needs. Nonfiction**—book excerpts; how-to; interview/profile; photo feature; columns. Suggested word length—feature articles: 2500; columns: 2000. **Short stories** (nonfiction)—number per year: 3.

**Initial Contact.** Article proposal with subject outline.

**Acceptance Policies.** Byline given: yes. Submit seasonal material 3 months in advance. Simultaneous submissions: no. Response time to initial inquiry: 2 weeks. Average time until publication: 3-6 months. **Payment**: varies with type of article. Payment made: upon acceptance. Kill fee: no. Writer's expenses on assignment: no. Publishing rights: first North American serial rights. Computer print-outs: yes. Dot matrix: yes. Disk submissions: no.

**Photography Submissions.** Format: transparencies. Film: color. Photographs should include: captions; identification of subjects. **Payment**: $30 per photo. Photographic rights: first rights.

**Additional Information.** Tips: All material must have a strong law enforcement slant. Writer's guidelines: SASE.

**PORTS O'CALL.** PO Box 530. Santa Rosa, CA 95402. (707) 542-0898. Submissions Editor: William A. Breniman. *See* **SPARKS JOURNAL.**

**POWDER, THE SKIERS' MAGAZINE.** PO Box 1028. Dana Point, CA 92629. (714) 496-5922. Submissions Editors: Pat Cochran (features); Steve Casimiro (dept. material); Jackie Mathys (fashion/accessories); Casey Sheahan (cross country/backcountry). Type: skiing. Frequency of publication: 7 times per year. Circulation: 150,000. Freelance submissions: 90%. Number of manuscripts bought each year: 30.

**Editorial Needs.** **Nonfiction**—book excerpts; book reviews; entertainment reviews; general interest; health/fitness; historical; humor; interview/profile; photo feature; travel. Suggested word length—feature articles: 1500-2000. Short stories—number per year: 2.

**Initial Contact.** Query letter; article proposal with subject outline; entire article. Any okay, just no phone queries.

**Acceptance Policies.** Byline given: yes. Submit seasonal material 5 months in advance. Simultaneous submissions: no. Response time to initial inquiry: 6-8 weeks. Average time until publication: 2-3 months. **Payment**: n/i. Payment made: on publication if article on spec; on acceptance if assigned. Kill fee: 50% for assigned articles only. Writer's expenses on assignment: if approved in advance. Publishing rights: first rights. Computer print-outs: yes. Dot matrix: no. Disk submissions: Macintosh.

**Photography Submissions.** Format: transparencies. Film: color. Photographs should include: captions; model releases; identification of subjects. **Payment**: $50-$500 depending on size used. Photographic rights: first rights only.

**Additional Information.** Articles should be directed to advanced to expert skiers only! Tips: Read back issues for style. Writer's guidelines: write and request.

**POWERBOAT MAGAZINE.** 15917 Strathern St. Van Nuys, CA 91406. Submissions Editor: Bob Nordskog. Type: recreational power boating (high performance); water skiing. Frequency of publication: monthly. Circulation: 82,000. Freelance submissions: 60%. Number of manuscripts bought each year: n/i.

**Editorial Needs.** **Nonfiction**—how-to photo essays; competition coverage; interviews/profiles; new products. Suggested word length—feature articles: 1500-2000.

**Initial Contact.** Query letter required.

**Acceptance Policies.** Byline given: yes. Response time to initial inquiry: 2 weeks. Average time until publication: 3 months. **Payment**: $150-500. Payment made: upon publication. Kill fee: no. Writer's expenses on assignment: sometimes. Publishing rights: all; first North American serial rights. Computer print-outs: yes. Dot matrix: letter quality. Disk submissions: query.

**Photography Submissions.** Format and film: 35mm kodachrome slides.

**Additional Information.** We are interested in how our readers can maximize their high performance boating experiences. Writer's guidelines: free sample copy.

**PRIVATE PILOT.** PO Box 6050. Mission Viejo, CA 92690. (714) 855-8822. Submissions Editor: Mary F. Silitch. Type: for owner/pilots of private planes. Frequency of publication: Circulation: 120,000. Freelance submissions: 75%. Number of manuscripts bought each year: 75+/-.

**Editorial Needs. Nonfiction**—general aviation field; flying techniques; new products; test reports; columns. Suggested word length—feature articles: 1000-4000; columns: 1000.

**Initial Contact.** query letter.

**Acceptance Policies.** Byline given: n/i. Simultaneous submissions: no. Response time to initial inquiry: 8 weeks. Average time until publication: 6 months. **Payment**: $75-$300; $50-$125 (columns). Payment made: upon publication. Kill fee: Writer's expenses on assignment: Publishing rights: first North American serial rights. Computer print-outs: yes. Dot matrix: double-spaced; upper and lower case. Disk submissions: query.

**Photography Submissions.** Format and film: 8x10 black and white glossy prints; color transparencies (cover). Photographs should include: n/i. **Payment**: $15 (black and white); $150 (cover). Photographic rights: same as article.

**Additional Information.** Our audience is particularly knowledgeable; articles should be well-researched and written to that level. Writer's guidelines: SASE.

**PROFESSIONAL CAREERS.** Writers Connection. 1601 Saratoga-Sunnyvale Rd., Ste. 180. Cupertino, CA 95014. Submissions Editor: Meera Lester. *See* **HIGH TECHNOLOGY CAREERS.**

**PROPHETIC VOICES.** 94 Santa Maria Dr. Novato, CA 94947. (415) 897-5679. Submissions Editors: Ruth Wildes Schuler; Goldie L. Morales; Jeanne Leigh Schuler-Farrell. Type: literary, poetry. Frequency of publication: twice yearly. Circulation: 400. Freelance submissions: most. Number of manuscripts bought each year: n/i.

**Editorial Needs. Nonfiction**—poetry; art. Short stories—rarely.

**Initial Contact.** Submit complete material.

**Acceptance Policies.** Byline given: n/i. Simultaneous submissions: prefer exclusive. Response time to initial inquiry: 2 weeks. Average time until publication: varies. **Payment**: contributor's copy. Computer print-outs: yes. Dot matrix: n/i. Disk submissions: no.

**Additional Information.** Tips: No religious poetry. Prefer poetry of social significance.

**PUBLISH!, THE HOW-TO MAGAZINE OF DESKTOP PUBLISHING.** 501 Second St. San Francisco, CA 94107. (415) 546-7722. Submissions Editor: c/o Submissions Editor. Type: desktop publishing. Frequency of publication: monthly. Circulation: 100,000. Freelance submissions: 80%. Number of manuscripts bought each year: 120.

**Editorial Needs. Nonfiction**—book excerpts; new products; interview/profile; technical information. Suggested word length—feature articles: 300-2500.

**Initial Contact.** Query. Include clips; photo availability.

**Acceptance Policies.** Byline given: yes. Response time to initial inquiry: 3 weeks. Average time until publication: n/i. **Payment**: $300-$2000. Payment made: upon acceptance. Kill fee: no. Writer's expenses on assignment: sometimes. Publishing rights: first international. Computer print-outs: yes. Dot matrix: letter quality. Disk submissions: query.

**Photography Submissions.** Format: contact sheets. Film: black and white. Photographs should include: captions; identification of subjects. **Payment**: n/i. Photographic rights: same as article.

**Additional Information.** Writer's guidelines: upon request.

**QUARRY WEST.** c/o Porter College. University of California. Santa Cruz, CA 95064. (408) 429-9403. (408) 429-9403. Submissions Editor: Ken Weisner. Type: literary. Frequency of publication: semiannual. Circulation: 700. Freelance submissions: n/i.

**Editorial Needs. Fiction**—literary. Short Stories—number per issue: 2-3. Other—poetry; art.

**Initial Contact.** Complete manuscripts. Include SASE.

**Acceptance Policies.** Byline given: yes. Simultaneous submissions: yes. Response time to initial inquiry: 6 weeks. Average time until publication: 1-3 months. **Payment**: 2 contributor copies. Publishing rights: first North American serial rights. Computer print-outs: yes. Dot Matrix: yes. Disk submissions: Macintosh.

**Additional Information.** Published in the fall and spring. Submitted material should be sent between September and May. Tips: We are interested in good writing—we've published first-time writers and experienced professionals. The only criteria is good writing. Writer's guidelines: call.

**RADIANCE, THE MAGAZINE FOR LARGE WOMEN.** PO Box 31703. Oakland, CA 94604. (415) 482-0680. Submissions Editor: Alice Ansfield. Type: women's; health; psychology; fashion. Frequency of publication: quarterly. Circulation: 40,000. Freelance submissions: 100%. Number of manuscripts bought each year: 70-80.

**Editorial Needs. Nonfiction**—book excerpts; book reviews; entertainment reviews; general interest; health/fitness; historical; how-to; humor; inspiration; interview/profile; opinion; photo feature; poetry; self-improvement. Suggested word length—feature articles: 2000; columns: 1500. **Fiction**—women's (prefer if stories are related to large women). Short stories—number per year: 2.

**Initial Contact.** Article proposal with subject outline; entire article (would be nice).

**Acceptance Policies.** Byline given: yes. Submit seasonal material 6 months in advance. Simultaneous submissions: yes. Response time to initial inquiry: 2 1/2 months. Average time until publication: varies—our issues have themes (1-6 months). **Payment**: $50-$100 per article at this point, plus issue in which article appears. Payment made: upon publication. Kill fee: $25, only if we requested article. Writer's expenses on assignment: most of the time. Publishing rights: we're negotiable and open. Computer print-outs: yes. Dot matrix: letter quality only. Disk submissions: not at this time.

**Photography Submissions.** Format and film: black and white: prints 5x7; contact sheets; color: slides. Color for cover, inside black and white. Photographs should include: captions; identification of subjects; photo credit. **Payment**: $20 per inside photo used; $50 for cover. Photographic rights: n/i.

**Additional Information.** We're an upbeat, supportive magazine for the larger woman. We like good, strong profiles, interviews. We cover health, fashion, cultural/social views of body size, and more. Our focus is self-esteem. Tips: Send for sample copy at $1.50 to get the flavor of our magazine first. Writer's guidelines: SASE.

**RADIUS/ ARC.** PO Box 1547. Mendocino, CA 95460. (707) 937-4494. Submissions Editor: K. Larsen. Type: community arts resource listings (management, funding, services, etc.); and feature stories on rural arts issues. Frequency of publication: twice monthly. Circulation: 2000. Freelance submissions: 100%.

**Editorial Needs. Nonfiction**—community arts resource listings and articles on rural arts planning and management. Suggested word length—feature articles: 1500.

**Initial Contact.** Query letter.

**Acceptance Policies.** Byline given: yes. Simultaneous submissions: yes. Response time to initial inquiry: 2 months. Average time until publication: 6 months. **Payment**: referral to funding sources for grants and fellowships. Publishing rights: n/i. Computer print-outs: yes. Dot matrix: yes. Disk submissions: no.

**Photography Submissions.** Format: n/i. Film: black and white. Photographs should include: captions; identification of subjects. **Payment**: none. Photographic rights: n/i.

**Additional Information.** We're nonprofit, low budget, with few ads. We publish for a very interesting but specialized audience interested in making the arts a vital part of the fabric of community life. Tips: We do reach a very intelligent readership. Though there's no pay, there's good reader response.

**REAPER, THE.** 403 Continental St. Santa Cruz, CA 95060. (408) 426-5539. Submissions Editors: Robert Mc Dowell, Mark Jarman (poetry; essays; reviews); Thomas Wilhelmus (fiction). Type: literary. Frequency of publication: twice yearly. Circulation: 700. Freelance submissions: 100%.

**Editorial Needs. Nonfiction**—entertainment reviews; opinion; poetry. Suggested word length—feature articles: 2000. **Fiction**—literary; women's. Short stories—number per year: 2.

**Initial Contact.** Query letter.

**Acceptance Policies.** Byline given: n/a. Submit seasonal material 3 months in advance. Simultaneous submissions: yes. Response time to initial inquiry: 1 month. Average time until publication: 6-12 months. **Payment**: copies. Publishing rights: first North American serial rights. Computer print-outs: yes. Dot matrix: yes, but not encouraged. Disk submissions: no.

**RIDER.** 29001 Agoura Rd. Agoura, CA 91301 Submissions Editor: Tash Matsouka. Type: motorcycle commuting, touring, and sport riding. Frequency of publication: monthly. Circulation: n/i. Freelance submissions: 60%. Number of manuscripts bought each year: n/i.

**Editorial Needs. Nonfiction**—directly related to camping, sport riding, travel; safety; how-to; technical; personal experience; historical; opinion. Suggested word length—feature articles: varies.

**Initial Contact.** Query first.

**Acceptance Policies.** Byline given: n/i. Submit seasonal material 3 months in advance. Response time to initial inquiry: 1 month. Average time until publication: 6 months. **Payment:** $100 (short feature); $350-$500 (major articles). Payment made: upon publication. Kill fee: no. Writer's expenses on assignment: sometimes. Publishing rights: first time rights only. Computer print-outs: yes. Dot matrix: no. Disk submissions: no.

**Photography Submissions.** Format: n/i. Film: n/i. Photographs should include: captions. **Payment**: included with manuscript. Photographic rights: same as article. Tips: Direct your article to the well-informed reader. Photo quality is stressed and very important. Writer's guidelines: SASE.

**ROAD AND TRACK.** 1499 Monrovia Ave. Newport Beach, CA 92663. (714) 720-5300. Submissions Editor: Thos L. Bryant. Type: for car enthusiasts. Frequency of publication: monthly. Circulation: n/i. Freelance submissions: 10%.

**Editorial Needs. Nonfiction**—in-depth exploration of subject area.

**Initial Contact.** Query letter.

**Acceptance Policies.** Byline given: n/i. Response time to initial inquiry: 6 weeks. Average time until publication: 2 years. **Payment:** $.25-$.50 per word. Publishing rights: first rights. Computer print-outs: yes. Dot matrix: n/i. Disk submissions: no.

**Additional Information.** Tips: We buy very few articles.

**RV BUSINESS.** 29901 Agoura Rd. Agoura, CA 91301. (818) 991-4980. Submissions Editor: Katherine Sharma. Type: RV industry personnel. Frequency of publication: semimonthly. Circulation: 25,000. Freelance submissions: 60%. Number of manuscripts bought each year: 75; columns 100-120.

**Editorial Needs.** **Nonfiction**—directed toward dealership owners, manufacturers, suppliers: article on marketing; how-to; business; interview/profile; legal; verifiable statistics; columns (guest editorial; RV people). Suggested word length—feature articles: 1000-1500; columns: 50-500.

**Initial Contact.** Query letter (send one or more ideas with outline of article). State photo availability; or send complete manuscript (include photos). Include clips.

**Acceptance Policies.** Byline given: yes. Submit seasonal material 6 months in advance. Response time to initial inquiry: 3-6 weeks. Average time until publication: 2 months. **Payment:** $500; $10-$200 (columns). Payment made: upon acceptance. Kill fee: 50%. Writer's expenses on assignment: sometimes. Publishing rights: first North American serial rights. Computer print-outs: yes. Dot matrix: letter quality. Disk submissions: query.

**Photography Submissions.** required. Format and film: 35mm transparencies; 8x10 black and white. Photographs should include: captions; model releases; identification of subjects. **Payment:** included with article. Photographic rights: buys one-time or all rights. (Unused photos returned.)

**Additional Information.** Writer's guidelines: #10 SASE; sample copy 9x12 SASE, 3 first class stamps.

**RX HOME CARE, THE JOURNAL OF HOME HEALTH CARE AND REHABILITATION.** 1640 5th St. Santa Monica, CA 90401. (213) 395-0234. Submissions Editor: Cliff Henke. Type: professionals in the home health care field; medical supply dealers. Frequency of publication: monthly. Circulation: 18,000. Freelance submissions: 40%. Number of manuscripts bought each year: 50.

**Editorial Needs.** **Nonfiction**—how-to (market medical equipment); technical (non-invasive therapy); columns (legislative news; dealerships; computer). Suggested word length—feature articles: 900-3500. columns: 500-2000.

**Initial Contact.** Query by phone first.

**Acceptance Policies.** Byline given: yes. Response time to initial inquiry: 3 weeks. Average time until publication: 6 months. **Payment:** $.12 per word; $100 (columns). Payment made: upon acceptance. Kill fee: Writer's expenses on assignment: yes. Publishing rights: all rights; work-for-hire. Computer print-outs: yes. Dot matrix: n/i. Disk submissions: no.

**Additional Information.** Our magazine is slanted toward legislation, technological advances and their effect on our readers in their professional capacity. Tips: While you do not have to be a medical professional to write for us, you must be conversant with medical terminology and conform to the American Medical Association handbook. All work is reviewed by a professional editorial board.

**SACRAMENTO MAGAZINE.** PO Box 2424. Sacramento, CA 95812-2424. Submissions Editor: Nancy Curley. Type: regional. Frequency of publication: monthly. Circulation: 25,000. Freelance submissions: 60%. Number of manuscripts bought each year: 15.

**Editorial Needs.** **Nonfiction**—local issues pertinent to Sacramento region. Suggested word length—feature articles: 2000-3000. Columns—business; home and garden; parenting; politics; travel; sports; arts. Suggested word length—1000-1500.

**Initial Contact.** Query letter. Include photo availability.

**Acceptance Policies.** Byline given: yes. Response time to initial inquiry: 8 weeks. Average time until publication: 3 months. **Payment**: $65-$300. Payment made: upon publication Kill fee: no. Writer's expenses on assignment: sometimes. Publishing rights: first North American serial rights; second serial rights (rarely). Computer print-outs: yes. Dot matrix: letter quality. Disk submissions: no.

**Photography Submissions.** Format: n/i. Film: n/i. Photographs should include: captions (identification, location and date). **Fee**: varies. Photographic rights: one-time rights.

**Additional Information.** Writer's guidelines: SASE; sample copy $4.50.

## SAN DIEGO HOME/GARDEN.

PO Box 1471. San Diego, CA 92112. (619) 233-4567. Submissions Editor: Peter Jensen. Type: regional. Frequency of publication: monthly. Circulation: 33,000. Freelance submissions: 50%. Number of manuscripts bought each year: 60+\-.

**Editorial Needs. Nonfiction**—homes; gardens; home entertainment; food; local travel; architecture; interior design; arts; environment. Suggested word length—feature articles: 700-2000.

**Initial Contact.** Query letter. Include clips.

**Acceptance Policies.** Byline given: yes. Submit seasonal material 3 months in advance. Response time to initial inquiry: 2 month. Average time until publication: 6 months. **Payment**: $50-$400. Payment made: upon acceptance. Kill fee: no. Writer's expenses on assignment: sometimes. Publishing rights: first North American serial rights. Computer print-outs: yes. Dot matrix: n/i. Disk submissions: no.

**Additional Information.** Regional, unique to San Diego area only. Writer's guidelines: SASE.

## SAN DIEGO READER.

PO Box 80803. San Diego, CA 92138. (619) 231-7821. Submissions Editor: James E. Holman. Type: general interest for the San Diego area only. Frequency of publication: weekly. Circulation: 129,000. Freelance submissions: 15%. Number of manuscripts bought each year: 50.

**Editorial Needs. Nonfiction**—general interest. Short stories—(nonfiction)—number per issue: 2-3.

**Initial Contact.** Query letter.

**Acceptance Policies.** Byline given: yes. Simultaneous submissions: yes. Response time to initial inquiry: 10 days. Average time until publication: 15-30 days. **Payment**: $500-$1500 shorter features; $1500-$2000 longer features. Payment made: upon publication. Kill fee: no. Writer's expenses on assignment: only extraordinary. Publishing rights: first rights. Computer print-outs: yes. Dot matrix: yes. Disk submissions: CPM or MS-DOS.

**Additional Information.** Only local San Diego items. Tips: Don't call us. Writer's guidelines: write and request.

## SAN FERNANDO POETRY JOURNAL.

18301 Halsted St. Northridge, CA 91325. (818) 349-2080. Submissions Editor: Richard Cloke. Type: social protest poetry; women's liberation; minority rights; peace issues; environmental concerns. Frequency of publication: quarterly. Circulation: 500. Freelance submissions: 100%.

**Editorial Needs. Nonfiction**—poetry which urges or implies struggle to alter our system.

**Initial Contact.** Send poetry.

**Acceptance Policies.** Byline given: yes. Submit seasonal material 12 months in advance. Simultaneous submissions: yes. Response time to initial inquiry: 1 week. Average time until publication: 1 year. **Payment**: in copies. Publishing rights: one-time rights only. Computer print-outs: yes. Dot matrix: yes. Disk submissions: no.

**Additional Information.** Tips: We like to see work with energy, well-thought out and with compelling ideas. See our guidelines first. Writer's guidelines: SASE.

**SAN FRANCISCO BAY GUARDIAN.** 2700 19th Street. San Francisco, CA 94110. (415) 824-7660. Submissions Editors: Jean Field (entertainment); Eileen Ecklund (lifestyle, books, and features); Tim Redmond (news); John Schmitz (illustrations, photos). Type: alternative newsweekly, with an emphasis on news, entertainment, consumer and lifestyle features. Frequency of publication: weekly. Circulation: 65,000. Freelance submissions: 80%. Number of manuscripts bought each year: 60-200.

**Editorial Needs. Nonfiction**—book reviews; entertainment reviews; general interest; health/fitness; interview/profile; travel; news on local and statewide issues. Suggested word length—feature articles: 2500; columns: 800-1000.

**Initial Contact.** Article proposal with subject outline; entire article. Include resumé, clips.

**Acceptance Policies.** Byline given: yes. Submit seasonal material 2 months in advance. Simultaneous submissions: no. Response time to initial inquiry: 1 month. Average time until publication: varies. **Payment:** $40-$250, depending on length and scope. Payment made: upon acceptance plus. Kill fee: no. Writer's expenses on assignment: yes. Publishing rights: first rights. Computer print-outs: yes. Dot matrix: yes. Disk submissions: CPM or MS-DOS; please include print-out.

**Photography Submissions.** Format: n/i. Film: black and white. Photographs should include: captions; model releases; identification of subjects. **Payment:** $40. Photographic rights: first rights.

**Additional Information.** We only print high-quality individual features. Tips: Read the paper to learn our style and types of features. Write queries, don't call!

**SAN FRANCISCO BUSINESS TIMES.** 325 Fifth St. San Francisco, CA 94107. (415) 777-9355. Submissions Editor: Tim Clark. Type: local business. Frequency of publication: weekly. Circulation: 30,000. Freelance submissions: 15-25%. Number of manuscripts bought each year: 25.

**Editorial Needs. Nonfiction**—interview/profile; opinion. Suggested word length—feature articles: 800-1000; columns: 800.

**Initial Contact.** Query letter.

**Acceptance Policies.** Byline given: yes. Simultaneous submissions: inform us; not to publication in our area Response time to initial inquiry: 2-3 weeks. Average time until publication: 3 months. **Payment:** $100-$150. Payment made: upon publication. Kill fee: no. Writer's expenses on assignment: yes. Publishing rights: first North American serial rights; second serial rights. Computer print-outs: yes. Dot matrix: yes. Disk submissions: ASCII, no control characters.

**Photography Submissions.** Format: prints, 5x7. Film: black and white. Photographs should include: captions; identification of subjects. **Payment:** $35. Photographic rights: first rights.

**Additional Information.** Stress Bay Area business language. Tips: No puff pieces. Writer's guidelines: upon request.

**SAN FRANCISCO FOCUS.** 680 Eighth Ave. San Francisco, CA 94103. (415) 553-2800. Submissions Editors: Mark Powelson (features); Amy Renner (entertainment; fashion); Adair Lara (fiction); Alice Thibeau (events). Type: general interest. Frequency of publication: monthly. Circulation: 250,000. Freelance submissions: n/i. Number of manuscripts bought each year: 5-10.

**Editorial Needs. Nonfiction**—entertainment reviews; fillers; general interest; health/fitness; historical; humor; interview/profile; travel. Suggested word length—feature articles: 1500. **Fiction**—literary. Short stories—yes.

**Initial Contact.** Query letter. Include resumé; clips.

**Acceptance Policies.** Byline given: yes. Submit seasonal material 2 months in advance. Simultaneous submissions: no. Response time to initial inquiry: 2-3 weeks. Average time until publication: 2-3 months. **Payment:** $50-$150 (50-500 words); $300-$750 (departments and features of 1500-3000 words). Payment made: upon acceptance. Kill fee: 25% of publication payment. Writer's expenses on assignment: yes. Publishing rights: first North American serial rights. Computer print-outs: yes. Dot matrix: no. Disk submissions: no.

**Additional Information.** Writer's guidelines: SASE.

**SAN JOSE STUDIES.** San Jose State University. San Jose, CA 95192. (408) 924-4476. Submissions Editors: Fauneil J. Rinn (general); O.C. Williams (poetry). Type: interdisciplinary—sciences, humanities and arts, social sciences; business and technology. Frequency of publication: winter; spring; fall. Circulation: 500+/-. Freelance submissions: 100%.

**Editorial Needs. Nonfiction**—articles which will provoke intellectual pleasure; poetry. Suggested word length—feature articles: 5000. **Fiction**—literary. Short stories—number per issue: 1-3; per year: 6-8.

**Initial Contact.** Entire article (double-spaced, normal margins).

**Acceptance Policies.** Byline given: yes. Simultaneous submissions: no. Response time to initial inquiry: 6-8 weeks. Average time until publication: 1 year. **Payment:** 2 copies of issue in which article appears. Publishing rights: first North American serial rights. Computer print-outs: yes. Dot matrix: no. Disk submissions: no.

**Additional Information.** Each February a $100 award is given to the author of the best essay, short story or poem appearing in the previous volume, along with a year's subscription. Writer's guidelines: SASE.

**SANTA CRUZ COUNTY HISTORICAL REVIEW.** PO Box 246. Santa Cruz, Ca 95061-0246. (408) 425-2450. Stanley Stevens. *See* **SANTA CRUZ COUNTY HISTORICAL TRUST** (book division).

**SCP JOURNAL.** PO Box 4308. Berkeley, CA 94704. Submissions Editor: Robert J.L. Burrows. Type: analysis of new age movements from a Christian viewpoint. Frequency of publication: quarterly. Circulation: 16,000. Freelance submissions: 5%. Number of manuscripts bought each year: 10.

**Editorial Needs. Nonfiction**—book excerpts; essays; interview/profile; opinion; personal experience; book reviews (most available to freelancers). Suggested word length—feature articles: 2500-3000.

**Initial Contact.** Query letter; photo availability; clips.

**Acceptance Policies.** Byline given: yes. Simultaneous submissions: yes. Response time to initial inquiry: Average time until publication: 6 months. **Payment:** $25-$30 per typeset page. Payment made: upon publication. Kill fee: no. Writer's expenses on assignment: no. Publishing rights: n/i. Computer print-outs: yes. Dot matrix: n/i. Disk submissions: no.

**Photography Submissions.** Format: contact sheets and prints. Film: black and white. Photographs should include: captions; model releases; identification of subjects. **Payment**: included with manuscript. Photographic rights: one-time rights.

## SEA MAGAZINE.

PO Box 1579. Newport Beach, CA 92663. (714) 646-3963. Submissions Editors: Linda Yuskaitis, Cathi Douglas (features; columns); Eston B. Ellis (new boats; new products); Cathi Niese (new books, calendar listings). Type: recreational boating; sportfishing; sailing; cruising. Frequency of publication: monthly. Circulation: 60,000. Freelance submissions: 70%. Number of manuscripts bought each year: 300.

**Editorial Needs.** **Nonfiction**—book excerpts; book reviews; general interest; historical; how-to; humor; interview/profile; photo feature; travel. Suggested word length—feature articles: 1000-3000; columns: 100-850. Short stories—(nonfiction news stories)—number per issue: 10-20; per year: 120-240.

**Initial Contact.** Complete query letter including description of proposed story. Include brief bio; clips. State availability of photos.

**Acceptance Policies.** Byline given: yes. Submit seasonal material 6-8 months in advance. Simultaneous submissions: yes. Response time to initial inquiry: 4-6 weeks. Average time until publication: 3-6 months. **Payment**: $25-$300 depending on length, content and topic. Payment made: upon publication. Kill fee: negotiable. Writer's expenses on assignment: sometimes. Publishing rights: first North American serial rights; second serial rights (sometimes). Computer print-outs: yes. Dot matrix: yes; letter quality. Disk submissions: IBM compatible; Word Star.

**Photography Submissions.** Format: prints, 5x7 or 8x10; contact sheets; negatives; transparencies (preferred). Film: black and white; color (preferred). Photographs should include: captions (need not accompany pictures, but we should receive enough information to write them ourselves); identification of subjects. **Payment**: $25-$250, depending on size. Photographic rights: n/i.

**Additional Information.** We are *the* magazine of Western boating, and our audience is made up of experienced boat owners. They seek well-informed, lively articles about the sport and its participants. Tips: A well-written, concise query letter accompanied by writing samples and, if possible, some photographs depicting your subject will be received and read with interest. Writer's guidelines: SASE (includes sample copy).

## SENIOR WORLD.

1000 Pioneer Way. El Cajon, CA 92020. (619) 442-4404. Submissions Editors: Ronald Miller (health); Sandy Pasqua (lifestyle); Gerald Goodrum (travel). Type: senior adults 55 years and older. Frequency of publication: monthly. Circulation: 390,000 in 7 Southern California counties. Freelance submissions: 10% Number of manuscripts bought each year: 15-20.

**Editorial Needs.** **Nonfiction**—News—local, state, national; Living—celebrities, remarkable seniors; consumer, finance and investment, innovative approaches to housing, sports, hobbies, etc. Travel—destinations, how-to. Health—health and medicine emphasizing wellness and preventive care; latest medical updates. Suggested word length—feature articles: 1000-1200; columns: 800 (will consider query and sample column).

**Initial Contact.** Query letter. State article availability; photo availability.

**Acceptance Policies.** Byline given: yes. Submit seasonal material 4 months in advance. Simultaneous submissions: yes; exclusive one-time rights in our circulation area. Response time to initial inquiry: 60 days. Average time until publication: 3 months. **Payment**: $50-$100. Payment made: upon publication. Kill fee: no. Writer's expenses on assignment: no. Publishing rights: first rights; rights to syndicate through our in-house news service. Computer print-outs: no. Dot matrix: no. Disk submissions: no.

**Photography Submissions.** Format: prints, 5x7, 8x10. Film: black and white. Photographs should include: captions; model releases; identification of subjects. **Payment**: $10-$15. Photographic rights: same as written material.

**Additional Information.** All accepted material will be made available to all of our publications and to our Senior News Service. Tips: Read the publication. Adhere to guidelines. Do not make telephone inquiries. Include your phone on all submissions. Poor spelling and presentation will automatically disqualify submissions. Writer's guidelines: upon request; sample copy $2.

**SIERRA.** 730 Polk Street. San Francisco, CA 94109. (415) 923-5656. Submissions Editor: Annie Stine. Type: environmental protection; outdoor recreation. Frequency of publication: every 2 months. Circulation: 350,000. Freelance submissions: 90%. Number of manuscripts bought each year: 100.

**Editorial Needs. Nonfiction**—book reviews; interview/profile; travel; environmental protection and politics; outdoor adventure. Suggested word length—feature articles: 2000-3000; columns: 500-1000.

**Initial Contact.** Query letter. Include clips.

**Acceptance Policies.** Byline given: yes. Submit seasonal material 6 months in advance. Simultaneous submissions: no. Response time to initial inquiry: 4-6 weeks. Average time until publication: 2-4 months. **Payment**: $75-$350 (departments); $500-$1000 (features). Payment made: upon acceptance. Kill fee: no. Writer's expenses on assignment: phone only; no travel. Publishing rights: first North American serial rights. Computer print-outs: yes. Dot matrix: yes. Disk submissions: We make arrangements with author.

**Photography Submissions.** Photo research is conducted separately.

**Additional Information.** Tips: Get to know the magazine so that you are familiar with the departments and what we've published recently. Writer's guidelines: SASE.

**SIERRA LIFE MAGAZINE, THE MAGAZINE OF THE HIGH SIERRA.** 699 West Line St. Bishop, CA 93514. (619) 873-3320. Submissions Editor: Steve Boga. Type: Sierra region. Frequency of publication: bimonthly. Circulation: n/i. Freelance submissions: 50%. Number of manuscripts bought each year: 18.

**Editorial Needs. Nonfiction**—book excerpts; general interest; historical; how-to; interview/profile; personal experience; photo feature; travel; arts; outdoor; wildlife; current events; poetry; recreation. Suggested word length—feature articles: 500-10,000.

**Initial Contact.** Query letter. Include photo availability.

**Acceptance Policies.** Byline given: yes. Submit seasonal material 6 months in advance. Simultaneous submissions: yes. Response time to initial inquiry: 3 months. Average time until publication: 6 months. **Payment**:$20-$400. Payment made: upon publication. Kill fee: no. Writer's expenses on assignment: sometimes. Publishing rights: second serial rights. Computer print-outs: yes. Dot matrix: letter quality. Disk submissions: no.

**Photography Submissions.** Format and film: 5x7 black and white prints; color transparencies (our request). Photographs should include: identification of subjects. **Payment**: $5 (black and white); $10-$50 (color). Photographic rights: two-time rights.

**Additional Information.** Writer's guidelines: SASE.

**SILVER WINGS.** PO Box 1000. Pearblossom, CA 93553-1000. (805) 264-3726. Submissions Editor: Jackson Wilcox. Type: inspirational poetry; affirmatively Christian and ecumenical in nature. Frequency of publication: quarterly. Circulation: 500. Freelance submissions: 100% Number of manuscripts bought each year: 200.

**Editorial Needs. Nonfiction**—inspiration; poetry. Suggested word length—no more than 20 lines.

**Initial Contact.** Entire article; cover letter listing poet's credentials. Include SASE for return.

**Acceptance Policies.** Byline given: yes. Submit seasonal material 9 months in advance. Simultaneous submissions: yes; first rights. Response time to initial inquiry: 10-30 days. Average time until publication: 3-18 months. **Payment:** $7 subscription plus $2 copy of issue ($9 per poem in value). Payment made: upon publication. Publishing rights: first rights. Computer print-outs: yes. Dot matrix: yes. Disk submissions: no.

**Additional Information.** Our purpose is to encourage poetry to lift the spirit of humankind to God. Tips: We also sponsor contests which result in chapbooks, as *Thanatopsis Wings* and *New Life Wings*. Writer's guidelines: SASE.

**SINISTER WISDOM.** PO Box 3252. Berkeley, CA 94703. Submissions Editor: Elana Dykewomon. Type: lesbian literary, art and political journal (since 1976). Frequency of publication: quarterly. Circulation: 3000. Freelance submissions: 90%.

**Editorial Needs. Nonfiction**—book reviews; historical; opinion; poetry. Suggested word length—feature articles: under 3000 words preferred. **Fiction**—1989 themes issues: Italian/American Lesbians; Lesbians and Disability; Lesbian Friendships. Short stories—number per issue: 4-9; per year: 20-40.

**Initial Contact.** n/i.

**Acceptance Policies.** Byline given: yes. Simultaneous submissions: no. Response time to initial inquiry: 2 weeks for inquiry; up to 9 months for acceptance or rejection decision. Average time until publication: 2-4 months. **Payment:** 2 copies. Publishing rights: all rights remain with author. Computer print-outs: yes. Dot matrix: yes. Disk submissions: Macintosh Word or Write.

**Photography Submissions.** Format: prints, 5x7. Film: black and white. Photographs should include: captions; model releases. **Payment:** 2 copies. Photographic rights: none.

**Additional Information.** Send 2 copies, SASE; and postcard for acceptance notification. Tips: Read *Sinister Wisdom* first. Writer's guidelines: SASE.

**SIPAPU.** (Division of Konocti Books). Route 1, Box 216. Winters, CA 95694. (916) 752-1032. Submissions Editor: Noel Peattie. Type: small press for librarians interested in Third World cultures; alternative and independent presses. Frequency of publication: twice yearly. Circulation: 400. Freelance submissions: 10%. Number of manuscripts bought each year 1-2.

**Editorial Needs. Nonfiction**—interview/profile. Suggested word length—feature articles: 1000.

**Initial Contact.** Query letter.

**Acceptance Policies.** Byline given: yes. Simultaneous submissions: no. Response time to initial inquiry: 1 week. Average time until publication: 6 months. Payment: $.05 per word. Payment made: upon publication. Kill fee: no. Writer's expenses on assignment: no. Publishing rights: first North American serial rights. Computer print-outs: yes. Dot matrix: no. Disk submissions: no.

**Additional Information.** Query before sending. Tips: Read *Sipapu*.

**SKIN DIVER MAGAZINE.** 8490 Sunset Blvd. Los Angeles, CA 90069. (213) 854-2960. Submissions Editor: Bill Gleason. Type: broad coverage of topics related to scuba diving. Frequency of publication: monthly. Circulation: 225,000. Freelance submissions: 85%. Number of manuscripts bought each year: 200.

**Editorial Needs. Nonfiction**—how-to; interview/profile; personal experience (no "how I learned to . . .); travel (no Caribbean); photo feature; fillers; cartoons. Suggested word length—feature articles: 1200 preferred.

**Initial Contact.** Complete manuscript. Include photos.

**Acceptance Policies.** Byline given: yes. Submit seasonal material 6 months in advance. Simultaneous submissions: no. Response time to initial inquiry: 3 months. Average time until publication: 9 months. **Payment**: $50 per published page; $25 (cartoon). Payment made: upon publication. Kill fee: Writer's expenses on assignment: Publishing rights: one-time rights. Computer print-outs: yes. Dot matrix: n/i. Disk submissions: no.

**Photography Submissions.** Format and film: 35mm transparencies; 8x10 prints. Photographs should include: captions; identification of subjects. **Payment**: $50 per published page. Photographic rights: one-time rights.

**Additional Information.** Tips: Write for areas of interest. Writer's guidelines: upon request.

**SOCCER AMERICA MAGAZINE.** PO Box 23704. Oakland, CA 94623. (415) 549-1414. Submissions Editor: Lynn Berling-Manuel. Type: for soccer fans. Frequency of publication: weekly. Circulation: 20,000. Freelance submissions: 20%. Number of manuscripts bought each year: 75.

**Editorial Needs. Nonfiction**—interview/profile; photo feature; technical; historical; expose; special issues (query for subject). Suggested word length—feature articles: 200-1500.

**Initial Contact.** query letter.

**Acceptance Policies.** Byline given: yes. Submit seasonal material 3 months in advance. Response time to initial inquiry: 2 months. Average time until publication: 2 months. **Payment**: $.50 per inch minimum. Payment made: upon publication. Kill fee: Writer's expenses on assignment: Publishing rights: all. Computer print-outs: yes. Dot matrix: letter quality. Disk submissions: query.

**Photography Submissions.** With or without manuscript; query. Format: 5x7+ glossy prints. Film: Black and white. Photographs should include: captions. **Payment**: $12. Photographic rights: n/i.

**Additional Information.** Tips: Read the publication! Writer's guidelines: $1.

**SONOMA MANDALA.** Dept. of English, Sonoma State University. 1801 E. Cotati Ave. Rohnert Park, CA 94928. (707) 664-2140. Submissions Editor: Elizabeth Herron, Faculty Advisor. Type: literary magazine. Frequency of publication: annual. Circulation: 700. Freelance submissions: 100%.

**Editorial Needs. Nonfiction**—humor; poetry. **Fiction**—literary; general. Short stories—number per year: 5-8.

**Initial Contact.** Send 10 pages of fiction; 3-5 poems.

**Acceptance Policies.** Byline given: yes. Simultaneous submissions: inform us. Response time to initial inquiry: 3-6 months. Average time until publication: 6 months. **Payment**: 2 copies. Publishing rights: first North American serial rights. Computer print-outs: yes. Dot matrix: yes. Disk submissions: no.

**Photography Submissions.** Our art does not illustrate text, but stands on its own. Art is reviewed in May. Format: prints, 8x10 high contrast. Film: black and white. Photographs should include: artist's name, address and phone on back; with title. **Payment**: contributor's copy. Photographic rights: all rights revert to artist.

**Additional Information.** We accept submissions between September 1 and December 15 only. Writer's guidelines: SASE.

## SPARKS JOURNAL and QTC Newsletter SOWP. PO Box 86. Geyserville, CA 95441. (707) 857-3434. Submissions Editor: Waldo T. Boyd. Type: professional and amateur radio operators. Frequency of publication: quarterly. Circulation: 5000. Freelance submissions: varies.

**Editorial Needs.** **Nonfiction**—historical. Suggested word length—feature articles: 1000. Short stories—true "stories" only.

**Initial Contact.** Query letter. State writer's source for the historical material; qualifications.

**Acceptance Policies.** Byline given: yes. Simultaneous submissions: no. Response time to initial inquiry: 2 weeks. Average time until publication: 3 months. **Payment**: 3 copies of QTC; 1 copy of *Sparks Journal*. Publishing rights: all rights. Computer print-outs: yes. Dot matrix: yes. Disk submissions: 8" floppy; TRS-DOS format; SCRIPSIT.

**Photography Submissions.** Format: print 4x5. Film: black and white. Photographs should include: captions. Payment: no cash payment. Photographic rights: one-time use.

**Additional Information.** The publisher, Society of Wireless Pioneers, is a nonprofit professional, historical corporation. Tips: Know your subject thoroughly! You cannot fool an "old salt" who has been there!

## STAR-WEB PAPER. PO Box 40029. Berkeley, CA 94704. (415) 845-2740. Submissions Editor: Thomas Michael Fisher. Type: literary; arts. Frequency of publication: irregular. Circulation: n/i. Freelance submissions: 100%.

**Editorial Needs.** **Nonfiction**—book excerpts; fillers; general interest; photo feature poetry; self-improvement. Suggested word length—feature articles: 1000. **Fiction**—literary; women's; general. Short stories—number per issue: 2.

**Initial Contact.** Entire article. Include biographical note.

**Acceptance Policies.** Byline given: yes. Simultaneous submissions: no. Response time to initial inquiry: 2 weeks. Average time until publication: 1 year. **Payment**: copies. Publishing rights: copyright in name of author. Computer print-outs: yes. Dot matrix: no. Disk submissions: no.

**Photography Submissions.** Format: prints, any size. Film: black and white. Photographs should include: identification of subjects. **Payment**: copies. Photographic rights: copyright in name of photographer.

**Additional Information.** Sample copy available for $5.

## STONE SOUP, THE MAGAZINE BY CHILDREN. PO Box 83. Santa Cruz, CA 95063. (408) 426-5557. Submissions Editor: Gerry Mandel. Type: literary magazine of work by children through age 13. Frequency of publication: every other month. Circulation: 10,000. Freelance submissions: 100%. Number of manuscripts bought each year: 60.

**Editorial Needs.** **Nonfiction**—book reviews; poetry. **Fiction**—literary. Short stories—number per issue: 6; per year: 30.

**Initial Contact.** Entire article.

**Acceptance Policies.** Byline given: yes. Submit seasonal material 6 months in advance. Simultaneous submissions: no. Response time to initial inquiry: 4 weeks. Average time until publication: 10 weeks. **Payment**: copies and discounts. Publishing rights: all rights. Computer print-outs: yes. Dot matrix: yes. Disk submissions: no.

**Additional Information.** We have a preference for work based on real-life experiences. Tips: Read a couple of issues of our magazine to get a sense of the kind of work we like. Sample: $4. Writer's guidelines: SASE.

**SUNSET MAGAZINE.** 80 Willow Rd. Menlo Park, CA 94025. (415) 321-3600. Does not accept freelance submissions.

**SURFER MAGAZINE.** PO Box 1028. Dana Point, CA 92629. (714) 496-5922. Submissions Editors: Matt Warshaw (features); Ben Marcus (columns); Jeff Divine (photography). Type: surf specialty. Frequency of publication: monthly. Circulation: 112,000. Freelance submissions: 40%. Number of manuscripts bought each year: 50-60.

**Editorial Needs. Nonfiction**—book reviews; health/fitness; historical; how-to; humor; inspiration; interview/profile; opinion; photo feature; travel. Suggested word length—feature articles: 1500-3500; columns: 500-1200. **Fiction**—surf related. Short stories—number per issue: 1.

**Initial Contact.** Query letter; or article proposal with subject outline.

**Acceptance Policies.** Byline given: yes. Submit seasonal material 3 months in advance. Simultaneous submissions: yes; no responsibility, no obligation. Response time to initial inquiry: 60-90 days. Average time until publication: 90 days. **Payment**: $.10-$.15 per word as published. Payment made: upon publication. Kill fee: no. Writer's expenses on assignment: yes. Publishing rights: first North American serial rights. Computer print-outs: yes. Dot matrix: yes. Disk submissions: no.

**Photography Submissions.** Format: transparencies only. Film: K64 color. Photographs should include: identification of subjects; photographer identification. Payment: $30-200. Photographic rights: first rights.

**Additional Information.** Articles should be aimed at intermediate to advance surfers. Writer's guidelines: SASE.

**THIS WORLD** (San Francisco Chronicle Sunday Feature Magazine). 901 Mission St. San Francisco, CA 94103. (415) 777-7050. Submissions Editors: Lyle York. Type: features, columns, analysis. Frequency of publication: weekly. Circulation: 750,000. Freelance submissions: 20%. Number of manuscripts bought each year: 100.

**Editorial Needs. Nonfiction**—book excerpts; general interest; health/fitness; historical; humor; interview/profile; opinion; photo feature; science; psychology; technology. Suggested word length—feature articles: up to 4000 words; columns: up to 2000 words. **Fiction**—literary. Short stories—number per issue: 1; per year: 5. Very rarely used.

**Initial Contact.** Query letter; or entire article. State author's qualifications if appropriate.

**Acceptance Policies.** Byline given: yes. Submit seasonal material 1 month in advance. Simultaneous submissions: yes. Response time to initial inquiry: 4 weeks. Average time until publication: 10 weeks. **Payment**: $75-$300 per piece. Payment made: upon publication. Kill fee: no. Writer's expenses on assignment: no. Publishing rights: first rights; second serial rights. Computer print-outs: yes. Dot matrix: no. Disk submissions: no.

**Photography Submissions.** Format: prints. Film: black and white. Photographs should include: identification of subjects. **Payment**: $40 or less. Photographic rights: one-time use.

**Additional Information.** Phone queries not acceptable. All articles must be submitted on spec. Tips: Send finished manuscript with SASE. Don't call.

**THREEPENNY REVIEW.** PO Box 9131. Berkeley, CA 94709. (415) 849-4545. Submissions Editor: Wendy Lesser. Type: literary magazine in the area of politics, and the arts. Frequency of publication: quarterly. Circulation: 8,000. Freelance submissions: 100%. Number of manuscripts bought each year: 40.

**Editorial Needs.** **Nonfiction**—(best area for freelancers) reviews (book, film theater, dance, music, art); interview/profile; personal experience; historical; essays; exposes; poetry (free verse, traditional). Suggested word length—feature articles: 1500-4000. **Fiction**—literary. Suggested word length—800-4000.

**Initial Contact.** Query. Include clips.

**Acceptance Policies.** Byline given: yes. Response time to initial inquiry: 1-2 months. Average time until publication: 1 year. **Payment**: $50. Payment made: upon acceptance. Kill fee: no. Writer's expenses on assignment: no. Publishing rights: first North American serial rights. Computer print-outs: yes. Dot matrix: letter quality. Disk submissions: no.

**Additional Information.** Writer's guidelines: SASE.

**TOTAL HEALTH.** 6001 Topanga Cyn Blvd., Ste. 300. Woodland Hills, CA 91367. (818) 887-6484. Submissions Editor: Robert L. Smith. Type: health and fitness. Frequency of publication: every other month. Circulation: 85,000. Freelance submissions: 80%. Number of manuscripts bought each year: 40.

**Editorial Needs.** **Nonfiction**—health/fitness; inspiration; self-improvement. Suggested word length—feature articles: 1600-1800.

**Initial Contact.** n/i.

**Acceptance Policies.** Byline given: yes. Submit seasonal material 3 months in advance. Simultaneous submissions: yes. Response time to initial inquiry: 4 weeks. Average time until publication: 6-8 weeks. **Payment**: $50-$75 depending on length and professional experience. Payment made: upon publication. Kill fee: no. Writer's expenses on assignment: no. Publishing rights: first rights. Computer print-outs: no. Dot matrix: n/i. Disk submissions: no.

**Photography Submissions.** Format: prints, 5x7 or 8x10 glossy. Film: black and white; color. Photographs should include: captions; model releases. **Payment**: n/i. Photographic rights: n/i.

**Additional Information.** We look for the holistic approach: body, mind and spirit. Writer's guidelines: $1 plus postage for sample copy and guidelines.

**TRADESWOMEN.** PO Box 40664. San Francisco, CA 94140. (415) 821-7334. Submissions Editor: Molly Martin. Type: for blue-collar working women. Frequency of publication: quarterly. Circulation: 900. Freelance submissions: 75%

**Editorial Needs.** **Nonfiction**—book excerpts; book reviews; general interest; health/fitness; inspiration; interview/profile; photo feature; fillers. Suggested word length—feature articles: 1000-2000. **Fiction**—women's (related to work in the trades). Short stories—number per issue: 2.

**Initial Contact.** Query letter; article proposal with subject outline. Include phone.

**Acceptance Policies.** Byline given: yes. Submit seasonal material: write or call for next deadline. Simultaneous submissions: yes. Response time to initial inquiry: 4-6 weeks. Average time until publication: 4-8 weeks. **Payment**: sorry, none. Kill fee: no. Writer's expenses on assignment: no. Publishing rights: share rights with author. Computer print-outs: yes. Dot matrix: yes. Disk submissions: Macintosh.

**Photography Submissions.** Format: prints; contact sheets. Film: black and white. Photographs should include: captions; identification of subjects. Payment: up to $25. Photographic rights: none.

**Additional Information.** Looking for articles by or about women in blue-collar occupations.

**TRAILER BOATS.** 20700 Belshaw Ave. Carson, CA 90746. (213) 537-6322. Submissions Editor: Chuck Coyne. Type: boating for people who own powerboats 26 feet and less. Frequency of publication: monthly. Circulation: 65,000. Freelance submissions: 20%. Number of manuscripts bought each year: 10.

**Editorial Needs. Nonfiction**—fillers; historical; how-to; humor; photo feature; travel. Suggested word length—feature articles: 1000-1500.

**Initial Contact.** Query letter. Include samples of published work if available.

**Acceptance Policies.** Byline given: yes. Submit seasonal material 4 months in advance. Simultaneous submissions: yes. Response time to initial inquiry: 30 days. Average time until publication: 3-6 months. **Payment:** $.07-$.10 per word. Payment made: upon publication. Kill fee: no. Writer's expenses on assignment: no. Publishing rights: first rights. Computer printouts: yes. Dot matrix: yes. Disk submissions: ASCII.

**Photography Submissions.** Format: prints, 8x10. Film: black and white; color (preferred, depending on story). Photographs should include: captions; model releases; identification of subjects. **Payment:** $10-50 per photo. Photographic rights: first rights.

**Additional Information.** No articles on sailboats; powerboats only. Tips: Read our magazine and be familiar with our format. Writer's guidelines: SASE. Sample magazines are $1.50.

**TRAILER LIFE.** 29901 Agoura Rd. Agoura, CA 91301. (213) 991-4980. Submissions Editor: Submissions Editors: Barbara Leonard (features, travel); Bob Livingston (technical). Type: for the dedicated RV owner. Frequency of publication: monthly. Circulation: 340,000. Freelance submissions: 60%. Number of manuscripts bought each year: 100.

**Editorial Needs. Nonfiction**—health/fitness; photo feature; travel. Suggested word length—feature articles: 1000-2000.

**Initial Contact.** Query letter; article proposal with subject outline.

**Acceptance Policies.** Byline given: yes. Submit seasonal material 4 months in advance. Response time to initial inquiry: 2-4 weeks. Average time until publication: 6 months. **Payment:** $50-$500. Payment made: upon acceptance. Kill fee: yes if assigned article.. Writer's expenses on assignment: sometimes. Publishing rights: first rights. Computer printouts: yes. Dot matrix: no. Disk submissions: IBM compatible.

**Photography Submissions.** Buys some supplemental photography. Format and film: contact sheets; transparencies; 8x10 black and white prints. Photographs should include: captions. **Payment:** $75-$250. Photographic rights: first North American.

**Additional Information.** Tips: Guidelines will help determine areas most open to freelancers. Make sure you have the expertise to write about RV life. Writer's guidelines: upon request.

**UNIX WORLD.** Tech Valley Publishing. 444 Castro Street. Mountain View, CA 94041. (415) 940-1500. Submissions Editors: Vanessa Schnatmeier (new products); Dr. Becca Thomas (tutorial); Michael Tucker (East Coast and features); Alan Winston (features); Omri Serlin (features); Augie Hansen (industry news). Type: trade. Frequency of publication: monthly. Circulation: 42,000. Freelance submissions: less than 5%.

**Editorial Needs. Nonfiction**—book reviews; how-to. Suggested word length—feature articles: 3000; columns: 1500-1800.

**Initial Contact.** Query letter; article proposal with subject outline.

**Acceptance Policies.** Byline given: yes Submit seasonal material 4 months in advance. Simultaneous submissions: no. Response time to initial inquiry: 1-3 months. Average time until publication: 3-4 months. **Payment**: $300-$900 for 3000 words. Payment made: upon publication; when the story is typeset, 30 days after deadline. Kill fee: n/i. Writer's expenses on assignment: yes. Publishing rights: first North American serial rights. Computer print-outs: yes. Dot matrix:n/i. Disk submissions: ASCII; 5 1/4" IBM.

**Photography Submissions.** Format: transparencies. Film: black and white; color. Photographs should include: captions; identification of subjects. **Payment**: included in text transaction. Photographic rights: first run.

**Additional Information.** The cover says "Open Systems Computing." This is a magazine for networked and multitasking systems. Writer's guidelines: upon request.

## VALLEY MAGAZINE.

16800 Devonshire, Ste. 275. Granada Hills, CA 91344. (818) 368-3353. Submissions Editor: Barbara Wernick. Type: issues and concerns related to residents of the San Fernando Valley and Southern California. Frequency of publication: monthly. Circulation: 35,000. Freelance submissions: 70%. Number of manuscripts bought each year: 100.

**Editorial Needs. Nonfiction**—adventure; agriculture; art; book reviews; business opportunities; career; child care; children; economics; entertainment reviews; general interest; health/fitness; interview/profile; photo feature; self-improvement; travel. Suggested word length—feature articles: 1200-1800; columns: 800-1000.

**Initial Contact.** Query letter; or article proposal with subject outline; or entire article. Include bio; clips.

**Acceptance Policies.** Byline given: yes. Submit seasonal material 3 months in advance. Simultaneous submissions: yes; we want first rights. Response time to initial inquiry: 4 weeks. Average time until publication: 8 weeks. **Payment**: $200-$400 depending on length and topic. Payment made: upon acceptance. Kill fee: 20%. Writer's expenses on assignment: no. Publishing rights: first rights. Computer print-outs: yes. Dot matrix: yes. Disk submissions: no.

**Photography Submissions.** Format: transparencies. Film: black and white; color. Photographs should include: identification of subjects. **Payment**: depends on assignment. Photographic rights: n/i.

**Additional Information.** Everything we do, except travel, somehow relates to the San Fernando Valley. Tips: Articles should be upbeat, positive and geared to enhancing the quality of our readers' lives. Writer's guidelines: SASE.

## WAYSTATION, FOR SCIENCE FICTION WRITERS.

(Subsidiary of Unique Graphics). 1025 55th St. Oakland, CA 94608. (415) 655-3024. Submissions Editor: Millea Kenin. Type: how-to for science fiction and fantasy writers. Frequency of publication: quarterly. Circulation: 1500. Freelance submissions: 99%. Number of manuscripts bought each year: 15+/-.

**Editorial Needs. Nonfiction**—book reviews; how-to; interview/profile; only useful, informative material by and for science fiction writers. Suggested word length—feature articles: 2000; columns: no unsolicited. **Fiction**—only from people who are familiar with our magazine or have received our guidelines. Short stories—1 per issue, to be critiqued in print.

**Initial Contact.** Query letter; article proposal with subject outline. No complete article from first-time submitters.

**Acceptance Policies.** Byline given: yes. Simultaneous submissions: no. Response time to initial inquiry: 1-3 weeks. Average time until publication: 1-12 months. **Payment**: contributor's copies; 4 issue subscription. Payment made: upon publication. Kill fee: 4 issue subscription plus back issues. Writer's expenses on assignment: no. Publishing rights: first North American serial rights; second serial rights. Computer print-outs: yes. Dot matrix: letter quality. Disk submissions: any Macintosh or IBM compatible text format.

**Photography Submissions.** Format: prints, up to 8x10. Film: black and white. Photographs should include: captions; identification of subjects. **Payment**: same as for articles. Photographic rights: one-time rights. Line art (black and white), any size, is also encouraged.

**Additional Information.** Most of the material is by people well-known in the genre SF community, so competition is stiff. Tips: If you are not familiar with genre SF, forget it. Even if you are, get our guidelines first! Writer's guidelines: #10 SASE with postage for 2 oz.; only one needed for both *Owlflight* and *Waystation.*

**WEST.** 750 Ridder Park Dr. San Jose, CA 95190. (408) 920-5000. Submissions Editor: Charles Matthews. Type: general interest with a Bay Area focus. Frequency of publication: weekly. Circulation: 320,000. Freelance submissions: 33%. Number of manuscripts bought each year: 200.

**Editorial Needs. Nonfiction**—book excerpts; general interest; health/fitness; how-to; humor; interview; profile; photo feature; travel. **Fiction**—rarely accept any.

**Initial Contact.** Query letter. Include clips.

**Acceptance Policies.** Byline given: Submit seasonal material 2 months in advance. Simultaneous submissions: no. Response time to initial inquiry: 3 weeks. Average time until publication: 2 months. **Payment**: $150 and up per text. Payment made: upon acceptance. Kill fee: 25%. Writer's expenses on assignment: no. Publishing rights: first North American serial rights. Computer print-outs: yes. Dot Matrix: yes. Disk submissions: yes.

**Additional Information.** Tips: We expect authors to familiarize themselves with our magazine. Writer's guidelines. none.

**WESTART.** PO Box 6868. Auburn, CA 95604. (916) 885-0969. Submissions Editor: Martha Garcia. Type: current reviews of art for the artist/craftsman and people who enjoy art. Frequency of publication: semimonthly tabloid. Circulation: 6000. Freelance submissions: n/i. Number of manuscripts bought each year: 6-8/.

**Editorial Needs. Nonfiction**—information; photo-feature; interview/profile. Suggested word length—feature articles: 700-800.

**Initial Contact.** Query letter; or complete manuscript. Phone queries accepted.

**Acceptance Policies.** Byline given: yes. Response time to initial inquiry: n/i. Average time until publication: n/i. **Payment**: $.50 per column inch. Payment made: upon publication. Kill fee: no. Writer's expenses on assignment: no. Publishing rights: all. Computer print-outs: n/i.

**Photography Submissions.** purchase with or without article. Format: prints. Film: black and white. Photographs should include: n/i. **Payment**: $.50 per column inch. Photographic rights: n/i.

**Additional Information.** Tips: deadlines critical. Writer's guidelines: upon request; sample copy $1.

**WESTERN AND EASTERN TREASURES.** 5440 Ericson Way. PO Box 1095. Arcata, CA 95521. (707) 822-8442. Submissions Editor: Rosemary Anderson. Type: treasure hunting as hobby and sport. Frequency of publication: monthly. Circulation: 100,000. Freelance submissions: 100%. Number of manuscripts bought each year: 300+/-.

**Editorial Needs. Nonfiction**—book reviews; fillers; how-to; interview/profile; opinion; travel. Suggested word length—feature articles: 1500.

**Initial Contact.** Entire article; cover letter listing amount of experience in the hobby/sport of treasure hunting.

**Acceptance Policies.** Byline given: yes. Submit seasonal material 6 months in advance. Simultaneous submissions: no. Response time to initial inquiry: 4 weeks. Average time until publication: 3-12 months. **Payment**: $.02 per word. Payment made: upon publication. Kill fee: n/i. Writer's expenses on assignment: no. Publishing rights: all. Computer print-outs: yes. Dot matrix: no. Disk submissions: no.

**Photography Submissions.** Format: prints, 3x5. Film: black and white; color. Photographs should include: captions; model releases; identification of subjects. **Payment**: $5 per photo; more for cover. Photographic rights: all.

**Additional Information.** Tips: Read guidelines first; follow them. I'm especially looking for how-to material. Writer's guidelines: upon request.

**WESTERN OUTDOORS.** PO Box 2027. Newport Beach, CA 92559-1027. (714) 546-4370. Submissions Editor: Jack Brown. Type: fishing, hunting. Frequency of publication: 10 times per year. Circulation: 143,000. Freelance submissions: 70%. Number of manuscripts bought each year: 70+/-.

**Editorial Needs.** **Nonfiction**—interviews/profile; how-to; where-to. Suggested word length—feature articles: 1500.

**Initial Contact.** Query letter. Include published credits.

**Acceptance Policies.** Byline given: yes. Submit seasonal material 6 months in advance. Simultaneous submissions: no. Response time to initial inquiry: 4 weeks. Average time until publication: 4-6 months. **Payment**: $400+/-. Payment made: upon acceptance. Kill fee: no. Writer's expenses on assignment: no. Publishing rights: first North American serial rights. Computer print-outs: yes. Dot matrix: no. Disk submissions: no.

**Photography Submissions.** Format: transparencies. Film: color. Photographs should include: captions; model releases. **Payment**: included in package. Photographic rights: included.

**Additional Information.** Tips: Avoid first-person writing. Writer's guidelines: SASE.

**WESTERN PUBLISHER, A TRADE JOURNAL.** PO Box 591012, Golden Gate Station. San Francisco, CA 94159. (415) 661-7964. Submissions Editor: Paula von Louwenfeldt. Type: publishing and the book industry in the Western United States and Pacific Rim. Frequency of publication: monthly tabloid. Circulation: 10,000. Freelance submissions: 25%. Number of manuscripts bought each year: 100.

**Editorial Needs.** **Nonfiction**—books excerpts; general interest; historical; how-to; interview-profile; new product; opinion; photo feature; technical; short reviews. Suggested word length—feature articles: open; reviews: 250.

**Initial Contact.** Query letter; or send complete manuscript. Include clips.

**Acceptance Policies.** Byline given: yes. Submit seasonal material 3 months in advance. Simultaneous submissions: yes. Response time to initial inquiry: 1 week. Average time until publication: 1 month. **Payment**: varies. Payment made: upon publication. Kill fee: negotiable. Writer's expenses on assignment: no. Publishing rights: one-time rights. Computer print-outs: yes. Dot matrix: letter quality. Disk submissions: no.

**Additional Information.** Tips: Short book reviews are freelancers best bet. Writer's guidelines: sample copy $2.

**WESTWAYS.** Automobile Club of Southern California). PO Box 2890, Terminal Annex. Los Angeles, CA 90051. Submissions Editor: Mary Ann Fisher. Type: regional publication with emphasis on Western and world travel. Frequency of publication: monthly. Circulation: 490,000. Freelance submissions: 90%. Number of manuscripts bought each year: 125.

**Editorial Needs. Nonfiction**—general interest; history; humor; interview/profile; photo feature; travel; columns (Wit and Wisdom). Suggested word length—feature articles: 1500; columns: 750-900.

**Initial Contact.** Query; or complete manuscript. Include clips.

**Acceptance Policies.** Byline given: yes. Submit seasonal material 6 months in advance. Response time to initial inquiry: 2 weeks. Average time until publication: 6 months. **Payment**: $50-$350. Payment made: 30 days before publication. Kill fee: $75. Writer's expenses on assignment: sometimes. Publishing rights: first North American serial rights. Computer print-outs: yes. Dot matrix: letter quality. Disk submissions: no.

**Photography Submissions.** send with queries or manuscripts. Format: 35mm transparencies. Film: color. Photographs should include: captions; model releases; identification of subjects. **Payment**: $50; $400 (full color cover). Photographic rights: one-time rights.

**Additional Information.** Writer's guidelines: upon request; sample copy: 9x12 SASE plus $1.

**WIDE OPEN MAGAZINE.** 116 Lincoln St. Santa Rosa, CA 95401. (707) 545-3821. Submissions Editor: Clif Simms, Lynn Simms. Type: works with viable solutions to widespread problems . Frequency of publication: quarterly. Circulation: 500. Freelance submissions: 99%. Number of manuscripts bought each year: 8-12.

**Editorial Needs. Nonfiction**—opinions on world problems expressed logically. Suggested word length—feature articles: 500-2500 (required). **Fiction**—problems that people face in the world today with a realistic, purposeful solution; no blind luck or the intervention of the fates. Short stories—number per issue: 1-3; per year: 4-12.

**Initial Contact.** Entire article (Do not send bio or clips). Include SASE.

**Acceptance Policies.** Byline given: yes. Simultaneous submissions: yes. Response time to initial inquiry: 1-6 months. Average time until publication: 2 months. **Payment**: $5-$25; 1 copy. Payment made: upon publication. Kill fee: no. Writer's expenses on assignment: no. Publishing rights: one-time rights only. Computer print-outs: yes. Dot matrix: yes. Disk submissions: no.

**Additional Information.** Our prose requirements are very strict. We also charge a $5 reading fee for prose, refundable if we accept your manuscript. Tips: Study our guidelines and copies of our magazines. Samples are $6. Writer's guidelines: #10 SASE.

**WINES AND VINES.** 1800 Lincoln Ave. San Rafael, CA 94901. Submissions Editor: Philip E. Hiaring. Type: professionals in all phases of the wine industry. Frequency of publication: monthly. Circulation: 4500. Freelance submissions: 20%. Number of manuscripts bought each year: 4.

**Editorial Needs. Nonfiction**—general interest to the trade; how-to; history; technical; interview/profile; new products. Suggested word length—feature articles: 1000-2500.

**Initial Contact.** Query letter.

**Acceptance Policies.** Byline given: n/i. Submit seasonal material 3 months in advance. Response time to initial inquiry: 2 weeks. Average time until publication: 3 months. **Payment**: $.05 per word. Payment made: upon acceptance. Kill fee: n/i. Writer's expenses on assignment: sometimes. Publishing rights: first North American serial rights; simultaneous rights. Computer print-outs: yes. Dot matrix: no. Disk submissions: no.

**Photography Submissions.** Format: 4x5, 8x10 prints. Film: black and white. Photographs should include: captions. **Payment**: $10. Photographic rights: same as article.

**Additional Information.** Contact us for special subject each month. Writer's guidelines: 10x12 SASE.

**WINE SPECTATOR.** Opera Plaza, Suite 2014. 601 Van Ness Ave. San Francisco, CA 94102. (415) 673-2040. Submissions Editor: Jim Gordon. Type: for the wine consumer. Frequency of publication: twice monthly. Circulation: 80,000. Freelance submissions: 10%. Number of manuscripts bought each year: n/i.

**Editorial Needs. Nonfiction**—general interest; humor; interview/profile; opinion; photo feature. Suggested word length—feature articles: 100-2000.

**Initial Contact.** Query letter.

**Acceptance Policies.** Byline given: yes. Submit seasonal material 3 months in advance. Response time to initial inquiry: 3 weeks. Average time until publication: 2 months. **Payment**: $50-$300. Payment made: upon publication. Kill fee: no. Writer's expenses on assignment: no. Publishing rights: first-time rights; work for hire. Computer print-outs: yes. Dot matrix: legible. Disk submissions: query.

**Photography Submissions.** Format and film: color transparencies. Photographs should include: captions; model releases; identification of subjects. **Payment**: $25+. Photographic rights: all.

**Additional Information.** Tips: Succinct query letter detailing the article is a must. Writer's guidelines: upon request; sample copy $2.

**WINE WORLD MAGAZINE.** 6433 Topanga Blvd., Ste. 412. Canoga Park, CA 91303. Submissions Editor: Dee Sindt. Type: wine information for the consumer. Frequency of publication: quarterly. Circulation: n/i. Freelance submissions: n/i. Number of manuscripts bought each year: 50.

**Editorial Needs. Nonfiction**—history; profile/interview; new products; technology. (No first person). Suggested word length—feature articles: 750-2000.

**Initial Contact.** query letter.

**Acceptance Policies.** Byline given: n/i. Simultaneous submissions: yes; inform us. Response time to initial inquiry: n/i. Average time until publication: n/i. **Payment**: $50-$100. Payment made: upon publication. Kill fee: no. Writer's expenses on assignment: no. Publishing rights: first North American serial rights. Computer print-outs: n/i.

**Additional Information.** Writer's guidelines: $2.

**WISE WOMAN, THE.** 2441 Cordova St. Oakland, CA 94602. (415) 536-3174. Submissions Editor: Ann Forefreedom. Type: women's, feminist issues; feminist spirtuatlity; feminist withcraft. Frequency of Publication: quarterly. Circulation: small but influential. Freelance submissions: almost all; except poetry and cartoons.

**Editorial Needs. Nonfiction**—book reviews; entertainment reviews; fillers; general interest; health/fitness; historical; how-to; humor; inspiration; interview/profile; opinion; photo feature; poetry; self-improvement; travel; news analysis; annotated songs; spiritual rituals; goddess lore; political cartoons on feminist issues. Suggested word length—keep it brief. **Fiction**—generally no; if brief, and clearly feminist and relevant to feminism and feminist spirituality. **Other**—poetry.

**Initial Contact.** Query letter; entire manuscript. State whether article has been submitted elsewhere. Include SASE.

**Acceptance Policies.** Byline given: yes. Submit seasonal material at least 3-6 months in advance. Simultaneous submissions: yes; include where the material has been submitted. Response time to initial query: usually within several months. Average time until publication: varies. **Payment:** 1 copy of the issue in which submission appears. Publishing rights: first rights; second serial rights. Computer print-outs: yes. Dot matrix: letter quality. Disk submissions: no.

**Photography Submissions:** Format: prints, any size. Film: black and white. Photographs should include: captions; identification of subjects; model releases. Include name and address on each photo. **Payment:** copies. Photographic rights: n/i.

**Additional Information.** Since the publication is a quarterly, articles should be timely within 3-6 months, and appropriate for *The Wise Woman.* We have been publishing quarterly since February, 1980 and are listed in feminist and new age directories. Tips: Keep materials as short as possible—space is always tight. Editorial revisions may be necessary; I usually check with the author. Writer's guidelines: SASE; sample copy $4.

**WOMAN IN THE MOON PUBLICATIONS (WIM).** 2215 R Market St., Box 137-Dept CAS. San Francisco, CA 94114. (209) 667-0966. Submissions Editor: S. Diane Bogus. Type: women's; African-American; gay poetry. We accept chapbook manuscripts April-August each year. Frequency of publication: yearly (2-4 books). Circulation: n/i. Freelance submissions: 100%. Number of manuscripts bought each year: 2-4; we give 1/2 press run to author.

**Editorial Needs. Fiction**—literary.

**Initial Contact.** Query letter.

**Acceptance Policies.** Byline given: yes. Simultaneous submissions: yes; inform us. Response time to initial inquiry: 2-6 weeks. Average time until publication: one year. **Payment:** 1/2 of press run. Publishing rights: second serial rights. Computer print-outs: yes. Dot matrix: no. Disk submissions: 3 1/2" diskettes; ASCII; Word Perfect.

**Additional Information.** We offer a poetry test for practicing and novice poets; useful for Marketing, analysis and to check skills, and for fun. Tips: Writing must have a real voice and come from human experience. Writer's guidelines: free upon request. Catalog: SASE, $.45 postage.

**WOMAN'S ENTERPRISE.** 28210 Dorothy Dr. Agoura, CA 91301. (818) 889-8740. Submissions Editor: Caryne Brown. Type: small-business magazine for women. Frequency of publication: bimonthly. Circulation: 150,000. Freelance submissions: 50%. Number of manuscripts bought each year: 200.

**Editorial Needs. Nonfiction**—book reviews; how-to; small business facts. Suggested word length—feature articles: 1800.

**Initial Contact.** Query letter.

**Acceptance Policies.** Byline given: yes. Simultaneous submissions: no. Response time to initial inquiry: 4 weeks. Average time until publication: varies. **Payment:** $.20 per word. Payment made: upon acceptance. Kill fee: n/i. Writer's expenses on assignment: only if assignment originates with us. Publishing rights: all rights. Computer print-outs: yes. Dot matrix: yes. Disk submissions: ASCII.

**Photography Submissions.** Format and film: prints (black and white); transparencies (color). Photographs should include: captions; model releases; identification of subjects. **Payment:** $40. Photographic rights: all.

**Additional Information.** Tips: The more specific financial information, profit/expense information, the better. Writer's guidelines: SASE.

**WORKING CLASSICS.** 298 Ninth Ave. San Francisco, CA 94118. (415) 387-3412. Submissions Editor: David Joseph. Type: literary and general interest creative work of working people. Frequency of publication: occasional. Circulation: 2000. Freelance submissions: 95%.

**Editorial Needs.** Nonfiction—book excerpts book reviews; entertainment reviews; general interest; historical; how-to; humor; interview-profile; opinion; photo feature; poetry. Suggested word length—feature articles: 1000-3700. Fiction—literary workers' stories. Short stories—number per issue: 2; per year: 4.

**Initial Contact.** Query letter. Include work background.

**Acceptance Policies.** Byline given: yes. Simultaneous submissions: yes; let us know if accepted elsewhere. Response time to initial inquiry: 1-4 weeks. Average time until publication: varies. **Payment**: in copies. Publishing rights: first rights. Computer print-outs: yes. Dot matrix: yes. Disk submissions: query.

**Photography Submissions.** Format: prints. Film: black and white. Photographs should include: captions. **Payment**: copies. Photographic rights: first rights.

**Additional Information.** This magazine showcases the lives of working people, the creativity involved, and the innovative methods used to juggle a busy life, which includes the work place and a place for creativity. Writer's guidelines: upon request.

**WORMWOOD REVIEW.** PO Box 8840. Stockton, CA 95208-0840. (209) 466-8231. Submissions Editor: Marvin Malone. Type: contemporary poetry. Frequency of publication: quarterly. Circulation: 700. Freelance submissions: 100%. Number of manuscripts bought each year: varies.

**Editorial Needs. Nonfiction**—book reviews. **Other**: prose-poetry; poetry.

**Initial Contact.** Entire article.

**Acceptance Policies.** Byline given: yes. Simultaneous submissions: no. Response time to initial inquiry: 4-8 weeks. Average time until publication: 4-8 months. **Payment**: 2-35 copies or cash equivalent. Payment made: upon publication. Publishing rights: all rights. Computer print-outs: no. Dot matrix: no. Disk submissions: no.

**Additional Information.** We have been operating since 1959. We concentrate on the Prose-Poem and contemporary concerns. Writer's guidelines: SASE.

**WRITERS CONNECTION.** 1601 Saratoga-Sunnyvale Rd, Ste. 180. Cupertino, CA 95014. (408) 973-0227. Submissions Editor: Jan Stiles. Type: how-to for writers. Editorial content covers writing, publishing, technical writing and desktop publishing topics. Frequency of publication: monthly. Circulation: 2700. Freelance submissions: 40%.

**Editorial Needs. Nonfiction**—writing-related strategies; how-to. Suggested word length—feature: 1800-2000; secondary articles: 100-1400; columns: staff written.

**Initial Contact.** Query letter; or entire article.

**Acceptance Policies.** Byline given: yes. Submit seasonal material 3 months in advance. Simultaneous submissions: no. Response time to initial inquiry: 1 month or less. Average time until publication: 2-6 months. **Payment**: trade out for Writers Connection membership, subscription, or seminars. Publishing rights: first North American serial rights. Computer print-outs: yes. Dot matrix: letter quality. Disk submissions: ASCII or Microsoft Word; disk must be accompanied by formatted manuscript.

**Additional Information.** We like to see articles stress nuts-and-bolts information and present the information in a logical, concise, and easy-to-read style. Tips: Study our publication and request the guidelines. Writer's guidelines: SASE; free sample copy on request.

**WRITERS' RENDEZVOUS.** 3954 Mississippi St., #8. San Diego, CA 92104. (619) 296-2758. Submissions Editor: Karen M. Campbell. Type: for freelance writers. Frequency of publication: quarterly. Circulation: unknown. Freelance submissions: 75%. Number of manuscripts bought each year: 20.

**Editorial Needs. Nonfiction**—book reviews; fillers; how-to; humor; inspiration; interview/profile; opinion; poetry; anything about freelance writers and writing, or pen pal correspondence. Suggested word length—feature articles: 750-1000; columns: 750-1000. Short stories—number per issue: 1; per year: 4. **Fiction**—literary; women's; genre; freelancing; penpalling.

**Initial Contact.** Query letter; entire article.

**Acceptance Policies.** Byline given: yes. Submit seasonal material 2-3 months in advance. Simultaneous submissions: yes. Response time to initial inquiry: 1-2 weeks. Average time until publication: 3-6 months. **Payment**: 1 copy; contest offers cash prize. Publishing rights: one-time rights. Computer print-outs: yes. Dot matrix: yes, true descenders only. Disk submissions: no.

**Additional Information.** W.R. is specifically for freelancers and penpals. If article is not on these topics it will automatically be rejected, no matter how well-written. Tips: Read our guidelines carefully. Orient towards novice writers. Check spelling and grammar. Consider entering annual contest and review the contest winners. Writer's guidelines: SASE (includes contest rules); $3 sample issue.

**YELLOW SILK, JOURNAL OF EROTIC ARTS.** PO Box 6374. Albany, CA 94706. (415) 841-6500. Submissions Editor: Lily Pond. Type: erotica. Frequency of publication: quarterly. Circulation: 14,000. Freelance submissions: 90%. Number of manuscripts bought each year: 5 (nonfiction); 16 (fiction).

**Editorial Needs. Nonfiction**—book excerpts; humor; reviews; poetry; columns (reviews, emphasis on erotic content). Suggested word length—feature articles: any. **Fiction**—erotica; fantasy; humor; mainstream; novel excerpts; science fiction.

**Initial Contact.** Complete manuscript.

**Acceptance Policies.** Byline given: yes. Response time to initial inquiry: 3 months. Response time to initial inquiry: 6-8 weeks. Average time until publication: 1 month to 3 years. **Payment**: $10 minimum, 3 copies (nonfiction); $10 minimum, copies (fiction, columns); $5 minimum, copies (poetry). Payment made: upon publication. Kill fee: no. Writer's expenses on assignment: no. Publishing rights: all (revert to author after 1 year). Computer print-outs: yes. Dot matrix: letter quality. Disk submissions: no.

**Photography Submissions.** May be submitted without manuscript. Also, 4 color, black and white art work. Format: photocopies; transparencies; contact sheets; prints. Film: black and white; color. Photographs should include: n/i. **Payment**: varies. Photographic rights: one-time; reprint.

**Additional Information.** Our policy is to emphasize the erotic through well-crafted literature; no brutality or minute descriptions or personal accounts. Tips: Sample copy $6.

**YOGA JOURNAL.** 2054 University Ave. Berkeley, CA 94704. (415) 841-9200. Submissions Editor: Stephan Bodian. Type: new age. Frequency of publication: bimonthly. Circulation: 50,000. Freelance submissions: 75%. Number of manuscripts bought each year: 40.

**Editorial Needs. Nonfiction**—book excerpts; how-to; interview/profile; opinion; photo feature; travel; inspirational; columns (book and music reviews); cooking; psychology; interviews). Suggested word length—feature articles: 750-3500.

**Initial Contact.** Query letter.

**Acceptance Policies.** Byline given: yes. Submit seasonal material 4 months in advance. Simultaneous submissions: yes. Response time to initial inquiry: 6-8 weeks. Average time until publication: 6 months. **Payment**: $75-$250 (nonfiction); $25-$100 (columns). Payment made: upon publication. Kill fee: $50. Writer's expenses on assignment: no. Publishing rights: first North American serial rights. Computer print-outs: n/i.

**Photography Submissions.** Format: prints. Film: black and white. Photographs should include: model release; identification of subjects. **Payment**: $15-$25; $200-$300 (color transparencies, cover). Photographic rights: one-time.

**Additional Information.** While our focus is on yoga, we feature a monthly subject or personality in the broader new age field. Tips: We read all manuscripts and encourage submissions. Writer's guidelines: upon request.

**ZYZZYVA.** 41 Sutter St., Ste. 1400. San Francisco, CA 94104. (415) 982-3440. Submissions Editor: Howard Junker. Type: literary. Frequency of publication: quarterly. Circulation: 3500. Freelance submissions: 100%. Number of manuscripts bought each year: 80.

**Editorial Needs.** **Fiction**—2 per issue. Short stories—number per issue: 4.

**Initial Contact.** Entire story.

**Acceptance Policies.** Byline given: yes. Simultaneous submissions: no. Response time to initial inquiry: prompt. Average time until publication: varies. **Payment**: $25-$100. Payment made: upon acceptance. Kill fee: no. Writer's expenses on assignment: no. Publishing rights: first North American serial rights. Computer print-outs: yes. Dot matrix: no. Disk submissions: no.

**Additional Information.** Writer's guidelines SASE.

# Newspapers

Many writers first break into print with a published column in a local newspaper. While the pay may be nominal, writing for a newspaper provides an opportunity to learn about writing within editorial requirements, targeting specific markets, and meeting deadlines.

## How to Use the Information in This Section

Our listings are alphabetized by the name of the newspaper or by the area serviced. There are also several newspaper publishing groups that are listed alphabetically by the name of the group. We felt it would be more useful to do it this way since writers are often writing for a specific audience in a specific area. If the name of the area is in parenthesis, do not include it when sending material to the newspaper; it is for your use in determining the geographical area served by that publication.

The initial entry identifies the name of the publication, its location, and phone number.

**Submissions Editor:** Direct your initial contact to the appropriate editor.

**Book Review Editor:** Send press releases and review copies of your book to this individual.

**Freelance submissions:** If the text indicates that the newspaper accepts freelance submissions, write to the editor requesting writer's guidelines and information about the editorial needs of the newspaper's special sections. This is a particuarly good idea if the answer to whether or not the paper accepts freelance material is seldom, or rarely.

**Circulation:** This number helps you judge the size of your market.

## Abbreviations

n/i means no information was given to us by the newspaper.

**AGOURA ACORN.** 5226 Chesebro Rd. Agoura Hills, CA 91301-2202. (818) 706-0266. Submissions Editor: Keteri Alexander. Freelance submissions: rarely. Circulation: 26,000.

**ALAMEDA COUNTY/BAY AREA OBSERVER.** PO Box 817. San Leandro, CA 94577. (415) 483-7119. Submissions Editor: Ad Fried (also book reviews). Freelance submissions: no. Circulation: 135,000.

**ANTIOCH LEDGER/POST DISPATCH.** 1650 Cavallo Rd., PO Box 2299. Antioch, CA 94531-2299. (415) 757-2525. Submissions Editor: Clay Kallam (lifestyles); Robert Weaver (Editor). Freelance submissions: yes. Circulation: 22,000.

**AZUSA HERALD PRESS.** 234 E. Foothill Blvd. Azusa, CA 91702. (818) 969-1711. Submissions Editor: Lynn Schnier. Freelance submissions: rarely. Circulation: 359,000.

**BAKERSFIELD CALIFORNIAN.** PO Box 440. Bakersfield, CA 93301. (805) 395-7249. Submissions Editor: Bob Bentley. Book Review Editor: John Irby. Freelance submissions: yes. Circulation: 83,000 daily, 89,000 Sunday.

**BERKELEY DAILY CALIFORNIAN, THE.** 2150 Dwight Way. Berkeley, CA 94704. (415) 849-2482. Submissions Editor: Jim Harris. Freelance submissions: no. Circulation: 25,000.

**BERKELEY EAST BAY EXPRESS.** PO Box 3198. Berkeley, CA 94703. (415) 652-4610. Submissions Editor: John Raeside. Book Review Editor: Rob Hurwitt. Freelance submissions: yes. Circulation: 55,000.

**BLYTHE PALO VERDE VALLEY TIMES.** PO Box 1159. Blythe, CA 92226. (619) 922-3181. Submissions Editor: Tim Dewar. Book Review Editor: George Zieman, PO Box 567, Bullhead City, AZ 86430. Freelance submissions: yes, but generally local. Circulation: 4,000.

**CALISTOGAN, THE.** PO Box 385. Calistoga, CA 94515. (707) 942-6242. Submissions Editor: Jack Kenny (also book reviews). Freelance submissions: no. Circulation: n/i.

**CAMARILLO NEWS.** PO Box 107. Camarillo, CA 93011. (805) 987-5001. Submissions Editor: Harold Kinsch. Book Review Editor: Donna de Paolo. Freelance submissions: no. Circulation: 11,500.

**CAPISTRANO VALLEY NEWS.** 23811 Via Fabricante. Mission Viejo, CA 92691. (714) 768-3631. Submissions Editor: David McAdam (also book reviews). Freelance submissions: yes. Circulation: 131,888.

**CARLSBAD JOURNAL.** PO Box 878. Encinitas, CA 92024. (619) 729-2345. Submissions Editor: Stacy Nickerson (also book reviews). Freelance submissions: possible. Circulation: 3,609.

**CARMEL AND MONTEREY/KEY MAGAZINE.** PO Box 223859. Carmel, CA 93922. (408) 624-3411. Submissions Editor: Penny Green. Freelance submissions: no. Circulation: 37,000.

**CENTRAL NEWS-WAVE PUBLICATIONS.** 2621 W. 54th St. Los Angeles, CA 90043. (213) 290-3000. Submissions Editor: Alice Marsh. Book Review Editor: Tomas Lewis. Freelance submissions: no. Circulation: 289,000.

**CERES COURIER.** PO Box 7, 2940 Fourth St. Ceres, CA 95307. (209) 537-5032. Submissions Editor: Jeff Benziger. Freelance submissions: no. Circulation: 15,500.

**CHICO NEWS AND REVIEW.** 353 East Second St. Chico, CA 95928. (916) 894-2300. Submissions Editor: George Thurlow. Book Review Editor: Bob Speer. Freelance submissions: some. Circulation: 40,000.

**CHINO VALLEY NEWS.** 13179 9th St., PO Box 607. Chino, CA 91708-0607. (714) 628-5501. Submissions Editor: Charles Ferrell. Freelance submissions: seldom. Circulation: 8,000 daily, 15,000 Wednesday.

**CHULA VISTA STAR NEWS.** 835 Third Ave. Chula Vista, CA 92010. (619) 427-3000. Submissions Editor: Dale Morton. Freelance submissions: n/i. Circulation: 84,000.

**CLAREMONT COURIER.** PO Box 820. Claremont, CA 91711-0820. (714) 621-4761. Submissions Editor: Martin Weinberger (also book reviews). Freelance submissions: yes. Circulation: 6,000.

**CLOVIS INDEPENDENT.** PO Box 189. Clovis, CA 93613. (209) 298-8081. Submissions Editor: Judith House. Freelance submissions: n/i. Circulation: 4,000.

**COACHELLA VALLEY SUN.** 45-140 Towne St. Indio, CA 92201. (619) 347-3313. Submissions Editor: Nadine Rivera (also book reviews). Freelance submissions: n/i. Circulation: n/i.

**COAST DISPATCH GROUP.** PO Box 878. Encinitas, CA 92024. (619) 753-6543. Submissions Editor: James Baumann (also book reviews). Freelance submissions: rarely. Circulation: 23,000.

**COAST MEDIA NEWSPAPER GROUP.** 4034 Irving Place. Culver City, CA 90232. (213) 839-5271. Submissions Editor: John Hartmire. Freelance submissions: yes. Circulation: 17,000.

**CONTRA COSTA TIMES.** PO Box 5088. Walnut Creek, CA 94596. (415) 935-2525. Submissions Editor: Michael Laumiere (features). Book Review Editor: Carol Fowler. Freelance submissions: sometimes. Circulation: 100,000.

**COPLEY LOS ANGELES NEWSPAPERS.** 5215 Torrance Blvd. Torrance, CA 90509. (213) 540-5511. Submissions Editor: Jean Adelsman. Book Review Editor: Don Lechman. Freelance submissions: n/i. Circulation: 126,037 Sunday, 92,754 weekly.

**CORONADO JOURNAL.** PO Box 8. Coronado, CA 92118. (619) 435-3141. Submissions Editor: Sue Timmons (city; also book reviews). Freelance submissions: n/i. Circulation: 6,500.

**(CORTE MADERA) TWIN CITIES TIMES.** PO Box 186. Corte Madera, CA 94925. (415) 924-8552. Submissions Editor: Matt Maguire. Freelance submissions: local only. Circulation: 5,500.

**COVINA INTER-CITY EXPRESS.** PO Box 1259. Covina, CA 91722. (818) 962-8811. Submissions Editor: Joe Blackstock. Freelance submissions: no. Circulation: 62,000.

**CRESCENT CITY DEL NORTE TRIPLICATE.** PO Box 277. Crescent City, CA 95531. (707) 464-2141. Submissions Editor: Larry Wells (Managing Editor). Freelance submissions: no. Circulation: 7,650.

**DAILY VARIETY.** 1400 N. Cahuenga Blvd. Hollywood, CA 90028. (213) 469-1141. Submissions Editor: Rick Bozanich. Book Review Editor: Peter Pryor. Freelance submissions: no. Circulation: 23,000.

**DAVIS ENTERPRISE, THE.** 315 G Street (95616), PO Box 1470. Davis, CA 95617. (916) 756-0800. Submissions Editor: Debbie Davis. Book Review Editor: Del McColm. Freelance submissions: very rarely. Circulation: 10,000.

**DESERT SENTINEL.** PO Box 338. Desert Hot Springs, CA 92240. (619) 329-1411. Submissions Editor: Kathryn Koch (also book reviews). Freelance submissions: accepts, but no payment. Circulation: 10,000.

**DRAMA-LOGUE.** PO Box 38771. Los Angeles, CA 90038. (213) 464-5079. Submissions Editor: Faye Vordy (also book reviews). Freelance submissions: yes. Circulation: 18,000.

**(EL CAJON) DAILY CALIFORNIA, THE.** PO Box 1565. El Cajon, CA 92022. (619) 442-4404. Submissions Editor: Ray Bordner. Book Review Editor: Karen Barnett. Freelance submissions: no. Circulation: 22,500.

**EL SEGUNDO HERALD.** PO Box 188. El Segundo, CA 90245. (213) 322-1830. Submissions Editor: Linda Collins (also book reviews). Freelance submissions: no. Circulation: 13,000.

**(EUREKA) TIMES-STANDARD.** PO Box 3580. Eureka, CA 95501. (707) 442-1711. Submissions Editor: Rhonda Pialorsi. Freelance submissions: sometimes. Circulation: 22,000.

**(FAIRFIELD) DAILY REPUBLIC.** 1250 Texas St., PO Box 47. Fairfield, CA 94533. (707) 425-4646. Submissions Editor: Rick Jensen. Book Review Editor: Ian Thompson. Freelance submissions: rarely. Circulation: 19,000 Monday-Saturday, 20,400 Sunday.

**FOLSOM TELEGRAPH.** PO Box 157, 825 Sutter St. Folsom, CA 95630. (916) 985-2581. Submissions Editor: Cris Angell. Freelance submissions: no. Circulation: 25,850

**FREMONT ARGUS.** 37427 Centralmont Place, PO Box 5100. Fremont, CA 94536. (415) 794-0111. Submissions Editor: Bob Cuddy. Book Review Editor: Barry Caine. Freelance submissions: seldom. Circulation: 30,000.

**FRESNO BEE.** 1626 "E" St. Fresno, CA 93786. (209) 441-6111. Submissions Editor: Dana Heupel (metro). Book Review Editor: Eddie Lopez. Freelance submissions: yes. Circulation: 180,000.

**FULLERTON NEWS TRIBUNE.** 70l W. Commonwealth. Fullerton, CA 92632. (714) 871-2345. Submissions Editor: John Kane (also book reviews). Freelance submissions: no. Circulation: 42,000.

**GARDENA VALLEY NEWS.** PO Box 219. Gardena, CA 90247. (213) 329-6351. Submissions Editor: Robert Murray. Freelance submissions: generally, no. Circulation: 14,000.

**GILROY DISPATCH.** 6400 Monterey Rd., PO Box 22365. Gilroy, CA 95021-2365. (408) 842-6411. Submissions Editor: Mark Derry. Freelance submissions: n/i. Circulation: 7,800.

**GLENDALE NEWS PRESS.** 111 N. Isabel St. Glendale, CA 91206. (818) 241-4141. Submissions Editor: Mike Montgomery. Freelance submissions: n/i. Circulation: 38,000.

**GOLETA SUN.** PO Box 1670. Goleta, CA 93116. (805) 683-1587. Submissions Editor: Star Smith. Freelance submissions: no. Circulation: 18,000.

**GRASS VALLEY UNION.** PO Box 1025. Grass Valley, CA 95945. (916) 273-9561. Submissions Editor: Judy Mooers. Book Review Editor: Linda Whittmore. Freelance submissions: no. Circulation: 15,000.

**HALF MOON BAY REVIEW.** PO Box 68. Half Moon Bay, CA 94019. (415) 726-4424. Submissions Editor: Kimberly Stein. Freelance submissions: no. Circulation: 6,800.

**(HAYWARD) DAILY REVIEW.** 116 W. Winton Ave. Hayward, CA 94544. (415) 783-6111. Submissions Editor: Scott Livingston. Freelance submissions: yes. Circulation: 45,000 daily, 47,000 Sunday.

**HEALDSBURG TRIBUNE.** PO Box 518. Healdsburg, CA 95448. (707) 433-4451. Submissions Editor: Rollie Atkinson. Freelance submissions: no payment. Circulation: 6,675.

**(HOLLISTER) PINNACLE.** 341 Tres Pinos Rd., Ste. 201. Hollister, CA 95023. (408) 637-6300. Submissions Editor: Herman Wrede (also book reviews). Freelance submissions: yes. Circulation: 12,000.

**HOLLYWOOD REPORTER, THE.** 6715 Sunset Blvd. Hollywood, CA 90028. (213) 464-7411. Submissions Editor: Therese Wells. Freelance submissions: no. Circulation: 22,000.

**HUMBOLDT BEACON.** PO Box 310. Fortuna, CA 95540. (707) 725-6166. Submissions Editor: Glen Simmons. Freelance submissions: no. Circulation: 4,200.

**HUNTINGTON BEACH NEWS.** PO Box 31. Huntington Beach, CA 92648. (714) 969-4335. Submissions Editor: Gray Hernandez (also book reviews). Freelance submissions: rarely. Circulation: 20,000.

**IMPERIAL VALLEY PRESS & BRAWLY NEWS.**
205 N. 8th St. (92243), PO Box 2770. El Centro, CA 92244. (619) 352-2211. Submissions Editor: J. R. Fitch. Book Review Editor: Don Quinn. Freelance submissions: rarely. Circulation: 19,200 (both papers combined).

**LA JOLLA LIGHT & LA JOLLA UNIVERSITY CITY LIGHT.**
450 Pearl St., PO Box 1927. La Jolla, CA 92038. (619) 459-4201. Submissions Editor: Patricia Walsh. Freelance submissions: yes. Circulation: 10,000 & 12,500.

**(LIVERMORE) DAILY REVIEW (& LIVERMORE TRI-VALLEY HERALD).** PO Box 5050. Hayward, CA 94540. (415) 783-6111. Submissions Editor: Scott Livingston (Managing Editor, all submissions). Freelance submissions: n/i. Circulation: n/i.

**LODI NEWS SENTINEL.** PO Box 1360. Lodi, CA 95241. (209) 369-2761. Submissions Editor: Bob Mishizaki. Freelance submissions: yes. Circulation: 17,700.

**LOMPOC RECORD.** PO Box 578. Lompoc, CA 93438. (805) 736-2313. Submissions Editor: Leeda Henning. Freelance submissions: sometimes. Circulation: 10,200 daily, 10,500 Sunday.

**(LONG BEACH) PRESS TELEGRAM.** 604 Pine Ave. Long Beach, CA 90844-0001. (213) 435-1161. Submissions Editor: Mike Schwartz. Book Review Editor: Tim Grobaty. Freelance submissions: sometimes. Circulation: 135,000 daily, 150,000 Sunday.

**LOS ALTOS TOWN CRIER.** PO Box F. Los Altos, CA 94023. (415) 948-4489. Submissions Editor: Cheryl Tendick. Freelance submissions: yes. Circulation: 20,000.

**(LOS ANGELES) ADVOCATE, THE.** 6922 Hollywood Blvd., 10th Fl. Los Angeles, CA 90028. (213) 871-1225. Submissions Editor: Gerry Kroll. Freelance submissions: yes. Circulation: 70,000.

**(LOS ANGELES COUNTY, NORTH) DAILY NEWS.** PO Box 4200. Woodland Hills, CA 91365. (818) 713-3000. Submissions Editor: Bob Burdick. Book Review Editor: Bruce Cook. Freelance submissions: travel & book reviews only. Circulation: 300,000.

**LOS ANGELES HERALD EXAMINER.** 1111 S. Broadway (90015). PO Box 2416, Terminal Annex. Los Angeles, CA 90051-0416. (213) 744-8000. Submissions Editor: Andrea Herman (Managing Editor of Features). Book Review Editor: Jeff Silverman. Freelance submissions: yes. Circulation: 240,000.

**LOS ANGELES SENTINEL.** 1112 East 43rd St. Los Angeles, CA 90011. (213) 232-3261. Submissions Editor: Timothy Lester. Book Review Editor: Betty Pleasant. Freelance submissions: sometimes. Circulation: 40,000.

**LOS ANGELES TIMES.** Times Mirror Square. Los Angeles, CA 90053. (213) 237-5000. Submissions Editor: Jean Patman (features). Book Review Editor: Jack Miles. Freelance submissions: yes. Circulation: 136,813.

**LOS GATOS TIMES TRIBUNE.** 236 N. Santa Cruz Ave. Los Gatos, CA 95030. (408) 354-3900. Submissions Editor: Iver Davidson (also book reviews). Freelance submissions: no. Circulation: n/i.

**LOS GATOS WEEKLY.** 20 S. Santa Cruz Ave., Ste. 110. Los Gatos, CA 95030. (408) 354-3666. Submissions Editor: Irving Shear (also book reviews). Freelance submissions: yes. Circulation: 19,000.

**(MAMMOTH LAKES) REVIEW HERALD, THE.** PO Box 110. Mammoth Lakes, CA 93546. (619) 934-8544. Submissions Editor: Claudia Silverman. Freelance submissions: yes, generally local. Circulation: 4,500.

**MARIN INDEPENDENT JOURNAL.** PO Box 330. San Rafael, CA 94915. (415) 883-8600. Submissions Editor: Joe Konte. Book Review Editor: Rebecca Larsen. Freelance submissions: yes. Circulation: 40,000.

**(MARYSVILLE) YUBA-SUTTER APPEAL-DEMOCRAT.** 1530 Ellis Lake Dr. Marysville, CA 95901. (916) 741-2345. Submissions Editor: Larry Badger. Book Review Editor: Bob Curry. Freelance submissions: yes. Circulation: 24,000.

**MERCED SUN STAR.** 3033 N. G St., PO Box 739. Merced, CA 95341-0739. (209) 722-1511. Submissions Editor: Mike Blaesser (also book reviews). Freelance submissions: seldom. Circulation: 23,000.

**MERCED SUN STAR.** 3033 N. G St., PO Box 739. Merced, CA 95341-0739. (209) 722-1511. Submissions Editor: Mike Blaesser (also book reviews). Freelance submissions: seldom. Circulation: 23,000.

**MILL VALLEY RECORD.** PO Box 848. Mill Valley, CA 94941. (415) 388-3211. Submissions Editor: Peter Seidman (also book reviews). Freelance submissions: yes. Circulation: 22,000.

**MODESTO BEE.** 14th and H St. Modesto, CA 95352. (209) 578-2000. Submissions Editor: Larry McSwain. Book Review Editor: Ms. M. A. Mariner. Freelance submissions: sometimes. Circulation: 80,000.

**MONTEREY HERALD.** Monterey Peninsula Herald Co. Monterey, CA 93940. (408) 372-3311. Submissions Editor: Reg Henry. Book Review Editor: Susan Bernhardt. Freelance submissions: sometimes. Circulation: 35-37,000.

**NAPA REGISTER.** 1615 Second St. PO Box 150. Napa, CA 94559. (707) 226-3711. Submissions Editor: Lynn Penny. Book Review Editor: Mary Wallace. Freelance submissions: no. Circulation: 22,000.

**NORTHEAST NEWSPAPER GROUP.** 5420 N. Figueroa. Los Angeles, CA 90042. (213) 259-6200. Submissions Editor: Roger Swanson. Book Review Editor: Charles Cooper. Freelance submissions: yes. Circulation: 90,000.

**OAKLAND PRESS PUBLICATIONS.** PO Box 10501, Grand Lake St. Oakland, CA 94610. (415) 547-4000. Submissions Editor: Ray Epstein. Book Review Editor: Jan Miller. Freelance submissions: no. Circulation: 27,000.

**(OAKLAND) TRIBUNE, THE.** 409 13th St. Oakland, CA 94623. (415) 645-2000. Submissions Editor: Robert Maynard. Freelance submissions: n/i. Circulation: 149,256 daily, 150,089 Sunday.

**OCEANSIDE BLADE-TRIBUNE.** 1722 S. Hill St., PO Box 90. Oceanside, CA 92054. (619) 433-7333. Submissions Editor: William Missett. Book Review Editor: Jan Molen. Freelance submissions: yes. Circulation: 40,000.

**ORANGE COAST PILOT.** PO Box 1560. Costa Mesa, CA 92626. (714) 642-4321. Submissions Editor: Tom Tait. Freelance submissions: yes. Circulation: 21,000.

**ORANGE COUNTY NEWS.** 9872 Chapman, Ste. 8. Garden Grove, CA 92641. (714) 530-7622. Submissions Editor: Dave Roque. Freelance submissions: sometimes. Circulation: 35,000.

**OROVILLE MERCURY-REGISTER.** PO Box 651. Oroville, CA 95965. (916) 533-3131. Submissions Editor: Carolyn Richards (also book reviews). Freelance submissions: no. Circulation: 9,000.

**OXNARD PRESS COURIER.** 300 W. Ninth St. Oxnard, CA 93030. (805) 483-1101. Submissions Editor: Ed Smith. Book Review Editor: Cathy Scott. Freelance submissions: no. Circulation: 20,000.

**PACIFICA TRIBUNE.** 59 Aura Vista, PO Box 1188. Pacifica, CA 94044. (415) 359-6666. Submissions Editor: Rene Deal (also book reviews). Freelance submissions: rarely. Circulation: 8,638.

**(PALM DESERT) PUBLIC RECORD.** PO Drawer J. Palm Desert, CA 92261. (619) 346-8177. Submissions Editor: Jane Curtis (also book reviews). Freelance submissions: sometimes. Circulation: 1,000.

**PALM SPRINGS DESERT SUN.** 611 S. Palm Canyon Dr., PO Box 190. Palm Springs, CA 92263. (6l9) 325-8666. Submissions Editor: Rick Martinez (also book reviews). Freelance submissions: no. Circulation: 43,000 daily, 55,000 Saturday.

**(PALO ALTO) TIMES TRIBUNE.** 245 Lytton Ave. Palo Alto, CA 94301. (415) 853-1200. Submissions Editor: William Shillstone. Book Review Editor: Liz Manning. Freelance submissions: yes. Circulation: n/i.

**PALO ALTO WEEKLY.** 703 High St. Palo Alto, CA 94302. (415) 326-8210. Submissions Editor: Becky Bartindale. (also book reviews). Freelance submissions: yes. Circulation: 45,000.

**PALOS VERDES PENINSULA NEWS.** 900 Silver Spur Rd. Palos Verdes, CA 90274. (213) 377-6877. Submissions Editor: Ann LaJaunesse. Book Review Editor: David Knoles. Freelance submissions: yes. Circulation: 18,000.

**PASADENA/ALTADENA WEEKLY, THE.** 155 S. El Molino. Pasadena, CA 91101. (818) 584-1500. Submissions Editor: Dan Hutson. Book Review Editor: David Crowe Freelance submissions: yes. Circulation: 50,000 subscribers, 125,000 readers.

**PASADENA STAR-NEWS.** 525 E. Colorado Blvd. Pasadena, CA 91109. (213) 681-4871. Submissions Editor: Jim Timmermann (city desk). Book Review Editor: Kathy Register. Freelance submissions: Yes (mostly features). Circulation: 40,081.

**PETALUMA ARGUS-COURIER.** 830 Petaluma Blvd. N., PO Box 1091. Petaluma, CA 94953. (707) 762-4541. Submissions Editor: Chris Samson. Book Review Editor: Nome Faingold (lifestyles). Freelance submissions: no. Circulation: 10,000.

**(PINOLE) WEST COUNTY TIMES.** 1660 San Pablo Ave., PO Box 128. Pinole, CA 94564. (415) 724-8400. Submissions Editor: Al Pacciorini (Managing Editor). Freelance submissions: yes. Circulation: 40,000.

**(PLACERVILLE) MOUNTAIN DEMOCRAT.** PO Box l088. Placerville, CA 95667. (916) 622-1255. Submissions Editor: Mike Raffety. Book Review Editor: Rosemary Moore. Freelance submissions: sometimes. Circulation: 14,700.

**(PLEASANTON) VALLEY TIMES.** 126 Spring St., PO Box 607. Pleasanton, CA 94566. (415) 462-4160. Submissions Editor: Marian Green (community) or Mary Lou Bustos. Book Review Editor: Anne Shalsant (lifestyle). Freelance submissions: sometimes. Circulation: 30,000.

**POINT REYES LIGHT, THE.** PO Box 210. Point Reyes Station, CA 94956. (415) 663-8404. Submissions Editor: David V. Mitchell (also book reviews, regional). Freelance submissions: sometimes. Circulation: 3,600.

**POMONA PROGRESS BULLETIN.** PO Box 2708. Pomona, CA 91769. (714) 622-1201. Submissions Editor: Bob Muir (also book reviews). Freelance submissions: sometimes. Circulation: 40,000.

**PORTERVILLE RECORDER.** 115 E. Oak, PO Box 151. Porterville, CA 93258. (209) 784-5000. Submissions Editor: Rick Elkins. Freelance submissions: seldom. Circulation: 14,000.

**REDDING RECORD-SEARCHLIGHT.** PO Box 492397. Redding, CA 96049-2397. (916) 243-2424. Submissions Editor: Kip Cady. Book Review Editor: Laura Christman. Freelance submissions: seldom. Circulation: 39,000.

**RIVERSIDE PRESS-ENTERPRISE.** PO Box 792. Riverside, CA 92502. (714) 684-1200. Submissions Editor: Michael Jordan. Book Review Editor: Joel Blain. Freelance submissions: generally not. Circulation: 147,000.

**(ROSEVILLE) PRESS TRIBUNE, THE.** 188 Cirby Way. Roseville, CA 95678. (916) 786-8742. Submissions Editor: Dennis Wyatt Freelance submissions: seldom. Circulation: 15,000.

**RUSSIAN RIVER NEWS.** PO Box 19. Guerneville, CA 95446. (707) 869-3520. Submissions Editor: John De Salvio. Freelance submissions: yes. Circulation: 3,200, 3,600-3,700 summer.

**SACRAMENTO BEE.** PO Box 15779. Sacramento, CA 95852. (916) 321-1000. Submissions Editor: Gregory Favre. Book Review Editor: Paul Craig. Freelance submissions: yes. Circulation: 250,000.

**SACRAMENTO UNION.** 301 Capitol Mall. Sacramento, CA 95812. (916) 442-7811. Submissions Editor: Patrick Joyce. Book Review Editor: Jerry Cox. Freelance submissions: no. Circulation: 90,000.

**SALINAS CALIFORNIAN.** PO Box 81091. Salinas, CA 93912. (408) 424-2221. Submissions Editor: Dave Doucette (also book reviews). Freelance submissions: yes. Circulation: 23,500.

**SAN BERNARDINO COUNTY SUN.** 399 no. "D" Street. San Bernardino, CA 92401. (714) 889-9666. Submissions Editor: Arnold Garson. Freelance submissions: yes. Circulation: 86,500 daily, 95,000 Sunday.

**SAN DIEGO BUSINESS JOURNAL.** 4909 Murphy Canyon Rd., Ste. 200. San Diego, CA 92123. (619) 277-6359. Submissions Editor: Christi Phelps. Freelance submissions: sometimes. Circulation: 12,000.

**(SAN DIEGO COUNTY) TIMES-ADVOCATE.** 207 E. Pennsylvania Ave. Escondido, CA 92025. (619) 745-6611. Submissions Editor: Kathie Hinnen. Book Review Editor: Tom Spain. Freelance submissions: no. Circulation: 46,000.

**SAN DIEGO UNION TRIBUNE.** PO Box 191. San Diego, CA 92112-4106. (6l9) 299-3131. Submissions Editor: Ray Kipp. Book Review Editor: Ed Hutchings. Freelance submissions: yes. Circulation: 270,000 daily, 400,000 Sunday.

**SAN FRANCISCO CHRONICLE.** 901 Mission St. San Francisco, CA 94103. (415) 777-1111. Submissions Editor: Rosalie Wright (special sections); Marjorie Rice (travel, food). Book Review Editor: Patricia Holt. Freelance submissions: yes. Circulation: 115,000.

**SAN FRANCISCO EXAMINER.** 925 Mission St. San Francisco, CA 94103. (415) 777-2424. Submissions Editor: Paul Wilner (special sections). Book Review Editor: Patricia Holt. Freelance submissions: yes. Circulation: 145,000 weekly, 715,000 Sunday.

**SAN FRANCISCO PROGRESS.** 909 Montgomery St. San Francisco, CA 94113. (415) 982-8022. Submissions Editor: Al Burgin. Freelance submissions: rarely. Circulation: 158,000 S.F., 64,200 Peninsula.

**SAN FRANCISCO SUN REPORTER.** 1366 Turk St. San Francisco, CA 94115. (415) 931-5778. Submissions Editor: Amelia Ward (also book reviews). Freelance submissions: no. Circulation: n/i.

**SAN JOSE MERCURY NEWS.** 750 Ridder Park Drive. San Jose, CA 95190. (408) 920-5000. Submissions Editor: Carol Muller (also book reviews). Freelance submissions: rarely. Circulation: 250,000.

**(SAN LUIS OBISPO) COUNTY TELEGRAM-TRIBUNE.** 1321 Johnson Ave., PO Box 112. San Luis Obispo, CA 93406. (805) 595-1111. Submissions Editor: Winston Caine. Book Review Editor: Bruce Miller. Freelance submissions: yes. Circulation: Circulation: 38,000.

**SAN MATEO TIMES.** 1080 S. Amphlett Blvd. San Mateo, CA 94402. (415) 348-4321. Submissions Editor: John Hubbard. Book Review Editor: Jack Russell. Freelance submissions: yes. Circulation: 40,000.

**(SANTA ANNA) ORANGE COUNTY REPORTER.** 1315 W. 5th St., PO Box 1846. Santa Ana, CA 92702-1846. (714) 543-2027. Submissions Editor: Lavonne Mason (also book reviews). Freelance submissions: no. Circulation: 150,000.

**SANTA BARBARA NEWS PRESS.** PO Drawer NN. Santa Barbara, CA 93102. (805) 564-5200. Submissions Editor: Ed Lawler. Book Review Editor: John Crowder. Freelance submissions: yes. Circulation: 52,000 daily.

**SANTA CRUZ SENTINEL.** PO Box 638. Santa Cruz, CA 95061. (408) 423-4242. Submissions Editor: Tom Honig. Book Review Editor: Chris Watson. Freelance submissions: sometimes. Circulation: 32,830.

**SANTA MARIA TIMES.** PO Box 400. Santa Maria, CA 93456. (805) 925-2691. Submissions Editor: Don Brown (also book reviews). Freelance submissions: rarely. Circulation: 22,000.

**(SANTA MONICA) GOOD LIFE INDEPENDENT JOURNAL.** 1032 Broadway. Santa Monica, CA 90401. (213) 393-0601. Submissions Editor: Don Murchie (also book reviews). Freelance submissions: sometimes. Circulation: 47,000.

**SANTA ROSA PRESS DEMOCRAT.** 427 Mendocino Ave. Santa Rosa, CA 95402. (707) 546-2020. Submissions Editor: George Manes. Book Review Editor: Susan Leathers. Freelance submissions: sometimes. Circulation: 87,000 daily, 93,000 Sunday.

**SANTA YNEZ VALLEY NEWS.** 423 Second St. PO Box 647. Solvang, CA 93463. (805) 688-5522. Submissions Editor: King Merrill. Book Review Editor: Pam Mowry. Freelance submissions: no. Circulation: 7,500.

**(SEASIDE) SENTINEL, THE.** 1760 Fremont Blvd., Ste. G1. Seaside, CA 93955. (408) 899-2305. Submissions Editor: David Bennett. Freelance submissions: no. Circulation: 20,000 weekly.

**SIMI VALLEY ENTERPRISE.** 888 Easy St. (93065). PO Box 869. Simi Valley, CA 93062. (805) 526-6211. Submissions Editor: Jacque Kampschroer (also book reviews). Freelance submissions: yes. Circulation: 16,800 daily, 17,400 Sunday.

**SISKIYOU DAILY NEWS.** PO Box 129. Yreka, CA 96097. (916) 842-5777. Submissions Editor: Jeff Lester. Book Review Editor: Jeff Wagner. Freelance submissions: n/i. Circulation: 6,000 daily, 9,743 Wednesday.

**(SONORA) UNION DEMOCRAT.** 84 S. Washington St. Sonora, CA 95370. (209) 532-7151. Submissions Editor: Buzz Eggleston. Book Review Editor: Kathe Waterbury. Freelance submissions: rarely. Circulation: 20,000.

**SOUTHERN CALIFORNIA COMMUNITY NEWSPAPER.** 8800 National Ave. South Gate, CA 90280. (213) 927-8681. Submissions Editor: Phil Villa. Book Review Editor: Art Aguilar. Freelance submissions: sometimes. Circulation: 356,685.

**STOCKTON RECORD.** PO Box 900. Stockton, CA 95201. (209) 943-6397. Submissions Editor: Richard Hamner. Book Review Editor: Philip Bookman. Freelance submissions: yes. Circulation: 59,000.

**THOUSAND OAKS NEWS CHRONICLE.** 2595 Thousand Oaks Blvd. (91360). PO Box 3129. Thousand Oaks, CA 91359. (805) 496-3211. Submissions Editor: David Becker. Book Review Editor: Shirley Appleman. Freelance submissions: no. Circulation: 25,000.

**TURLOCK JOURNAL.** PO Box 800. Turlock, CA 95381. (209) 634-9141. Submissions Editor: Don Hansen (also book reviews). Freelance submissions: sometimes. Circulation: 10,300.

**UKIAH DAILY JOURNAL.** 590 S. School St., PO Box 749. Ukiah, CA 95482. (707) 468-0123. Submissions Editor: Mary Greeley. Book Review Editor: Sae Woodward. Freelance submissions: seldom. Circulation: 9,200.

**VALLEJO TIMES HERALD.** PO Box 3188. Vallejo, CA 94590. (707) 644-1141. Submissions Editor: Colleen Truelsen. Freelance submissions: sometimes. Circulation: 28,000.

(Ventura County, Inland) *Daily News see* **(LOS ANGELES COUNTY, NORTH) DAILY NEWS**

**VENTURA COUNTY STAR-FREE PRESS.** PO Box 6711. Ventura, CA 93003. (805) 656-4111. Submissions Editor: John Bowman (or by department). Freelance submissions: very rarely. Circulation: 50,000.

**(VICTORVILLE) DAILY PRESS.** PO Box 1389. Victorville, CA 92393-0964. (6l9) 241-7744. Submissions Editor: John Iddings. Freelance submissions: sometimes. Circulation: 25,000.

**VISALIA TIMES DELTA.** 330 N. West St. Visalia, CA 93279. (209) 734-5821. Janet C. Sanford, Publisher. Submissions Editor: Nancy Hampel. Book Review Editor: Camille Nichols. Freelance submissions: sometimes. Circulation: 22,000.

**WATSONVILLE REGISTER PAJARONIAN.** PO Box 780. Watsonville, CA 95077. (408) 724-0611. Submissions Editor: Mike Wallace. Book Review Editor: Lauren Wilkins. Freelance submissions: yes. Circulation: 15,500.

**WHITTIER DAILY NEWS.** PO Box 581. Whittier, CA 90608. (213) 698-0955. Submissions Editor: Bill Bell. Book Review Editor: Glen Whipp. Freelance submissions: n/i. Circulation: 18,500.

# Literary Agents

There is no law which says that a writer must have an agent. However, for some writers the benefits of having an agent are well worth the 10-15 percent commission charged. For example, some publishers simply refuse to consider unagented manuscripts. The specific services and charges vary from agent to agent, but they usually include the following:

**Before sale**—Evaluates your manuscript, advises on the preparation of your proposal, talks to editors, sends out your submissions and informs you of results.

**During sale**—Negotiates contract with publisher and reviews the terms with you, after which you must decide to sign or not sign.

**After sale**—Receives and examines your royalty statements and payments, deducts the appropriate commission, and sends you the remainder. Pursues the sale of subsidiary rights retained by you in your contract.

Merely writing to one agent does not guarantee that you will be accepted as a client, so expect the search to involve several contacts. The following information has been gathered and organized to help you in the process of finding the right agency for your work.

### How to Use the Information in This Section

The first paragraph of each entry gives the basic contact information and identifies the agent to whom you should address your query.

### Subjects of Interest

We've included information on the type of material the agent prefers to handle. Your chances of a positive response to your initial inquiry are maximized when you approach an agent who is already interested in your subject matter. Books that the agent has previously sold indicate the contacts and success the agent has had. However, some agents prefer to keep this type of information confidential.

### Agency Policies

Many agents will only handle new writers if they have been referred by clients, editors, or other professional colleagues. Other agents will gladly encourage new writers and are eager to represent well-written manuscripts. Reading fees are charged by some agencies and do not guarantee that the agent will accept the work. Some only charge a first-time writer, and some will refund the fee if the manuscript sells. Agents may charge an additional fee to cover "out-of-pocket" expenses, such as long-distance phone calls, photocopying, express mail, etc.

Agents who do not handle all forms of subsidiary rights often will work in conjunction with other agents to get you the best deal possible. Agents will also work closely with their counterparts in Europe for sales of foreign rights, or in Hollywood for sales of dramatization, motion picture, and broadcast (performance) rights.

Agents try to respond to your submissions or queries in a reasonable length of time; make it easier for them by including a SASE.

**Commission:** This information represents the percentage of income from your writing that the agent takes as a fee for representing you. Most agents charge between 10 and 15 percent. You alone must decide if it is worth it to you to market your book yourself or pay an agent to do it.

### Initial Contact

Never send a complete manuscript unless requested by the agent. An initial query letter may include no more than an outline or brief summary of your story and idea. For nonfiction, include your qualifications. Always include a SASE.

### Additional Information

This section lists any other information the agent expects you to know, or wants you to know, about the agency.

### Abbreviations

n/i means no information was given to us by the agency.

n/a means that this particular question did not apply to the agency.

---

**LINDA ALLEN AGENCY.** 1949 Green St., #5. San Francisco, CA 94123. (415) 921-6437. Agent: Linda Allen.

**Subjects of Interest.** **Books**—Nonfiction: juvenile; young adult. Fiction: juvenile; young adult. Representative titles: *Suffer the Child* (Pocket Books); *dBase 4 Made Easy* (McGraw Hill); *Visiting Miss Pierce* (Farrar, Straus and Giroux). **Scripts**—not at present. Do not want: category fiction; westerns; science fiction.

**Agency Policies.** Previously unpublished authors: yes. Reading fee: no. Other fees: photocopying. Subsidiary rights all when appropriate; differs from contract to contract. Response time to initial inquiry: 6 weeks. **Commission:** 15%.

**Initial Contact.** Query letter; sample chapters. Include SASE.

**HARRY BLOOM AGENCY.** 1520 S. Beverly Glen Blvd., Ste. 404. Los Angeles, CA 90024. (213) 556-3461. Agents: Patricia Dale; Harry Bloom.

**Subjects of Interest.** **Books**—Fiction: yes. Nonfiction: yes. Other: biographies. Representative titles: confidential. **Scripts**—specials; miniseries; motion pictures. Do not want: science fiction; horror; religion.

**Agency Policies.** Previously unpublished authors: yes. Reading fee: no. Other fees: agency fee if we represent and sell the work. Subsidiary rights: all. Designated agents: n/a. Response time to initial inquiry: 2-4 weeks. **Commission:** 10%.

**Initial Contact.** Phone; query letter; query with synopsis or proposal.

## BOOKSTOP LITERARY AGENCY. 67 Meadow View Road. Orinda, CA 94563. (415) 254-2664. Agents: Kendra Bersamin.

**Subjects of Interest.** **Books**—Fiction: children's; young adult. Nonfiction: children's. Other—illustrated children's. Representative titles: *Letter to Letter* (Dutton); *Stable in Bethlehem* (Golden); *Jenny* (Macmillan). **Scripts**—handled by sub agent. Do not want: adult material.

**Agency Policies.** Previously unpublished authors: yes. Reading fee: no. Other fees: postage; photocopying; phone. Subsidiary rights: all. Designated agents: yes. Response time to initial inquiry: 4-8 weeks. **Commission:** 15%.

**Initial Contact.** Fiction, entire manuscript. Nonfiction, outline, 2 sample chapters.

**Additional Information.** BookStop Literary Agency sells quality fiction, nonfiction, illustration and manuscripts for books for children from six months to sixteen years old.

## CALDER AGENCY. 4150 Riverside Dr., Ste. 204. Burbank, CA 91505. (818) 845-7434. Agent: Maury Calder.

**Subjects of Interest.** **Scripts**—episodic TV; specials; miniseries; motion picture. Do not want: anything less than 1 hour.

**Agency Policies.** Previously unpublished authors: yes. Reading fee: no. Other fees: no. Subsidiary rights: first serialization; second serialization; reprint; dramatization, motion picture and broadcast; video distribution; sound reproduction and recording; direct mail or direct sales; computer and other magnetic and electronic media; commercial. Response time to initial inquiry: varies. **Commission:** 10%.

**Initial contact.** Query with short synopsis of proposal. Include SASE.

## MARTHA CASSELMAN. PO Box 342. Calistoga, CA 94515-0342. (707) 942-4341. Agent: Martha Casselman.

**Subjects of Interest. Books**—Nonfiction: looking for books dealing with contemporary concerns—including politics, biography; children's and YA (limited number); cookbooks and food-related works. Fiction: mainstream; literary; will consider "women's books." Recent publications: confidential, but publishers include Simon & Schuster, Harper and Row, Knopf, Holt, *Focus Magazine*. Do not want: genre fiction; computer; technical.

**Agency Policies.** Previously unpublished authors: yes, including short story writers. Reading fee: no. Other fees: copying; overnight mail; FAX; charge back. Subsidiary rights: all; depends on contract between author and publisher, agency controls all rights not contractually assigned to or held by publisher. Designated agents: chosen for specific projects. Response time to initial inquiry: 1 day to 1 month. **Commission:** 15%.

**Initial Contact.** Phone; query letter; query with synopsis or proposal. Include brief biographical material; for nonfiction also include analysis of market for book and the competition.

**Additional Information.** We cannot return long-distance query calls. Therefore, it is preferable to query by mail. If calling locally, office hours are Monday through Friday, 9-4; please do not expect us to return calls in the evening. I absolutely do not want material mailed by way of a computer-generated program that is sent to every agent in the country; do not send unsolicited full-length manuscripts, fiction or nonfiction.

**CINEMA TALENT INTERNATIONAL.** 7906 Santa Monica Blvd. #212. Los Angeles, CA 90046. (213) 656-1937. Agents: George Kriton; Maxine Arnald; Lawrence Athan.

**Subjects of Interest.** **Books**—Nonfiction: yes. Fiction: yes. **Scripts**—episodic TV; miniseries; motion picture. Do not want: anything that deals with drugs.

**Agency Policies.** Previously unpublished authors: yes. Reading fee: no. Other fees: no. Subsidiary rights: all. Response time to initial inquiry: n/i. **Commission:** 10%.

**Initial Contact.** Query letter; query with synopsis or proposal.

**RUTH COHEN, INC.** Box 7626. Menlo Park, CA 94025. (415) 854-2054. Agents: Ruth Cohen and Associates.

**Subjects of Interest.** **Books**—Nonfiction: quality writing and well-researched manuscripts. Fiction: quality adult and juvenile; mainstream novels; genre: mysteries, romances, historicals. Representative titles: *Boomerang Kids* (Little Brown)*; Killshot* (Bantam)*; No Way Out* (Harper & Row). Do not want: poetry; film scripts.

**Agency Policies.** Previously unpublished authors: yes. Reading fee: no. Other fees: photocopying; foreign cables and shipment. Subsidiary rights: first serialization; reprint; dramatization, motion picture and broadcast; translation and foreign; English language publication outside the United States and Canada. Designated agents (foreign or film rights): Joel Gotler of LA Literary Associates. Response time to initial inquiry: 3-4 weeks. **Commission:** 15%.

**Initial Contact.** Query with synopsis or proposal; 15 pages of opening of manuscript. Include SASE.

**Additional Information.** Actively seeking good writers of juvenile YA fiction and adult mysteries.

**SANDRA DIJKSTRA LITERARY AGENCY.** 1237 Camino del Mar, Ste. 515C. Del Mar, CA 92104. (619) 755-3115. Agent: Sandra Dijkstra, President; Katherine Goodwin, Associate Agent.

**Subjects of Interest.** **Books**—Nonfiction: biography/memoir; psychology; health and medicine; parenting; business; art and artists; self-help; finance; travel; essays; women's studies; politics; nature. Fiction: quality and contemporary and literary fiction; mainstream; mystery-suspense; horror; science fiction; historical romance. Representative titles: *If I'm So Wonderful, Why Am I Still Single* (Viking)*; The Joy Luck Club* (Putnam)*; White Rabbit: A Woman Doctor's Story of Addiction and Recovery* (Crown). **Scripts**—only from books we already represent; i.e. the original author doing his or her own screenplay. Do not want: textbooks; children's; dissertations; computer books; vanity press.

**Agency Policies.** Previously unpublished authors: occasionally. Reading fee: no. Other fees: in-depth evaluation of manuscript or proposal; fee depends on length. Subsidiary rights: all. Designated agents (foreign or film rights): Mildred Hird (translation); Abner Stein (British). Response time to initial inquiry: 3-4 weeks. **Commission:** 15%.

**Initial Contact.** Query letter; query with synopsis or proposal.

**ERIKSON LITERARY AGENCY.** 223 Via Sevilla. Santa Barbara, CA 93109. (805) 564-8782. Agents: George Erikson; Lois Shearer.

**Subjects of Interest.** **Books**—Nonfiction: yes. Fiction: yes. Representative titles: *Elvis, my Brother* (St. Martin's Press)*; The Don Juan Papers* (Brower)*; Imagine That* (Chicago Review Press). **Scripts**—motion picture. Do not want: poetry.

**Agency Policies.** Previously unpublished authors: yes. Reading fee: $100. Other fees: no. Subsidiary rights: all. Response time to initial inquiry: 6 weeks. **Commission**: 15%.

**Initial Contact**. Query letter. Include SASE.

## FELICIA ETH LITERARY REPRESENTATIVE.

140 University Ave., Ste. 62. Palo Alto, CA 94301. (415) 375-1276. Agent: Felicia Eth.

**Subjects of Interest. Books**—Nonfiction: health; psychology; history; popular science; women's issues; investigative journalism; contemporary issues. Fiction: high quality (no glitz). Representative titles: confidential. Do not want: juvenile; young adult; poetry; romance series; science fiction series; westerns.

**Agency Policies.** Previously unpublished authors: yes. Reading fee: no. Other fees: photocopying; telexes; any extraordinary expenses. Subsidiary rights: first serialization; newspaper syndication; reprint; video distribution; sound reproduction and recording; translation and foreign; commercial; English language publication outside the United States and Canada. Designated Agents: independent agents. Response time to initial inquiry: 3-6 weeks. **Commission:** 15%.

**Initial Contact**. Fiction, query letter; first 30 pages. Nonfiction, query with synopsis or proposal. Include credentials and SASE.

## CANDICE FUHRMAN LITERARY AGENCY.

30 Ramona Rd. PO Box F. Forest Knolls, CA 94933. Agent: Candice Fuhrman.

**Subjects of Interest. Books**—Fiction: adult; commercial. Nonfiction: self-help; how-to. Representative titles: *The Recovery Catalog* (Simon and Schuster); *The Dreams of Pregnant Women* (Tarcher); *Hassle-Free Homework* (Doubleday). Do not want: genre; children's.

**Agency Policies.** Previously unpublished authors: yes. Reading fee: no. Other fees: copying; postage. Subsidiary rights: all. Response time to initial inquiry: 2 weeks for queries; 4 weeks for manuscripts. **Commission:** 15%.

**Initial Contact.** Query with synopsis or proposal.

**Additional Information.** I'm especially interested in nonfiction self-help or how-to and am happy to work with new authors. Please include SASE with submissions if you want your materials returned.

## MITCHELL J. HAMILBURG AGENCY.

292 S. La Cienega Blvd., Ste. 312. (213) 657-1501. Agent: Michael Hamilburg.

**Subjects of Interest. Books**—Nonfiction: general. Fiction: general. Representative titles: *Helter Skelter; Von Ryan's Express; Logan's Run; Taxi Driver; Time after Time.*

**Agency Policies.** Previously unpublished authors: yes. Reading fee: no. Other fees: no. Subsidiary rights: first serialization; dramatization, motion picture and broadcast; video distribution; commercial. Response time to initial inquiry: 3-4 weeks. **Commission:** 10-15%.

**Initial Contact.** Query letter first.

## FREDRICK HILL ASSOCIATES.

1842 Union St. San Francisco, CA 94123. (415) 921-2910. Agents: Fredrick Hill; Bonnie Nadel.

**Subjects of Interest. Books**—Nonfiction: investigative journalism; biography. Fiction: literary. Do not want: no genre fiction (science fiction, romance, etc.).

**Agency Policies.** Previously unpublished authors: yes. Reading fee: no. Other fees: foreign rights, galleys sent overseas. Subsidiary rights: first serialization; newspaper syndication; dramatization, motion picture and broadcast; video; English language publication outside the United States and Canada. Designated Agents: agents in every country and Southern

California. Response time to initial inquiry: 4-8 weeks. **Commission:** 15%, domestic; 20%, foreign.

**Initial Contact.** Query with synopsis or proposal.

## ALICE HILTON LITERARY AGENCY. 13131 Welby Way. North Hollywood, CA 91606. (818) 982-2546. Agent: Alice Hilton.

**Subjects of Interest. Books**—Nonfiction and Fiction: sophisticated, civilized quality material. Representative titles: *Tax-Free America* (Witlauer). **Scripts**—episodic TV; specials; miniseries; motion picture; cartoons. Do not want: children's books; violence.

**Agency Policies.** Previously unpublished authors: yes. Reading fee: on book-length material, $2 per 1000 words (pica), for previously unpublished authors. Other fees: no. Subsidiary rights: all, as the need arises. Response time to initial inquiry: 4-6 weeks. **Commission:** 10%.

**Initial Contact.** Query letter.

## INDEPENDENT PUBLISHERS SERVICES. PO Box 135. Volcano, CA 95689. (209) 296-3445. Agent: Ruth Gottstein.

**Subjects of Interest. Books**—Nonfiction: yes. Fiction: children's books. I only handle foreign (translation) rights for already published books. Representative titles: represent Tomie dePaola for translation; *Waking Up*, published in United States by Shambala Press.

**Agency Policies.** Previously unpublished authors: no. Reading fee: no. Other fees: postage; telephone. Subsidiary rights: translation and foreign. Response time to initial inquiry: n/i. **Commission:** 20%.

**Initial Contact.** Query letter. Include SASE.

## JLM LITERARY AGENTS. 17221 E. 17th St. Santa Ana, CA 92701. (714) 547-4870. Agent: Judy Semler.

**Subjects of Interest. Books** —Nonfiction: general, new age, holistic health. Fiction: general. Representative titles: *Ghost of a Chance, Flying Wing, Light His Fire.*

**Agency Policies.** Previously unpublished authors: yes. Reading fee: no. Other fees: no. Subsidiary rights: first serialization; second serialization; reprint rights; dramatization, motion picture and broadcast; direct mail or sound reproduction and recording rights; direct sales rights; book club rights; English language publication outside the United States and Canada. Response time to initial inquiry: varies. Include SASE. **Commission:** 15%.

**Initial Contact.** Query letter; query with synopsis.

## WILLIAM KERWIN AGENCY. 1605 N. Cahuenga Blvd., #202. Hollywood, CA 90028. (213) 469-5155. Agent: William Kerwin.

**Subjects of Interest. Scripts**— movie of the week; pilots; feature films.

**Agency Policies.** Previously unpublished authors: yes. Reading fee: no. Other fees: no. Subsidiary rights: first serialization; second serialization; dramatization, motion picture and broadcast; video distribution; commercial; English language publication outside the United States and Canada. Response time to initial inquiry: 7 days, with SASE. **Commission:** 10%.

**Initial Contact.** Query letter; query with synopsis.

## LAKE AND DOUROUX, INC. 445 South Beverly Dr., Ste. 310. Beverly Hills, CA 90212. (213) 557-0700. Agents: Candace Lake; Michael Douroux.

**Subjects of Interest. Scripts**—main concentration: screen writers, directors, cinematographers in areas of episodic TV; specials; miniseries; motion picture; cartoons.

**Agency Policies.** Previously unpublished authors: no. Reading fee: no. Other fees: no. Subsidiary rights: first serialization; reprint; dramatization, motion picture and broadcast; book club. Response time to initial inquiry: 1 month average. **Commission:** 10%.

**Initial Contact.** Query letter.

**LARSEN/POMADA LITERARY AGENTS.** 1029 Jones St. San Francisco, CA 94109. (415) 673-0939. Agents: Michael Larsen; Elizabeth Pomada.

**Subjects of Interest.** **Books**—Fiction: literary; commercial; historical romance; "new voices." Nonfiction: pop psychology; business; popular science; biography; cultural affairs. Do not want: scripts; poetry; children's and YA.

**Agency Policies.** Previously unpublished authors: yes. Reading fee: no. Other fees: no. Subsidiary rights: all. Designated agents (foreign or film rights): yes. Response time to initial inquiry: 6-8 weeks. **Commission:** 15%.

**Initial Contact.** Phone; query letter; query with synopsis or proposal. 30 pages and synopsis, fiction; proper proposal, nonfiction. Include SASE with all proposals.

**Additional Information.** We are looking for good new ideas and new voices. We are charter members of ILAA.

**THE MAUREEN LASHER AGENCY.** PO Box 888. Pacific Palisades, CA 90272. (213) 459-8415. Agents: specialities decided in-house.

**Subjects of Interest.** **Scripts**—motion pictures; TV. Do not want: stage plays; radio.

**Agency Policies.** Previously unpublished authors: rarely. Reading fee: no. Other fees: no. Subsidiary rights: all. Response time to initial inquiry: 1 month. **Commission:** 15%.

**Initial Contact.** Nonfiction, query letter and proposal. Fiction, manuscript.

**IRVING PAUL LAZAR AGENCY.** 120 El Camino, Ste. 108. Bevery Hills, CA 90212. (213) 275-6153. Agent: Irving Paul Lazar. Not accepting any new material.

**LOS ANGELES LITERARY ASSOCIATES.** 8955 Norma Place. Los Angeles, CA 90069. (213) 275-6330. Agents: Joel Gotler; Howard Sanders.

**Subjects of Interest.** **Books**—Nonfiction: yes. Fiction: yes. Other: unpublished material which we sell to film/TV companies prior to sale to publishing companies. Representative titles: *Rockets Red Glare* (St. Martin's Press)*; About Faces* (Doubleday)*; Depraved Indifference* (NAL). Do not want: screenplays.

**Agency Policies.** Previously unpublished authors: yes. Reading fee: no. Other fees: extensive photocopying. Subsidiary rights: first serialization; dramatization, motion picture and broadcast; book club; translation and foreign; commercial. Designated agents (foreign or film rights): many agents (New York, London), as well as the publishers, handle my foreign rights. Response time to initial inquiry: promptly. **Commission:** 10%.

**Initial Contact.** Query letter; recommendation.

**Additional Information.** We see much of the material bought in Hollywood.

**MARGARET MCBRIDE LITERARY AGENCY.** PO Box 8730. La Jolla, CA 92038. (619) 459-0559. Agent: Margaret McBride.

**Subjects of Interest.** **Books**—Nonfiction: all categories. Fiction: literary; mainstream; commercial; suspense; action adventure; women's; science fiction. Representative titles: *One Minute Manager* (series) (Morrow)*; The Generals*: *Ulysses S. Grant and Robert E. Lee* (Knopf)*; Hand of Lazarus* (Zebra)*; High Priest* (New American Library). **Scripts**—film rights connected with literary properties. Do not want: magazine articles; poetry; short stories.

**Agency Policies.** Previously unpublished authors: query first. Reading fee: no. Other fees: n/i. Subsidiary rights: first serialization; second serialization; newspaper syndication; dramatization, motion picture and broadcast; sound reproduction and recording; translation and foreign; commercial; English language publication outside the United States and Canada. Designated agents (foreign or film rights): Winifred Golden. Response time to initial inquiry: 6-8 weeks. **Commission:** 15% literary rights; 10% audio and other nonliterary rights; 25% foreign rights.

**Initial Contact.** Query letter; query with synopsis or proposal.

## HELEN MCGRATH, WRITERS' REPRESENTATIVE. 1406 Idaho Ct. Concord, CA 94521. (415) 672-6211. Agent: Helen McGrath.

**Subjects of Interest.** **Books**—Fiction: all types. Nonfiction: new-age; self-help; biography; how-to. Representative titles: *Love Me True* (Harlequin); *Mass Dreams of the Future* (McGraw Hill); *Reckless Passage* (Lynx Communications). Do not want: scripts; cookbooks; poetry; religious; textbooks.

**Agency Policies.** Previously unpublished authors: yes. Reading fee: no. Other fees: photocopying. Subsidiary rights: all. Designated agents (foreign or film rights): Karen Schindler; Brazil; A.S. Bookman, Denmark, Sweden, Norway and Finland; Jane Conway-Gordon, British; Agence Hoffman, Germany and France; Michael Meller, Holland; Lorna Soifer, Israel; Erich Linder, Italy; Ursula Barnett, South Africa; Julio Yanez, Spain and Portugal. Response time to initial inquiry: 3 weeks to 3 months. **Commission:** 15%.

**Initial Contact.** Phone; query with synopsis and proposal. Include SASE.

## THE MITNICK AGENCY. 91 Henry St. San Francisco, CA 94114. (415) 864-2234. Agent: Samuel A. Mitnick.

**Subjects of Interest.** **Books**—Nonfiction: health; self-help; biography; science; business; cookbooks; humor; current affairs; history; some illustrated books. Fiction: mainstream; literary. Representative titles: see under "Additional Information" Do not want: science fiction; computers; juvenile.

**Agency Policies.** Previously unpublished authors: prefer published, but will consider after query. Reading fee: no. Other fees: photocopying. Subsidiary rights: all. Designated agents (foreign or film rights): Candace Lake (film); Carol Smith (England); Michael Meller (German language). Response time to initial inquiry: 2-4 weeks. **Commission:** 15%.

**Initial Contact. Query** letter; query with synopsis or proposal.

**Additional Information.** This is a new agency. I am a former publisher (HP Books, GP Putnam's) and editor in chief (HBJ, Dell, Da Capo Press).

## NEW AGE WORLD SERVICES AND BOOKS. 62091 Valley View Circle. Joshua Tree, CA 92252. (619) 366-2833. Agents: Rev. Victoria E. Vandertuin.

**Subjects of Interest.** **Books**—Nonfiction: metaphysical; parapsychology; occult; lost continents; yoga; mystical; UFO; alchemy; astrology; reincarnation; biblical prophecy; crystals channelling; health and beauty. Fiction: new age. Other: poetry; short stories; articles. Representative titles: confidential.

**Agency Policies.** Previously unpublished authors: yes. Reading fee: yes; depending on length. Other fees: manuscript typing service; critiquing service. Subsidiary rights: first serialization; second serialization; direct mail or direct sales; book club; commercial. Response time to initial inquiry: 4-6 weeks. **Commission:** standard.

**Initial Contact.** Phone; query letter and synopsis.

**Additional Information.** All submissions must be completed, typed manuscripts, in the new-age fields, either fiction or nonfiction. We also have a beautiful writer's retreat available in the high desert on a year-round basis. Write or phone for information.

## PUBLISHING ENTERPRISES/LITERARY AGENCY.

William Oliver: 4090 Ben Lomond Dr. Palo Alto, CA 94306. (415) 856-1062. Marjorie Gersh: 3100 Erin Lane. Santa Cruz, CA 95065. (408) 475-3045. Agents: William Oliver (computer, business, economics, general business, finance, marketing, travel); Marjorie Gersh (fiction, children's and YA, humanities, arts, new age).

**Subjects of Interest.** **Books**—Nonfiction: yes. Fiction: yes. Representative titles: *Family Camping* (Globe Pequot); *Street-Smart Real Estate Investing* (Dow Jones); *Microsoft Works for the Mac* (Compute! Books); *Gardens of Northern California* (Tioga). Do not want: scripts; poetry; short stories; essays.

**Agency Policies.** Previously unpublished authors: yes. Reading fee: no. Other fees: photocopying; postage; long-distance phone calls. Subsidiary rights: all. Designated agents (foreign or film rights): yes. Response time to initial inquiry: 4-6 weeks. **Commission:** 15%.

**Initial Contact.** Query letter; query with synopsis or proposal. Include SASE.

## SHERRY ROBB LITERARY PROPERTIES.

PO Box 2787. Hollywood, CA 90078. (213) 653-7734. Agents: Sherry Robb, Rosemary Sneeringer.

**Subjects of Interest.** **Books**—Nonfiction: commercial nonfiction especially in the areas of self-help. Fiction:literary, off-beat novels; serious literary novels; big commercial women's novels; mysteries and thrillers. Known for celebrities: *Dreamgirls* by Mary Wilson (St. Martin's); Jacqueline Stallone's *Starpower* (NAL); also books by Betty White (Doubleday) and Smokey Robinson (McGraw Hill); *No Easy Place to Be* (Simon & Schuster), mysteries, *The Daphne Decisions* (Bantam), *Finders Keepers* (McGraw Hill); mainstream, *My Enemy, My Love* (Dell), Mistresses (Pinnacle). Nonfiction: *The Agony of It All* (Tarcher). **Scripts**—episodic TV; specials; miniseries; motion picture; romantic comedy, both TV and features. Do not want: most poetry unless also a performer.

**Agency Policies.** Previously unpublished authors: yes; we've sold 60 first-time authors in five years. Reading fee: no. Other fees: Sometimes we recommend more intense editorial work and suggest a freelance editor to work with. Subsidiary rights: all (except for those handled by a publisher). Designated agents (foreign or film rights): We have 10 foreign agents around the world. Response time to initial inquiry: 2-4 weeks. **Commission:** 15% books, video, audio; 10% film.

**Initial Contact.** Fiction, query letter plus manuscript; except for romance, query letter plus 3 chapters. Nonfiction, query letter plus proposal. Include author biography. All queries or submissions must include SASE.

**Additional Information.** We edit and guide writers of fiction; help shape proposals for nonfiction writers.

## JACK SCAGNETTI TALENT AND LITERARY AGENCY.

5330 Lankershim Blvd. #210. North Hollywood, CA 91601. (818) 762-3871. Agent: Jack Scagnetti (nonfiction; novel-length fiction; screenplays; television plays).

**Subjects of Interest.** **Books**—Nonfiction: how-to; sports; films; biographies. Fiction: stories must be high quality type that lend themselves to screenplay adaptability. **Scripts**—screenplays; TV. Representative titles: *Highway to Heaven* (TV episodic script); *Family Ties* (TV episodic script). Do not want: poetry; magazine fiction.

**Agency Policies.** Previously unpublished authors: yes. Reading fee: no. Other fees: one-way postage on multiple submissions. Subsidiary rights: first serialization; newspaper syndication; reprint; dramatization, motion picture and broadcast; video; sound reproduction and recording; book club. Response time to initial inquiry: 4-6 weeks. **Commission:** 10%; 15% foreign rights.

**Initial Contact.** Query letter; query with synopsis or proposal.

**Additional Information.** More emphasis on screenplays than books; more interested in nonfiction books than fiction.

## SEBASTIAN AGENCY. PO Box 1369. San Carlos, CA 94070. (415) 598-0310. Agents: Laurie Harper.

**Subjects of Interest.** **Books**—Nonfiction: adult (except cookbooks or poetry). Fiction: adult (except horror or occult). Representative titles: *God Was An Atheist Sailor* (W. W. Norton); *Step-by-Step: How to Actively Ensure the Best Care for Relatives* (Warner); *Higher Ground* (Mercury House). **Scripts**—motion picture only. Do not want: Vietnam novels at this time.

**Agency Policies.** Previously unpublished authors: yes. Reading fee: no. Other fees: in depth critique, upon request. Subsidiary rights: first serialization; second serialization; reprint; dramatization, motion picture; book club; translation and foreign; commercial; English language publication outside the United States and Canada. Designated agents (foreign or film rights): Thomas Schluck (foreign, Germany); Shorr, Stille and Associates (film). Response time to initial inquiry: 3-4 weeks. **Commission:** 15% domestic; 20% foreign.

**Initial Contact.** Query letter; query with synopsis or proposal. No submissions in February or September.

**Additional Information.** We are seeking multiple-book authors more than single-book; interested in helping to guide the writing career of an author.

## SINGER MEDIA CORPORATION. 3164 Tyler Ave. Anaheim, CA 92801. (714) 527-5650. Agents: Diane Ward (special project manager); Kurt D. Singer (everything).

**Subjects of Interest.** **Books**—Nonfiction: business; computers; psychological self-help; ethnic cook books; how-to. Fiction: romances, westerns, horror. Other: juvenile activities. **Scripts**: specials; miniseries; motion picture; cartoons; in the areas of international celebrities, health and travel material for world-wide syndication only. Do not want: local histories; war; science fiction; children's stories.

**Agency Policies.** Previously unpublished authors: yes. Reading fee: $250 for new book manuscript. Other fees: no. Subsidiary rights:first serialization; second serialization; newspaper syndication; reprint; book club; foreign; computer and other magnetic and electronic; English language publication outside the United States and Canada. Designated agents (foreign or film rights): several New York agents. Response time to initial inquiry: 2 weeks. **Commission:** 15% domestic; 20% foreign; 50% subsidiary.

**Initial Contact.** Query with synopsis or proposal.

**Additional Information.** We have contracts with German and Italian publishers for romances.

## H. N. SWANSON, INC. 8523 Sunset Blvd. Los Angeles, CA 90069. (213) 652-5385. Agents: H. N. Swanson; Ben Kamsler; Michael Siegel.

**Subjects of Interest.** **Books**—Nonfiction: yes. Fiction: yes; first novels. Representative titles: *Freaky Deaky* (Morrow/Arbor House); *Killshot* (Morrow/Arbor House); *Dirty Money* (St. Martin's Press) Arthur Hailey's *Strong Medicine*. **Scripts**—episodic TV; specials; miniseries; motion picture (emphasis). Do not want: individual short stories; unfinished manuscripts.

**Agency Policies.** Previously unpublished authors: yes. Reading fee: no. Other fees: no. Subsidiary rights: all; foreign rights. Response time to initial inquiry: variable. **Commission:** 10%.

**Initial Contact.** Query letter with synopsis or proposal; with referral.

**Additional Information.** H. N. Swanson, Inc., is the oldest literary agency in Los Angeles. Past clients include Raymond Chandler, James M. Cain, John O'Hara, Pearl Buck. We are very selective, but remain committed to new and exciting talent.

**PATRICIA TEAL LITERARY AGENCY.** 2036 Vista del Rosa. Fullerton, CA 92631. (714) 738-8333. Agent: Patricia Teal.

**Subjects of Interest.** **Books**—Nonfiction: how-to; self-help. Fiction: category and mainstream (the latter usually from authors with publishing credits); specialize in romance literature both contemporary and historical. Representative titles: *Honorbound* (Franklin Watts); *Sunflower* (Berkley Publishing Group); *Polo Solo* (St. Martin's Press). Do not want: children's; YA; poetry; short stories.

**Agency Policies.** Previously unpublished authors: yes. Reading fee: no. Other fees: $35 marketing fee to cover postage and telephone. Subsidiary rights: all. Designated agents (foreign or film rights): Sandra Watt and Associates for film rights. Response time to initial inquiry: 2 weeks; 4 weeks, synopsis and chapters. **Commission:** 10%; 15% mainstream.

**Initial Contact.** Query letter.

**Additional Information.** With all correspondence a SASE must be included for a response. Include a SASE postcard for confirmation of material arrival.

**WATERSIDE PRODUCTIONS, INC.** 832 Camino Del Mar, Ste. 2. Del Mar, CA 92014. (619) 481-8335. Agents: William Gladstone (computer books and software, general nonfiction); Julie Castiglia (fiction, nonfiction, juvenile, women's issues); Tracy Smith (technology, general nonfiction; based in New York).

**Subjects of Interest.** **Books**—Nonfiction: computer; business biographies; how-to; self-help. Fiction: literary; genre. Representative titles: *Hyper Card Handbook* (Bantam); *Never Be Tired Again* (Macmillan); *The Art Biz* (Contemporary Books). **Scripts**: new area.

**Agency Policies.** Previously unpublished authors: yes. Reading fee: $200-$500 for first-time novelists; no fee for nonfiction proposals. Other fees: mailing and related documentable expenses charged back. Subsidiary rights: all (except book club). Designated agents (foreign or film rights): Richard Gollner (U.K.); various agents in Germany, Japan, etc. Response time to initial inquiry: 2-6 weeks (fiction, nonfiction); 1 week (computer-related). **Commission:** 15%.

**Initial Contact.** Query letter.

**Additional Information.** Waterside Production, Inc., is a full service literary agency which has placed over 900 titles since 1982. Waterside represents more computer book authors than any agency in the world. We have recently opened a New York office at 1 Union Square West, #209. New York, NY 10003. (212) 645-7123.

**SANDRA WATT AND ASSOCIATES.** 8033 Sunset Blvd., Ste. 4053. Los Angeles, CA 90046. (213) 653-2339. Agents: Sandra Watt (books, books-to-film); Robert Drake (books); Corey Eglash (film, TV).

**Subjects of Interest.** **Books**—Nonfiction: psychology; diet; sex; general interest. Fiction: category fiction; literary; gay/lesbian; young adult. Representative titles: *Lemons . . . & Lemonade* (NAL); *Sex and the Single Parent* (Henry Holt); *Hungry Women* (Warner). **Scripts**—motion picture; literary screenplays; movies of the week; independent films. Do not want: poetry; variety scripts; right-wing tracts; unprofessional work.

**Agency Policies.** Previously unpublished authors: yes. Reading fee: no. Other fees: On signing, first-time authors pay a marketing fee used solely for the promotion and marketing of their work. The fee is nominal. Subsidiary rights: all. Designated agents (foreign or film rights): We are a full-service agency with foreign reps in over seven countries. Response time to initial inquiry: 6-8 weeks. **Commission:** 10% (film); 15% (books); 20% (foreign).

**Initial Contact.** Query letter.

**Additional Information.** Liberal bent, possesses integrity and is willing to work with new, and as yet, unproven talent.

## WRITERS' ASSOCIATES LITERARY AGENCY.

3960 Laurel Canyon Blvd., Penthouse Ste. 219. Studio City, CA 91604. (213) 851-2488. Agents: Barbara Dempsey (screenplays); Steve Stratton, Mike Dudley (novels, print media).

**Subjects of Interest.** **Books**—Nonfiction: varied. Fiction: main line contemporary fiction; historical novels; short stories. Other: plays. Representative titles: *See the Woman* (Worldwide); *Tawny* (Marquis); *The Chateau* (C. Gunn, London). **Scripts**—episodic TV; motion pictures; cartoons; TV movies. Do not want: children's fare.

**Agency Policies.** Previously unpublished authors: yes. Reading fee: It is minimal and refunded upon sale. Only unpublished writers are so charged. Other fees: no. Subsidiary rights: first serialization; second serialization; newspaper syndication; dramatization, motion picture and broadcast; video distribution; book club; translation and foreign; commercial; English language publication outside the United States and Canada. Response time to initial inquiry: 6 weeks. **Commission:** 10%.

**Initial Contact.** Query with synopsis or proposal.

**Additional Information.** We are especially receptive to new writers, and their development.

## WRITER'S CONSULTING GROUP.

PO Box 492. Burbank, CA 91503. (818) 841-9294. Director: Jim Barmeier.

**Subjects of Interest.** **Books**—Fiction: we will look at all manuscripts. Nonfiction: all. Representative titles: Craig Smith espionage story; Smurfs (Hanna-Barbera). **Scripts**—we will look at all scripts.

**Agency Policies.** Previously unpublished authors: yes. Reading fee: no. Other fees: no. Subsidiary rights: dramatization, motion picture and broadcast; video distribution. Response time to initial inquiry: 1-3 months. **Commission:** 10%.

**Initial Contact.** Phone; query letter.

**Additional Information.** Mr. Barmeier is a graduate of Stanford University's Master's Degree in Creative Writing Program and provides ghostwriting/editing services for interested writers.

# Professional Organizations

Membership in one or more professional organizations can enhance your resumé, expand your network of professional contacts, and be a source of industry information and news. No two organizations are exactly alike, as you'll see from reading this section. Membership criteria, dues, and activities vary as does the contact information.

Some organizations maintain an office where you can request information; others use branch members' homes or work addresses and phone numbers. A few organizations prefer queries be directed to their national headquarters. In any case, with dozens to choose from, you are sure to find one that's right for your writing field and geographic area.

## How to Use the Information in This Section

The first paragraph of each entry identifies the name of the organization, address and phone number of its national headquarters, and name and professional title of a contact person. We've listed the date when the organization was founded, number of members nationally, and annual dues (at the national level).

Information that applies to both the national and branch (or chapter) levels, such as membership criteria, activities, and benefits, is listed under the national entry. If the information applies only at the chapter level, it is found there.

## Local Chapters

To help you find a chapter or branch in your area, we've listed the name and address and/or phone number of a local contact person. Some organizations prefer all inquiries to be directed to their national headquarters since annual elections render the current information inaccurate. Some organizations were very generous in supplying information about their activities, and thus their entries are comprehensive; others are quite concise.

**Purpose:** Most of the organizations we surveyed listed a statement of purpose which often emphasized the organization's role in the pursuit of excellence in writing, advancement of members' career goals and communication skills, and dissemination of information.

**Membership criteria:** Some organizations list only an interest in writing and payment of dues as their criteria for membership; others offer several types of membership and require different levels of professional achievement as criteria.

**Dues:** When appropriate, we listed national dues and branch dues. While some organizations require only branch dues, others require dues to be paid at both the branch and national levels. Still others require a one-time processing fee in addition to the dues.

**Members:** This figure represents the number of members of the chapter at the time it was surveyed.

**Activities:** Most organizations sponsor monthly meetings, often with guest speakers. Seminars, critique group sessions, and annual conferences are also common. If an organization lists conferences as one of its activities, there may be additional information in the Conferences section. Some organizations sponsor conferences in a different state each year. We've limited our listings to those conferences using Calfornia sites.

**Newsletters:** In addition to providing information to its members, some organizations' newsletters accept freelance material (though usually not for pay) and publish book reviews and/or press releases of events or news.

**Editor:** This entry specifies the name of the newsletter editor.

**Frequency:** The newsletter publication schedule is indicated here.

**Submissions:** This section lists the types of written material the publication accepts.

**Additional publications:** Some organizations produce a variety of publications or resources. Those publications other than newsletters are listed here.

### Abbreviations

n/i means no information was given to us by the organization.

---

**AMERICAN MEDICAL WRITERS ASSOCIATION.** 9650 Rockville Pike. Bethesda, MD 20814. (301) 493-0003. Executive Director, Lillian Sablack. Founded: 1940. Members: 3100 (national); 375 (California); 190 (NCA chapter). Dues: $55.

Purpose: To further clarity in medical communications. Membership criteria: interest in medical communications. Benefits: curriculum of workshops leading to a certificate in their specialty area of medical communications; networking; including annual conference (location varies); medical and life insurance. Meetings: 8-10 times annually (chapter); annually (national). Activities: meetings, chapter events, workshops/seminars, conferences

Newsletter: *The Pacemaker*. Editor: Judith Windt. Frequency: eight times yearly. Submissions: articles for quarterly journal only. Additional publications: freelance directory, quarterly journal.

**Northern California Chapter**: Contact Person: President, Daniel Liberthson, Ph.D., c/o Syntex Laboratories. 3401 Hillview Ave., MS 13-10, Palo Alto, CA 94304. (415) 759-7617.

**Pacific Southwest Chapter** (Southern California, Arizona, Nevada, Hawaii): Contact Person: President, Beverly Sloane, 1301 North Santa Anita Ave., Arcadia, CA 91006. (818) 355-8915. Members: 250. Activities: bimonthly meetings with prominent speakers, annual one-day conference co-sponsored with Independent Writers of Southern California.

## AMERICAN SOCIETY FOR TRAINING AND DEVELOPMENT.

National office: (703) 683-8100. Founded: 1946. Members: 23,000 (national). National dues: $120.

Purpose: To provide leadership, service, and education for the training and development of individuals, organizations, and the community. Membership criteria: Any person who is interested in the training and development of individuals is eligible for membership. Benefits: directory.

**El Camino Chapter.** Contact Person: President, Mark Shaw, 800 Menlo Ave., #215, Menlo Park, CA 94025. (415) 743-0476. Members: 500-600. Dues: $60. Benefits: discounts on all functions/events, free directory, monthly newsletter (job referral), networking opportunities, a chance to gain insight to the active training field. Meetings: second Tuesday of each month. Activities: meetings, workshops/seminars, conferences, contests. Newsletter: *The Update.* Editor: Sandy Pokras. Frequency: monthly. Submissions: press releases and articles upon editor's approval.

**Golden Gate Chapter.** Contact Person: Administrative Director, Al Williams, 5229 Harbord Dr., Oakland, CA 94618. (415) 652-5340. Members: 850. Dues: $40 (plus one-time $10 processing fee). Benefits: discount on monthly meeting fees and workshops, monthly newsletter, directory, position referral service, special interest groups, networking opportunities. Meetings: dinner meeting on second Wednesday of the month. Activities: meetings, workshops/seminars, conferences, trade shows. Newsletter: *The ASTD Reporter.* Frequency: monthly. Submissions: press releases regarding members.

**Inland Empire Chapter.** Contact Person: Bob Hack, 8631 Rush Street. Rosemead, CA 91770. (818) 302-5467.

**Los Angeles Chapter.** Contact Person: President, Frank Rabwin, 2410 Beverly Blvd., Ste. #1, Los Angeles, CA 90057. (213) 387-7432.

**Los Padres Chapter.** 5128 Moonstone Way. Oxnard Shores, CA 93035. (805) 985-9721.

**Mt. Diablo Chapter.** Contact Person: Membership Chairperson, Kathy Block, PO Box 1646, Danville, CA 94526. (415) 932-2374. Members: 100. Dues: $30. Meetings: Third Tuesday of every month.

**Orange County Chapter.** Contact Person: President, Lynn McCann, 195 South "C" St., Ste. 250, Tustin, CA 92680. (714) 544-1733.

**Pacific Delta Chapter.** Contact Person: Lou Surles, PO Box 30115, Stockton, CA 95213. (209) 983-6480. Members: 102. Dues: $20. Newsletter: *The Dateline.* Editor: Gail Wax. Frequency: monthly. Activities: monthly meetings (except July), two workshops annually.

**Sacramento Chapter.** Contact Person: President, Cheri Douglas, PO Box 5280, Auburn, CA 95604. (916) 443-4305. Members: 300. Dues: $45 (for new members). Meetings: third Tuesday of the month. Newsletter: yes. Frequency: monthly. Submissions: press releases, articles.

**San Diego Chapter.** Contact Person: Marcie Jordan, 1360 Rosecrans, Ste. I, San Diego, CA 92106. (619) 224-2783. Members: 583. Dues: $55. Activities: monthly lunch meeting, last Wednesday of month.

## AMERICAN SOCIETY OF INDEXERS.

1700 18th St., N.W. Washington, D.C. 20009. President, Dr. Bella Hass Weinberg, Division of Library and Information Science, St. John's University, Jamaica, NY 11439. (718) 990-6200. Founded: 1980s. Members: 1000 (national); 110 (California). Dues: $40.

Purpose: To improve the quality of indexes, increase awareness of indexing among publishers and public. Membership criteria: interest in indexing. Benefits: informative newsletter and conferences. Offer medical, life and disability insurance. Meetings: bimonthly. Activities: meetings, workshops/seminars, conferences, trade shows, potluck informal gatherings.

Newsletter: *Entry Points*. Editor: Barbara Newcombe. Frequency: quarterly. Submissions: articles, press releases. Additional publications: membership directory, many aids to indexers (national level).

**Golden Gate Chapter**. Contact Person: President, Elinor Lindheimer, 990 Winery Canyon Rd., Templeton, CA 93405. (805) 434-2330.

**AMERICAN SOCIETY OF JOURNALISTS & AUTHORS, INC.** 1501 Broadway, Ste. 1907. New York, NY 10036. (212) 977-0947. Executive Director, Alexandra Cantor; President, David W. Kennedy. Founded: 1948. National dues: $120.

Purpose: to establish high ethical standards and further pursuit of excellence in writing nonfiction. Membership criteria: professional published nonfiction writers. Benefits: medical benefits package, dial-a-writer referral service, membership directory. Branch-level activities: meetings, workshops, seminars, annual conference, discussion groups, networking with professionals. Refer all requests for information to national office.

Newsletter: *ASJA Newsletter*. Frequency: monthly. Additional publications: *The Complete Guide to Writing Nonfiction, A Treasury of Tips for Writers, How to Make Money Writing Magazine Articles, Prose by Professionals, A Guide to Successful Magazine Writing*.

**San Francisco Chapter**: Contact Person: Chairperson, Shimon-Craig Van Colli, 881 Haight St., San Francisco, CA 94117. (415) 864-6369.

**ASIAN AMERICAN JOURNALISTS ASSOCIATION.** 1765 Sutter St., Room 1000. San Francisco, CA 94115. (415) 346-2051. Executive Director, Diane Yen-Mei Wong. Founded: 1981. Members: 600 (national); 400 (California). Dues: $36 (paid at branch level).

Purpose: to increase employment of Asian/American (A/A) journalists; to assist A/A students pursuing journalism careers; to encourage fair and accurate news coverage of A/A issues; to provide support for A/A journalists. Membership criteria: includes categories for professional members; full members (journalists); associate members (non-journalists, retired, or part-time); student members. Benefits: reduced rates for organization conventions, directory, job bank. Activities: workshops, seminars, conferences. Meetings: two times annually; chapters meet monthly.

Newsletter: *Asian/American Journalists Association*. Frequency: quarterly. Submissions: press releases, articles. Additional publications: periodic studies and handbook.

**San Francisco Chapter**. Contact Person: President, Lisa Chung. (415) 835-5834. Members: 150. Meetings: monthly. Activities: quarterly events. Newsletter: *SF Chapter AAJA Newsletter*.

**Los Angeles Chapter**. Contact Person: President, Joanne Ishimine. (213) 669-7536. Members: 150. Meetings: monthly.

**Sacramento Chapter**. Contact Person: President, Mr. Lonni Wong, 2705 23rd St., Sacramento, CA 95818. (916) 454-4548. Members: 50. Meetings: monthly. Activities: workshops, community service projects. Newsletter: *AAJA Sacramento Chapter*.

**San Diego Chapter**. Contact Person: President, Jon Funabiki, PO Box 882076, San Diego, CA 92108. (619) 293-1220. Members: 50. Meetings: monthly.

**BAY AREA BOOK REVIEWERS ASSOCIATION.** 50 The Uplands. Berkeley, CA 94705. (415) 655-6724. Contact, Henry Mayer. Founded: 1981. Members: 24. Dues: none.

Purpose: to provide a forum for book reviewers and to sponsor the annual awards ceremony (BABRA) honoring excellence in books. Membership criteria: freelance and staff book reviewers. Meeting: monthly.

**BOOKBUILDERS WEST.** PO Box 883666. San Francisco, CA 94188-3666. President, Larry Lazopoulos (408) 476-6990; Membership Chair, Roy Wallace (415) 934-1440. Founded: 1969. Members: 325. Dues: $75, companies with four or more employees; $40, for companies with three or fewer employees.

Purpose: educational and social resource for book publishers and their suppliers (freelance designers and production services, typesetters, color separators, printers, etc.) in 13 Western states. Membership criteria: publishers, suppliers, or individuals engaged in book publishing or offering services to book publishers; must be located or do business within the 13 Western states; publishers must publish books with Western states imprint or register copyright in one of the states. Benefits: monthly dinner meetings, seminars, access to job bank, bimonthly newsletter, biannual trade show/conference. Meetings: monthly (except July and August). Activites: meetings, worships/seminars, conferences, annual Bookbuilders West book show.

Newsletter: *Bookbuilders West*. Editor: Pat Brewer, Wadsworth Publishing Company. Frequency: bimonthly. Submissions: press releases rewritten for Calendar or Industry News; articles are solicited, but appropriate submissions are considered. Additional publications: *The New Directory* (includes membership and other book-production resources), book show catalog (annual).

**CALIFORNIA PRESS WOMEN.** 114 21st Ave. San Francisco, CA 94121. (415) 584-1455. President, Myra Bailey. Membership Chairperson, Mary Woolcott. Members: 75. Dues: $41.

Meetings: monthly board meeting. Activities: workshops, seminars, student scholarships, essay contest. Newsletter: *Proof Sheet*. Frequency: quarterly. Submissions: press releases and articles.

**CALIFORNIA WRITERS' CLUB.** 2214 Derby St. Berkeley, CA 94705. (415) 841-1217. Secretary, Dorothy Benson. Founded: 1909. Members: 800. Dues: $25 annually, the same for all chapters. $20 to join.

Purpose: nonprofit professional organization open to writers to provide writing and market information and to promote fellowship among writers. Membership criteria: publication for active membership; expected publication in five years for associate membership. Benefits: workshop opportunities, monthly newsletter, discounted conference fee, contests. Meetings: monthly. Activities: meetings, workshops/seminars, conferences, contests. An all-branch meeting is held once a year. Dues: the same for all chapters—$20 to join plus $25 annually.

**Berkeley Branch**. Contact Person: President, Ray Nelson, 333 Ramona Ave., El Cerrito, CA 94530. (415) 526-7378. Members: 118. Meetings: monthly. Newsletter: *California Writers' Club Bulletin*. Editor: Dorothy V. Benson. Frequency: monthly. Submissions: press releases, article submissions. Additional publications: *West Winds* (anthology).

**Mt. Diablo Branch** (Danville area). Contact Person: President, Jay Lloyd Luff, 1155 Daniel Hills Ct., Benicia, CA 94510. Members: 70.

**Peninsula Branch**. Contact Person: President, James McLaughlin, 3313 Plateau Dr., Belmont, CA 94002. Members: 103.

**Redwood Branch** (Santa Rosa area). Contact Person: President, Marion J. McMurtry, 912 Humbolt St., Santa Rosa, CA 95402. Members: 61.

**Sacramento Branch**. Contact Person: President, Sharon Schneider, 6825 Lincoln Ave., Carmichael, CA 95608. Members: 166.

**San Fernando Valley Branch**. Contact Person: Secretary, Betty Freeman, 5115 Vesper Ave., Sherman Oaks, CA 91403. (818) 784-1944. Members: 96.

**South Bay Branch** (San Jose area). Contact Person: President, Tom Mach, 1072 Alderbrook Ln., San Jose, CA 95129. Founded: 1987. Members: 58. Activities: monthly meetings, conferences, contests. Newsletter: *CA Writers' Club, South Bay Branch.* Editor: Madge Saksena. Frequency: monthly.

**COMEDY/HUMOR WRITERS ASSOCIATION.** PO Box 211. San Francisco, CA 94101. (415) 626-3292. President, Karen Warner; Membership Chairperson, Kate Pudenz. Founded: 1986. Members: 50. Dues: $30.

Purpose: to provide friendship, contacts and educational activities for comedy/humor writers. Membership criteria: actual or aspiring comedy/humor writer. Benefits: discount on monthly dinners and annual conference. Meetings: monthly. Activities: conferences.

Newsletter: *C/H Writers Association Newsletter.* Editor: Don Stevens. Frequency: monthly. Submissions: press releases; query for article submissions. Additional publications: membership directory.

**COSMEP, THE INTERNATIONAL ASSOCIATION OF INDEPENDENT PUBLISHERS.** PO Box 703. San Francisco, CA 94101. (415) 922-9490. Executive Director, Richard Morris. Founded: 1968. Members: 1400. Dues: $50.

Purpose: trade association of small publishers. Membership criteria: must be publishers of books or periodicals; self-publishers are eligible to join. Benefits: information available on request; medical and life insurance offered. Meetings: annually. Activities: conferences.

Newsletter: *COSMEP Newsletter.* Editor: Richard Morris. Frequency: monthly. Submissions: press releases.

**CUPERTINO WRITERS CLUB.** 180 West Rincon Ave. Campbell, CA 95008. (408) 370-2205. Coordinating Chairperson, Barbara Johnson. Founded: 1973. Members: 60. Dues: $3 annually.

Purpose: To meet regularly to share information and to critique members' work. Selections of 10 pages or less are read aloud; critiques are written following each reading. Occasional speakers. Membership criteria: be actively writing, attend three meetings, and read at least once prior to joining. Benefits: first-first-book signings for members to honor a first published book; directory. Meetings: twice monthly.

**EDITCETERA.** 2490 Channing Way, #507. Berkeley, CA 94704. (415) 849-1110. Membership Chairperson, Hazel White. Founded: 1971. Members: 65. Dues: $60.

Purpose: a nonprofit mutual benefit corporation designed to help freelancers improve their skills, share resources, and find work. Membership criteria: strong background in book publishing or technical documentation, freelance status, successful completion of editcetera tests and work reviews. Benefits: directory. Meetings: none. Activities: workshops/seminars.

**INDEPENDENT WRITERS OF SOUTHERN CALIFORNIA.** PO Box 19745. Los Angeles, CA 90019. (213) 470-9654. President, Cheryl Crooks. Members: 400. Dues: $55 plus $55 one-time initiation fee.

Purpose: a professional service and support organization for self-employed writers, focusing on the business of writing. Membership criteria: principle occupation must be writing (professional); producers of services for writers (associates); students. Benefits: medical and dental insurance, networking, directory, job referral service. Meetings: monthly. Activities: workshops, conferences, specialty groups within the organization, including health writers' caucus and script writers' caucus.

Newsletter: *The IWOSC Independent.* Editor: Ellen Alperstein. Frequency: monthly. Submissions: press releases, articles.

## INTERNATIONAL ASSOCIATION OF BUSINESS COMMUNICATORS.

One Hallidie Plaza, Ste. 600. San Francisco, CA 94102. (415) 433-3400. President, Norm Leaper. Membership Coordinator, Angie Vallecillo. Founded: 1964. Members: 1200. International dues: $140 plus $30 applicant fee.

Purpose: to further excellence in the area of business communication. Membership criteria: qualification and payment of fees. Benefits: directory; applicants are sent a packet outlining services. Activities: chapter meetings, workshops, international conferences. Newsletter: *IABC.*

**Long Beach-South Bay Chapter**: Contact Person: Andra Miller, Downey Community Hospital, 11500 Brookshire Ave., Downey, CA 90241. (213) 904-5066. Members: 50. Dues: $45.

**Los Angeles Chapter**: Contact Person: Jean Jarvis, Times Mirror Co., Times Mirror Square, Los Angeles, CA 90053. (213) 237-3935. Members: 305. Dues: $60.

**Orange County Chapter**: Contact Person: Jeanie Herbert, Beckman Instruments, Inc., 2500 Harbor Blvd., B-26-A, Fullerton, CA 92634. (714) 773-8762. Members: 125. Dues: $40.

**Peninsula Chapter**: Contact Person: President, Laura Mills, Alza Corporation, 950 Page Mill Rd., PO Box 10950, Palo Alto, CA 94303-0802. (415) 494-5042. Dues: $30.

**Sacramento Chapter**: Contact Person: Tracy Thompson, Carlson Associates, 3445 American River Dr., Sacramento, CA 95864. (916) 973-0600. Members: 23. Dues: $70.

**San Diego Chapter**: Contact Person: Anne Cox, Cox Company, 4350 La Jolla Village Dr., Ste. 300, San Diego, CA 92122. (619) 546-4342. Members: 84. Dues: $39.

**San Francisco Branch**: Contact Person: President, Paul Morton, Communication Center, 106 Camino Pablo, Orinda, CA 94563. (415) 254-1105. Members: 286. Dues: $40.

## INTERNATIONAL FOOD, WINE, AND TRAVEL WRITERS ASSOCIATION.

PO Box 1532. Palm Springs, CA 92263. (619) 322-4717. President, Don Jackson; Executive Director and Membership Chairperson, Ray Kabaker. Founded: 1956. Members: 350 (international); 250 (California). Dues: $60.

Purpose: to provide a gathering point and resource base for professionals engaged in the food, wine, travel, and hospitality industries. Membership criteria: open to individuals, companies, and organizations maintaining professional interests in the above industries; must be nominated by a member or an officer. Benefits: access to current information on press trips and other professional travel benefits, official IFW&TWA working press card, confidential membership directory; special discounts on rental cars, travel, hotel accommodations; writer participation in Annual Guide Book; networking relationship with worldwide members and associate member organizations. Activities: local and regional meetings; annual conclave; awards based on nominations by regular members, including the *Golden Fork Award.*

Newsletter: *Hospitality World.* Editor: Ray Kabaker. Frequency: monthly. Submissions: press releases, articles from members. Additional publications: *Window to the World* (guidebook).

**MARIN SMALL PRESS ASSOCIATION.** Box 1346. Ross, CA 94957. President, Mel Boyce. Founded: 1979. Members: 160. Dues: $25.

Purpose: to help members publish their written, spoken or visual materials. Membership criteria: actively pursuing self-publishing. Benefits: market and production information. Meetings: monthly. Activities: meetings, workshops/seminars, conferences, trade shows.

Newsletter: *SPEX*. Editor: Karen Misuraca. Frequency: six times a year. Submissions: press releases, article submissions. Additional publications: membership directory.

**MEDIA ALLIANCE.** Fort Mason, Bldg. D. San Francisco, CA 94123. (415) 441-2557. Executive Director, Dr. Mikha Peled. Founded: 1976. Members: 2500. Dues: $50 first year; $40 renewal.

Purpose: to provide resources to writers and media people. Membership criteria: none. Benefits: health plan, access to credit union, attorney referral service, educational programs, job listings for writers. Activities: meetings, workshops, seminars, conferences.

Newsletter: *Mediafile*. Frequency: bimonthly. Submissions: press releases and articles. Additional publications: three books.

**MYSTERY WRITERS OF AMERICA.** 236 West 27th St., Room 600. New York, NY 10001. (212) 255-7005. President, Tom Chastain; Membership Chairperson, Priscilla Ridgeway. Founded: 1945. Members: 2200 (international). Dues: $50, $25 for correspondent members.

Purpose: to promote interests of mystery writers; to maintain recognition of mystery writing in publishing industry and reading public; to disseminate information and share benefits of associating with others interested in mystery writing. Membership criteria: includes categories for people actively writing mysteries, those published in other fields, those published outside the United States, and those who are unpublished or fans.

Newsletter: *The Third Degree*. Frequency: nine issues yearly. Activities: conferences, Edgar Allen Poe annual awards dinner always held in New York City in May.

**Northern California Chapter**. Contact Person: Regional Vice-President, Robert J. Bowman, 38 Seal Rock Dr., San Francisco, CA 94121. (415) 457-5179. (415) 752-4884. Members: 250. Membership criteria: unpublished writers of mystery (associate); professionals in allied fields—editors, agents, libraries, etc.; and published writers of fiction or nonfiction in the crime/mystery/suspense field (active). Benefits: association with writers sharing common interests; access to national organization's publicity, pamphlets, marketing information; participation in local meetings, seminars; publicity efforts. Meetings: nine times a year. Activities: meetings, workshops/seminars, trade shows, manuscript critiquing service. Membership directory: yes. Newsletter: *Lineup*. Editor: Meg O'Brien. Frequency: 10 issues yearly. Submissions: press releases.

**Southern California Chapter**. Contact Person: Regional Vice President, Elizabeth James, 14600 Saticoy St., #204, Van Nuys, CA 91405. (213) 278-9500. Newsletter: *March of Crime*.

**NATIONAL LEAGUE OF AMERICAN PEN WOMEN.** Pen Arts Building. 1300 17th Street, NW. Washington, D.C. 20036-1973. (202) 785-1997. President, Juanita C. Howison. Founded: 1897. Members: 6000 (national); 1300 (California). Dues: $30, paid at branch level (200 U.S. branches).

Purpose: to further professional contacts and excellence in the arts. Membership criteria: rigorous qualification process. Activities: national meeting every spring. National membership directory: yes.

Newsletter: *PenWoman* (magazine). Editor: Martha Snyder Byron. Frequency: nine times annually, includes book reviews and members' achievements report.

**Berkeley Branch.** Contact Person: President, Rosemary Wilkinson, 3146 Buckeye Court, Placerville, CA 95667. (916) 626-4166. Members: 18. Activities: monthly meetings (except summers), workshops, seminars, contests. Membership directory: yes. Newsletter: *Berkeley Branch Newsletter*. Editor: Rosemary Wilkinson. Submissions: articles.

**Butte County Branch.** Contact Person: President, Lois H. McDonald, 14609 Skyway, Magalia, CA 95954. (916) 873-0769. Members: 20. Dues: $30. Meetings: monthly.

**Carmel Valley Branch.** Contact Person: President, Jerry Motto, 515 Ramona Court #15, Monterey, CA 93940.

**Diablo Alameda Branch.** Contact Person: President, Jean Lucken, 10 Fieldbrook Place, Oakland, CA 94619.

**El Camino Real Branch.** Contact Person: President, Judith Daniels, Box 38, 19081 Alameda de las Pulgas, Belmont, CA 94002. (415) 364-8468. Members: 27. Dues: $30. Activities: monthly meetings, workshops, seminars, conferences, contests. Membership directory: yes.

**Hollywood-Los Angeles Branch.** Contact Person: President, Ruth Crisman, 742 1/2 West Glenoaks Blvd., B-1, Glendale, CA 91202.

**La Jolla Branch.** Contact Person: President, Kathyrn Nordquist, 2473 Geranium St., San Diego, CA 92109.

**Laguna Beach Branch.** Contact Person: President, Virginia Ryder, 31687 Crystal Sands Dr., Laguna Nigel, CA 92677.

**Las Artes Branch**: Contact Person: President, Nettie Tays Campbell, 891 Terrace Dr., Los Altos, CA 94022.

**Modesto Branch**: Contact Person: President, Martha Knight, 10155 Peppermint Circle, No. 69, Jamestown, CA 95327.

**Napa Valley Branch.** Contact Person: President, Toni Tacona Brent, 3051 Foothill Blvd., Calistoga, CA 94515.

**Nob Hill Branch.** Contact Person: President, Vicki Lavorini, 2730 39th Ave., San Francisco, CA 94116.

**Palomar Branch.** Contact Person: President, Helen Des Ermia, 30641 Rolling Hills Dr., Valley Center, CA 92082.

**Redwood Branch.** Contact Person: President, Kathy Ray Pierson, 132 Azalea Way, Eureka, CA 95501. Founded: 1969. Members: 12. Meetings: nine times annually. Newsletter: *Writing Behind the Redwood Curtain*. Editor: Carolyn Moore, PO Box 111, Arcata, CA 95521. Frequency: six times annually. Submissions: press releases, articles. Directory: yes.

**Sacramento Branch.** Contact Person: President, Doris Pichly, 4221 Devon Ln., Sacramento, CA 95825.

**San Bernadino Branch.** Contact Person: President, Alice G. Hall, 17227 Hall Ranch Rd., San Bernadino, CA 92407.

**Santa Clara Branch.** Contact Person: President, Thyra Tegner-Rogers, 226 Via La Posada, Los Gatos, CA 95030.

**Santa Cruz Branch.** Contact Person: Treasurer, Esther Schulz, 100-63 N. Rodeo Gulch Rd., Soquel, CA 95073. (408) 475-5514. Members: 32. Dues: $30. Membership directory: yes. Newsletter: yes. Editor: Beverly Levine. Frequency: monthly, except summer. Activities: monthly meetings, except summers, workshops, conferences, occasional art shows.

**Santa Monica Branch.** Contact Person: President, Knarig Boyadjian, 2924 St. George St., Los Angeles, CA 90027.

**Simi Valley Branch.** Contact Person: President, Mary M. Harris, 5349 Maricopa Dr., Simi Valley, CA 93063.

**Sonoma County Branch**. Contact Person: President, Betty Aust, 242 Dover Court North, Santa Rosa, CA 95403. (707) 546-8944. Members: 35. Dues: $40. Meetings: monthly. Membership directory: yes. Newsletter: monthly bulletin for members.

**Stockton Branch**. Contact Person: President, Mabel Ellen Myers, 1215 West Park St., Stockton, CA 95203.

**Victor Valley Branch**. Contact Person: Treasurer, Wilma Vielda Terrill, Box 7263, Spring Valley Lake, Victorville, CA 92392.

**NATIONAL WRITERS UNION.** 13 Astor Pl., Seventh Floor. New York, NY 10003. (212) 254-0279. Executive Director, Kim Fellner. Founded: 1983. Members: 2600 (national); 500 (California). Dues: $50-$120 (sliding scale).

Purpose: trade union for freelance writers; to gain equity, fair standards, and payment for freelance writers through collective action. Membership criteria: publish a book or play, three articles, five poems, one short story, or an equivalent amount of newletter, publicity, technical, commercial, governmental, or institutional copy; or have similar portfolio of unpublished work, actively seeking publication. Benefits: medical insurance, collective bargaining, individual contract advice, press credentials, grievance handling. Activities: delegates' assembly annually first weekend in June, chapter meetings, workshops, conferences.

Newsletter: *The American Writer*. Editor: Ira Wolfman. Frequency: quarterly. Additional publications: Boston chapter has published *An Insider's Guide to Freelance Writing in New England.*

**San Francisco Bay Area Local #3**: Contact Person: President, Bruce Hartford, 236 West Portal Ave., #232, San Francisco, CA 94127. (415) 654-6369. Members: 300. Membership criteria: all qualified writers, and no one shall be barred, or in any manner prejudiced within the union, on account of age, disability, ideology, national origin, race, religion, sex, or sexual preference. Benefits: medical insurance, negotiates union contracts with national and local publications; establishes grievance committees; job hotline for technical writers; contract advisory committee to assist authors; trade group meetings. Meetings: monthly. Activities: workshops/seminars, conferences, contests. Newsletter: *Bay Area Writer*. Editor: Kathleen White (415) 285-6946. Frequency: quarterly. Submissions: press releases, articles (from members only). Additional publications: *The American Writer* (national).

**Los Angeles Local**: Contact Person: President, Kathy Seal, (213) 452-2769. Members: 180. Meetings: monthly. Activities: conferences, workshops. Newsletter: *LA Writer*. Frequency: monthly. Submissions: press releases.

**Santa Cruz/Monterey Local #7**: PO Box 2409. Aptos, CA 95001-2409. (408) 427-2950. Co-Chair, Elizabeth Schilling (Santa Cruz); Co-Chair, Ray March (Monterey); Grievance Chair, Steve Turner. Founded: 1982. Members: 70. Dues: $60 minimum. Benefits: grievance protection in or outside contracts, databases evaluating agents and publications, job hotlines. Activities: monthly steering committee meetings, workshops, seminars, conferences, contests, sponsors annual nationwide poetry competition. Newsletter: *Cows Bigger Than Barns*. Frequency: quarterly. Submissions: press releases. Additional publications: *Frequent Flyer*, calendar published between newsletters.

**NORTHERN CALIFORNIA BOOK PUBLICISTS ASSOCIATION.** c/o U.C. Press. 2120 Berkeley Way. Berkeley, CA 94720. (415) 642-4562. President, Jo Lynn Sanders; Membership Chairperson, Mary Ann Guilderbloom. Founded: 1975. Members: 120. Dues: $35 (associate); $50 (full).

Purpose: forum for the communication of ideas concerning the publicizing, promoting and marketing of books. Membership criteria: not limited to publishing industry; membership includes authors, literary agents, retailers, investment bankers Benefits: discount at all functions, voting privileges. Meetings: 11 times annually. Activities: monthly meetings, luncheons with guest speakers, half-day spring and fall breakfast workshop, workshops, seminars, conferences, book fair (1989).

Newsletter: *News from the Northern California Book Publicists Association.* Editor: Pat Anderson. Frequency: bimonthly. Submissions: articles.

**NORTHERN CALIFORNIA WOMEN IN FILM AND TELEVISION.** PO Box 89. San Francisco, CA 94101. (415) 431-3886. President, Mimi Riley. Founded: 1982. Members: 2500 (national); 180 (chapter). Dues: $55 plus one-time initiation fee.

Purpose: to increase equal opportunity of employment of women in film and television. Membership criteria: minimum two years' experience in the the film or related industries. Benefits: directory, support network. Meetings: monthly. Activities: workshops, seminars, weekly breakfasts.

Newsletter: *On Screen.* Editor: Scott French. Frequency: bimonthly. Submissions: press releases, articles.

**PENINSULA PRESS CLUB.** PO Box 5341. San Mateo, CA 94402. (415) 637-1953. President, Bill Workman. Founded: 1974. Members: 160. Dues: $30.

Purpose: to provide a forum for the interchange of ideas and opinions between professionals in the various news and public relations media. Membership criteria: must earn a major source of one's income or spend a major portion of one's working time as a paid employee in the one of the journalistic professions. Benefits: directory, use of a hotel pool/health facilities. Activities: conferences, contests, workshops, social networking events, annual picnic, professional awards banquet.

Newsletter: *The Peninsula Press Club News.* Editor: Joe Hood. Frequency: monthly. Submissions: press releases, articles.

**POETS & WRITERS, INC.** 72 Spring St. New York, NY 10012. (212) 226-3586. Executive Director, Elliott Figman. Founded: 1973. Members: 9500 (national), 900 (California) listed writers. Dues: none; ($5 listing fee).

Purpose: nonprofit corporation organized for literary and educational purposes. Membership criteria: publication requirements in order to be listed. Activities: Writers Exchange Program, competitions, Readings/Workshops Grants Program which offers matching grants to writers in New York and California; National Literary Information Center (NLIC).

Newsletter: *Poets & Writers Magazine.* Editor: Darylyn Brewer. Frequency: bimonthly. Submissions: articles. Additional publications: references, source books, how-to guides, several newsletters.

**Poets & Writers West** (West Coast Office): 1862 Euclid Ave., Box 292. Berkeley, CA 94709. (415) 548-6618. West Coast Coordinator, Stuart Robbins. Activities: competitions and Writers Exchange Program.

**PRESS CLUB OF SAN FRANCISCO.** 555 Post St. San Francisco, CA 94102. (415) 775-7800. Founded: 1888. President, Roy Pasini. Membership Chairperson, Joyce Cirimelli. Members: 2000. Dues: n/i.

Purpose: private social club, to promote better understanding between cultures. Membership criteria: application reviewed by category (students, professional journalists). Benefits: privileges of club and reciprocal clubs, parties, conferences, athletic facilities. Meetings: annual and designated, no set number. Activities: junior scholarship program, meetings, press conferences.

Newsletter: *The Scoop.* Editor: Teresa Barnett. Frequency: bimonthly. Submissions: articles.

**PUBLISHERS MARKETING ASSOCIATION.** 2401 Pacific Coast Highway, Ste. 206. Hermosa Beach, CA 90254. (213) 372-2732. Executive Director, Jan Nathan. Founded: 1983. Members: 1000. Dues: vary; start at $75 for companies having up to nine employees.

Purpose: to cooperatively market our titles and to educate the independent publisher. Membership criteria: must be a publisher or about to become a publisher. Benefits: cooperative marketing programs to libraries, bookstores, schools and speciality markets. Meetings: monthly. Activities: workshops, seminars, conferences, trade shows, contests. Newsletter: *PMA Newsletter*. Editor: Jan Nathan. Frequency: monthly. Submissions: press releases, articles. Membership directory: yes.

**ROMANCE WRITERS OF AMERICA, INC.** 5206 FM. 1960 West, Ste. 208. Houston, TX 77069. (713) 440-6885. Members: 4000 (national); 820 (California). Dues: $45 plus $10 one-time processing fee.

Purpose: support and education for romance writers. Membership criteria: must join national organization before joining local. Activities: annual national conference (1000+ attendees).

Newsletter: *Romance Writer Report*. Frequency: bimonthly.

**Central Coast Chapter**. Contact Person: Chapter Advisor, Carol Bennett, 6775 Rocky Canyon Rd., Creston, CA 93432. (805) 238-6939. Members: 15. Dues: $12 plus per meeting charge. Meetings: monthly.

**Fresno Chapter**. Contact Person: Chapter Advisor, Deborah Lynn Chance, 5212 North Valentine, Apt. #101, Fresno, CA 93711. (209) 275-5267. Members: 62. Dues: $20. Meetings: monthly meetings, workshops, one-day conferences.

**Gold Coast Chapter**. Contact Person: President, Bobbie Grabendike, 1215 Anchors Way, #47, Ventura, CA 93001. (805) 642-7195. Members: 30. Dues: $12. Benefits: audio tape library of conference workshop presentations, synopses packet (collection of synopses of published books), Meetings: monthly.

**Inland Valley Chapter** (Riverside County). Contact Person: Chapter Advisor, Miriam Pace, 11079 Mars Pl., Mira Loma, CA 91752. (714) 681-5392. Members: seven. Dues: $18. Meetings: monthly. Benefits: lending library, personal relationship and critique at monthly meetings.

**Los Angeles Chapter**. Contact Person: Regional Advisor, Aline Thompson, 13400 Bromwich, Arleta, CA 91331. (818) 876-8246. Meetings: monthly.

**Monterey Bay Chapter**. Contact Person: Chapter Advisor, Courtney Henke, PO Box 723, Seaside, CA 93955. (408) 899-7974. Founded: 1988. Members: 35. Dues: $20. Membership criteria: actively engaged in writing romance. Benefits: support, friendship, helpful hints. Meetings: second Saturday of the month. Activities: meetings, workshops. Newsletter: *MBC*. Frequency: monthly. Submissions: press releases, articles.

**Orange County Chapter**. Contact Person: Co-Advisor, Susan Phillips, 6528 Conant St., Long Beach, CA 90808. (213) 429-5660. Members: 244. Dues: $21 first year, $18 for renewal. Benefits: lending library of audio tapes. Meetings: monthly. Activities: yearly contest for unpublished romance writers, mentor program, editors, and celebrity romance writers host special meetings.

**Sacramento Chapter**. Contact Person: Chapter Advisor, Georgia Bockoven, 5937 Allan Dr., Rocklin, CA 95677. (916) 624-7333. Members: 72. Dues: $20. Meetings: monthly.

**San Diego Chapter**. Contact Person: Chapter Advisor, Betty Duran, 585 El Miraso, Vista, CA 92083. (619) 724-5146. Members: 70. Dues: $18. Meetings: second Saturday monthly. Benefits: lending library. Activities: mentor program, matching unpublished writers with published mentor, "Write for the Money" program, roses for book sales. Newsletter: *Romantically Speaking*.

**San Francisco Chapter**. Contact Person: Membership Chairperson, Pamela Collins, 374 Riviera Dr., San Rafael, CA 94901. (415) 485-0960. President, Nadine Haag, 3781 Boxwood Ct., Concord, CA 94519. (415) 687-5025. Members: 100. Dues: $20. Benefits: critique groups; lending library of books, tapes, and transcripts of national conferences, seminars, panels. Meetings: monthly, first Saturday of month. Activities: hosts several romance editors yearly, conferences, workshops, seminars, contests. Membership directory: yes. Newsletter: *San Francisco Area Chapter Newsletter*. Editor: Barbara Turner. Frequency: monthly. Submissions: press releases with romance writing tie-in, articles.

**SAN DIEGO WRITERS AND EDITORS GUILD.** 3235 Homer St. San Diego, CA 92106. (619) 223-3634. President, Lynn Ford; Membership Chairperson, Betty Smith. Founded: 1979. Members: 120 (California). Dues: $25; $40 (writer plus spouse); $12.50 (student).

Purpose: to help writers and to form a professional network. Membership criteria: for professional membership, three published works for pay or one play produced or one published book (not vanity press); for associate membership, serious interest in writing. Activities: meetings, conferences, annual conferences.

Newsletter: *San Diego Writers/Editors News*. Frequency: monthly. Additional publications: directory.

**SCIENCE FICTION WRITERS OF AMERICA.** Contact Person, Ray Nelson. 333 Ramona Ave. El Cerrito, CA 94530. (415) 526-8356. President, Greg Bear. 506 Lakeview Rd. Alderwood Manor, WA 98036. West Coast Regional Director, Stephen Goldin. 6251 Havenside #4. Sacramento, CA 95831. Founded: 1965. Members: 1000 (national); 100 California. Dues: $75.

Purpose: to inform science-fiction writers of professional matters; to promote professional welfare; to help in dealing with publishers, agents, editors, and anthologists. Membership criteria: sale to professional publishers (reduced subscription rate available to unpublished writers). Benefits: medical insurance, model contracts, legal advice and representation under certain circumstances, meeting room at conventions, bookstore discounts, free review copies of books and magazines, numerous quarterly publications. Activities: conferences, weekly meetings, small meetings at many science fiction conventions, annual awards banquet. (The annual Nebula Trophy is the most important award in the science fiction genre.)

Newsletter: *Bulletin of the Science Fiction Writers of America*. Editor: Pamela Sargent, Box 486, Johnson City, NY 13790. Frequency: quarterly. Submissions: press releases, articles. Additional publications: membership directory, *Science Fiction Forum* (letters), *Awards Report* (Nebula Trophy).

**SOCIETY FOR TECHNICAL COMMUNICATION.** 815 15th Street NW. Washington, D.C. 20005. (202) 737-0035. Founded: 1953. Members: 11,100 (national); 2000 (California). Dues. $75, $10 one-time initiation fee; $25 student rate, payable at national level.

Purpose: the advancement of the theory and practice of technical communication in all media. Criteria: be engaged or have an interest in any phase of technical communication. Meetings: open to the public in all chapters. Activities: annual arts and publication contest; annual international conference in May, held in continental United States (Santa Clara/1990).

Newsletter: *Technical Communication* (quarterly journal), *Intercom* (monthly newsletter).

**Berkeley Chapter**. Contact Person: Ray Bruman, PO Box 1007, Berkeley, CA 94701. (415) 549-1509. Members: $75. Activities: monthly meetings including speakers, field trips, demonstrations. Newsletter: *Ragged Left*. Frequency: monthly. Submissions: press releases, article.

**Costa Mesa Chapter**. Contact Person: Don Pierstorff, Orange Coast College, Costa Mesa, CA 92626. (714) 432-5716.

**East Bay Chapter**. Contact Person: Claudette LaBreche Gesner, 365 Adagio Dr., Danville, CA 94526. Additional contact, Vince Swanson (415) 595-1414.

**Los Angeles Chapter**. Contact Person: President, Dana Brown, 11114 Fairbanks Way, Culver City, CA 90230. (213) 398-5877.

**Monterey Bay Chapter**. Contact Person: Susan Dumonde, 711 Archer St., Monterey, CA 93940. (408) 372-4690.

**Orange County Chapter**. Contact Person: Dorothy Duplissey, PO Box 16535, Irvine, CA 92713. (714) 842-2860. Members: 230. Meetings: monthly (September through June). Newsletter: *Techniscribe*. Frequency: ten issues annually. Submissions: articles, press releases.

**Sacramento Chapter**. Contact Person: President, Joan Levers, PO Box 1292, Roseville, CA 95661. (916) 782-2211. Membership Criteria: must be actively engaged in the field or interested in the field. Benefits: quarterly journal, monthly newsletters, national conferences, local programs, conferences and workshops, employment referral service. Meetings: monthly. Activities: workshops/seminars, conferences, contests. Newsletter: *Capitol Letter*. Editor: Nancy Watson. Frequency: monthly. Submissions: press releases, articles. Additional publications: employment referral brochure, membership directory.

**San Diego Chapter**. Contact Person: President, Linda Oestreich, 2938 30th St. #A., San Diego, CA 92104. (619) 553-4791. Members: 200. Dues $75 (includes local and international). Meetings: monthly, September through June. Activities: participates in annual national arts and publication contest. Newsletter: *Signature*. Frequency: monthly. Submissions: press releases, articles from members.

**San Diego State Student Chapter**. Contact Person: President, Dr. Sheri Little, English Dept., San Diego State University, San Diego, CA 92182. (619) 265-6584.

**San Francisco Chapter**. Contact Person: President, Meryl Natchez, PO Box 2706, San Francisco, CA 94126. (415) 932-0257. Members: 250. Dues: $75. Meetings: third Wednesday of the month. Activities: participation in arts and publication contest. Newsletter: *The Active Voice*. Editor: Kathy Tobin. Frequency: monthly. Submissions: press releases, articles.

**Santa Barbara Chapter**. Contact Person: President, Yvonne G. DeGraw, c/o Signal Technology, 5951 Encina Rd., Goleta, CA 93117. (805) 683-3771. Members: 38. Meetings: fourth Thursday of the month. Newsletter: *The Dispatch*. Submissions: articles.

**Sierra-Panamint Chapter**. Contact Person, Ramona Bernard, PO Box 1792, Ridgecrest, CA 93555. (619) 446-6451. Members: 30. Meetings: monthly. Newsletter: *The Petroglyph*.

**Silicon Valley Chapter**. Contact Person: Judith Wilton, PO Box 700944, San Jose, CA 95170. (415) 940-6394.

## SOCIETY OF AMERICAN TRAVEL WRITERS.
1120 Connecticut Ave., Ste. 940. Washington, D.C. 20036. (202) 7850-5567.

## SOCIETY OF CHILDREN'S BOOK WRITERS.
PO Box 296. Mar Vista Station. Los Angeles, CA 90066. (818) 347-2849. Executive Director, Stephen Mooser; Chairperson of Board of Directors, Sue Alexander. Founded: 1968. Members: 5000 (national). Dues: $35.

Purpose: to serve as a network of information and support for professional writers and illustrators of children's literature. Membership criteria: full members (published writers of children's literature) and anyone interested in children's literature. Benefits: manuscript exchange, writing grants, medical insurance. Activities: meetings, workshops, seminars, conferences (national conference every August), annual awards.

Newsletter: *The Bulletin*. Editor: Stephen Mooser. Frequency: bimonthly. Submissions: from members only.

**Northern California Chapter**: Contact Person: Regional Advisor, Gay Finkelman, PO Box 505, St. Helena, CA 94574. (707) 963-0704. Members: 400. Dues: $15. Meetings: last Saturday of the month. Newsletter: *Galleys*. Editor: Alice Salerno. Frequency: bimonthly. Submissions: press releases, articles.

**Orange County Chapter**. Contact Person: Regional President, Dianne MacMillan, 7530 East Vista del Sol, Anaheim, CA 92808. (714) 637-6586. Members: 120. Activities: two workshops annually, "talkshops" held eight times annually. Newsletter: yes. Frequency: quarterly.

**Santa Barbara/Ventura/Oxnard/Camarillo Chapter**: Contact Person: Regional Advisor, Jean Stange, 1658 Calle La Cumbre, Camarillo, CA 93010. (805) 482-1075. Members: 96. Activities: two conferences annually.

**Southern California Chapter**. Contact Person: Co-Regional Advisor, Judith Ross Enderle, 29636 Cuthbert Rd., Malibu, CA 90265. (213) 820-5601. (213) 457-3501. Members: 900. Dues: none (payable at national level). Meetings: none. Activities: conferences including national conference in August; Illustrators' Day in November.

## WESTERN WRITERS OF AMERICA. 1753 Victoria. Sheridan, WY 82801. (307) 672-2079. Membership Chairperson, Barbara Ketcham. Founded: 1950. Members: 500 (international). Dues: $60.

Purpose: to advertise professional writers and help promote their books. Membership criteria: associate member must have published one book or several articles; full member must have published 3 books or 22 articles. Benefits: promotion and publicity. Meetings: none. Activities: annual conference, fourth week in June, location varies. Membership directory: yes. Newsletter: *WWA Newsletter* (monthly) and *The Roundup* (quarterly magazine including reviews of members' books).

## WOMEN IN COMMUNICATION, INC. 2101 Wilson Blvd., Ste. 417. Arlington, VA 22201. (703) 528-4200. President, Judy Rowcliffe (415) 397-5525. Founded: 1909. Members: 11,000 (national), 600 (California). National dues: $55 plus $25 one-time processing fee.

Purpose: a national organization of women and men who work to unite all communications professionals, support First Amendment rights, recognize outstanding communication achievements, and promote the advancement and equitable treatment of women communicators. Membership criteria: must have worked at least two years as a professional in creative communications (professional status), or work 20 hours weekly in a professional capacity (associate status); student memberships also available. Activities: annual national convention, workshops, seminars, advancement fund for scholarship and awards programs.

Newsletter: *The Professional Communicator* (magazine). Editor: Linda Russman. Frequency: bimonthly. Submissions: press releases, articles. Membership directory: yes.

**Los Angeles Chapter**. Contact Person: Lisa Gates. (818) 957-4807. Members: 300. Dues: $50 (plus national dues). Meetings: monthly. Activities: program meetings, focus seminars, conferences, awards, scholarships. Newsletter: *The Signal*. Frequency: monthly. Submissions: press releases. Additional publications: directory.

**Orange County Chapter**. Contact Person: Ilene Schneider. (714) 786-6270.

**San Francisco Chapter**. Contact Person: President, Joyce Steele, 2757 16th St., San Francisco, CA 94103. (415) 346-1816. Dues: $25.

**Santa Barbara Chapter**. Contact Person: Louise Polis. (805) 683-2060.

**WOMEN IN FILM.** 6464 Sunset Blvd., Ste. 660. Los Angeles, CA 90028. (213) 463-6040. President, Marian Rees. Founded: 1973. Members: 1500. Dues: $100.

Purpose: to increase equal opportunity of employment of women in film and television and create greater visibility of work by women. Membership criteria: three years' professional
Purpose: to increase equal opportunity of employment of women in film and television and create greater visibility of work by women. Membership criteria: three years' professional
experience in film and television. Benefits: medical insurance, contacts with professionals, other benefits outlined in membership information. Meetings: bimonthly. Activities: workshops, seminars, conferences, 10+ meetings annually. International organization with branches in United States.

Newsletter: *W/F Newsmagazine*. Editor: Melissa Miller. Frequency: bimonthly.

**WOMEN'S NATIONAL BOOK ASSOCIATION, INC.** 160 5th Ave. New York, NY 10010. (212) 675-7805. President, Cathy Rentschler. Founded: 1917.

Purpose: a nonprofit, tax-exempt corporation providing educational and literary programs to those interested in the publishing industry; also serves as a channel of communication for topics of interest in the book world. Membership criteria: open to women and men in all occupations associated with the publishing industry.

Newsletter: *The Bookwoman*. Additional publications: directory.

**Bay Area Chapter**. Contact Person: Vice President and Membership Chairperson, Linda Meade, 379 Burning Tree Ct., Half Moon Bay, CA 94019. (415) 726-3969. Members: 125. Dues: $15. Meetings: monthly, September through May. Activities: contests, scholarships. Newsletter: yes. Frequency: bimonthly. Submissions: press releases, articles.

**Los Angeles Chapter**. Contact Person: Sue MacLaurin, PO Box 807, Burbank, CA 91503-0807. (818) 501-3925. Members: 160. Dues: $20. Meetings: monthly (September through June). Activities: annual writers conference, workshops, monthly program with speakers, annual writing contest (poetry, essay, short story).

**WORLD ACADEMY OF ARTS AND CULTURE.** Contact Person: Secretary General, Rosemary Wilkinson. 3146 Buckeye Court. Placerville, CA 95667. (916) 626-4166. Dues: $30 first year, $10 annual renewal.

Purpose: international organization which gathers world poets in biannual conference to promote world brotherhood and peace through poetry. Activites: liason for information for poets, international conferences.

Newsletter: *The Voice of Poets*. Frequency: biannually (before and after international conference).

**WRITERS CONNECTION.** 1601 Saratoga-Sunnyvale Rd., Ste 180. Cupertino, CA 95014. (408) 973-0227. Membership Chairperson, Mardeene Mitchell. Founded: 1983. Members: 2000. Dues: $40 a year (individual); $180 a year (corporate membership for six named individuals, $30 each additional person).

Purpose: to provide a wide-range of services to writers and other publishing professionals and to act as a facilitator for connections between writers and members of the publishing and film industries. Membership criteria: an interest in writing and writing/publishing related topics. Benefits: substantial discount on seminars and services, conferences, and special events. Members may also purchase books at a discount from our bookstore. Meetings: ongoing seminars and events. Activities: meetings, workshops, seminars, conferences.

Newsletter: *Writers Connection*. Editor: Jan Stiles. Frequency: monthly. Submissions: press releases, articles. Additional publications: Writers Connection Event Reports, two seminar catalogs, and the *California Publishing Marketplace* directory.

**WRITERS GUILD OF AMERICA, WEST.** 8955 Beverly Blvd. Los Angeles, CA 90048. (213) 550-1000. Public Relations Director, Cheryl Rhoden. Founded: 1933. Members: 9000 (Western United States). Dues: $1500 initiation; then 1.5 percent of annual income plus $25 per quarter.

Purpose: collective bargaining agency representing writers. Membership criteria: rigorous qualification process. Benefits: pension plan, medical and dental insurance. Activities: annual meeting of membership, conferences. Membership directory: yes.

Newsletter: *The Journal*. Editor: Martin Sweeny. Frequency: monthly.

**WRITERS' SOCIETY OF AMERICA.** 11684 Ventura Blvd., Ste. 868. Studio City, CA 91604. President, Colton Gunn. Founded: 1987. Members: 148. Dues: $100.

Purpose: to help end exploitation of freelance writers receiving payment on publication; to achieve group medical and retirement benefits; to heighten freelance writer's status in the literary scene. Membership criteria: must be producing writers, although they need not have sold at time of joining; must have professional respect for the craft. Benefits: consultation with editorial advisory panel regarding writing problems; intervention in disputes regarding payment for writing product. Meetings: n/i. Activities: annual writers' convention will be planned when viable.

Newsletter: *The Activity*. Editor: Colton Gunn. Frequency: quarterly. Submissions: press releases.

# Conferences

Conferences are a great place to make professional contacts, discover new information, and get motivated. In this section we've listed over 32 conferences covering a diverse range of writing and publishing topics.

## How to Use the Information in This Section

We've listed conferences by their official names and included other pertinent information such as sponsors' names, addresses, and telephone numbers. We've also included founding dates and a contact person (often the conference director).

**Theme:** If a conference lists a theme, its workshops and seminars will often tie in to that theme.

**Place:** This information pinpoints the location of the conference; location often varies from year to year.

**Date:** We have listed specific dates for 1989 or 1990 wherever possible. If the information was not available, we listed the time of the year the conference is usually held.

**Frequency:** Most conferences are held annually. However, some are offered every two years.

**Fee:** The conference fee may cover tuition, accommodations, meals, and special activies, or it may cover only tution.

**Attendees:** This indicates the number of people expected to attend the conference.

**Length:** This indicates the length of the conference, from one day to twelve weeks.

**Subjects:** The subjects a particular conference covers may be broad with many offerings in all categories, or it may be narrowly focused.

**Format:** This information indicates the method by which a subject is presented and how much time is allotted to its presentation. Formats vary from hourly workshops, formal and informal panel discussions, and guest speaker presentations to intensive daylong sessions. Request the conference brochure and check to see if the subject areas and format appeal to you.

**Special events:** In addition to educational activities, conferences sometimes include activities such as sunset cruises, banquets, wine tastings, receptions, job fairs, silent auctions, book signings, awards presentations, and informal night-owl sessions.

**Faculty:** The total number of guest speakers, teachers, workshop facilitators, and the like is given here.

**Additional information:** Any other information that the conference director wants you, the prospective attendee, to know is included in this section.

### Abbreviations

n/i means no information was given to us by the conference sponsor.

---

**AMERICAN RIVER COLLEGE WRITING WORKSHOP.** Sponsored by American River College. 4700 College Oak Dr. Sacramento, CA 95841. (916) 484-8643. Founded: 1978. Contact Person: Raynelle Revell.

Place: American River College. Date: March 18, 1989. Frequency: annual, third weekend in March. Length: one day. Fee: $55. Included: lunch. Attendees: 250.

Theme: Selling What You Write. (Theme varies annually.) Subjects: poetry, fiction, nonfiction, scriptwriting. Format: workshops, guest speakers, panels. Special events: appointments with editors and agents. Faculty: 30.

**AMERICAN SOCIETY OF INDEXERS 21ST ANNUAL MEETING.** 1700 18th St., NW. Washington, DC 20009. Founded: 1968. Contact Person: Nancy Mulvany. 265 Arlington Ave. Kensington. CA 94707. (415) 524-4195.

Place: varies, San Francisco/1989. Date: May 19-20, 1989. Frequency: annually. Length: two days. Fee: ASI members—$45 (Friday), $35 (Saturday, $65 (both); nonmembers $60, $50, $95. Included: meals on Friday only. Attendees: 200+/-.

Theme: Indexing in the '90s. Subjects: indexing of traditional trade books; technical documentation; online text. Format: individual speakers, panel discussions. Special events: presentation of the Wilson Awards, indexing software publishers exhibition.

Additional information: 1989 will be the first time in 21 years that the meeting will be held on the West Coast.

**ASIAN AMERICAN JOURNALISTS ASSOCIATION NATIONAL CONVENTION.** Sponsored by Asian American Journalists Association. 1765 Sutter St., Room 1000. San Francisco, CA 94115. (415) 346-2051. Founded: 1987. Contact Person: Diane Yen-Mei Wong.

Place: varies, San Francisco/1989. Date: April 5-8, 1989. Frequency: annually. Length: four days. Fee: $150/members. Included: meals. Attendees: 600.

Theme: Visions for a New Decade. Subjects: newspaper, magazine. Format: speakers, workshops, panels. Special events: banquet, job fair, receptions, silent auction.

**ASILOMAR ADVENTURE.** Sponsored by National League of American Pen Women, Northern California. 2730 39th Ave. San Francisco, CA 94116. (415) 564-9453. Contact Person: Vicki Lavorini.

Place: Asilomar Conference Center. Pacific Grove. Date: February 17-20, 1989. Frequency: annually. Length: weekend. Fee: $136. Included: room and board. Attendees: n/i.

Theme: Tapping Your Unconscious for Higher Creativity. (Theme varies.) Subjects: poetry, art of seeing, music, sculpture, women, image and creativity. Special events: art show.

Additional information: individual sessions or days available at reduced rate.

**BAY AREA WRITERS' WORKSHOPS.** Sponsored by Co-directors Elizabeth Sprague and Laura Jason. PO Box 620327. Woodside, CA 94062. (415) 430-3127. Founded: 1988. Contact person: Laura Jason.

Place: Mills College, Oakland. Date: August 6-12, 1989. Frequency: annually in August. Length: one week. Fee: $400. Included: workshops and sessions only; room and board available separately. Attendees: 120.

Subjects: fiction, poetry, agents/editors, translation, small press relating to larger publishing houses, writers and taxes, surviving as a writer. Format: morning workshops, special afternoon sessions, evening readings by participants, panel discussions. Special events: welcoming reception for faculty and attendees. Faculty: 9.

Additional information: scholarships and work study positions (30 hours each) available.

**BIOLA UNIVERSITY WRITERS INSTITUTE.** Sponsored by Biola University. 13800 Biola Ave. La Mirada, CA 90639. (213) 944-0351, ext. 3441. Founded: 1984. Contact Person: Susan Titus.

Place: Biola University. Date: July 23-26, 1989 (always in late July). Frequency: annually. Length: 4 days. Fee: $180; $160, early registration. Special members fee. Extra fees: $55/meals; $70/3 nights' accommodations. Attendees: 400.

Theme: "Guard my words . . ." (Proverbs 7:23). Subjects: beginning writing, fiction, nonfiction book writing for children, advanced writing. Format: seven major morning classes, 42 afternoon classes, held concurrently seven at a time. Special events: morning plenary sessions, professional music, evening plenary speakers and panel discussions, banquet and awards. Faculty: 35-40.

**CALIFORNIA WRITERS' CLUB ASILOMAR CONFERENCE.** Sponsored by California Writers' Club. 2214 Derby St. San Francisco, CA 94705. Founded: 1909. Contact Person: Dorothy V. Benson. (415) 841-1217.

Place: Asilomar Conference Center, Pacific Grove, California. Date: July 14-16, 1989. Frequency: biannually. Length: Friday noon to Sunday lunch. Fee: $219/CWC members; $249/nonmembers; $150/commuter rate. Included: accommodations, meals, winetasting, parking. Attendees: 400.

Theme: Winning the Writing Game. Subjects: agents; mainstream, historical, romance, mystery, horror, humor, science fantasy, travel, young adult, middle-grade and children's books; nonfiction; short fiction; scriptwriting; newspaper syndication; research; revision; book proposals; synopsis; interviewing techniques; photography, and contracts. Format: panels of magazine editors, book editors and agents; appointments with agents; one-hour seminars on the above genres. Special events: Paul Erdman, keynote speaker, winetasting, night-owl sessions on various disciplines; bookstore where members may bring their own books to sell. Faculty: 60.

Additional information: manuscript critique service available. (Submit before conference.) Contact Person: Ethel Bangert, 1343 Vallejo Way, Sacramento, CA 95818.

**CLARK POETRY SEMINARS.** Sponsored by Clark Productions. PO Box 24824. San Jose, CA 95154. (408) 269-8933. Founded: 1984. Contact Person: Gail Clark.

Place: Asilomar Conference Center, Pacific Grove. Date: weekends in February, at Easter, in June, October, and December. Frequency: five times annually. Length: Friday through Sunday. Fee: $250; Commuter registration, $95 plus meals. Reduced rate available for individual sessions. Included: accommodations and meals. Attendees: 20 maximum per weekend.

Theme: poetry writing. Subjects: writing and marketing poetry. Format: workshop. Special events: open reading on Saturday nights. Faculty: 1-2.

**COMEDY/HUMOR WRITERS ASSOCIATION ANNUAL CONFERENCE.** Sponsored by Comedy/Humor Writers Association. Box 211. San Francisco, CA 94101. (415) 751-6725. Founded: 1987. Contact Person: Kate Pudenz.

Place: Marto Bar & Grill, San Francisco. Date: last week of September. Frequency: annually. Length: one day. Fee: $70. Reduced rate for members. Attendees: 50+.

Theme: comedy/humor writing. Subjects: comedy/humor. Format: six speakers giving 30-minute lectures with 15 minutes for questions and answers. Special events: after hours "schmooze" session.

**COSMEP PUBLISHERS CONFERENCE.** Sponsored by COSMEP, The International Association of Independent Publishers. PO Box 703. San Francisco, CA 94101. (415) 922-9490. Founded: 1968. Contact Person: Richard Morris.

Place: New York, Chicago, San Francisco, and Los Angeles in alternate years. Date: September. Frequency: annually. Length: three days. Fee: $75 (1 day) to $115 (3 days), member rate. Attendees: 120-130.

Theme: Book Marketing. Format: Three one-day seminars. Faculty: number varies.

**FIESTA/SIESTA.** Sponsored by San Diego Writers/Editors Guild. 3235 Homer St. San Diego, CA 92106. (619) 223-5235. Founded: 1982. Contact Person: Peggy Lipscomb.

Place: Murietta Hot Springs Resort. Date: April. Frequency: annually. Length: Friday evening through Sunday afternoon. Fee: conference fee only: $125; $200/double occupancy; $280/single occupancy. Reduced rates for members. Included: some meals, accommodations. Day rate: $45/members; $60/nonmembers, including lunch. Attendees: 75 maximum.

Theme: Fiesta/Siesta. Subjects: fiction (various genres), screen and TV, nonfiction, computer law for writers, children's plays, photography, self-publishing, agents, publishers. Format: seminars, small group interaction with seminar speaker. Special events: relaxing, stress-free weekend including evening parties; networking with outstanding professionals in the field. Faculty: 10-12.

**GATEWAY TO THE '90s.** Sponsored by Women in Communication, Inc., San Francisco Chapter. Pier 39. PO Box 3730. San Francisco, CA 94119. (415) 981-8030. Contact Person: Denise Rasmussen. Founded: 1989 (new).

Place: San Francisco. Date: spring 1989. Frequency: annually. Length: weekend. Fee: $180/members; $225/nonmembers; $90/students, retired members. Included: meals. Attendees: 100.

Theme: Gateway to the '90s. Subjects: public relations, communications, photojournalism, video, journalism. Format: panels, guest speakers, roundtable discussions. Special events: welcome sunset cruise, one-on-one portfolio review, exhibits, door prizes, fashion show. Faculty: 11.

**IDYLLWILD CREATIVE WRITING WORKSHOPS.** Sponsored by Idyllwild School of Music and the Arts. PO Box 38. Idyllwild, CA 92349. (714) 659-2171. Winter: (213) 622-0355. Contact Person: Steven Fraider, Director of Summer Programs.

Place: Idyllwild campus. Date: summer. Frequency: annually. Length: 12-week summer program, one-week classes. Fee: $300 per week. Included: tuition only. Housing $40 (camping) to $325 (private room with meals) per week. Attendees: 500 per week.

Subjects: creative writing, science fiction/fantasy, marketing and publishing, poetry, scriptwriting classes. Special events: art shows, concerts, special events related to the arts.

Additional information: beautiful, 205-acre campus.

**THE INTERNATIONAL WOMEN'S WRITING GUILD CONFERENCE.** Sponsor: The International Women's Writing Guild. PO Box 810. Gracie Station. New York, NY 10028. (212) 737-7536. Founded: 1982. Contact Person: Hannelore Hahn, Executive Director and Founder.

Place: Sonoma/1989. Date: March. Frequency: annually. Length: weekend. Fee: $215, $110/commuter registration. Included: room and board. Attendees: under 100.

Subjects: poetry, fiction, nonfiction, artwork, meditation, yoga. Format: workshops, presentations, networking, critiques, evening readings. Special events: appointments with agents (occasionally). Faculty: 7.

Additional information: individual days available at reduced rate.

**MOUNT HERMON CHRISTIAN WRITERS CONFERENCE.** Sponsored by Mount Hermon Christian Conference Center. PO Box 413. Mount Hermon, CA 95041. (408) 335-4466. Founded: 1969. Contact Person: Elaine Colvin.

Place: Mount Hermon Christian Conference Center. Date: Easter week, Monday through Friday between Palm Sunday and Easter Sunday. Frequency: annually. Length: five days, four nights. Fee: $175 tuition, plus room and board available in three levels—deluxe, moderate, economy. Commuter registration: tuition plus a registration fee and meals. Housing not required with the conference. Included: meals must be taken with the conference. Attendees: 250-300.

Theme: writing for the religious market. Subjects: fiction, nonfiction, short story, children's literature, curriculum, poetry, inspirational, major books, articles, journaling, computer aids, research methods, etc. Format: daily workshops and general sessions; all meals taken together, family style; daily group critique sessions; individual appointments with faculty. Special events: author's autograph party, Good Friday Communion service, writer-of-the-year awards. Faculty: 40-50.

Additional information: Advance manuscript critique service included.

**NAPA VALLEY WRITERS' CONFERENCE.** Sponsored by Napa Valley College, Community Education Office. Napa, CA 94558. (707) 253-3070. Founded: 1980. Contact Person: Sherri Hallgren.

Place: Napa Valley College. Date: poetry—last week of July; fiction—first week of August. Frequency: annually. Length: one week. Fee: $350 per session; $50 nonrefundable deposit. Attendees: 40 each session.

Subjects: plotting, characterization, revision, publishing. Format: Each participant submits a manuscript for critiquing and receives copies of other participants' manuscripts. Two to three manuscripts are critiqued during each three-hour daily workshop. Also faculty lectures, panels. Special events: Evening parties and readings, either on campus or at private homes or wineries around Napa. Faculty: 10-20 including authors, poets, agents, directors, publishers.

**NATIONAL WRITERS UNION ANNUAL CONFERENCE.** Sponsored by the National Writers Union. Local #3. 236 West Portal Ave., #232. San Francisco, CA 94127. (415) 654-6369. Founded: 1986. Contact Person: Bruce Hartford.

Place: San Francisco or Berkeley. Date: spring. Frequency: annually. Length: one day. Fee: $45/NWU members; $40/students, low income; $60/others. Attendees: 300-400.

Theme: writing. Subjects: technical writing, travel writing, freelance contracting, agent/author relationship, third world authors, contracts, environmental writing, rights of writers, and others. Format: panels and workshops. Special events: keynote speaker, party.

**PMA ANNUAL SEMINAR.** Sponsored by Publishers Marketing Association. 2401 Pacific Coast Hwy., Ste. 206. Hermosa Beach, CA 90254. (213) 372-2732. Founded: 1985. Executive Director, Jan Nathan.

Place: various locations. Date: late spring. Frequency: annually. Length: two days. Fee: $50 per seminar. Included: workshops, sessions only. Attendees: 150+.

Theme: A Book Publishing Course. Subjects: marketing, design, editing, proofing, desktop publishing, financial considerations, publicity. Format: three-hour seminar tracks. Faculty: 20+.

Additional information: reduced rates for members and individual sessions.

**PROFESSIONAL WRITERS LEAGUE OF LONG BEACH WRITERS CONFERENCE.** PO Box 20409. Long Beach, CA 90801. (213) 423-1527. Founded: 1972. Contact Person: Mrs. Dorathea Wolford.

Place: Elks Lodge. Date: October 14, 1989. Frequency: annually. Length: one day. Fee: $25. Included: meals. Attendees: 100.

Theme: Know the Markets. Subjects: poetry, specific tips on marketing, writing the romance novel, writing for children, how to sell what you write, research. Topics vary each year. Format: three lectures with question and answer periods, morning, luncheon speaker, four afternoon workshops of two sessions each. Exchange of information with faculty and other participants very popular and helpful.

**PUBLISHING WEEKEND.** Sponsored by Para Publishing. PO Box 4232-853. Santa Barbara, CA 93140-4232. (805) 968-7277. Founded: 1984. Contact Person: Monique Tihanyi.

Place: Santa Barbara. Date: 1989—January 14-15; March 11-12; May 27-28; August 26-27; November 4-5. Frequency: five times each year. Length: two days. Fee: $295. Included: all meals. Attendees: limited to 16.

Theme: nonfiction book promotion and marketing. Format: lecture, discussion, exercises and tours of publishing facility. Many resources and handouts. Special events: networking with typesetters, artists and other resource people. Faculty: 2.

**ROMANCE WRITERS OF AMERICA ANNUAL CONFERENCE.** Sponsored by Romance Writers of America. 5206 FM. 1960 West #208. Houston, TX 77069. (713) 440-6885. Founded: 1980. Contact Person: Bobbi Stinson.

Place: Boston/1989; San Francisco/1990. Date: July 20-23, 1989. Length: three days. Fee: $210. Included: workshops, agent/editor appointments, meals. Reduced rates available for members. Attendees: 1000.

Theme: A Boston Teaparty—RWA Style. Subjects: anything pertaining to romance genre; also information on screenwriting. Format: keynote address, 62 workshops, writing award for contest that precedes the conference, agent/editor appointments (10 minutes each). Special events: Linda Barlowe, Jane Anne Krantz, special guest speakers, champagne party hosted by Avon Books; publishing houses sponsor special activities. Faculty: 180 speakers.

**SAN DIEGO SCHOOL OF CHRISTIAN WRITING.** Sponsored by San Diego County Christian Writers' Guild (cosponsored by Point Loma Nazarene College). Box 1171. El Cajon, CA 92022. (619) 748-0565. Founded: 1989. Contact Person: Candace Walters.

Place: Point Loma Nazarene College, San Diego. Date: June 15-18, 1989. Frequency: annually. Length: Thursday through Sunday. Fee: $250; rates for individual sessions. Commuter registration: $100 per day. Included: meals; accommodations. Attendees: 200 or more.

Theme: training writers to get published. Subjects: all kinds of writing by Christians. Format: plenary lectures, specialized workshops, continuing classes. Special events: closing banquet with Marabel Morgan, speaker; special awards. Faculty: 24.

**SANTA BARBARA WRITERS' CONFERENCE.** Sponsored by Barnaby Conrad. PO Box 304. Carpinteria, CA 93013. (805) 684-2250. Founded: 1972. Contact Person: Mary Conrad.

Place: Miramar Hotel, Santa Barbara. Date: June 23-30, 1989. Frequency: annually. Length: one week. Fee: $750/single, $550/double occupancy, $300/day students. Includes: room (no board), all workshops and lectures, first and final nights' al fresco dinners. Attendees: 300+.

Theme: all aspects of writing specialities. Subjects: fiction, nonfiction, scriptwriting, travel writing. Format: A.M. and P.M. workshops; afternoon and evening panels and lectures by best-selling authors; all-night panels. Faculty: 50+.

**SANTA CLARA VALLEY CHRISTIAN WRITERS' SEMINAR.** Sponsored by Santa Clara Valley Christian Writers. 71 Park Village Pl. San Jose, CA 95136. (408) 281-8926. Founded: 1975. Contact Person: Pamela Erickson.

Place: First Covenant Church. 790 Coe Ave. San Jose. Date: third Saturday in October. Frequency: annually. Length: one day. Fee: $25. Attendees: 100.

Theme: inspirational writing. Subjects: basic and advance workshops in fiction and nonfiction writing; marketing. Format: two major sessions with guest speakers (often editors) and multiple workshops. Special events: faculty book table, free sample magazines and guidelines. Faculty: 8-12.

**SELLING TO HOLLYWOOD.** Sponsored by Writers Connection. 1601 Saratoga-Sunnyvale Rd., Ste. 180. Cupertino, CA 95014. (408) 973-0227. Founded: 1987. Contact Person: Meera Lester.

Place: Sunnyvale Hilton, Sunnyvale. Date: August 11-13, 1989. Frequency: annually. Length: weekend. Fee: $340-360 (may increase slightly). Reduced rate for members. Commuter rate: usually $70 less than full registration. Included: meals, accommodations. Attendees: 200-300.

Theme: Selling to Hollywood. Subjects: All workshops and panel discussions provide information specific for writers interested in selling literary properties to the film industry. Format: panels of producers, story editors and literary agents; individual presentations and workshops; one-on-one consultations; keynote address. Special events: winetasting, individual consultation with film industry professionals, bookstore, autograph session (if appropriate) with keynote speaker. Faculty: 12-20.

**SIERRA WRITING CAMP.** 18293 Crystal St. Grass Valley, CA 95949. (916) 272-8047. Founded: 1975. Contact Person: Karen Newcomb.

Place: Columbia Junior College, Sonora; Idyllwild, Southern California. Date: July. Frequency: annually. Length: six days. Fee: $450. Included: meals, accommodations. Attendees: 100

Theme: "nuts and bolts" approach to writing and marketing. Subjects: fiction, nonfiction, screenwriting, travel, photography, humor, juvenile. Format: daily classroom instruction, one-on-one teacher/student critiquing, work on in-progress manuscript. Special events: guest speakers. Faculty: 12.

**SOCIETY FOR TECHNICAL COMMUNICATION'S 37TH INTERNATIONAL CONFERENCE.** Sponsored by Society for Technical Communication (STC). 815 15th St. NW. Washington, D.C. 20005. (202) 737-0035. Founded: 1953.

Place: Santa Clara Convention Center/1990. Date: May 20-23, 1990. Frequency: annually (location varies). Length: four days. Fee: approximately $200/members; $285/nonmembers. Accommodations: n/i.

Theme: Communication: In the Chips. Subjects: the changing role of the technical communication specialist considering factors such as technology, literacy levels, corporate and national cultures, and international business.

Additional information: Submissions of papers, workshops, panels, and discussion topics for the conference are invited.

**SOCIETY OF CHILDREN'S BOOK WRITERS CONFERENCE.** Sponsored by the Society of Children's Book Writers, Northern California Chapter. PO Box 505. St. Helena, CA 94574. (707)963-0704. Founded: 1985. Contact Person: Bobi Martin (707) 426-6776.

Place: Asilomar Conference Center, Pacific Grove. Date: February 16-18, 1990. Frequency: annually. Length: two days. Fee: $150. Included: accommodations. Attendees: 60.

Theme: writing and illustrating for children's books and articles. Format: lectures, small workshops, critique sessions. Faculty: 3.

**SQUAW VALLEY COMMUNITY OF WRITERS ANNUAL WORKSHOP.** Sponsored by Squaw Valley Creative Arts Society. PO Box 2352. Olympic Valley, CA 95730. (916) 583-5200. Founded: 1969. Contact Person: Carolyn Doty, fiction; Gil Dennis, scriptwriting.

Place: Squaw Valley (conference center). Date: second week in August. Frequency: annually. Length: one week. Fee: $450 per program. Included: one dinner meal. Attendees: 150.

Theme: to help the writer attain his or her potential by providing the concentrated attention of established writers, editors, agents and fellow participants to the writer's work. Subjects:

prose, poetry, screenwriting. Format: small, intensive workshops. Special events: movies, poetry readings, fiction readings. Faculty: 25.

Additional information: separate one-week, concurrent programs for prose, poetry, and screenwriting; afternoon meetings open to public.

**STANFORD PUBLISHING COURSE.** Sponsored by Stanford University. Stanford Alumni Association. Bowman House. Stanford, CA 94305-4005. (415) 725-1083; FAX (415) 723-8597. Founded: 1977. Contact Person: Della Van Heyst, Director of Publications, Stanford Alumni Association. (415) 497-2021.

Place: Stanford University. Date: July 16-29, 1989. Frequency: annually in July. Length: 12 days. Fee: $1850; $1810/Stanford Alumni Association members. Included: books, working materials, receptions, all luncheons, opening banquet, closing barbecue. Attendees: less than 100.

Subjects: new publishing technologies, editing, design, production, finance and marketing, functions of publishing. Format: lectures, hands-on workshops. Faculty: 50.

Additional information: Application deadline is April 28. Preview videotape available for loan. Admissions standards are a minimum of three years' experience in professional publishing, or a waiver at the discretion of the Course Director must be granted.

**WESTERN REGIONAL CONFERENCE OF THE AMERICAN MEDICAL WRITERS ASSOCIATION.** Sponsored by the American Medical Writers Association. Contact Person: Michele Vivirito. c/o Herbert Laboratories. 1202 E. Wakeham Ave. Santa Ana, CA 92705. (714) 752-4629.

Place: Asilomar Conference Center, Pacific Grove. Date: spring. Frequency: annually. Length: five days. Fee: $300/AMWA members; $325/nonmembers. Included: accommodations (double occupancy), meals. Attendees: limited to 50.

Theme: medical writing. Subjects: evolution of medical journals, writing in the pharmaceutical industry, on-line medical databases, what editors and writers should know about publishing, business aspects of a freelance writing career. Faculty: 20+.

**WORLD CONGRESS OF POETS.** Sponsored by the World Academy of Arts and Culture. 3146 Buckeye Court. Placerville, CA 95667. (916) 626-4166. Founded: 1969. Contact Person: Rosemary C. Wilkinson.

Place: Cairo, Egypt. (Location varies.) Date: 1990. Frequency: biannually, by invitation of Cultural Minister/Minister of Education of host nation. Length: five-day symposium. Fee: not yet set for 1990. Reduced rates available for organization members. Attendees: 400+.

Theme: World Brotherhood and Peace through Poetry. Subjects: poetry and literature. Format: plenary sessions with afternoon workshops and evening cultural events. Special events: side trips to museums, ancient sites, libraries, etc. Faculty: 10+.

**WRITER IN THE WORKPLACE.** Sponsored by Society for Technical Communication and American River College. PO Box 1292. Roseville, CA 95661. (916) 484-8430. Founded: 1988. Contact Person: Connie Warloe.

Place: American River College, Sacramento. Date: February. Frequency: annually. Length: one day. Fee: $55. Included: meals. Attendees: 150.

Theme: changes every year. Subjects: technical and business writing. Format: keynote address and workshops. Special events: reception at end of day. Faculty: 16.

**WRITERS' JAMBOREE.** Sponsored by Creative States Quarterly, Inc. PO Box 22438. Carmel CA 93922. Founded: 1986. Contact Person: Ray Mungo.

Place: Carmel-Monterey. Date: third weekend in November. Frequency: annually. Length: weekend. Fee: $20-50. Attendees: 50-350.

Subjects: fiction, nonfiction, publishing, agents, getting published. Format: two-hour seminars and workshops with several speakers followed by question and answer sessions; party Saturday night. Special events: writers lunch, Jamboree Ball. Faculty: 50+.

# Books for Writers

The following writing- and publishing-related books are available from the Writers Connection bookstore. Writers Connection members are entitled to a 15% discount off the retail prices listed. To order books, use the order form on page 249.

## Fiction

### CHARACTERS AND VIEWPOINT
Orson Scott Card
How to invent, construct, and animate vivid, credible characters and choose the best eyes through which to view the events of your short story or novel. F36—$13.95

### THE CHILDREN'S PICTURE BOOK
Ellen Roberts
How to write it, how to sell it. F3—$16.95

### DIALOGUE
Lewis Turco
How to get your characters talking to each other in a way that vividly reveals who they are, what they're doing,and what's coming next in your story. F45—$12.95

### FICTION IS FOLKS: HOW TO CREATE UNFORGETTABLE CHARACTERS
Peck
Lively, fun-to-read advice from a prolific writer. F7—$8.95

### THE FICTION WRITER'S RESEARCH HANDBOOK
Mona McCormick
How to locate historical data using various sources. F44—$8.95

### HANDBOOK OF SHORT STORY WRITING
Jean M. Fredette
Volume II—37 chapters of practical instruction. F31—$15.95

### HOW TO WRITE A DAMN GOOD NOVEL
James N. Frey
A step-by-step no-nonsense guide to dramatic storytelling. F32—$13.95

## HOW TO WRITE AND ILLUSTRATE CHILDREN'S BOOKS
Treld P. Bicknell
Covers constructing a story, illustration, and getting published. F38—$22.50

## HOW TO WRITE ROMANCES
Phyllis T. Pianka
Everything you need to know about writing and selling the romance novel, including a sample query and synopsis. F33—$13.95

## HOW TO WRITE TALES OF HORROR, FANTASY & SCIENCE FICTION
J. N. Williamson
How-to essays from 26 top speculative fiction writers. F16—$15.95

## MYSTERY WRITER'S HANDBOOK
The Mystery Writers of America; revised edition
Top mystery writers share tricks of the trade. F17—$10.95

## 1989 CHILDREN'S WRITER'S & ILLUSTRATOR'S MARKET
Connie Wright Eidenier
Constructing a story, illustration, and getting published. F39—$14.95

## 1989 NOVEL & SHORT STORY WRITER'S MARKET
Writer's Digest
Formerly Fiction Writer's Market. F40—$17.95

## THE POET'S HANDBOOK
Judson Jerome
Detailed instruction in the mechanics and art of writing poetry. F42—$10.95.

## PLOT
Ansen Dibell
How to build short stories and novels that don't sag, fizzle, or trail off in scraps of frustrated revision, and how to rescue stories that do. F35—$13.95

## STORYCRAFTING
Paul Darcy Boles
The art and craft of writing fine short stories. F21—$10.95

## WRITING FICTION THAT SELLS
Louise Boggess
Proven techniques for plot, viewpoint, dialogue, etc. F24—$6.95

## WRITING FOR CHILDREN AND TEENAGERS
Lee Wyndham
Revised and updated: step-by-step instruction on how to hold a young reader's attention, where to find ideas, and vocabulary lists based on age level. F25—$12.95

## WRITING MYSTERY AND CRIME FICTION
Sylvia K. Burack
Twenty-six successful crime and mystery writers describe tested procedures for writing and selling all types of mystery writing. F27—$12.95

## WRITING SHORT STORIES FOR YOUNG PEOPLE
George E. Stanley
How to write and sell juvenile short fiction. F28—$15.95

## WRITING THE MODERN MYSTERY
Barbara Norville
How to research, plot, write, and sell a modern mystery. F29—$15.95

## WRITING THE NOVEL FROM PLOT TO PRINT
Lawrence Block
Every step is fully described. F30—$10.95

### WRITING YOUNG ADULT NOVELS
Hadley Irwin
How to write the stories today's teens want to read. F34—$14.95

## Nonfiction

### ARTICLE TECHNIQUES THAT SELL
Louise Boggess
Turning ideas into the nine basic types of articles. NF2—$6.95

### HOW TO SELL AND RE-SELL YOUR WRITING
Duane Newcomb
Manage your writing time and market your nonfiction to maximize your income; top return on your research time investment. NF8—$11.95

### HOW TO WRITE A BOOK PROPOSAL
Michael Larsen
A step-by-step guide a leading literary agent. NF11—$10.95

### HOW TO WRITE AND SELL A COLUMN
Julie Raskin
Write and sell columns to a variety of periodicals; choosing a subject and format, establishing your credentials. NF13—$10.95

### HOW TO WRITE AND SELL THE 8 EASIEST ARTICLE TYPES
Helene Schellenberg Barnhart
Complete instructions on writing nonfiction articles. NF14—$14.95

### HOW TO WRITE AND SELL YOUR PERSONAL EXPERIENCES
Lois Duncan
Turn everything that happens to you into writing that sells. NF44—$10.95

### HOW TO WRITE FILLERS AND SHORT FEATURES THAT SELL
Louise Boggess
Includes types of fillers, techniques, and addresses of markets. NF18—$6.95

### HOW TO WRITE IRRESISTIBLE QUERY LETTERS
Lisa Collier Cool
How to craft powerfully persuasive letters that connect with an editor's imagination—and sell your work. NF19—$11.95

### AN INTRODUCTION TO CHRISTIAN WRITING
Ethyl Herr
Effective techniques and marketing strategies for Christian writers. NF1—$8.95

### THE TRAVEL WRITER'S HANDBOOK
Louise P. Zobel
How to travel more and make more money writing about it. NF26—$11.95

### TRAVEL WRITER'S MARKETS
Elaine O'Gara
Details on over 400 markets. NF27—$8.95

### WRITER'S DIGEST HANDBOOK OF MAGAZINE ARTICLE WRITING
Jean M. Fredette
Complete writing and marketing instruction on every type of article. NF45—$15.95

### WRITE TO $ELL
Ruth Wucherer
How to add dollars to your income writing nonfiction articles and getting them published.
NF42—$9.95

### WRITING CREATIVE NONFICTION
Theodore A. Rees Cheney
Use fiction techniques to make your nonfiction more vivid.
NF29—$15.95

---

## Publishing

---

### A BEGINNER'S GUIDE TO GETTING PUBLISHED
Kirk Polking
Answers the beginning writer's most-asked questions about getting into print. PB1—$11.95

### EDITING YOUR NEWSLETTER
Mark Beach
A complete guide to writing and producing a successful newsletter—on schedule and within budget. PB20—$18.50

### HOW TO BULLET-PROOF YOUR MANUSCRIPT
Bruce Henderson
How to check manuscripts for potential libel and other legal problems. PB6—$9.95

### HOW TO MAKE BIG PROFITS PUBLISHING CITY & REGIONAL BOOKS
Marilyn and Tom Ross
How to get a winning "area" book idea, research it, generate working capital, handle editorial development, as well as sales and promotion ideas. PB8—$14.95

### LITERARY AGENTS
Debby Mayer
A writer's guide, includes interviews with well-known agents. PB30—$6.95

### LITERARY AGENTS, HOW TO GET AND WORK WITH THE RIGHT ONE FOR YOU
Michael Larsen
A guide to selecting and working with an agent. PB12—$9.95

### PROFESSIONAL ETIQUETTE FOR WRITERS
William Brohaugh
Guidelines for etiquette, manners, and protocol for professional writers. PB14—$9.95

### PUBLISHER'S LUNCH
Ernest Callenbach
A dialogue concerning the secrets of how publishers think and what authors can do about it.
PB32—$7.95

### THE SELF-PUBLISHING MANUAL
Dan Poynter
A complete guide to the self-publishing process. PB17—$14.95

### SELLING BOOKS IN THE BAY AREA
Karen Misuraca
A directory of over 2,000 listings and resources for producers, sellers, and promoters of books in the Bay Area. PB34—$17.95

### 12 KEYS TO WRITING BOOKS THAT SELL
Kathleen Krull
Develop a more professional attitude to writing and marketing your book. PB33—$12.95

### A WRITER'S GUIDE TO COPYRIGHT

Poets & Writers

A summary of the current copyright law for writers, editors, and teachers. PB29—$4.95

### THE WRITER'S LEGAL COMPANION

Brad Bunnin

How to deal successfully with copyrights, contracts, libel, taxes, agents, publishers, legal relationships, and marketing strategies. PB31—$14.95

---

## Reference

---

### CHICAGO MANUAL OF STYLE

University of Chicago Press

A comprehensive, authoritative guide to journalistic techniques. R24—$37.50

### THE DESKTOP PUBLISHER'S LEGAL HANDBOOK

Sitarz

How to make best use of your rights as a publisher and avoid infringing rights of others. R23—$19.95

### FINDING FACTS FAST

Alden Todd

Comprehensive research techniques to save you hours; a gold mine of information sources and research techniques. R4—$3.95

### KNOWING WHERE TO LOOK, THE ULTIMATE GUIDE TO RESEARCH

Lois Horowitz

The secrets of research. R5—$15.95

### THE NEW YORK TIMES GUIDE TO REFERENCE MATERIALS

Mona McCormick

How and where to look up almost anything. R7—$3.95

### 1989 POET'S MARKET

Writer's Digest

Where and how to publish your poetry. R20—$17.95

### 1990 WRITER'S MARKET

Writer's Digest

Where and how to sell what you write; thousands of markets for fiction and nonfiction articles, books, plays, scripts, short stories, and more. R25—$23.95

### THE WRITER'S DIGEST GUIDE TO MANUSCRIPT FORMATS

Writer's Digest

Illustrated, easy-to-follow guide to all types of manuscript formats, including books, articles, poems, and plays. R10—$16.95

### A WRITER'S GUIDE TO RESEARCH

Lois Horowitz

Up-to-date ways to find facts, people, quotes. R11—$9.95

---

## Scriptwriting

---

### THE ART OF DRAMATIC WRITING

Lajos Egri

Examines a play from the inside out; principles apply equally well to short stories, novels, and screenplays. SC1—$10.95

### THE COMPLETE BOOK OF SCRIPTWRITING
J. Michael Straczynski
All of the information you need to understand, write for, and break into dramatic scriptwriting for TV, radio, film, and theatre. SC3—$11.95

### THE CRAFT OF THE SCREENWRITER
John Brady
In-depth interviews with six successful screenwriters. SC15—$10.95

### THE ELEMENTS OF SCREENWRITING
Irwin R. Blacker
A no-nonsense guide for film and television writing including plot, character, conflict, crisis, climax, exposition, and dialogue. SC7—$4.95

### HOW TO WRITE A PLAY
Raymond Hull
Provides solid instruction on how to write a performable play with scenes that work effectively for actors and directors. SC6—$10.95

### MAKING A GOOD SCRIPT GREAT
Linda Seger
How to get the script back on track and preserve the original creativity; a guide for writing and rewriting. SC8—$8.95

### SCREENPLAY
Syd Field
The foundations of screenwriting; a step-by-step guide from concept to finished script. SC9—$8.95

### THE SCREENWRITER'S WORKBOOK
Syd Field
Exercises and step-by-step instruction for creating a successful screenplay; a workshop approach. SC10—$8.95

## Writing

### ART AND CRAFT OF NOVEL WRITING
Oakley Hall
Excerpts from great writers show, rather than tell, how to write great novels. W42—$16.95

### ASSOCIATED PRESS STYLEBOOK AND LIBEL MANUAL
Addison-Wesley
Authoritative word on rules of grammar, punctuation, and the general meaning and usage of over 3,000 terms; insight into journalistic techniques. W2—$10.95

### BEGINNING WRITER'S ANSWER BOOK
Kirk Polking
Answers to nearly 900 questions most often asked writers; organized subject areas. W4—$13.95

### BEYOND STYLE: MASTERING THE FINER POINTS OF WRITING
Gary Provost
Form, tone, subtlety, pacing, tension, metaphor, theme, viewpoint, slant, flashbacks for fiction and nonfiction writers. W24—$15.95

### COPYEDITING, A PRACTICAL GUIDE
Karen Judd
A comprehensive field guide to copyediting, publishing. W5—$17.95

**DARE TO BE A GREAT WRITER**
Leonard Bishop
329 keys to powerful fiction to help fiction writers polish their skills. W25—$15.95

**GETTING THE WORDS RIGHT**
Theodore A. Rees Cheney
A guide to revising, editing, and rewriting. W8—$15.95

**IS THERE A BOOK INSIDE YOU?**
Dan Poynter
"Join the ranks of those who shape society." W11—$9.95

**MAKE EVERY WORD COUNT**
Gary Provost
Basic techniques of good writing, fiction or nonfiction. W12—$9.95

**THE MENTOR GUIDE TO PUNCTUATION**
William C. Paxson
Quick and easy answers to punctuation problems organized for easy access. W13—$3.50

**PINCKERT'S PRACTICAL GRAMMAR**
Robert C. Pinckert
A grammar usage, punctuation, and style guide for all writers. W14—$14.95

**REVISION**
Kit Reed
How to find and fix what isn't working, and strengthen what *is*, to build vivid, powerful fiction. W43—$13.95

**REWRITE RIGHT!**
Jan Venolia
Most writing can be improved the simple process of review and rewriting. W15—$6.95

**TIME MANAGEMENT FOR WRITERS**
Ted Schwarz
How to utilize writing time to the fullest to increase output and income. W29—$10.95

**THE 29 MOST COMMON WRITING MISTAKES & HOW TO AVOID THEM**
Judy Delton
An anecdotal guide. W17—$9.95

**WRITE RIGHT!**
Jan Venolia
The best summary of grammar available for writers. W32—$5.95

**THE WRITING BUSINESS**
The editors of Coda: Poets and Writers Newsletter
Practical advice on the business side of being a writer. W36—$11.95

**WRITING AFTER FIFTY**
Leonard L. Knott
How to start a writing career after you retire. W37—$12.95

**WRITING DOWN THE BONES**
Natalie Goldberg
Guidelines for freeing the writer within. W38—$8.95

# Book Subject Index

This index is alphabetized using the letter-by-letter system and is divided into three sections: nonfiction, fiction, and subsidy presses.

## Nonfiction

## Fiction

## Subsidy Presses

# Magazine Subject Index

This index is alphabetized using the letter-by-letter system and is divided into two sections: nonfiction and fiction.

## Nonfiction

## Fiction

# Comprehensive Index

This index is alphabetized using the letter-by-letter system. Magazine and newspaper listings are in italic.

# Order Form

## Information

❑ Send me a free sample newsletter

❑ Send me a general (fiction/nonfiction) seminar catalog

❑ Send me a business communications seminar catalog

❑ Send me more information on Writers Connection

❑ Send me information on the next edition of the *California Publishing Marketplace*

## Membership/Subscription

❑ Enroll me as a Writers Connection member includes subscription—$40 per year $ _______

❑ Send me 12 issues of the *Writers Connection* newsletter without membership—$12 per year $ _______

## Books

Writers Connection members can deduct 15 percent on all book orders. Please enter code, title, and price for each book below.

❑ Send me _____ copies of the *California Publishing Marketplace* directory—$14.95 each $ _______

❑ Send me the following titles:

_______________________________________ $ _______

_______________________________________ $ _______

_______________________________________ $ _______

Book subtotal $ _______

Calif. residents add 7% sales tax $ _______

Add $1.25 per book for postage and handling $ _______

Book total $ _______

Total $ _______

Name _______________________________________

Address _______________________________________

City ____________________ State ______________ Zip __________

**Daytime phone** ____________________ Membership number ______________

❑ Check or money order enclosed

Please charge my: ❑ Visa ❑ MasterCard Account # ____________________

Expiration date ______________ Signature ____________________

Please return to:

**Writers Connection**

1601 Saratoga-Sunnyvale Rd., Suite 180, Cupertino, CA 95014

Phone orders using a Visa or MasterCard are accepted: **(408) 973-0227**